Second Generation Voices

Religion, Theology, and the Holocaust
Alan L. Berger, *Series Editor*

Second Generation Voices

Reflections by Children of Holocaust
Survivors and Perpetrators

Edited by

Alan L. Berger *and* Naomi Berger

Syracuse University Press

First Edition 2001

02 03 04 05 06 07   7 6 5 4 3

Permission to reprint from the following sources is gratefully acknowledged: *Pardes* 21 (1995) for "A Yiddish Writer Who Writes in French," by Myriam Anissimov; New York University Press for "On the Yiddish Question," by Anita Norich in *Mapping Jewish Identities,* ed. by Laurence Silberstein. Reprinted by permission of New York University Press. "The Journey to Poland" by Michal Govrin appeared as part of a longer piece in the *Partisan Review* (Fall 1999).

The paper used in this publication meets the minimum requirements of American National Standard for Information Sciences—Permanence of Paper for Printed Library Materials, ANSI Z39.48-1984.∞™

Library of Congress Cataloging-in-Publication Data

Second generation voices : reflections by children of Holocaust survivors and
perpetrators / edited by Alan L. Berger and Naomi Berger.

    p. cm.

  ISBN 0-8156-2884-6 (alk. paper). ISBN 0-8156-0681-8 (pbk. : alk. paper)

  1. Children of Holocaust survivors—Psychology.   2. Children of Holocaust
survivors—Biography.   3. Holocaust, Jewish (1939–1945)—Influence.   4. Children of
Nazis—Psychology.   I. Berger, Alan L., 1939–   II. Berger, Naomi.
D804.195.S43 2001
940.53'18—dc21   00-046205

To the memory of
Judith (8), Vera (6), George (4), and Reuven (2)—
Naomi's half brothers and sisters,
who were murdered at Auschwitz in September 1944

Contents

PART SIX

Confronting a Repressed Past

PART SEVEN

Is Dialogue Possible?

Acknowledgments

This book could have come to fruition only with the participation of contributors from various parts of the world, Jews and Germans, who were willing to share their reflections on second-generation identity after Auschwitz. We are grateful to all of them for contributing to this project and for writing about their journeys of self-discovery. In addition, several people provided their expertise and time at various stages of the book's development. David Anderson and Hugh Nissenson read and commented on earlier drafts of the manuscript. Barbara Appelbaum, Rachel Feldhay Brenner, Susan E. Nowak, Bruce Warshal, and Chana Winer helped us with logistical and other support. We are especially pleased to acknowledge the assistance of Dan Berger, our youngest son, who put us in contact with one of the contributors. Nahum Sarna provided wise counsel. Mr. Marvin Skorman, our dear friend, whose insights, support, and encouragement were important in the birthing of this work, is owed a special debt of gratitude.

Earlier portions of the manuscript were typed by Samantha Rowe and Evelyn Mermonstein. Susan Kohnken-French typed the entire manuscript. Her patience and skill are much appreciated. Thanks go as well to my assistant, Bonnie Lander, for her invaluable help in preparing the manuscript for publication. We are grateful to the Florida Atlantic University Foundation for their support.

We acknowledge with thanks the following for permissions to republish: Helen Epstein for "Returning," Michal Govrin for "The Journey to Poland," and Nava Semel for "Intersoul Flanking."

Contributors

Myriam Anissimov was born in a refugee camp in Switzerland. The author of twelve books, she lives in Paris.

Liesel Appel was born as a "special gift to Hitler." She turned her back on family and homeland when she discovered her legacy, and now lives in the United States as a converted Jew.

Dan Bar-On is the David Lopatie Chair of Psychological Post-Holocaust Studies and a social and clinical psychologist at the Department of Behavioral Sciences at Ben Gurion University. He is also the codirector of PRIME (Peace Research Institute in the Middle East). Among his books are *Legacy of Silence, Fear and Hope,* and *The Indescribable and the Undiscussable: Reconstructing Human Discourse after Trauma.*

Alan L. Berger holds the Raddock Eminent Scholar Chair of Holocaust Studies, at Florida Atlantic University, where he directs both the Holocaust and Judaic Studies B.A. program and the Center for the Study of Values and Violence after Auschwitz. Among his books are *Crisis and Covenant, Judaism in the Modern World* (ed.), and *Children of Job.* He is the author of numerous essays and book chapters.

Naomi Berger is a licensed marriage and family therapist, clinical supervisor, and certified addiction counselor. She was born in Czechoslovakia and raised in Israel. Naomi is in private practice in Boca Raton and writes a weekly column on personal and relationship issues for a south Florida newspaper. She and her husband, Alan, have three sons.

Melvin Jules Bukiet is the author of *Sandman's Dust, Stories of an Imaginary Childhood, While the Messiah Tarries, After, Signs and Wonders,* and, forthcoming, *Strange Fire*. He teaches at Sarah Lawrence College and lives in New York City.

Helen Epstein is the author of several award-winning books, including *Children of the Holocaust, Joe Papp: An American Life,* and *Where She Came From: A Daughter's Search for Her Mother's History*. She lives in Massachusetts with her husband and two sons.

Barbara Finkelstein is the author of the novel *Summer Long-a-Coming*, and *The First Year of Nursing*.

Eva Fogelman is a psychologist in private practice in New York City who pioneered group methods for generations of the Holocaust. She is a senior research fellow at the Center for Social Research of CUNY Graduate Center.

Julie C. Goschalk is a daughter of Holocaust survivors, born and raised in postwar Germany. She is a clinical social worker in private practice, and lives with her husband and daughter in Boston.

Miriam Tabak Gottdank Isaacs holds a doctorate in linguistics and specializes in Yiddish language, sociolinguistics, and bilingualism. She teaches Yiddish language, culture, and literature for the University of Maryland at College Park. She honors her ancestors by passing on their ways to future generations.

Michal Govrin is a writer and poet, and an award-winning director of experimental theater. She received her Ph.D. from the University of Paris. Govrin was awarded the Israeli Prime Minister's Prize for Writers, and her novel *The Name,* the first one to be translated into English, won the Kugel Literary Prize. Her literary works have been largely anthologized, and have been translated into many languages. Born in Tel Aviv, Govrin currently lives in Jerusalem.

Björn Krondorfer is assistant professor of religious studies at St. Mary's College of Maryland. Among his books are *Remembrance and Reconciliation: Encounters Between Young Jews and Germans*. Recently, he edited Edward Gastfriend's *My Father's Testament: Memoir of a Jewish Teenager, 1938–1945*. He is series editor of the Cultural Criticism Series of Scholars Press and serves on the editorial board of *Living Text: The Journal of Contemporary Midrash*.

Wendy Joy Kuppermann is a second-generation "witness appointee" of the Holocaust, a writer, poet, photographer, painter, and scholar, whose creative and academic works addressing the second-generation experience have been published, anthologized, and exhibited widely. She lectures on the subject nationwide and practices the Dharma of Compassion toward all living things, even human beings.

Asher Z. Milbauer is a professor of English at Florida International University. Before accepting his present appointment, he taught literature and English in the former Soviet Union, in Israel, and at the University of Washington. He is the author of *Transcending Exile: Conrad, Nabokov, I. B. Singer,* and coeditor of *Reading Philip Roth.* His study *The Image of Eastern Europe* was published in *American Jewish Literary Experiences: An Analytical Guide to Themes and Sources,* and his essay on I. B. Singer was included in *Literary Exile in the Twentieth Century.* His most recent publication is "Rescue Missions: Vasily Grossman and the Holocaust" in *Literature and Belief.*

Anita Norich is associate professor of English and Judaic Studies at the University of Michigan. She teaches, lectures, and publishes on topics concerning Yiddish language and literature, modern Jewish culture, Jewish-American literature, and Holocaust literature.

Abraham J. Peck is director of the Center for Post-Holocaust Jewish and Christian Studies at the University of Southern Maine, Portland, where he also teaches in the department of history. He is co-editor (with Michael Berenbaum) of *The Holocaust and History.*

Eugene L. Pogany is a clinical psychologist. He lives in Newton, Massachusetts, with his wife and two sons. His book *In My Brother's Image* is an account of the relationship between his father, a Jewish survivor of the Holocaust, and his father's identical twin brother, who was a devout Roman Catholic priest.

Lisa Reitman-Dobi is a freelance writer. She is recently remarried and "lives happily ever after" in New York with her husband, Steve, and daughters, Danielle and Emily.

Barbara Rogers is a piano teacher, and lives with her second husband in Chicago and Mexico. She loves to write, to paint, to create photos, and to share her joy of music with others by playing chamber music and teaching her students.

Menachem Z. Rosensaft, a partner in the law firm of Ross & Hardies and foundation executive, is the founding chairman of the International Network of Children of Jewish Holocaust Survivors and a former national president of the Labor Zionist Alliance. He is the editor of *Life Reborn, Jewish Displaced Persons 1941–1945,* published by the United States Holocaust Memorial Museum. He has contributed articles to the *New York Times, Newsweek,* the *Los Angeles Times,* and other publications.

Anna E. Rosmus has dedicated her life to uncovering the Nazi past of her hometown and to combating the neo-Nazis in Germany. As a freelance writer, she has written seven books, initiated several movies, and contributed numerous essays to magazines and newspapers, such as *La Pensée et les Hommes, Holocaust and Genocide Studies,* the *New York Times,* the *European,* and *Aufbau.*

Elka Rottgardt is an organizational psychologist and lives in Köln, Germany.

Julie Salamon is the author of *The Net of Dreams, The Devil's Candy, White Lies,* and *The Christmas Tree.* She is a former film critic of the *Wall Street Journal,* and has written for the *New York Times, The New Yorker, Vanity Fair, Vogue,* and *The New Republic.*

Nava Semel was born in Israel. She has published nine books and three plays, and also writes scripts and translates plays for the Israeli theater. Her work focuses on children of Holocaust survivors, Israeli split identity, and on growing up in a scarred society. Her books have been published in the United States, Germany, Italy, Czech Republic, Spain, Holland, France, and Romania. *Becoming Gershona* received the 1990 National Jewish Book Award. *Flying Lessons* was published by Simon and Schuster in 1995. She received the Prime Minister's Award for Literature in 1996.

Christian Staffa was born in 1959 in Essen, Germany. He studied Protestant theology in Berlin, Tubingen, and Prague. In 1989, he left his church career and founded, together with a sociologist, an institute for comparative history studies in Berlin. In April 1999, he became the executive director of Action Reconciliation Service for Peace, which also has a branch in Philadelphia.

Daniel Vogelmann was born in Florence, Italy, on May 28, 1948; his parents were Schulim and Albna Mondolfi Passigli. In his youth he wrote some books of poems, and then he became publisher of Editrice la Giuntina, a small publishing house specializing in books on Jewish subjects.

Gottfried H. Wagner was born in Bayreuth, Germany, in 1947. He received a doctorate in musicology, philosophy, and German philology at the University of Vienna. Dr. Wagner lectures internationally and is a stage and video director, music historian, and writer (central topic: German-Jewish history and art of the nineteenth and twentieth centuries). He is active, with Abraham Peck, as cofounder of the Post-Holocaust Dialogue Group. The English translation of his autobiography, *Twilight of the Wagners: The Unveiling of a Family Legacy,* appeared in 1999 in the United States.

Diane Wyshogrod is a writer and clinical psychologist in private practice. Born and raised in New York, she now lives in Jerusalem with her husband and three sons.

Second Generation Voices

Introduction

The story is told of a Jewish youth in the time of King Herod. Leaving Jerusalem for Rome, the young man brings with him a pillow on which he always slept. One night the pillow caught on fire—the night the Temple in Jerusalem burst into flames. Commenting on this tale by Uri-Zvi Greenberg, Elie Wiesel observes that "yes, one can live a thousand miles away from the Temple and see it burn. One can die in Auschwitz after Auschwitz."[1] Jewish second-generation witnesses to the Holocaust rest on such a fiery pillow. Although they were *not* in Auschwitz, their lives are lived in the shadow of death camps. These witnesses once removed have a plethora of questions about their identity as Jews and as children of survivors. The core question for the second generation remains. What is their connection to the Holocaust? How do they define their relationship to their parents? Their parents suffered, but what have been the effects on the offspring?

Where does the second generation fit in the history of the Shoah? For this generation, the Holocaust means the eternal *presence of an absence*, that is those who were murdered in the Shoah. The legacy of the Holocaust is present in a variety of ways for the second generation, issues of intergenerational communication, parental enmeshment, and separation concerns. This legacy also undergirds their identity, their sensitivity to multicultural issues, and their concern for social justice. The contributors from the Jewish second generation represented in this book reflect an *intensely personal* relationship to this legacy and a distinctive voice in responding to the *presence of the absence*.

There is, however, another second generation, descendants of perpetrators, about whom far less is known. How do they define their relationship to their parents? What have been the effects on the offspring? Thus, while

---

1. Elie Wiesel, *One Generation After*, trans. Lily Edelman and Elie Wiesel (New York: Schocken Books, 1985), 168–69.

1

Prof. Ernestine Schlant Bradley correctly asserts that "the Holocaust is as much a permanent part of German history as it is of Jewish history,"[2] memory of the Shoah and the role it plays in the interpsychic lives of the descendants varies between the two generations. The German second generation needs to confront a repressed past in which the fate of the Jews is never acknowledged by the perpetrator generation. Moreover, the German "generation after" may choose not to consciously acknowledge the impact of the Shoah.

Although both second generations were raised in partial or total silence about the past, the reason for this silence was different. For Jewish survivors the past contained painful and oppressive memories. The perpetrators were silent because of their guilt. Our contributors reveal much about the similarities and differences between these generations.

Both groups share the need to find out who they are, which, in turn, necessitates their dealing in a healthy way with their parents. This "working" through," about which more will be said shortly, may empower the second generation to confront their Holocaust legacy. Contributors to this book seek a healing of the self (*tikkun atzmi*) and many are determined to achieve—insofar as possible—a repair of the world (*tikkun olam*).

Children of Survivors

Sons and daughters of *survivors* are like the children of Job of antiquity. Born into homes marked by the millennial problem of theodicy, they are "replacement" children. Unlike their mythic forebears, however, the contemporary children of catastrophe inhabit a world deeply scarred by their parents' Holocaust experience.

Their post-Auschwitz legacy is one of questions. Moreover, the questions change as the children of Job themselves grow and become parents. For example, as children, the second generation wonder why their friends have grandparents and extended families while they have none. Later, they wonder what happened to their parents' first families, and why their parents had to suffer. Theologically, the issue involves attempting to bridge the gulf between pronouncements about a God who intervenes in history and the existence of death camps. The Jewish second generation is committed to transmitting their legacy to their children, the third generation.

---

2. Ernestine Schlant, *The Language of Silence: West German Literature and the Holocaust* (New York: Routledge, 1999), 20. Hereafter this work will be cited as *The Language of Silence*.

The legacy of survivors also has a life-affirming impact. Many of the second generation witnesses seek a post-Auschwitz mending of the world. For instance, numerous children of survivors enter the helping professions, for example, marriage and family therapists, mental health counselors, psychologists, psychiatrists, social workers, writers, attorneys, and teachers. Furthermore, many of the Jewish second generation speak with a moral voice, on issues ranging from social justice to peace in the Middle East to counseling children of Vietnamese boat people.

At the June 1981 World Gathering of Holocaust Survivors held in Jerusalem, one thousand of the second generation conducted their own sessions and accepted the legacy of their parents to bear witness to the world. Later that year an International Network of Children of Jewish Holocaust Survivors was established and Menachem Z. Rosensaft became its founding chairperson. The first International Conference of Children of Holocaust Survivors convened in New York City (1984) and was addressed by the late Rabbi Dr. Gerson D. Cohen and Elie Wiesel.

The Jewish second generation emerged as a distinct group in the midseventies, and gathered momentum in the eighties and early nineties. Its members expressed their Holocaust inheritance through a variety of genres: art, essays, film, memoirs, novels, poetry, and short stories.[3] This generation soon assumed the dimensions of a social movement whose members were united by their legacy; their common experiences enabled them to communicate across geographical and linguistic borders.

The second generation is intimately connected to the Holocaust by both a physical and psychic umbilical cord. Helen Epstein captures the relationship of this generation to the Shoah:

> Remembering the Holocaust is not an issue for us: we are, in our parents' minds, the answer to the Holocaust. We are, in our own minds, the guardians of a problematic, unique and volatile legacy. We do not need to be reminded of it: rather, we need to learn how to translate our

3. For a study of literary and cinematic responses of the second generation, see Alan L. Berger, *Children of Job: American Second Generation Witness to the Holocaust* (Albany: SUNY Press, 1997). Second-generation poetry is gathered in Stewart J. Floresheim, ed., *Ghosts of the Holocaust: An Anthology of Poetry by the Second Generation* (Detroit: Wayne State Univ. Press, 1989), and Charles Fishman, ed., *Blood to Remember: American Poets on the Holocaust* (Lubbock: Texas Tech Univ. Press, 1991). Second-generation artistic responses are discussed in Vivian Alpert Thompson, ed., *A Mission in Art: Recent Holocaust Work in America* (Macon, Ga: Mercer Univ. Press, 1988).

consciousness of evil, our skepticism, our sense of outrage into constructive action.[4]

Children of Perpetrators

Offspring of the *perpetrators,* however, need to confront the enormous
conflict between love for their parents and the fact that their progenitors
were Nazis, Nazi sympathizers, informers for the Third Reich, or passive
witnesses who watched as their friends and neighbors were humiliated,
robbed, and deported. Many of the German parents, uncles, or grandparents were themselves murderers—what Telford Taylor described as the "running dogs" of murder, some were prominent industrialists who exploited
slave labor (Alfried Krupp), others were cultural icons of National Socialism, such as Richard Wagner. The German second generation inherits the
sins of the fathers (and mothers) through no fault of their own, much in
the manner described in Jeremiah: "The fathers have eaten a sour grape and
the children's teeth are set on edge" (31:29).

○ Although collective guilt is a sterile and unfounded notion, the German
second generation inherits a dark legacy.●They struggle to reconcile their
image of German identity with the murderous anti-Semitic history of their
country. All of this occurs amidst a background of familial silence about the
Shoah. Martin Rumscheidt, a pastor and son of perpetrators, identifies this
silence as the cause of the pain of the German second generation. "Six
million Jews dead, gone," he writes. "I never knew you, but how present
you are to me in the silence which marks my generation. Indeed, it is the
protest against that silence which makes us a generation, especially to ourselves."[5] This phenomenon among the perpetrator generation is described
by Alexander and Margarete Mitscherlich as "the inability to mourn." The
Mitscherlichs describe many in the German *second* generation as "orphans
with parents."

Here one needs to keep in mind Jeremiah's further admonition: "But
every one shall die for his own iniquity; every man that eateth the sour
grape, his teeth shall be set on edge" (31:30). Elie Wiesel observes that

4. Helen Epstein, "Guardians of the Legacy," in *Jerusalem Post Supplement—Holocaust
Survivors Gathering,* June 14, 1981, p. 7.

5. Martin Rumscheidt, "Children of Perpetrators: The Generation after Auschwitz," in
What Kind of God? Essays in Honor of Richard L. Rubenstein. ed. Betty Rogers Rubenstein and
Michael Berenbaum (Lanham, Md.: Univ. Press of America, 1995), 51.

"the children of perpetrators are not guilty of the crimes, but they are responsible for perpetuating the memory of what their parents have done."[6]

Dark Lullabies, a film made by a Canadian, Irene Lilienheim-Angelico, German-born daughter of survivors, underscores the difference between the two second generations. The filmmaker has a discussion with Harald Lüders, her German counterpart who says:

> For all children of survivors you can go into the past and it will make you closer to your people. But I think, in a way, for some Germans it is effectively the other way around. The more you kind of go into it, the more it takes you away at least from a big part of your own people; from a huge part of the history of your own country. I envy you that you could do that, feel close to your people.

What emerges from this film is the fact that for the German second generation to confront the repressed past, it is first necessary, in the words of the granddaughter of the vice-commandant of Auschwitz, "to live in complete opposition to what the generation before me did,"

The second generation of victims has no extended family, but seeks—and cherishes—a memory. The second generation of perpetrators has an extended family, who actively oppose memory of the Holocaust. Moreover, this generation does not necessarily feel compelled to explore the past. They may ignore, deny, or repress their Nazi legacy. Some, neo-Nazis, either deny or celebrate the murder of the Jewish people.

Julie Goschalk, a German-born daughter of survivors, succinctly describes the different emotions confronting the two second generations as they work through relationships with parents. "Children of survivors," she writes, "can for the most part look to our parents with pride and admiration. The children of perpetrators, however, see themselves reflected in the eyes of evil."

The reflections in this book reveal how the two second generations deal with their Holocaust legacy. All of the writers report that this is the most personal and formidable piece they have ever written. Not difficult in research or intellectual understanding, but difficult in the sense that only the intensely personal can be. Authentically encountering who one is and what shapes one's identity is always difficult. Connecting to family, and to self,

---

6. Elie Wiesel, in a telephone discussion with Alan L. Berger's seminar at Florida Atlantic Univ., Mar. 29, 2000.

unlocking the unconscious, naming that which for so long had gone without a name—all are actions that require commitment and courage.

Julie Salamon, in *The Net of Dreams,* a memoir of the author's journey to Hungary and Poland with her survivor mother and stepfather, tells of visiting the set of *Schindler's List.* She reports receiving a "cheery" fax from Spielberg's publicist telling her that "Auschwitz was easy to get to." Salamon's response? "It's getting *away* from it that really is very difficult."[7] The book's contributors describe not so much a getting away from Auschwitz; that is impossible for the second generation. Rather, these responses tell how Auschwitz continues to wound, and how the second-generation witnesses work through and transmit their legacy. It remains to be seen whether the world will heed their witness.

Working Though

Working through does not mean "getting over" the Holocaust. Rather, it is appropriate to understand working through in the therapeutic sense of the term. Here, one revisits the source of pain by speaking about it, analyzing its impact on an individual's perception of psychosocial life, his/her religious perspective, and his/her view of the "other." In the process, one seeks to detoxify the issues involved so that further exploration and understanding can occur without the various psychic barriers that can block self-understanding. In contrast to Dominick LaCapra's "reading scars," to master the traumatic past, this way of working through enables one to be in touch with the past without being paralyzed by its legacy.[8] Commenting on LaCapra's terminology, Helen Epstein observes that "scars are covers that have become dry and static over wounds."[9] For Epstein, working through means having achieved the capacity for confronting the Shoah while at the same time placing the catastrophe within the broader perspective of Jewish history.

The question needs to be asked what the offspring do with their inherited memory. Emmanuel Levinas's insight concerning memory of Auschwitz and Judaism provides a useful clue. He writes:

7. Julie Salamon, *The Net of Dreams: A Family's Search for a Rightful Place* (New York: Random House, 1996), 31.

8. LaCapra is cited by Janet Burstein in "Traumatic Memory and American Jewish Writers: One Generation After the Holocaust" in Modern Jewish Studies vol. 2, 1999, 189.

9. Helen Epstein, letter to Alan L. Berger, Nov. 25, 1998.

> It is not memory itself which is essential but the reading, the interpretation of the facts of memory. The work of memory consists not at all of plunging into the past, but of renewing the past through new experiences, new circumstances, new wonders or horrors of real life. And from this point of view, it is the future that is important and not purely the past. . . . The essential is to always find the actuality of the lessons of the Holocaust.[10]

Levinas's call for each generation to interpret *and* renew the "facts of memory" requires everyone to experience a foundational event in history, such as the Exodus in the Passover Haggadah. Like much of the modern, and postmodern, world, Levinas invests individuals with the responsibility for reading, that is, shaping, the experience.

Studies of the Second Generation

Two pioneering works on the Jewish second generation were published in the late 1970s. One, an anthology, *Living after the Holocaust: Reflections by Children of Survivors in America* (edited by Lucy Y. Steinitz and David M. Szonyi, 1979), delineates the existence of the second generation and some of the interpsychic issues specific to its identity. This book reflects the offspring at a different time in their lives, for example, before many of them became parents themselves and before the time that their own parents' testimony became important to the culture at large. Although the Shoah occurred before they were born, all of the contributors attest that it is the most important event in their lives.

The second work is Helen Epstein's *Children of the Holocaust: Conversations with Sons and Daughters of Survivors* (1979). Frequently referred to as the "bible" of the second generation, Epstein's book speaks about offspring of survivors in a way that did much both to alert the public to the second-generation phenomenon, that is, a group having a distinctive angle of vision on the legacy of the Holocaust and its impact on Jewish identity, and to focus attention on the fact that the second-generation consists of an inordinately high proportion of articulate and high-functioning individuals. Epstein put into words what most in the second generation feel.

She writes of an "iron box buried so deep inside me that I was never sure just what it was. I knew I carried slippery, combustible things more

10. Levinas, as cited by Ellen Fine in "Transmission of Memory: The Post-Holocaust Generation in the Diaspora," in Efraim Sicher, ed., *Breaking Crystal: Writing and Memory after Auschwtiz* (Urbana: Univ. of Illinois Press, 1998) 185–86.

secret than sex and more dangerous than any shadow or ghost. Ghosts had shape and name. What lay inside my iron box had none. Whatever lived inside me was so potent that words crumbled before they could begin to describe." This observation struck with great resonance among children of survivors both nationally and internationally.

In the late eighties and early nineties, Art Spiegelman's *Maus* volumes, which depicted Jews as mice and Nazis as cats, focused international attention on the psychosocial legacy of the Shoah for both survivors and the second generation.

Responses by the German second generation were much slower in coming. Two works published in the late eighties brought public attention to this group. Peter Sichrovsky, an Austrian-born Jewish journalist, conducted a series of interviews with children of Nazi families. First published in 1987 as *Schuldig geboren: Kinder aus Nazifamilien,* Sichrovsky's work appeared in English one year later as *Born Guilty: Children of Nazi Families* (New York, Basic Books). In fifteen interviews, Sichrovsky revealed a variety of German second-generation attitudes. For example, some in this generation are protective of their fathers. Many, reports Sichrovsky, view their families as victims. "For the children of Nazis," he writes, "the unconditional love of parents is an indulgence they cannot afford."

Dan Bar-On's *Legacy of Silence: Encounters with Children of the Third Reich* (Harvard Univ. Press, 1989) is the first scholarly study in English that examines the impact of children's Nazi legacy on the German second generation. Bar-On, an Israeli professor of social psychology whose parents fled Vienna before the Anschluss, conducted more than fifty interviews with descendants of perpetrators. He reports two dominant images that emerge from the interviews: "the dark side of the mind and the quest for hope."[11] Bar-On links the first image to the clinical terms *denial* and *repression,* which indicate "knowledge or awareness that has been shifted away from consciousness."[12]

The quest for hope, attests Bar-On, is a "working through" process that moves away from parental euphemisms and distortions and toward acknowledging what happened during the Holocaust, "and what meaning those events have, especially for those who suffered."[13] This working through is hampered by the persistent repression of memory by perpetrator parents. Although when Bar-On published his book there was little public discussion

11. Dan Bar-on, 330.
12. Ibid., 331.
13. Ibid.

of this topic, he rightly observed a characteristic difference between the second generations. Children of survivors, he notes, were charged with the task of biological survival. Children of victimizers appear fearful that they will perpetuate a "bad seed."[14]

Second Generation Voices contains works by the offspring of survivors *and* perpetrators in a global perspective. Consequently, it contributes to the ongoing dialogue between these groups while at the same time acknowledging the barriers involved on both sides. For many years the two second generations were unable to speak to each other. This situation is slowly beginning to change. Books and films dealing with the German second generation have begun to appear.[15]

There are significant differences between the two generations, which are described in detail in part 6. At this point, it will suffice to indicate the differences by observing the following. The Jewish second generation response is unified by a search to *connect* with the past. The path to achieving this rootedness includes understanding their parents better and sharpening their own identity in relation to Jewish history. Among the German second generation that chooses to confront the repressed Nazi past, its response is built on a *rejection* of this repression. For example, we note themes of exile, rejection of parents, country, and language. Moreover, there is a cutting off from family in an attempt to gain one's own identity before seeking to confront Germany's Holocaust history.

There is, however, also disagreement on the possibility and need for dialogue. Some believe strongly in the necessity of speaking to each other (see part 7). Others are adamantly opposed, as seen in the following paragraph.

14. *Legacy of Silence,* 330.

15. Gerald L. Posner, *Hitler's Children: Sons and Daughters of the Third Reich Talk about Themselves and Their Families* (New York: Random House, 1991); Niklas Frank, son of Hans Frank the governor-general of the Nazi généralgouvernement in Poland, wrote a memoir, *In the Shadow of the Reich* (New York: Knopf, 1991), condemning his father and Nazism; and the searing poetry of Ursala Duba's *Tales from a Child of the Enemy* (New York: Penguin, 1995). See also Michael Verhoeven's 1990 film, *Nasty Girl,* based on the activities of Anna Rosmus in exposing the Nazi past of Passau, her Bavarian hometown. Björn Krondorfer, *Remembrance and Reconciliation: Encounters Between Young Jews and Germans* (New Haven: Yale Univ. Press, 1995), speaks insightfully about the third generation and the creative dance ritual that helps them work through their Holocaust legacy. For an insightful discussion of literary works by the German second generation, see Schlant's *The Language of Silence,* esp. chap. 9, which analyzes the work of "post-unification" writers Bernhard Schlink, Peter Schneider, and W. G. Sebald.

[Despite this book's aims two of the writers in it, Melvin Jules Bukiet and Anita Norich, nearly withdrew their essays when they belatedly realized that it included Germans as well as Jews, while a third, Barbara Finkelstein, expressed deep reservations about "bridge-building" exercises.] Ms. Finkelstein views any implied community between these two groups as perverse and disrespectful to the martyred dead. Likewise, Ms. Norwich has refrained from engaging in "dialogue" in the past and sees no reason to begin now that it has become more common. She believes that such attempts to create a false and necessarily shallow sense of connectedness between the heirs of Holocaust victims and their murderers is an insult to history and to the Jewish people whose loss we continue to mourn. Mr. Bukiet has said in public that he holds guilty "not only the octogenarian perpetrators but . . . their children and their children's children and the yet unborn tainted by their German blood." In short, he does not keep company with the descendants of his ancestors' killers. Yet, because of Ms. Norich's and Mr. Bukiet's and Ms. Finkelstein's contractual obligations to the publisher and their personal affection for the editor, they all agreed not to remove their work in return for this paragraph.

As the torch of remembrance is being passed from survivors to the second generation, so, too, is this generation preparing its own rituals, attitudes, and memories to be passed to the third generation. (See especially parts 3 and 4). This generation also addresses the postmodern concern with memory and ethnic identity in a clear and focused way that speaks to a great many groups having shared interest in issues of self, family, community, and culture. Second-generation—children of survivor—groups exist in many cities across America; new groups are being formed. For example, a Boston based organization called One by One brings together offspring of survivors and of perpetrators. A German-Jewish dialogue group, also located in Boston, began in 1987. These encounters help participants get past stereotypes of the *other*, while acknowledging the impact of their Holocaust legacy.

Like the ripples caused by a rock thrown into a river, the six millionfold shock waves caused by the Shoah continue to emanate throughout the generations. Daughters and sons of survivors are helping shape the contours of Holocaust memory for the future. Thus, sons and daughters of survivors add their own chapter to the historical book of intergenerational Holocaust representation.

A word is in order to explain the inception of this project. The editors have both an intellectual and personal connection to the Holocaust and its legacy. Naomi Berger was born after the war. Her parents survived Auschwitz where they lost all their extended family. Her father's first wife and four children were gassed. Her mother lost her three sisters and her first husband, who was shot to death by the Nazis. Naomi's clinical training as a marriage and family therapist, and her work with individuals and families, was a natural outgrowth of her interest in the impact of family history on one's emotional development and well-being. In the early seventies, following Eva Fogelman's encouragement, she became one of the core members of a second-generation support group in Syracuse, New York. The group met regularly for seven years and crystallized common issues shared by the second generation.

At the same time, Naomi had an opportunity to supervise a German graduate student in the Marriage and Family Therapy Program of Syracuse University. The student had left Germany in her late teens as a reaction to her family, who were Nazi sympathizers. Getting to know this woman sparked Naomi's interest in looking at the second generation of Germans, and led to recognizing their deep issues concerning their parent's wartime roles. It was a revelation to discover that some of the issues plaguing the children of perpetrators are like children-of-survivor issues. Several crucial events then ensued. After a psychoanalytic experience, a journey of self-discovery that helped work through the emotional issues connected to growing up in a survivor household, and visits to a number of death camps, the Holocaust and its lessons came to the forefront of her conscious life. A course in psychopathology required a paper titled "Personal Journey." This served as incentive for Naomi to put in writing some reflections about her second-generation experience.

Alan Berger has spent twenty-five years teaching, researching, and writing about the Holocaust. In the midseventies he arranged a symposium on the Shoah and its meanings for Christianity and Judaism. The event took place at Syracuse University on a dark, snowy, and blustery January day. Inside Hendricks Chapel, the speakers, Professors Emil L. Fackenheim and Franklin H. Littell, generated much heat—and anger. Alan's series of unending questions about the role of both God and humanity in the catastrophe of the Jewish people found earlier expression in his readings of the works of Elie Wiesel and Irving "Yitz" Greenberg. In 1977 he initiated the first Holocaust course ever taught for academic credit at Syracuse University.

Listening to his mother-in-law speak of gas chambers and children murdered in the camps became integral to Alan's Friday evening ritual. While celebrating God's world-creating activities, and preparing to hallow the Sabbath, tales were told—and heard—about deportations and about Auschwitz, about children who never became adults, and about an indifferent world. Alan and Naomi took their young sons to Mauthausen, another camp, where the grandfather they never knew had been imprisoned.

Alan began reading and writing about the second generation in the late eighties. He discovered many novels and poems, films, and short stories that had been written and made by sons and daughters of survivors. His book *Children of Job* stimulated Alan to seek out additional second-generation voices so that their witness be heard. Moreover, he has been in dialogue with the German second generation concerning their own Holocaust legacy.

As we conceptualized the format for this anthology, we asked the contributors to write personal reflections that reveal the second generations' coming to terms with their parents and themselves. The call for manuscripts included five areas ranging from the impact of the Holocaust as reflected in personal experience at home, school, work and in interpersonal relationships to issues of faith and belief after Auschwitz. The contributions to this anthology address the following topics: *Family Ties,* which, in turn, is subdivided into two portions, *The Search for Roots* and *Inheriting Parental Trauma; The Journey to Parents' Birthplaces and to Death Camps; Issues of Faith and Religion; Identity and the Yiddish Language; Confronting a Repressed Past; Is Dialogue Possible?*

These distinctions are fluid. Moreover, each of the reflections is concerned with more than one issue. However, the topics are self-contained and offer a glimpse at how the legacy of the Holocaust continues to be felt in the lives of its second-generation witnesses. Our main interest was in stimulating these witnesses to share their experiences and personal reflections in a manner that allows the most honesty and openness.

We hope that this anthology will provide readers with a sense of what issues the second generation is, like Jacob of antiquity, wrestling with, and how this generation is working through its inheritance. We also hope that this book can in some way help the two generations open a fruitful and honest dialogue. In an age that is increasingly defined by victims and offspring of tragedy, such as, boat people, refugees, genocides, and "ethnic cleansing," this drama has universal significance.

PART ONE

Family Ties

The Search for Roots

Introduction

Writings in this part reveal the complex and continuing legacy of the Holocaust as it manifests itself in family ties. Witnessing their parents continuing survival, the second generation inherits both positive and negative dimensions of their legacy. For instance, strong family ties mark survivor households. Feelings of mutual responsibility are punctuated by the desire of parents and children to protect each other from pain and suffering. On the other side of the coin, however, the trauma of the Holocaust continues to manifest itself in such an intense manner that some in the second generation view themselves as living in an emotional concentration camp.

Contributors to this part discuss their relationship dynamics and how their parents' Holocaust experience shaped the type of bond they established with their parents, which is reflected in their relationships with their own children, and their capacity for intimacy. The reflections in this part deal with a variety of second generation familial issues, including feelings of loyalty and the complexity of separation and differentiation. In addition, there is a meditation concerning the lifesaving action of a Christian helper during the Holocaust.

Once Removed

LISA REITMAN-DOBI

In early July of 1996, my father and I drove my eight-year-old daughter to her first sleep-away camp. Becky is the center of his universe. On the way home, he wiped a tear from his eye and said, "I can't imagine that she'll be away all summer. It seems like an eternity. You know," he added, "it's amazing. She's only here because of the war." "You mean because Mommy came here after the war?" I asked. "No," he said. "I felt that if every family had one more child, that we could make up for the six million that were murdered." My father is American. But my mother is the daughter of an Austrian father and a Polish mother. I was the extra child, born nearly a decade later than my two older sisters. All my life, I've felt a tremendous weight on me, something that I could not understand, although I knew it had to do with the Holocaust. Although my father is from the Bronx and my mother did not go through the camps, I felt different, lonely, with a keen sensitivity to suffering. I also felt loads of anger and grief, emotions that seemed rampant and unjustified because I had virtually nothing to pin them on. Why should I care? I didn't go through the war, my mother had gotten out of central Europe in time to take refuge in Morocco, and met my father in the forties when she arrived here alone. I was born in New York City. I was privileged. I was safe. Why was I miserable when I seemed to have "everything going for me" (a phrase my mother has repeated over the years)? What more did I want? I felt that I had no right to be unhappy, to feel deprived, to mourn for that which I never really knew or lost because the war had had nothing to do with me. Or had it?

The information came to me at a time when I had been grappling with terrible depression and was questioning every decision I've ever made. Why had I never lived away from my parents? Why did I feel such urgency to generate a family, to have children for my parents to hold? Even though I had been excited at the prospect of going to college in New England, I was miserable once I got there. I felt out of place and intimidated. Everyone seemed to be blond, rowed on the crew team, and wore Bermuda shorts. In short, it was not a Jewish school. But it was a secular school. I had never gone to a Jewish school, though my own schools had been primarily composed of Jewish students. It just didn't make sense. An intelligent girl who has traveled extensively should be able to adjust to and enjoy college! Depressed, I came back home. I was counseled and treated as sensitive, introspective, creative, poetic, and simply unhappy. Besides, depression could also be taken for the common angst of youth and early adult life. I transferred to a university in Manhattan, where my parents had moved to an apartment. During my sophomore year in college, I moved in with my boyfriend. Our apartment happened to be eleven city blocks away from my parents' home. We got married when I turned twenty-two the weekend after graduation. Still connected to my family of origin by irresistant, invisible strings, I was resolved to start my own family. And I did this, safe in the wake of my mother's course. During the second pregnancy, I joked with my parents. "Now there's one for each of you." But behind every joke, there is a little grain of truth. I wanted to present them with another generation. Why? I didn't know. It was something I felt. Throughout my experiences with therapy, I resisted the idea that my life is "too entwined" with that of my mother. I responded that family is too valuable to throw away and ignore. With all my mother went through, with all the loss she endured, I felt a pressing responsibility to be in her life.

Much of the time I felt that there has been something missing in my life. But I managed to stay two steps ahead of my anxieties the only way I knew how, the way I had seen my mother cope. I kept busy. I immersed myself in the caretaking of others. When I turned thirty, I hit an emotional low point. I began to see a therapist, who recognized what had gone unseen for so long. It turned out that she had worked with children of survivors.

She began to ask me about my mother, the war, many questions that I had never thought were particularly significant. My mother never sat down to deliver a detailed account of her childhood itinerary. Over the years, information about her childhood and the effects of the war came in scattered pieces. They still do.

"Where was your mother during the war?"

"The war? She was in North Africa."

"So she's a survivor."

"No, she's not." I answered in the same rehearsed way I had always answered questions about my foreign-born mother. My mother sees herself as a worldly expatriate, a lucky, intelligent woman whose energy, resourcefulness, and optimism carried her through. Her childhood was difficult, it's true. But she did not identify herself as a survivor. Of course I felt something about the Holocaust. As a Jew, who wouldn't? Dreams? Nightmares? Sure. All my life, I've had the recurring nightmare of the SS coming to our house.

I am in my parents' bedroom in the house I grew up. I am on their bed looking out the window and I'm scared because Nazis are parked across the street and they're on their way over. Our dog (a German shepherd) is barking fiercely and I don't know if they can get in anyway. I'm frightened and alone.

My dreams weren't always specifically about Nazis, but of forced detainment, fear, and persecution.

I accepted that there may be some truth to the idea that the war had impacted my thoughts. But it had been such a big event for everyone . . . hadn't it? Didn't everyone have deportation nightmares?

I had never thought of my mother as a survivor. I knew I felt sorry for her, losing her parents at a young age, living in foreign countries, growing up during a war. "We didn't *flee*," she has told me numerous times. "We *left*." "Escape" was a stronger word that she reserved for others, like her young cousins in Paris. It was "extremely upsetting" when the cousins came home from school one day to find that their mother, sister, and brother had been rounded up and deported. But a neighbor saw the girls and pulled them into her home. Their story of survival began there. Isn't that lucky?

My mother's "family," aside from the handful in Switzerland and Israel, existed in yellowing photographs that lived in old boxes from Saks Fifth Avenue and Best & Company. The pictures were not displayed. While I grew up, they sat silently on a shelf in her closet. I liked to look through them, but to do that, I had to make an effort. I would drag a chair into her closet, stretch up on my toes, and carefully take down one box and then another. Those boxes were weak and heavy from the weight of the many pictures and postcards. I always felt scared that I would drop them. The contents seemed eerily sacred; it would be like spilling bones, because this was all that was left. The pictures show gatherings in Austria with many aunts and uncles and children. There are photos of a Purim party, very festive but not particularly religious. All the children are dressed in elaborate costumes. Old photographs seem to make even children's faces appear older, more wizened. I already knew that they had disappeared under traumatic circumstances, and to me, it showed on their faces. But everyone pictured is elegant and smiling. There is also a priest in one of the pictures. He must have been a family friend. My grandfather's family lived a completely secular, assimilated lifestyle. They were Austrian first, and then Jewish. Some of the pictures were studio-style portraits that doubled as postcards. There is scratchy, elaborate German script on the back. I would stare at the loopy foreign words and try to figure out what they said. I even ventured to ask my mother. She was of no help. She would take a quick look and say, "It says 'Dear Petr'—that's my father—'We are . . .' no, I don't understand their writing." I was frustrated. She wasn't even trying to figure it out. I wanted to know more. This was my family. Wasn't it?

As I got older, I became more inquisitive. My modern American Life, a world of TV dinners, hula hoops, and "Romper Room," did not succeed in eclipsing the past. I knew that the war, the Holocaust specifically, was a topic that had been relegated to the topmost shelf, something that wouldn't be directly addressed. By the time I was in fifth or sixth grade, I was aching to know details, morbid details. I craved more information. I assumed that the truth must be awfully grotesque for it to be constantly avoided or shrouded in fantasy and romanticism. I was not completely ignorant. On the contrary. It was because I knew a fair bit about the war that my curiosity was piqued. I had always known about the Holocaust. I had always known about the concentration camps. I can't say how. It's as if I were born with a degree of information that had been genetically installed, like my brown hair and brown eyes. I knew that an isolated, distant horror, something that could never happen again, mind you, had severed the past from the present without a trace. I knew my mother's family had been shattered by the war, but she herself had survived, and had never referred to herself as anything other than strong and lucky. I had never seen her mourn or cry or show any anger at the injustice during her childhood. I sensed that I was required to appreciate the rich childhood that had been denied my mother. But instead of happy, I felt sad. I felt sad for my mother, sad for everyone, and then guilty for feeling sad. Everyone called me a "sensitive child." The reality was that I was in a perpetual state of mourning for that which I had never known, as much as there was to know. But for that, I had to prod. I felt badly for my mother. I didn't want to be mean to her and insensitive by stirring up sadness. So I tried to play dumb and asked her questions in an offhand way. This way, I could feel less guilty. But my mother played dumb too. When I asked her about relatives who had stayed in Europe, my mother shrugged and said, "I don't know," or, "I don't remember." My memory is of her "running away" from these conversations. She flew around the house, tossing laundry into the machine, running back upstairs to take care of a million small tasks. She was always in motion. I spent a lot of time following her around despite my awareness that she might feel upset. I was persistent. I think I badgered her.

"What happened if someone hadn't left like you did?"

"They were deported." She squirted Windex and ran a dust cloth after it.

"What's 'deported' "?

"Taken away." She went to the other end of the room. I went with her.

"Was anyone actually in a camp?"

"Of course. But no one knows."

"What do you mean 'no one knows'?"

"It's difficult to explain. Do you have homework to do?"

"I will. When they got deported, didn't they get sent to camps?"

"Probably."

"Did anyone live through a camp?"

"Probably not."

"How do you know?"

"They died. Everyone died."

"Of what?"

"Disease."

"What kind?"

"What kind? Typhus, different things."

"Why?"

"Because of the conditions."

"All your relatives?" I must have exasperated her.

"I was little. I don't remember very well."

"Some got out, Mom. Like Hana and Alena."

"That was unusual." She moved books from left to right and pushed the dust from side to side.

"Not everybody died."

"Not everyone. Most. Did you practice the piano?"

"I will. How do you know no one got out?"

"They were usually exterminated. You must practice."

"I will. How do you know?"

"They kept records." And then I remember her looking away, as if picturing something. She even slowed down a bit. "I think I had a cousin who did survive Auschwitz."

"So what happened to him?"

"I think he went to England. He woke up at five every morning screaming. He died." She dusted the piano. "It's a pity. You have an amazing ear."

"I will practice, I will. What happened to him?"

"He was very creative, just like my mother." She turned to look at me. "Maybe you have cousins in England! Wouldn't that be something?"

It was infinitely more appealing and appeasing to hang onto malleable illusions. That way, you could add your own ironic twists and happy endings.

"Do you think there are other cousins who survived?"

"I have no way of knowing. I'm sure they were exterminated."

My mother casually used words such as exterminated, gassed, murdered. She was offhand about it, treating the annihilation of her family in such a nonchalant way that it seemed normal. Whether there were cousins in England or in Spain, whether they had been shot, cremated, worked to death, or hanged, were all equally plausible, and to live with that, they had to be unilaterally acceptable. She clung to particular memories, focusing on the talents and qualities that were her birthright. What she chose to remember were the traits that she eagerly passed down to her children. She was selective, choosing only the positive, legendary traits. "You have Malka's writing talent." Or "You have the Lichtenstein creativity." Those who were killed became canonized, and with her indispensable perspective turned a time of trauma and confusion into a canvas for reinvention and potential.

Where I grew up, on the south shore of Long Island, mine was "the mother with the accent." Even her name, Jana, was difficult for most Americans to pronounce. (She gave all three of her daughter's international names, "just in case," she says). When she was on the phone, she spoke French. She didn't play tennis or golf. She didn't belong to any clubs and never socialized with our immediate neighbors. We lived in a suburb, which she regarded as a cultural wasteland, and so she brought us into Manhattan frequently for concerts, museums, browsing in Doubleday or Barnes and Noble bookstores. A well-educated, intellectual woman, she taught in the literature department at a nearby university. Her friends were European. They consisted of a few people she had met through the university and a handful of women she had known in Morocco. They too, had married American men. Some of them lived only twenty minutes away but they didn't come over much and certainly never visited to play cards or sit by a pool. Like my mother, they were all busy with their children. Their children were the center of their universe. My mother always put us first. She is protective, to put it mildly. When I went out as a teenager, I heard "have-fun-be-careful" as one phrase. I was always the one to call home when an evening got late. My parents always knew where I was. To me, this seemed normal. As I got older, I knew that it was not as standard as I had thought, not for my American peers. "You're calling *home?*" Of course! But I began to realize it was different and I became a bit embarrassed. I started to call home when no one was around. Yet, it remained institutional. To this day, my mother knows where I am, and I know where she is virtually all the time. Now I understand that it is typical behavior in survivor families.

My mother went out of her way to make sure that my sisters and I had educations, good values, and lessons in ballet, music, and art. She always made sure that we were dressed well and looked appropriate and present-able. She did anything and everything to ensure our happiness and safety. It was as if she had developed a unique mathematical formula. There had been enough sadness in the world! The quota has been filled! Her children could be completely happy. There was so much misery to make up for. Life was to be lived with a vengeance. I believe that my mother had basic living confused with being in perpetual motion. The only reason to stop moving was fatigue and even that was not an acceptable state of affairs. "When I came to this country from Palestine, I didn't speak English and I had to learn English to be a nurse here, and, do you know, I went to Columbia and I worked at Mount Sinai. I never slept."

"How could you never sleep?"

She shrugged. "I was young. And we took Dexedrine."

Sometimes, my mother seemed melancholy, which in itself is no crime. Her refusal to admit any sadness, grief, or negativity created a visible struggle, a battle I could see on her face as she made dinner, lips pursed together, an aura of anger and anxiety simmering just below the surface. Sometimes she cried and pretended that it was because of an onion she was peeling, or fatigue. Occasionally, there was an outburst. I remember an evening that my parents had company. I was upstairs, in my room. My sisters were away in college. For whatever reason, my mother became upset. I heard a crash, and then I heard the front door slam. The car started up and pulled out of the driveway. I ran to the top of the stairs in time to see the Chevrolet's taillights disappear into the dark. I sat there and cried, with my arm around my dog. Soon she came back, composed and intent on cleaning up as if the only concern were to load up the dishwasher and put away the perishables. The next morning, the wall facing her seat in the dining room was stained with red wine, which streaked down the cream-colored wall like watery blood. The painter came on Monday. I was only relieved that she was back. To cut and run was the only way she had ever known to deal with conflict, grief, or anger. It simply had to be shut down.

Other than her in-laws, my mother had no family. Our neighbors across the street seemed to have an endless flow of aunts, uncles, and cousins in and out every weekend. When I complained about this, particularly around holidays, she shrugged and said simply that she was an only child and that she had lost her parents young. She went overboard to downplay her loss. In general, holidays were strange. We were not at all religious. On Yom Kippur, my mother stayed in bed and fasted. This, she said, was not to atone for any sins, but was in memory of her parents. But there was no mourning, no pity, and no family involvement. No one interfered. It was a solitary experience.

My mother was born in Prague when Europe was on the threshold of Nazism. Her mother, Ida Lichtenstein, an independent, creative woman from a large, close family, had been born in Poland. Her father, Petr Beutler, was from the Austro-Hungarian Empire. He came from a wealthy family. He had been raised to enjoy the activities of the assimilated Renaissance man, playing the violin, dabbling in chemistry. They met in Austria. My mother remembers her parents as being more avant garde than their immediate families. She says that they were also very much in love. My mother saved the postcards they sent to each other during a prolonged separation. I have them now. And I've read and reread the German script, not knowing what the words said, but touching the black ink as if I could feel what they meant. I wanted to know. By the time my mother was born, Ida was well established as a popular hat designer. Her professional name was Ida Blanche. She had shows, ran workshops, and was often written up in German, French, and Austrian fashion columns. Petr kept a scrapbook of newspaper articles about his wife. Throughout her relocations, my mother has held onto this tattered black book. As a child, I loved looking on the backs of each clipping to see original advertisements for Charlie Chaplin movies and ads for remedies that we would today consider snake oil. During World War I, my mother's father fought for Austria. He received two medals from the emperor Franz Joseph. One is the Iron Cross. My mother shows them to me, remarking, "Look! Two medals from the country that later tries to kill him! Isn't that something!" She says this as if it had been written by someone for a serendipitous effect. My mother depersonalized a lot of things this way. By novelizing events and giving esoteric meaning to disaster, she could accept life and even love it. Two or three years after my mother's birth, it became apparent to her father that Jewish safety in Belgium was becoming dubious. But her father was in the minority in his foresight to leave Europe. Aunts, uncles, cousins, friends stayed in France, Belgium, Poland. From Prague, the three of them went to Portugal.

While writing all of this, I asked more about her life in Portugal. Until now, her stock answer was, "I had tapeworm!" I know, I know. Growing up, I never had a rare steak or an al dente vegetable. I had coq au vin and choucroute garni. These native dishes were beyond well cooked. They were stewed. Yes, you had tapeworm. What else? She is vague about this period of her life, as if she hasn't quite decided whether to edit it out or keep it in. Now, perhaps at this stage of her life, she was ready to answer them.

"My father, upon losing his job, left Lisbon for Morocco. He wanted to establish himself there first, some manner of earning money, living. My mother and I stayed behind."

"For how long?"

"Oh, about two years."

"You mean you didn't see your father for two whole years?"

My mother shrugged. "I guess not."

"Didn't you want to know why he wasn't with you?"

"I don't know. I just accepted it."

"What was your reaction when you finally saw him?"

She hesitated, thinking, "I don't remember. I just remember being very frightened by the long head wraps that the Arabs wore."

In Lisbon, Ida, who had been such a successful hat designer, was reduced to becoming a live-in maid in a non-Jewish household. In my mother's words, she was "treated like dirt." This is painful to write. I can feel the shame, guilt, and anger that my mother must have been carrying around for her whole life.

"Where were you when she was with that family?"

"She put me with, you know, a non-Jewish family. I had to pretend not to be Jewish. I was very young but I understood that I had to be careful. Sometimes it was by making an error. During a dinner conversation one evening, the topic of temples, churches, and such came up. I don't know why. Maybe it was about some synagogues being burned. I said that my father had gone to a synagogue. Everyone stared at me. They stared! I knew right away that it was a mistake and quickly added, 'Only to visit . . . out of curiosity.' You see? Even at that age I knew what to do! I think Becky is like that. She would know. I don't know about Sasha."

Could she really be calculating the survival skills of her grandchildren? I think so. I know I did it for myself as a child. I did it when I walked home from school in the snow and my feet were cold. I knew they weren't really that cold, because there had been people who marched in the snow for miles with nothing on their feet. I calculated and measured my feelings this way. The synagogue incident was not presented as a personal case history of anti-Semitism, fear, or hiding. Indirectly, as usual, she wanted me to garner some survival skills. That was what counted. I can understand now the origins of her general distrust of people and her insistence.

"After Hitler came to power, my mother had a hard life. I didn't make it any easier. I was terribly headstrong and difficult." After her mother's death, she lived alone with her father until she was fourteen. "He died of a broken heart. I wouldn't let him remarry." He died of a heart attack. During World War I he had been exposed to some sort of gas and it had severely weakened his heart. To my mother, the physical issues were anecdotal to the emotional. The power of the mind was clearly a two-edged sword, strong enough to command life and sharp enough to ordain death. That's a lot of power. That's a lot of pressure.

During the summers, I did not go to camp. I went with my mother to Europe and Israel. She is proficient in several languages. She communicates in French, English, Hebrew, and even a bit of Italian and Spanish. But German was her first language. "My father taught me to memorize German poetry when I was barely old enough to speak. All the great poets." I've only heard her speak German once. We were on an island off the coast of Spain. My parents had bought an apartment there before the trend had kicked in and the island became commercialized. They sold it after that. (This is what they said, but the truth is that more and more Germans bought homes and condos near us and it was uncomfortable). Early on, when we were there, a number of Germans were on the island, but only one German family was living in the same apartment complex. I remember their son, Bruno. He would be cute, I thought, if he weren't German. Look how my mind works! One morning, my mother and I went down to the pool. They were there. They greeted us and my mother answered them in German. I was very surprised. It hadn't occurred to me that she could speak that language. It sounded very strange. It wasn't just that it sounded rusty and broken. It sounded deferential and young. Her daily demeanor shifted from that of an elegant woman in her fifties with a fabulous figure to that of a shy child. She hadn't spoken German since she was four. I haven't heard her speak it since.

My mother took great pride in the fact that at a moment's notice, she could pack us all up and fly to Zurich. "I threw everything into a suitcase and just left with all three of you!" Adaptability and proficiency were valuable assets. I had a passport before I had a tooth. My mother always has an updated passport. It bothers me that mine has expired—as recently as three days ago.

The summer before I turned nine, my mother and I went to Vienna. She wanted me to see the beauty of her family's country, and I was there to protect her, providing tangible proof that the past was done. Despite the Austrian position during the Third Reich and their continuing unmitigated anti-Semitism, my mother has held on to the notion that still buried inside was another Austria, the homeland of her father, a place that gave birth to Mozart, Beethoven, Goethe, and Strauss. She longed to identify with the culture of her parents, with the poetic German of her father. She held on to the past by a string, and kept a safe distance, like a spy. In Austria, we met a fair-haired and broad-shouldered man who was in his thirties. He took us around Vienna. He bought me a mocha ice cream cone. I remember enjoying that very much. We walked on cobblestone roads and took a tour of Mozart's home. Throughout the day, my mother asked him questions about present-day Austria. He spoke with pride of the Austrian recovery after the Second World War. He spoke enthusiastically of the resurgence of anti-Semitism, pleased with the fact that, according to him, Austria had never expressed regret for its part in the mass extermination of European Jewry. My mother listened. She was polite and charming. "Yes, yes, I see. Really? How interesting. Oh, I see!" Late that night, he drove us back to our hotel in his sports car. I sat in the back. When we arrived at the hotel, he said good night. Then he took her hand and kissed it. She looked at him, with her green eyes and in her inimitable fashion, closed the evening with the irony that had always lifted her above a petty, dirty world. "Thank you for a lovely day. You have just kissed the hand of a Jewish woman."

I admired and loved my mother and I felt loved and protected by her. Yet, I resented her for being different. There was a gap between my world and hers, and it was not the "generation gap" that everyone talked about. Anything that felt wrong I began to associate not with the war, necessarily, but with her as an immigrant. I craved something and I associated that something with the seemingly calm American mothers around me. They appeared so well grounded. How could my mother relate to my childhood? Sometimes, her experiences slipped out as I struggled with my adolescence. When children were catty at school, she groped for what to say to me. Because her standard of childhood pain was conditioned by abstracted trauma, genuine commiseration with me was virtually impossible. Out of frustration, she would tell me to rise above it all. There was a time when, girls being cliquish girls, I was left out and teased. She told me that they were behaving "like little Nazis." It was not a successful comfort tool. I think that out of frustration, she described her experience with mean girls. "When I was in Portugal, just before we left, a bunch of schoolgirls pulled me into an alley and beat me. They knew I was Jewish. They took away my underpants! They told me never to tell anyone. And I haven't until now! You see?" This was my mother doing her best to empathize with me. I didn't know what to make of it. Her pain was worse, so mine was ridiculously small? If she could hold that in for upward of forty years, I could deal with my small-time conflict. She was really desperate to help me. She couldn't stand to see one of her children upset. She called the teacher directly, and he ended up reprimanding the girls in my class out loud, in front of everyone, which naturally just made things worse. I was very angry with my mother; all I wanted was for her to put her arms around me, to acknowledge my misery, to agree that childhood was hard, and that it did indeed hurt. But my mother, who had lost her family so young, didn't have the resources to identify with this level of pain. It came out of a part of childhood that she had missed. She did her best. She wanted me to be happy, but that desire became a requirement that did not permit acknowledging those small, necessary losses that are the rites of passage in girlhood.

Looking back, I see how deeply my mother's life affected me and my sisters. Fear and faith created a relentless twofold directive to reassure her children that everything would be fine, while it was painfully obvious to us that everything had not been fine, that the world was a dangerous place. She struggled so to present an optimistic image, and the result was that her childhood pain and confusion trickled out, unmanaged and unacknowledged. The metaphor of the elephant in the living room suits my childhood perfectly. We all walked around it, and she even dusted it. Eventually, we all stepped in its refuse, and had to learn to tread lightly in-between the nasty clumps, constantly cleaning our fancy shoes with one hand while we held our noses with the other. I suppose I could find irony in a retrospective view of events. My mother was thirty-eight when she had me, the age her mother was at the time of her death. My oldest sister was eleven when I was born, the age my mother was when she became motherless. Maybe having me was an action, an act of will, that would outsmart fate. It showed that she chose life over death. After all, my mother has always prided herself on "good instincts." My birth was, perhaps, her victory over death, her link to the future.

The fact that my mother suffered secondary casualties of the war and that she denied the impact the Holocaust had had on her made it awkward for me or any of my sisters to attribute her behavior to any specific cause. I was consistently reminded how difficult her childhood had been, but at the same time, she rejected the notion that she had been directly victimized by the Holocaust and maintained a disconnection from the mass murders that had colored her childhood. On an intellectual level, I was told that she had been untouched. But on an emotional level, I knew a different story. I bore witness to her wound and I responded to her pain. I was the good daughter, the good mother, and the creator of a new generation of happy Jewish children. To rebel would have caused her more pain, and from what I understood, her mother had died knowing only a rebellious daughter. I patterned my life after her example of breakneck speed and productivity, as if activity kept you a step ahead of fate, and caring for children gave you a reason to live. Only now, at thirty-three, can I see the effect that the Holocaust had on my mother, and the trickle-down effect it has had on me. When I began to explore this topic, my mother became agitated. She told me this in her usual way, indirectly.

"I just want you to be happy."

"I'm fine."

"I just want you and your children to be happy."

"Mom, please."

"I just want everyone to be healthy."

"Everyone is fine."

She developed sciatic pain. "Your father is worried," she told me. "He feels that all this attention on the Holocaust might be upsetting you."

Upsetting me? "Mom, this is nothing new. It's been there my whole life." *Upsetting* me?

"But I'm not a survivor!"

"OK, Mommy."

"I had a bad night."

"What is it, your back?"

"No, I had a terrible dream."

"What was it?"

"I was standing on the street with Becky and Sasha [my daughters] and I was holding their hands. You were crossing the street to come to us. A car pulled up. And you vanished! And then, Becky and Sasha were gone. I started screaming for them. I was screaming and screaming for them. But their names weren't Becky and Sasha. I was screaming 'Anna! Ava!' I woke up very upset."

"Who are Anna and Ava?"

"No one. I don't know."

"You don't know? Can't you remember?"

"No, I don't know. Have your heard from Becky? Now I'm concerned."

"She's fine. She's getting used to camp."

"Is she unhappy? She said she wanted to come home."

"Mom, kids have to get used to camp. It's normal."

Pause

"My grandmother's name was Anna. I think her name was Anna."

"Anna?"

Silence

"I don't know. It was so long ago. I don't know who Ava was. Oh, well. It doesn't matter."

While writing this, I had to ask myself many questions, and in turn, ask questions of my mother. Obviously, my probing was not at first well received. But I now see a significant change in her comfort level and to my great surprise, in her feelings. My younger daughter is fair, with my own mother's green eyes and fair skin. Shasha likes to read in her room. Recently, my mother stood in the doorway, watching her. "Look at her. She is a prize. She looks like those children in the pictures. All those pictures of those big gatherings. All those children." I nodded and looked at her face. We were both crying.

Teaching to Remember

ASHER Z. MILBAUER

> . . . I have set before you life and death, blessing and
> curse. . . . choose life . . . that thou . . . may live.
> —Deut. 30:19

> Auschwitz is modern civilization's declaration of bankruptcy.
> —Alexander Donat, *Jewish Resistance*

Shortly after moving to Miami in the early eighties, I received a phone call from someone representing a group composed mostly of young people whose parents survived the concentration camps. In what seemed to me a chirpy way, the person on the other end of the line invited me and my wife to join the informal discussion group she helped found about three weeks earlier. She wanted me to share my experiences of growing up in a survivor family. Without waiting for my reply—the tone of her voice suggested she expected to hear nothing but a yes—she told me that everyone in the group was eager to meet me because they never had a chance to listen to someone who grew up in Russia. "It will be interesting to compare notes," she said. "After all, you must have thought about your predicament, must have noticed the difference between you and those whose parents were 'normal' people, must have felt acutely the traumas associated with the second generation."

I felt as if I were presented with an outline of the talk everyone else but me assumed I would follow. The more she talked, the more I resented the tone of the conversation, or should I call it a monologue. I felt uncomfortable with her taking my consent for granted; and I fully rejected the implied assumption that I was somehow touched, negatively, of course, by my

30

parents' loss, suffering, and survival. Contrary to my normal practice, I interrupted her in midsentence with a firm no, a negative I had to repeat three times for her to recognize that I was declining the invitation. Somewhat taken aback, she quickly recovered and demanded an explanation. For the sake of civility, I answered that I had no intention to intellectualize my parents' experiences by indulging a pseudosearch for an identity I did not care to have forced upon me. Her retort is still reverberating in my ears: "You seem bitter and angry," she said, "Come, you'll benefit from talking to us."

In fact, I was neither bitter nor angry. Actually, I felt happy; happier, indeed, than I have been for many years. My sense of elation at having landed a professorship in a dry academic market was boundless. And although my move to Miami raised a few eyebrows among my former colleagues, I was nevertheless happy to join the faculty of a young and upwardly mobile university in a city populated by thousands of exiles, immigrants, refugees, and expatriates whose existential condition was not unlike my own. I shared their desire to succeed against all odds and to reconfirm the resiliency of the human spirit. Moreover, during my exploratory visit, the chair of the English department inquired what could play a role in helping me make a decision to accept an appointment. Without taking the time to think over my answer, I blurted out that it was important for me to live in a city with a large Jewish population and find fellow Jews who could share my love for Yiddish, the secret language of my childhood. He motioned me to get into his car, and in less than half an hour I found myself face to face with a motley bunch of older Jews, most of them from New York and other East Coast cities, who, after a brief introduction, wanted to know my marital status and whether I knew cousin Mendel in a little *shtetle* hundreds of miles away from my birthplace. At that moment I knew I could be happy in Miami.

The conversation with the founder of the second-generation group left an unpleasant aftertaste in my mouth. For some inexplicable reason, it mattered to me that she not think I intentionally divorced myself from the subject of the Holocaust. Of course, the circumstances of my birth were different from those of many others who grew up in a free society. It goes without saying that my parents' concerns in surviving their survival were different from the issues faced by survivors in America or Israel. Furthermore, one need not be a psychologist or psychiatrist to understand the consequences a family history has upon children. To be sure, there is no reason to shy away from discussing these complicated matters. If anything, they must be treated not as curiosities, but in a larger context. The Holocaust must be remembered for the sake of both the dead and the living. Children of survivors have an important role to play in carrying out this mission. Yet, when asked to speak to people sharing with me a past not of our own making, I refused.

At the time of the ill-fated conversation, I was, in fact, reading, writing, and talking about the Holocaust. My nearly completed study on the novel of exile included the writings of I. B. Singer, whose books are a monument to the savagely destroyed world of eastern European Jewry. I also taught a seminar based on exile writers, which afforded me the opportunity to test my theories and interpretations in Miami, a natural laboratory of exile. Most of the English majors enrolled in the class were either transplants or children of immigrants. Consequently, they took a genuine interest in the works of exiled writers, Nabokov and Conrad among them, whose fictional creations reminded them of their own plight. As students are apt to put it, they could "relate" to the characters and situations in these novels. This identification, however, extended mostly to the exile landscapes presented by Nabokov and Conrad. They understood, sometimes intuitively, that I. B. Singer's exiles, most of them Holocaust survivors, while sharing with them and their parents the hardships of transplantation to America, required different treatment. Of course, they were right in differentiating their approaches to the experiences of individual exiles and to those of a whole transplanted nation. And I was proud of them for displaying an intelligence more learned people often lack. What they did not know was that their instructor, as a result of studying and writing about Singer's transplanted Holocaust survivors, had himself been engaged in a discrimination he did not care to reveal to them, or to anyone else. The results of this discrimination yielded a feeling of satisfaction, or even a smug delight, which, if revealed, might cease to exist.

My road to Singer's fictions bore little resemblance to that of my counterparts who had the fortune and privilege to be born in countries where anti-Semitism was not institutionalized and where laws protected citizens from overt and brutal discrimination. I am saying this not to claim superiority or gain credibility for what follows. I am saying this to indicate that my views, opinions, and philosophy of life are marked by a simple fact: unlike my Western peers, who could read I. B. Singer, even in Yiddish if they so chose, I could not. Where I was born, I. B. Singer could not be published; his works are populated by Jews who ponder their faith, analyze their long history of suffering, speculate on the motives of their enemies' murderous animosity, and pass judgment on those who did nothing to prevent the slaughter of six million European Jews. Where I was born, Jewish faith, history, destiny held no interest to those in charge of the country. If the Soviet Communists had had their choice, the Jews would have been written out of history. As my parents nearly were.

Singer's Holocaust survivors, however, are not just question marks, means to make a point, or tools to raise issues. They are, as I was writing in my book *Transcending Exile,* complicated characters, full of dichotomies and contradictions. "They have a strong, almost heroic urge to live, yet they are convinced, on the basis of their past experiences, of life's worthlessness." While obsessed with the desire to have a family and raise children, "they are constantly fighting back the overwhelming natural instinct to multiply, that is, to start all over," for they are mortified at the prospects of yet again producing fuel for the death camp chimneys. "One moment the survivors vehemently deny the existence of God, who looked the other way when Jewish children were slaughtered, and the next they will reverently bow their heads before the Almighty in admission of the inexplicability of His ways."

More often than not, they "perceive themselves as walking corpses or as the souls of the dead. Frequently they think that being physically alive is not a joy but, rather, punishment. And although they are physically in America, mentally they are always looking backward toward past experiences, toward a world that keeps captive their true souls, which hover over the graves of their children, parents and grandparents. . . . Their emotions of loneliness, frustration, despair, and anger limit and paralyze them. . . . Their losses are so overwhelming and haunting that even the rare moments of joy and forgetfulness they sometimes experience turn later into feelings of guilt for yielding to the pleasures of everyday life and giving in to natural human instincts." Their everyday existence is aggravated by the "self-defeating inability to reconcile the longing to lead a 'normal life' with the acute awareness that all that was holy to them is buried under ashes."

When writing about I. B. Singer's artistic representation of Holocaust survivors, I thought of my parents. For some inexplicable reason, I found satisfaction in juxtaposing the experiences and destinies of fictional survivors with those of real survivors. Of course, I understand the fallacy imbedded in such comparisons. But compare I did, for in this exercise my parents came out ahead. Where the fictional characters seemed more dead than alive, my parents seemed so invincible, so stoic, so real, so normal.

In the years to come, my observations of Holocaust survivors went beyond the literary landscapes created by the American Singer, the Italian

Primo Levi, the French Elie Wiesel, or the Israeli Aharon Appelfeld. Living in Miami afforded me numerous opportunities to talk to survivors and to listen to their stories. I even created a ritual of engagement when approaching survivors. During my frequent visits to Miami Beach, I would seek out a cluster of Yiddish-speaking Jews lounging in the shadows of one of the many evenly spaced gazebos lining the recently built boardwalk, sit down at a respectable distance—close enough, however, to eavesdrop on their conversations—and at an opportune moment join in with a comment, usually in Yiddish.

The sound of Yiddish worked wonders. Surprised at first to hear Yiddish spoken by someone of their children's age, they would warm up to me almost immediately, then ignore me for a few minutes to debate the geographical origins of my accent, then finally appeal to me to resolve the issue before the discussion became a full-blown argument. I was happy to oblige. When I told them I was born in Mukachevo, or Munkach, as the town was known during the Hungarian and German occupations, they knowingly nodded their heads. They commented almost wistfully on the greatness of the Munkacher rabbi, on the world-famous yeshivot supported by a large Jewish population that dated its presence to the fifteenth century, and on the tragic fate Munkach shared with eastern European Jewry. Commenting on the virtues of my native town and its prewar Jewish population, they invariably shifted to reminiscing about their own places of birth, sorrowfully shaking their heads at the tragic fate that befell these towns and villages. They also told me how they tried to rebuild their lives in America; about their efforts to replicate the spirit and structure of the ravished communities they left behind; the struggles it took to regain confidence and succeed in this great land of opportunities; the desire to impart the legacy of the past to their children; the pride they took in raising funds to build memorials to commemorate the dead. Whatever they talked about, however, they never failed to point out that they felt lucky to have had a chance to cope with their past and succeed in their present in a free country, in America, the *Goldene Medine,* and that I, the newcomer, should never take this country for granted.

At moments like these, I thought about my parents and their predicament. Unlike their wonderful American counterparts, my parents, in an ironic twist of fate, found themselves under the rule of a dictator as ruthlessly anti-Semitic as Hitler was. Stalin, in fact, continued the devil's work. My parents had to face another catastrophe, whose result was to equal the annihilation of the Jewish spirit and Jewish identity. Thinking of what they had to go through after their liberation from concentration and labor camps, and juxtaposing their experiences with those of both fictional and real survivors whose lives have taken a very different course, I felt my parents came out ahead. At times, I felt guilty and ashamed for feeling good as a result of my mental score keeping. I feared being discovered and ridiculed. I kept my mouth shut, and cherished the self-imposed silence. I needed to be content. I needed to relish the dizzyingly delicious thought that Hitler failed in crippling my parents, and that Stalin and his successors did not succeed, no matter how hard they tried, in putting the finishing touches to the Judenrein landscape the giftless Austrian painter-turned-tyrant attempted to create through a unique medium of blood and ash. And if I ever get a chance to talk again to my Miami second-generation phone counterpart, I would tell her that what I tried to protect at the time of our conversation was the sweetness permeating my recollections of growing up in a household established by two very young and prematurely orphaned survivors deprived of the customary social, cultural, and spiritual networks so necessary for any marriage to survive, let alone one not destined to happen at all.

The precariousness of my parents' life was defined not only by their ethnicity but also by geographical circumstances. Born into a very volatile part of central Europe, they experienced firsthand the historical vicissitudes of one of the most politically eruptive regions. The history of Transcarpathian Ukraine, with Munkach as its major center, is almost as scarred by trauma and misfortune as their own lives. According to Transcarpathia's written record, which dates to the ninth century, there was hardly a time when it was not claimed by one or another political or ethnic entity. Whether Slavs, Hungarians, Mongols, or Turks happened to be victorious at any given moment, the respective occupation was invariably accompanied by wholesale slaughter and oppression, making life for the local Hungarians, Ruthenians, Rumanians, and Czechs, to name but a few of the area's ethnic groups, nearly unbearable.

If one were to rely solely on official Soviet historiography for understanding the region's historical development, as I and thousands of others enrolled in the Russian educational system had to, one would be left with the impression that the driving force behind this development reflected the desire of the local population, officially identified as primarily Slavic, to be constantly fighting for the reunification of Transcarpathia with the motherland. In classrooms and on field trips to historical museums, students were invariably presented with stories of glory associated with the benevolence of Lev I Danilovich, the Russian count who invaded the area in 1281; with narratives of the euphorious reception Bogdan Chmelnitski's ambassadors and the accompanying Cossacks received when they put in an appearance in 1649; with much regaled accounts of the welcome accorded the Russian soldiers, members of the Eighteenth Red Army division, whose commissar was none other than the future leader of Soviet Russia, Leonid Brezhnev, as they fought their way into the German-occupied region in October 1944.

What students were not told, however, was that the local population, against claims to the contrary by official Communist records, expected a full withdrawal of Russian troops after the defeat of Hitler's forces and the restoration of prewar Czechoslovakia and Hungary as independent sovereign countries. The Russians never left, and with much fanfare and amidst forced festivities, the region was annexed by the Soviet Union.

After their liberation from the camps, my parents undertook an arduous and taxing journey to their native town. The return, however, was void of the feelings of elation and happiness that any forcibly displaced or deported person would normally experience at the prospect of returning home. Although any life experience pales when compared to the horror each of them had so recently experienced, they could not forget the indifference, and in some cases the joy, with which many of their former neighbors and friends helped pave their way to hell. But they had to go back, for they needed to know who survived and for whom Kaddish must be recited.

When my parents returned to Munkach, they hoped to find the town under Czech rather than Hungarian rule. They found neither, for the town was already renamed and occupied by the Russians, with many Red Army soldiers and their families being resettled into the region in an effort to Russify it as soon as possible and make good on the centuries-old promise to reunify Transcarpathia with Russia. More important, however, my parents' dreams were dashed and shattered on yet another account: most of the members of their families were dead. My mother lost her parents, grandparents, and the entire family of her sister Rachel, who was pregnant with her third child at the time of deportations. Only my mother and three of her older siblings survived. On my father's side, he and a sister were the sole survivors of what used to be a large and thriving family.

Fresh from an ordeal that defies human imagination, barely out of their teens, orphaned and stateless, my parents had now to face a survival of a different kind. Many local residents were rather surprised when a few hundred Jewish survivors started to trickle back into Munkach, because, given their awareness, and in some cases too intimate a knowledge, of the efficiency of the German war machine, they took the demise of the Jewish population for granted. Moreover, some wished it. The miraculous emergence of a tiny fraction of what was left of the town's once large Jewish community could spell trouble for those who took yet another matter for granted—their inalienable right to hold on to the Jewish property they so shamelessly appropriated immediately after the deportation of the local Jews.

But it was not property or any worldly riches the ghostlike survivors craved. What they needed at the time was some sympathy, some under-standing of their plight. But instead of a kind word, they were often treated with an angry snarl lamenting Hitler's failure to rid the world of the Jews; instead of an extended helping hand came a wall of indifference; instead of condolences, hastily averted eye contact betraying a guilty conscience. Whom could they turn to? Where could they find solace? Would they ever be able to heal their wounds? Would the Russians, themselves a long-suffering people, be of any help?

The first contacts with the newly established Soviet order made it amply clear to my parents that if they ever hoped to re-create even the palest of replicas of their prewar existence they had to rely solely on their own inner strengths, complemented by the support of fellow survivors, both friends and relatives. They came to recognize that even though Russia contributed significantly to Hitler's defeat and paid dearly for her victory with substan-tial human losses, the Soviet regime, driven by the Marxist-Leninist doc-trine, failed to incorporate the lessons and legacies of the Third Reich, whose disregard for the sanctity of human life bore a remarkable resem-blance to Russia's own totalitarian order.

Nowhere was Russia's stubborn refusal to learn from history as appar-ent as in its treatment of Jews. Soviet apparatchiks asserted that the Jews were no different from other victims of World War II. Their claim of being singled out and punished for one reason only—the sinful audacity of being born Jewish—was pure rubbish. The early Russian revisionists called it yet another of many subversive Jewish inventions worthy of inclusion in THE PROTOCOLS OF THE ELDERS OF ZION, itself a notorious product of Russia's traditional anti-Semitism. For Russia to acknowledge the Jewish claim would be paramount to acknowledging how perniciously dangerous anti-Semitism could be when intertwined with a country's historical and political devel-opment. To accept that Hitler's war against the Jews was fundamentally different from Germany's aggression against the USSR and other eastern and central European countries would constitute a reversal of a longstanding assimilationist policy toward the Jews with far-reaching consequences, including the right of the Jews to practice their religion, study Jewish history, and develop a national consciousness.

By denying the Jews the most basic civil rights, the Russians denied them something that no human being should be deprived of at a time of a severe and irreversible loss—the right to grieve as a Jew. It was devastating to realize one would never see most of his or her family members alive; bad enough to find total strangers occupying a home once owned by one's own family; and downright demeaning to fight physically for the privilege to sleep in one's own bed. Adding insult to injury, these lonely, physically emaciated and mentally starved youngsters were forced to witness yet another utterly debilitating ordeal of synagogues being transformed into department stores, Hebrew schools into state-run educational facilities with a language of instruction they could not understand, of yeshivot emptied of their books and Torah scrolls and turned into warehouses, of community centers having their doors bolted down and windows boarded up.

Many times, while living my own joys and sorrows, I kept asking the same questions over and over again: Where did my parents derive the strength to go on living? How could they withstand yet another vicious attack on Jewish identity? What inspired them to seek out a minyan, a quorum of ten, to recite the prayer for the dead, the life-asserting Kaddish? How could they survive in a world without their fathers and mothers?

I do not have definitive answers to the above queries. What I do have are memories and recollections of growing up in a family where laughter always echoed through the L-shaped house divided now into three tiny apartments my mother and her siblings managed to reclaim from the greedy squatters. What I have are images of a happy childhood invariably associated with our sprawling yard, formerly the site of one of the local ghettos and now a magnet for all the neighborhood kids, cradled comfortably under the protective security of the age-old walnut tree. What I have are time-yellowed but still sharply focused mental pictures of family get-togethers; of friends and relatives stopping by; of Yiddish songs sung in a hushed voice around the coarsely built wooden kitchen table; of long silences children intuitively knew they had to respect. More important, however, I have stories I heard my parents tell each other; stories my aunts and uncles would weave into seemingly casual conversations over a weekend card game; stories shared by friends and visitors drawn to my family in search of companionship and solace.

Today, it strikes me as curious that, although many of the survivors' reminiscences invariably dealt with their survival of the concentration camps, and although the most frequently used term in their conversations was indeed the word *Lager*—camp in German—their accounts, usually told in a melodious Yiddish and most often in the presence of children, never seemed threatening, nightmarish, or potentially damaging to a child's tender ego. It is amazing how these young and inexperienced mothers and fathers, deprived of the benefits their parents could have provided them through wise counsel, and pointedly shared life experiences had they survived the Holocaust, found the means to impart to their offspring lessons about a past they felt imperative for their children to remember, without imposing upon them a burden too crippling to deal with or carry through life. Somehow, intuitively rather than in a consciously calculated way, they managed to have the most gruesome accounts permeated by humor, an occasional chuckle, and even laughter, all of a soothing and caressing quality devoid of kitsch and sugar coating.

I vividly recall an occasion—I must have been nine or ten at the time—as the entire family, my parents, aunts, uncles, and all the cousins, were getting ready to attend some kind of celebration held at the house of my uncle Yeno, the only one of the siblings living outside the "ancestral" home on the other side of the town. My mother and her sister Faigi sat at a kitchen table applying some powder and rouge to their faces in front of a picture frame–shaped mirror too small to accommodate both of them. They giggled and good naturedly tried to crowd each other's reflection out of the silvery surface, occasionally drawing me into their cosmetic tug-of-war by planting a bit of color on the tip of my nose or the middle of my forehead. Sulking at their impertinence to amuse themselves at my expense, I hardly noticed how their conversation took a very different turn. But when I decided that to be ignored could be far worse than made fun of, I inched closer to my mother, reminding her of a presence she had no right to forget.

Somewhat mechanically, but in a rather reassuring manner, she put her arm around my shoulder, drew me closer to her side, and resumed the animated dialogue prompted apparently by the activity at hand. "Look, Faigi," my mother was pointing to her face and patting first one and then the other side of it with all five slightly spread fingers of her free hand. "Don't my cheeks look as red as they did the morning you kept slapping them over and over again? That must have been some very special blush you used!" And, then, as if sensing how tense I became at the thought of the two of them fighting, my mother put the mirror and the blush back on the table, turned to me, and said with a chuckle, "Your aunt is a very good cosmetician. She can make anyone look beautiful and alive." Somewhat relaxed and reassured that the two sisters were not really enemies, I pressed them to tell me about what I thought was a childhood prank. They smiled, and then Aunt Faigi, after acknowledging my mother's compliment and reconfirming the fact that she indeed was a fine beautician, told me about a "minor" confrontation she had with my mother, prefacing her narrative, however, with her usual and always predictable piece of advice of how younger siblings deserved to be disciplined if they did not obey their older sisters or brothers.

My mother and Aunt Faigi shared a bunk bed in one of Auschwitz's overcrowded barracks. Somehow they managed to stick together and survive numerous selections. Shortly before liberation, my mother felt she had no strength to go on. Aunt Faigi grew desperate as she watched her younger sister rapidly slipping away, ignoring her older sister's selfless offering of an extra ration of soup and bread. As the heavy artillery shells exploding in the distance signaled the approaching end of the war, the SS accelerated the killings, with selections taking place more frequently. One morning, when ordered out of the barracks for yet another selection, my mother refused her older sister's urging to get out of the bunk bed. She was pale, emaciated, and void of energy. My aunt, in a fit of crazy anger and despair, dragged my mother out of the bunk bed and propped her up against the bed's wooden partition. She started mercilessly slapping and pinching my mother's pale face, desperately hoping to draw some color into her cheeks and make her look fit for a few more days of slave labor. Shocked by the savage beating administered by her own sister, my mother regained some energy and obediently followed Aunt Faigi down the narrow aisle alongside hundreds of other skeletonlike creatures pushing and shoving their way toward the open door. Just before exiting, my aunt stopped for a split second and slapped my mother's face again. With her cheeks aflame now, my mother rushed past the SS officer playing God for the day and into her sister's protective arms. Her face, exuding a temporary healthy radiance, fooled the SS man. Aunt Faigi's efforts paid off: the two women survived what turned out to be one of the last selections.

Each time I recall Aunt Faigi's narrative, I shudder at the thought of how much pain these two teenagers must have endured. But somehow my sense of horror and incredulity at their ordeal gets pushed into the background. What takes front stage is a feeling of admiration for the love, commitment, friendship, and loyalty suffusing their conduct under circumstances that often forced people to respond in ways unimaginable to those living a life of seeming normalcy. When questioned about their ability to withstand adversity and transcend what often appeared an unbearable challenge to human resiliency, my parents, aunts, uncles, and their friends invariably claimed their memories of prewar family life and Jewish communal values to be their sole source of strength in defying death. But they always hastened to add that one needed a great deal of luck, for the multitudes who perished had been endowed with the same values and principles that kept the lucky ones alive.

Through the years, I often heard them musing in bewilderment about the rules governing the tricky business of distributing that rarest of commodities—luck. I am sure, at moments like these, they must have felt haunted by the same demons that afflicted I. B. Singer's fictional characters when trying to cope with the shame caused by the ignominies they were forced to endure in the camps; when dealing with the guilt for staying alive while others did not; when confronting the crisis of faith they suffered when seeing God-fearing fellow Jews being burnt alive. But unlike their counterparts in Israel or America, they had no Jewish networks to assist them in the healing process. Trapped behind the Iron Curtain, they were left to their own resources to attempt to re-create a semblance of a world ravished and destroyed by forces beyond their control. Their efforts now were not only informed by the same values and standards that sustained them through the camps, but also by the sense of duty toward the memory of their own parents, grandparents, and siblings whose bones and ashes they could not gather for a dignified Jewish burial. They knew only one way to erect a memorial, a *matzeva,* to their loved ones: they defied Russia's assimilationist policies, ignored their neighbors' innate anti-Semitism, and fought off moments of darkness and depression generated by an irreversible loss. Consciously or subconsciously, they believed that the only way to commemorate the death of their loved ones was through giving birth to children, teaching them Yiddish, inspiring them to hope for a better future life beyond Russia's proverbial pale. Paradoxically, although common sense prompted them to abandon an identity that nearly got them killed and when life's vicissitudes provided them an opportunity to melt into a collective national Soviet landscape, they sought, instead, to re-create a way of life that would allow them and their children to remain Jews and retain an identity for which millions paid with their precious and waiting to be avenged lives.

Taking vengeance manifested itself in many different and often unexpected ways. I recall a story my mother relishes. After their return from the camps, the young survivors felt some irrational, even mystical, as they later used to claim, urge to find partners, marry, and raise a family. My parents were no exception, and although doctors warned my mother against having children, for medical reasons caused by a beating from a camp kapo, she decided to take a chance. What she really feared most was not dying in childbirth—somehow she felt confident she would make it—but how her impaired hearing might harm her ability to raise children. She also feared the deleterious effects of the unrelenting hum, reminiscent of the moving cattle trains, continuously shooting through her head.

When I came screaming into the world barely a year after my parents' marriage, their joy at producing a firstborn and naming him for a deceased parent proved short-lived. During the second week of nursing, my mother noticed how her baby's initial sense of contentment at being fed gave slowly into a restlessness soon followed by loud cries and convulsions. With no parent at her side to consult, she turned to her sister and sister-in-law, both inexperienced mothers themselves, for advice and solace. Their conclusion lacked comfort and encouragement—the baby was hungry and crying because my mother ran out of milk. Her breasts were dry, the nipples swollen, bleeding and cracked from the boy's fruitless efforts to make them yield what was deservedly his. There appeared to be only one way to remedy the situation. My mother had to find someone else to feed her baby.

Aunt Klara, who gave birth to cousin Malka just three weeks earlier, immediately volunteered her services. But when her milk ran out as well, my distraught mother took to the streets. Like a mad huntress in search of prey, she approached every single woman who happened to stroll by with a carriage, begging her to share some milk with her starving boy. A few obliged but most, following their own possessive motherly instincts, refused—some politely, others rudely. As the word in the neighborhood spread about the risks of being ambushed by a crazed Jewish woman in search of baby milk, most nursing mothers ducked into alleys and driveways when sensing or noticing the approaching danger.

One of the neighbors, however, was not quick enough, or, as my mother thinks was really the case, she might have thought that the disdain many felt for her collaborationist past would exempt her from my mother's pleading. She was wrong. Suppressing the hatred she felt for the woman with Jewish blood on her hands, my mother wasted no time and within seconds, the precious bundle quietly whimpering in her outstretched arms, she stood in front of the clearly apprehensive neighbor, meekly imploring her to feed the little boy. My mother's admonitions fell on deaf ears, and, when rejected and sternly shooed away, she felt an irresistible desire to spit into the neighbor's face and turn proudly away. As she turned to go, she suddenly noticed two Russian soldiers standing on the corner, waiting apparently for the local girls to meet them. Instinctively, she sought eye contact with the nursing neighbor about to leave now, and with a barely visible movement of her eyeballs she made her look toward the corner. The woman instantaneously understood the implied threat behind that motion, and, rather than face the consequences of an unpredictable confrontation with the authorities—given her own nature, she truly believed my mother would snitch on her—she resignedly sat down on a nearby bench, swung her ample breast out of what a minute ago seemed an impenetrable encasement, and let the little Jewish baby boy have his fill.

Not in her wildest dreams could my mother have ever pictured a former Nazi sympathizer nursing her son. Standing over the nursing mother and watching the baby eagerly suck and tug at the woman's nipples, she imagined that what was flowing out of those breasts was black rather than white, poison rather than a life-giving substance. But suddenly, as she would later recall, the sense of disgust slowly gave way to a feeling of satisfaction, and even ecstasy, at witnessing a confirmed anti-Semite breathing life into her baby boy rather than choking him to death. She never thought this bloodless revenge could feel so sweet and pure. She was proud, for she did well by her parents and by her child.

Stories that my parents, relatives, and friends told each other and their children nurtured in their offspring a sense of distinction and apartness from other kids they came to know later in their lives. Our parents had consciously instilled in us an awareness of being different, of being Jewish, figuring their actions would not only somehow pay tribute to the memory of their lost loved ones, but also help us if not dull then at least deal with the pain we would inevitably experience when rejected by what they perceived as an inhospitable foster home instead of a native land.

I can trace my sense of being different to early childhood. This awareness, however, did not entirely derive from the little mean things children do to one another on a playground. Of course, I did not like to be called four-eyes or a fatso or a dirty kike. With the first two offenses, however, I could live; after all, many other bespectacled and slightly overweight children were around me. With the third, the ethnic slur, I needed some help. After I complained bitterly to my mother about the carelessly hurled insult, she sat me down on a low stool by the kitchen sofa, and, with that ever-present twinkle in her eyes, told me the two things I never fail to recall when the real-life playground gets rough. First, I could do nothing about the naughty boys' accusations of being a Jew because I was Jewish. If anything, she insisted, I should be proud of it. Their assessment of my sanitary condition, on the other hand, was a different matter. This she took as a personal affront, for there was no truth in the false allegations. And, in what amounted to a concerted effort to prove the accusers wrong, she made me stand in front of a mirror, first motionless then in a light spin by turning me slowly on my heels, commenting all the while on how sparkling clean my clothes and face appeared in the mirror's reflection. Satisfied with the results of such close scrutiny, she then kissed me on the forehead, winked at me somewhat mischievously, and with a light shove to my back urged me to join my cousins' noisy card game in the shadows of the huge walnut tree standing sentry in our backyard for as long as anyone could remember.

My mother's propensity for using humor and laughter while delivering an important lesson in civic pride or allaying potentially damaging anxieties could go only so far. Other issues set me apart from many of my peers, concerns my parents could not laugh or wish away. Somehow, over the passing years all these issues merged somewhat magically into the unified image from my childhood I am about to invoke, an image that became an inseparable and inspiring companion in my life's journey.

I was seven when I began attending the Alexander Pushkin state school, fifteen minutes from my house. Because classes started at 6:30 A.M., it would still be dark when I and my cousin Malka set out, often accompanied by one of our parents, toward the school. It felt secure walking with a grown-up, especially when passing the corner favored by neighborhood bullies who rarely failed to call us names. With our hands firmly nestled in the warm palms of a guardian, we felt comfortable, eagerly looking forward to what often turned out to be a fun-filled day with friends and teachers.

Leaving school, however, often made me sad. Not because I was more studious, serious, or diligent than other pupils. I was not. And not because I feared the taunts of bad boys and girls—after a while you learn to live with them. My sadness is associated with a memory I have of myself, a bespec-tacled and always neatly dressed boy, standing by the tall and imposing doors of the school building waiting for my cousin Malka to join me on our way back home. While Malka tarried, I had a chance to survey the sur-roundings from the top step of a set of cement stairs descending toward a pavement separated from the busy thoroughfare by a line of majestic oak trees. Under the trees, usually in little clusters, stood the babushkas, shabbily dressed older women with kind wrinkled faces framed by broad and colorful kerchiefs the ends of which were tucked behind the pieces of string that lassoed their cotton-stuffed overcoats around their frail bodies to keep out the bitter winter cold. Jealous, I would observe this or another of my blue-eyed blond classmates snuggle up to his grandmother, give her a big hug, and thrust his hand into the deep warmth of her oversized fur-lined mitten. How wonderfully cozy that must have felt, I thought, watching the clusters slowly disappear, reforming now into pairs of grandmothers and grandchildren engaged in animated conversations.

In the years to come, that warm, fur-lined mitten metamorphosed into a vision of a constantly desired but never fully attainable destination, a place where children sit in the comfortable laps of their grandparents and listen to stories of a very different kind than the ones I listened to while growing up among survivors. This vision keeps pursuing me, wherever my personal or professional journeys happen to lead me. When teaching Kafka, for example, I cannot rid myself of the feeling that my childhood vision of the fur-lined mitten is somehow intricately connected to Gregor Samsa's longing for simple human contact, a longing invariably associated with the picture of the woman clad in fur he obsessively tries to keep from being moved out of his room and destroyed. While I am fully aware of the pathos permeating Gregor's existence—all he has left in life to cling to is a pin-up poster—I feel that for him to reach the woman's arm hidden in the depths of the fur muff is of paramount importance. Had he managed to touch it he could have achieved the happiness he so richly deserved.

Like Kafka's Gregor Samsa, I longed for and failed to benefit from the secret pleasures hidden in the fur-lined warmth of a grandmother's mitten. Unlike Gregor, however, I came very close to knowing how it would have felt had I reached the enclosed forearm for each time I and my cousin Malka were making our way home from school we felt our hearts beat faster and faster, eagerly anticipating the excitement of entering the house our grandparents built and being warmly greeted by our mothers, fathers, aunts, uncles, relatives, and friends ready to treat us to many more wonderful stories in the shadows of the age-old walnut tree.

The Coat

DIANE WYSHOGROD

December 11, 1995: My mother and I are in my kitchen in Jerusalem, and I am preparing to interview her yet again about her experiences during the war. She and my father have arrived only a few days ago from New York for a visit of several weeks' duration. It's early enough in the visit to feel relatively unencumbered by the sadness of the inevitable separation, the frustration of living so far apart, the tensions that often arise from so much expectation and emotion. But for now, the atmosphere is clear and uncluttered, like the airiness of the kitchen under the fourteen-foot ceiling.

Around us, the counters are filled with the debris of my everyday life, but I have cleared the round butcher block table of all but two mugs of warm tea and my little tape recorder. We sit opposite each other, ready to begin.

I sometimes wonder what she feels about my interviewing her in this way, whether she ever thinks about what I will do with all this material. When I tell her that I need her to answer some more questions, she agrees willingly. She never asks me, "what is this for?", never says she doesn't have the time. She makes herself available, my father obligingly busies himself with plans of his own, so that I can have my mother to myself in privacy.

From our previous conversations, I already know the main outlines of her story. My mother, Helen (Lutka) Rosenberg, an only child from a middle-class family, grew up in Zólkiew, a small town near Lwów, in southeastern Poland. The history of the Jews in Zólkiew dates to the beginning of the sixteenth century. The town enjoyed prosperity as part of the patrimony of Polish king Jan Sobieski under whose patronage the huge fortified synagogue was built in 1687. The "Sobieski shul," as it was known, was considered a national treasure for the beauty of its architecture and the ornate wood and brasswork that graced its interior.

46

Zólkiew's prewar population numbered about fifteen thousand, divided about equally between Poles, Ukrainians, and Jews. Despite its small size, it was extremely cosmopolitan, and the few former "Zólkiew-ites" with whom I have talked always glow when describing their bustling little town. Its Jewish citizens played a leading role in all aspects of its civic, cultural, and business life. Jews developed the town's fur and grain industries and expanded its public transportation. Its citizenry boasted many professionals, including doctors, lawyers, teachers, and pharmacists, one of whom was my grandfather, Jozef Rosenberg. Cultural life flourished. Jewish children learned Hebrew and Judaic subjects in the "Tarbut" school. Orphanages provided vocational training to boys and girls. The "Kultura" society fostered an appreciation for art and culture. The entire spectrum of Jewish life was represented, from freethinkers to Socialists to Chassidim. My mother's family was among the few assimilated Jews in the town, the rest being more traditional in their observance. However, there was a high degree of tolerance and mutual respect, both within the Jewish community and between the various ethnic groups.

All this came to an abrupt end with the advent of World War II. At first, the town came under Russian control, under the terms of the Hitler-Stalin Pact of 1939. Then, in 1941, Hitler reneged on his end of the bargain, overrunning the Russian forces and taking control of formerly Soviet territory. From then on, Zólkiew was under German control. Immediately upon occupying the town, the Germans destroyed the great synagogue, an act that presaged the misery to come. Forced to live within the confines of a ghetto on one side of town, the Jews were subjected to the viciousness of the German regime. Humiliation. Disease and starvation. Akcye, raids in which people were brutally rounded up and shipped to labor or death camps, most notoriously Belzec and Janowski Oboz. Over time, these Akcye became increasingly frequent and murderous. By March 1943, the situation of those left in the beleaguered community became more and more desperate. The realization began to sink in that it was probably just a matter of time before the worst happened and they were all shipped to the camps.

Fearing the increasing deadlines of each successive Akcya, my grandfather turned to a local Polish Christian couple for help. Emil Lozinski, a retired railway worker well into his seventies, and his wife, Maria, a woman in her sixties, were a devout Christian couple living in a small rickety cottage on the edge of town. In happier times, Mr. Lozinski used to spend hours in my grandfather's apothecary, debating politics and other affairs of the day. Now my grandfather asked Mr. Lozinski to hide him, his wife, Agatha, and daughter, Lutka, in the cellar of his house in the event of another Akcya. After discussing it among themselves, the Lozinskis agreed. When the start of the next raid was heralded by the sound of the whine of bullets and anguished screams, the Rosenbergs hurried into hiding.

It was only supposed to be for a few days. All previous roundups had lasted only several days, even at their worst. But this one was different. On March 25, 1943, the entire remaining Jewish population of Zólkiew was marched into a nearby forest by German troops and their Ukrainian assistants and shot to death, their bodies dumped into previously dug trenches. Thirty-five hundred men, women, and children were murdered on this one day. Jewish Zólkiew ceased to exist.

There was no place to return to now. To emerge from hiding would doom not only the Rosenbergs, but also their innocent saviors, the Lozinskis. There was no choice but to remain where they were. For the duration of the war, they sat in the earthen cellar by day, creeping upstairs to sleep in a small area of the little shack at night.

Zólkiew was liberated by the Russian army in July 1944. Only then did my mother and grandparents see daylight, for the first time in sixteen months.

There were five thousand Jews living in Zólkiew in 1941. Seventy survived the Holocaust.

I know this, and other facts besides. But there is so much more I need to understand. What was it like? What did my mother experience? How could anyone survive under such conditions, crouching in a cellar, in the dark, for so long?

So I keep asking, asking, fluttering, mothlike, around the flames, scraping away at layers of time and memory, trying to penetrate to the heart of the mystery.

"I want to go back to the couple who hid you, the Lozinskis," I say. "Whenever you talk about them, you always talk about *him*. You never talk about *her*."

"*Both* of them saved us," she declares. "*He* was the one who made the decision to let us hide in their cellar. He must've discussed it with her. I'm sure he discussed it with her. Because he said, 'I have to discuss it with her.' And then he came back to my father and said that they both decided, they agreed."

"Yes, but what was she like?" I ask.

"I told you. She was in her sixties. Wait. Grandma Agatha was born in 1895, so she was fifty at the end of the war. So it's impossible that Mrs. Lozinska was in her fifties. I know that my father said that Lozinski was retired, so he had to be at least in his seventies, and she was much younger, but how much, I don't know.

"You remember, I told you that Mrs. Lozinska came from Brzeżany, the same town my parents came from before they moved to Zólkiew. She apparently knew my grandfather, because it was a small town, and he was a lawyer, well-known. She certainly said that she remembered my grandmother, and my uncle. My father vaguely remembered her family name, but I don't. I don't even know when she came to Zólkiew. I never knew her before we went into hiding."

Again, I press. "What was she like as a person?"

"She could be very pleasant, but then sometimes if she got in a bad mood, then she would just, not abuse you, but, talk out. One time she talked about my mother's, your grandmother's, family in Brzeżany, and there was jealousy. She brought up an incident. It was in the evening, after we had come up from the cellar, and she was sitting and talking, and telling about her life in Brzeżany. She remembered my mother's family in Brzeżany. I don't know why, she said that my mother was always very well dressed. She mentioned that she wanted something once in a store window, I don't know what it was, some clothing, and her mother said they cannot afford it right now, but that they would try to save the money and buy it for Christmas. And when she finally saved the money and came to buy, she was told it was sold. And then she saw my mother wearing it. And she remembered it so many years later."

It's like an explosion going off in my head: ". . . she came to buy . . . it was sold . . . and then she saw my mother wearing it." Heat, like an electric current, shoots up my arms, while the nape of my neck contracts as though someone splashed ice water on it. I am riveted by the awful symmetry of this story, which I have never heard before. My mind reels, trying to absorb it. I think: what an unbelievable twist of fate! What a great scene for a movie! Then: what the hell's wrong with you? What movie? This is real! The psychologist in me salivates: what a mother lode of material: the relationships, the motives—this is amazing! The writer part of me worries: how will I ever do this story justice in the retelling?

And all the while the conversation continues, unwinding quietly, matter-of-factly, across the tabletop.

I ask, "How old was she then, a little girl?"

My mother answers, "I don't know. I don't know if that incident was right after World War I, or she was still talking about the times before. So I don't know what she wanted, and when it happened. We did not want to ask too many questions and elaborate. Whatever she said, we just let her talk. Nobody was going to get into arguments at that time. But there was some jealousy. But otherwise, she was nice. She tried to help us, she felt sorry for us."

Suddenly, there's an edge in her voice.

"She felt sorry for herself."

Then she pauses, and when she continues, her tone is softer.

"I mean, they were scared. It was very hard for them. To give food to three more people when you hardly have anything for yourself, and the situation was very difficult."

I feel as though I am swimming in a dark aquarium, submerged amid murky layers of meaning, coincidence, significance, like some fish trapped between dense growths of seaweed. I have to get out, to pull my thoughts together, have to react somehow to this revelation.

"Hard to imagine," my words emerge slowly, ponderously, "that the girl you were jealous of because she got the clothing you wanted, ends up hiding in your cellar with her husband and daughter, and you have to share your food and your clothing with them. . . .

This sounds all wrong. Forced. Strained. While my guts are quaking at the shock of this revelation. The drama begs for release: "This is unbelievable. This Mrs. Lozinski wanted something, and instead my grandmother got it . . . she must have been so upset, and disappointed, and jealous . . . and then my grandmother ends up in her cellar, at her mercy, in her power, so many years later . . . and she saves her!"

". . . Strange twist of fate, don't you think?" I hear myself finishing lamely.

And my mother's quiet reply, "Very. It is. She mentioned it once."

A scene unfolds in my head like a black-and-white movie from the forties. Characters with bobbed hairdos, and waisted dresses, pleated skirts tucked under narrowly cinched cloth-covered belts. . . .

It's a beautiful day, bitter cold, as is usual for Poland in midwinter. The air is brittle as glass and as crystal clear. The hard-packed snow crackles and crunches underfoot as Maria and her mother walk quickly toward the center of town. They've had to get up early to catch a ride on the next-door neighbor's wood wagon, from their little house on the edge of town, but it was worth it. Maria has been waiting for this moment for three months. Today, she is finally going to buy it, to make it her own.

She can still remember the thrill that had rushed through her when she'd first seen the coat. It was back in autumn. She'd been with her mother then too, the two of them walking, arm in arm, their shopping done, waiting for the hay wagon to drive them home. Even now, so many replays of the memory later, she can still feel the prickles of delight that rippled through her then, feel her breath sucked into an involuntary "oooh!!" of pure pleasure. Her mother, no less smitten, had still kept her head while she kept gabbing, "Oh, it's glorious! Oh, Mother, I must have it!!" Her mother's smile of pleasure had faded into a sigh, as reality set in. "I wish you could, Maria dear. But, the price . . ." Maria had felt her world crumble, the sun setting right in the middle of the day. The "oooh!" deflated, became an "oh," sagging and sorry. "But, look, Maria," trying to cheer her up a bit, "there's still time till Christmas. Let's see if we can save enough till then."

Christmas! Three whole months to wait! She'd thought it would never come! Yet it's here, in all its glittery splendor. And now she is on her way back to the tailor's shop. She keeps one hand firmly on her purse, with its precious store of zlotys, carefully saved up. She tucks her other arm firmly into the crook of her mother's, and the two of them trot across the *rynek* to the row of shops on the opposite side. The arcade shielding the stores is festooned with boughs of evergreens and colorful decorations. People heading to and from the market call cheerful holiday greetings to one another.

Maria almost drags her mother the last few feet and bursts into the shop, breathless from the cold, the pace, and mostly, from the excitement.

Slight, stooped, the tailor appears from behind the curtain at the back of the store and approaches them, bowing politely.

"Yes, what can I do for the ladies?"

"Oh, *prosze Pan*, please, sir, we're here to buy the coat you had on display in the window. Black, with shiny buttons, and a little fur trim at the neck."

"Ah, yes," he replies, smiling gently, "I know the coat."

"Oh, good!" cries Maria, happily, bouncing a bit in her eagerness.

"But, Panna," he says slowly, "Miss, I'm afraid I don't have it any more. It's been sold."

"Sold!" she gasps in dismay, and clutches at her mother. Her mouth goes dry. She opens it, but no sound comes out. Her mother tries to help.

"Are you sure?" she asks. "Maybe it's just in the back."

"Oh, no, Pani. I know the coat, madame. It was a lovely one. Panna has good taste. But I'm afraid it really is gone. Such a pity.

Perhaps the ladies would like to look at something else. I have some other ones, very nice—"

But Maria is already outside the shop, fighting back the tears that are beginning to freeze at the tips of her eyelashes. Her nose runs and she jabs at it with a mittened hand. Her mother comes up behind her softly and gives her a quick squeeze.

"Oh, my dear, I am so sorry. Come now. We must be getting back. Pan —ski will be waiting."

They trudge through the streets. Maria keeps slipping on the hardening snow, but she doesn't care. Keeping her eyes pointed stonily ahead, she plods on.

They stop at the corner to let a heavy wagon lumber by. As it creaks past, she prepares to step out over the snowdrift, and stops short. Stops so suddenly that she almost falls, and her mother grabs at her to steady her. On the opposite corner, stands *her* coat. Black, sleek, with a little fur trim, buttons twinkling in the sharp light. On someone else's body.

There is a strange roaring in her ears. She blinks to force her vision to clear. She recognizes the girl in the coat. She's seen her around. Her father's a lawyer, well-known in town. *Zydówka*. She's wearing a white muff that looked like whipped cream, soft and puffy and perfect against the dark fabric. She was always so well-dressed. And now she's dressed up, too—in *her* coat.

How little I know. I don't know when this incident took place, over what item of clothing, or how old Agatha and Maria were. All I have is—a few words. A bit of story. All the rest is my attempt to fill in the gaps, fit the pieces of the puzzle together. I am groping in the dark.

I have a photograph of my mother and grandmother striding arm-in-arm down some lane in postwar Poland. It's this image that I see when I imagine Maria and her mother setting out to make that special purchase. Just as my mother always accompanied my grandmother, who had a weak heart, on shopping expeditions in New York many years after the war.

I try to put myself in Maria's shoes. How did it feel to have wanted something desperately, to have saved for it, penny by penny, only to see it walk off on someone else's body? The disappointment. The jealousy.

But something doesn't quite fit. There weren't many stores in those days. People usually had clothes made to order from tailors or relatives. If so, if the display garment had been sold, and she had the money, why didn't she just order another one? Did she just give up? And why? Was she so overcome by disappointment? Was she generally passive, or passive-aggressive? Did she give it up because of vanity, because how can you wear the same garment as someone else? Did it matter that the "someone else" was Jewish? Or younger?

I can only guess at the possible motivations and emotions. And at their intensity. Was she resigned, or deeply hurt? Was she tolerant of her feelings, or, if they were strong, did they warrant confession, as she was deeply religious?

And by the time she revealed the incident to my grandmother, what had the passage of years done to the memory? Was the hurt still there, smoldering, seeking an accounting? Or had she developed a more philosophical view of the turn of events? What must that conversation between my grandmother and Mrs. Lozinska have been like?

They sit in the tiny kitchen, around the rickety old table. The windows are shuttered and draped with curtains and old blankets, and the light is dim, to save precious fuel and money, and to comply with wartime blackout regulations. It also protects them from possible prying eyes of neighbors and passersby. Not that there are likely to be any at this hour. It's past curfew, and the night is bitterly cold. Still, you never know.

Agatha wraps her hands around the chipped cup and sips slowly.

"Oh, for a cup of real coffee," she sighs to herself, not for the first time. "This is brown water. But at least it's warm."

She shivers slightly in her worn coat. The room is chilly but it's better than sitting on the earthen floor of the cellar, with the cold eating into your bones. She's tired. Those hours of sitting in the hole underground make you tired, even if you are doing nothing. Sitting, staring, whispering from time to time to her husband, her daughter, thinking and not thinking, trying not to think. She feels her eyes growing heavier, forces them open. Josef and Lutka look just as tired as she feels, but Maria is in a talkative mood. She has an audience. For her, it's a break after the long monotony of her day, scrounging for a few scrawny vegetables in the rock-hard garden, struggling to turn them into something edible and to stretch it to feed five people. It's so difficult for her, too: she can't do anymore what she used to, her eyes are bad—cataracts—and there's no money, and she's cooped up with us, this terrible, terrible war.

Maria's reminiscing again, saying something about Brzeżany. Funny that she should come from the same town as both Agatha and Josef, although they didn't know her then. Why would they—

different religions, different social circles. And anyway, she was at least ten years older than they were. Agatha stirs, forcing herself to perk up and pay attention.

"... a lovely town, *no wiesz ty,* isn't it so, Pani Rosenbergowa?"

Agatha nods tiredly, forcing her lips into what she hopes is a pleasant, social smile. She's not really listening, just letting the words wash over her. Some phrases stand out, borne on the waves of Maria's rising inflection.

"... Pani's father ... dis*tin*guished ... I remember. .... *Isn't* it so, Pani?"

Agatha keeps her head bobbing, struggling to focus.

"... and Pani too! ... oh, yes. Pani may not remember me, but I remember her."

Something has shifted in the way she is talking now. Agatha is not sure what, but something about the words slices through the fog of her fatigue.

"... I used to see Pani walking in the street sometimes, with her parents, or with friends. I always liked to see her, she was always so well dressed, isn't it so? So elegant ..."

Agatha gives a tiny shrug, a weak laugh, feeling self-conscious, not sure what to say, how to respond. Sitting here in much-mended clothes, it seems worlds away: pretty frocks? elegant white gloves? Why is she bringing it up now?

"... like it was yesterday. .... I love the shops with the pretty things in the window ... I would walk with my mother, strolling, you know ... and once I saw such a lovely coat. And it's funny, to think of this now ... it was in the tailor's window. .... It was dark, with shiny buttons, and fur, some kind of fur trim around the neck ... I wanted it so much. .... But, there was no money. .... My mother said, "Soon it will be Christmas. Maybe you can save enough till then. Your father and I were going to give you something anyway, so we will give you some money toward the coat." So I waited. You know how it is to wait, for something you want. .... So, I saved and saved, and then came Christmas, and I did get some money from my parents, and from some others, and it was enough. And I went to the tailor shop to buy the coat. But it was gone."

She pauses to take a sip of coffee. Agatha waits. Maria swallows, puts the cup down on the table.

"Ah, yes." She presses her lips together in a rueful kind of smile, nodding sadly. "It was gone. Someone else had bought it in the meantime."

Agatha feels her head nodding in rhythm with Maria. Poor thing. What a disappointment.

"I was so unhappy . . ." She sighs, drinks again, sets down the cup. "And do you know, it was some time later, and I saw Pani walking in the street, and she was wearing that same coat! Imagine . . ."

Agatha freezes. Her stomach contracts sharply, painfully, with the intake of breath. She sits absolutely still, gripping the cup.

"What?" Thoughts fly like frantic birds. "What did she say? I bought her coat? What coat? I don't remember. I never saw her. Oh, *Boże mój*, my God. What will happen now?"

She forces herself to keep her head moving, in that slow and stately tempo, nodding up and down, the two heads rising and dipping in tandem across the scarred table top. She says nothing, keeps her eyes locked on the other's face.

"No, *tak to jest*," murmurs Maria. "That's life . . . can you imagine . . . funny, no?" She stands up abruptly and collects the cups, to wash them in the sink.

This scenario comes out softer, more sympathetic than I'd have anticipated. Surprising me. But maybe it shouldn't, on reflection. When I first heard the story, first heard that my mother and her parents had been in the hands of someone with a potentially lethal grudge, I was frozen by the sense of threat. But my mother doesn't report it that way. There's no cataclysmic ending to the incident. Just Maria's telling the story, them receiving it in silence, and then on to something else. All the rest lives on in my head. All the drama lives in my head.

Did my grandparents discuss it later? They must have. But briefly, I would guess. In hurried whispers. There was no privacy, no place for lengthy discussions. Most likely the decision was: don't say anything. Just act normal. It happened a long time ago. Maybe she still bears a grudge but she agreed to take us in, so it can't be that bad. Anyway, there's nothing we can do about it now.

And Agatha, racking her brains, trying to remember the coat. But it was so long ago, who can remember? Better not tell her that, because it was so important to her, and here Agatha hardly remembers it at all. It seems to her that she did have a coat with a fur collar, but she doesn't really remember.

The Far Country Memoirs

Four Excerpts from a Work in Progress

WENDY JOY KUPPERMANN

1

When she was twelve her father ushered her into his musty leather-bound study and bade her for once sit still, saying, "I come from a place of chill and ash, of burning dreams and limestone powder. Every doorway reads *Wilkommen: Arbeit Macht Frei,*[1] each dark tower bruises the face of the sky. I come from a far country where nothing will grow, where quarries and smokestacks beckon unspeakable horror. I still do not believe that the world did not end. I still do not believe that the world did not rend the silence. I come from a world without answers. I come to a world without answers. I lie awake many nights, I lie trembling alone, and when I sleep, God have mercy, I dream."

He said, "I was barely a man, I was precisely human. I was just thirteen when my hair turned white. It was a clear crystal night when they took my mother. They took my mother with a goose step rhythm, with a heavy accent, with a uniform madness. They took my mother, I heard a scream of ghosts. They took my mother, they uncovered her head, then they shot her."

---

1. The entrance to Auschwitz, that most infamous of Nazi death camps, was framed by a large wrought-iron sign bearing the German motto "Arbeit Macht Frei," translated roughly as "Work Brings Freedom." The sign was intended to allay the fears of newly arrived prisoners and render them more docile by conveying falsely that the place was merely a forced labor camp rather than an extermination center.

He said, "Flesh of my flesh, breath of my soul, tell the truth, tell it all, tell it just as you see it. Tell your grief beyond grief, tell your hope beyond hope that the flesh reasserts itself and the soul never quenches. Tell all your love all the days of your life, the nights too. Tell all your love, tell all the truth just to survive."

She looked up then and her young eyes filled with water. She saw her sad lonesome father, his broken back, his open arm, his death camp devil's tattoo, its chilling numerical sequence. She saw her brave father, she saw through his existential weltschmerz, she saw through his barbeque terror. She saw the tenacity of his spirit, his regenerate charm. She saw his heart broken wide open to embrace all creation, and she understood him, the way a child understands intuitively without questions or answers, she understood him fully as a true love story unfolding.

2

When she was twelve her father packed up the car and they drove one hundred miles out to the heart of the Catskills, to Katz's Pine Away Valley Orthodox Lodge and Hotel to watch the leaves change, drift, and fall and to eat three kosher meals daily. They sat at a round table with two Old World rabbinical brothers, Meyer Culper the elder and the younger named Max. They ate everything on the menu because it was already paid for. They played shuffleboard and canasta, they belted down glasses of borscht, they said, "The smart money's in real estate," only they said it in Yiddish. Then they rang in the Sabbath with a little sponge cake, a little schnapps, and some dancing.

They wandered down a dirt road in their Saturday best, thanking God as they breathed the fresh mountain air. Three salt-of-the-earth dueling banjo–type homeboys rolled up in a pickup truck sounding like thunder. They rolled up and they rolled by flaunting naked red necks. They were hunting deer, they were sporting burly red sweatshirts that said, Yep, the Buck Stopped Here. They were shooting BB gun pellets and fighting words. The Old World rabbinical brothers stood still in their tracks like a couple of road kills, but her father took her hand and they just kept on walking.

They came together to a bump in the road. They looked down and saw it was a former rabbit crushed to the ground, its trim cottontail matted, a dark stain spread soaking below. Then her father looked up and he spoke of the war, shaking his head, sighing.

He said, "The very first dead I saw I just couldn't believe it. I was only thirteen, I was barely alive. I just could not believe it, that the world did not end." White tear streaks ran down his cheeks then like inverse stigmata, and she looked at her father, she saw him, and she loved him deeply.

She said, "I am not a boy, I am only a girl, but I would still really like to say Kaddish."[2] Her father lifted her chin, he said, "God will allow you to pray for the dead if you remember to pray for the living as well," and then he scooped up the rabbit and they both buried it deep. They stood up together, they spoke the Kaddish by heart, and the old words fell smoothly like stones damp with blood. As they walked on down the road, they admired the leaves falling, noting that no two were the same, just like snowflakes.

3

When she was grown she left her father's house for her very own studio apartment. She felt independent and competent, she felt fully adult and alive, and she promptly came down with the flu. Her father brought over a quart of chicken soup and the daily paper and they sat for a while discussing the news. There was more news of warfare around the globe.

Her father kissed her forehead to check for fever and he cracked open the window to air out the room. They could hear big-city sounds, the honking of horns, the squeaking of gears, whistles, sirens, bellows, and shrill indistinguishable voices. They heard the plaintive sound of a small frightened child crying or maybe it was just a Siamese cat in the alley below. They heard the loud steady sound of a hammer from a construction site nearby.

The hammering kept up an incessant tattoo. Her father shut the window to shut out the noise, then he took her hand and spoke softly.

He said, "In the ghetto, in Warsaw, I took my turn cleansing the dead. The morning shift was the cruelest because most passed away in the night. The first ones to die were the babies. The parents carried them in with the sunrise, silently screaming. I could not bear the look of their faces, I averted my eyes. I just could not believe it, that the world did not end. Outside the door, within sight of the wall, the carpenters never stopped working. They hammered through night and day at the dwindling wood, they pounded nails into tiny coffins. And I thought, This is the way the world will end, with a silent scream, with a small lifeless bundle. Every daybreak I heard the

2. Kaddish: Jewish prayer for the dead.

sound of war, I thought, This is the sound of the world when it ends, the hammering of nails into tiny coffins."

She drank down her soup and sank down under the covers. When her father opened the window again, the construction noises had stopped.

He said, "When you were a baby I would rush to your room at night just to watch you sleeping, just to touch you, just to check that you were still breathing. I could not believe that anything so beautiful could be mine and could still be alive. When you were a baby you ran very high fevers."

He said, "That very first Hanukkah you were so sick you had a temperature of a hundred and six. Your eyes would not open, you were not even moving. I lit the Hanukkah candles, I carried you into the kitchen and held you up to the sink as the cold water ran. I held you there under the tap, I wanted to pray, I opened my mouth but nothing came out. Still I held you there and the candles went out one by one. I sank down to my knees, I could not even scream, I felt cold water move through my veins. I heard the steady sound of a hammer. You coughed once in my arms, the hammering stopped, and then the fever broke. Of course I believe in miracles to this day."

She looked up from her pillow at her dear father's face and she saw he was smiling. Of course she believed in miracles, too. Because the hammering stopped, because the world did not end, because of the smile on his face, of course she believed in miracles too, and because there was more news of warfare around the globe she had no other choice.

4

When she was sixteen years old she was asked out on a date by a nice Jewish boy who admired her greatly. He was already pre-med, he knew what he wanted, he was a smart industrious freshman in a great metropolitan parochial college. He was a good kosher catch in a generic sort of way. She was only slightly excited but she knew it was time to discover for herself what dating was all about—and for all we know still is. She cautiously asked her father's permission, which he relinquished without much of an obvious struggle. He was always such a fine gentle man, was her sad soulful father.

Her father stroked his trim gray beard thoughtfully, leaned forward with his hands on his knees, and smiled wistfully.

He said, "I knew this was going to happen, that you would begin to be dating," pausing briefly to sigh. "I just did not think it would happen so soon."

She studied the elegant bones of her father's face and the watery deep hazel calm of his eyes. He looked soft and remote, like he was not even there. It was a look she knew well and she understood fully that he was traveling backward in time once again.

He said, "When I was a boy, maybe ten or eleven, before my Bar Mitzvah, before the storm started raging, there was a girl I admired, she was a breathtaking beauty. It is all very romantic. I still remember her name, it was Manya Krakowski. She was the most beautiful girl from Kraków to Warsaw. It all comes back so clearly, that Manya Krakowski, she was buxom and rosy, she was all natural beauty. She lived nearby on Alota Street, which is Gold Street in Polish. She was just a young girl but full grown like a woman."

He said, "Manya Krakowski hardly knew I existed. I was a young boy in knickers and she was nearly a woman. I always spied on her walking though it was strictly forbidden; I followed her footsteps, I was totally smitten. Ah, Manya Krakowski! When Manya went walking all the young men took notice, she was a breathtaking beauty like the young Rita Hayworth. I remember every detail of her, the long auburn gloss of her, her hair flowed wild down her back like a fire was raging there. Her petticoats rustled a sound just like laughter. Her lips were red and *poziomki,* tiny wild Polish strawberries, which she'd gather together in a large swinging basket and sell Friday mornings in the open air market."

She took quizzical note of the flush on Father's face. They both chuckled briefly with genuine amusement.

She said, "Tatte, I did not even suspect you were such a romantic." He said, "Your mother used to say I was not so romantic, but back then I could not even think to express it. The war changed everything. I was not merely empty; I was filled up with sorrow. I was only a man, I was living with horror. I just could not believe it, that the world did not end. But Manya Krakowski, I will always remember her. She set a sweet raging fire to me when I was only a boy. Most of all I remember her eyes, gently smiling. I can still see Manya's deep shining dark Jewish eyes, gently smiling."

A cloud passed over his brow and swept the smile from his face. He took his head between the mottled scoops of his hands and swept a curtain of tears out from under his eye.

He said, "After the war I returned to my hometown. There was nobody left in the old Jewish quarter. A young Pole was poking about the rubble and ashes. He carried a large burlap sack over his muscular shoulder. He was ruddy and careless, he was big-boned and sturdy, he was casually harvesting *memento mori.* I said, *'Przepraszam*—excuse me—do you know if there are any Jewish souls left here? He pointed toward the graveyard at the edge of the woods and he started off again laughing."

"I walked through the gate of the old Jewish graveyard. It was rusted and broken, it fell nearly off of its hinges. I saw a figure hunched beside a remnant of headstones. Most of the markers had been torn down long ago and carted off by the Germans for building foundations. It was a woman, I could tell by the sound of her weeping. I saw the look of her face, it was covered with scars like a cruel tortured road map. Her expression was stiff as if it were frozen in screaming. Her eyes were not merely empty, they were brimming with horror. They were foreign and frightening, they were vaguely familiar. I just could not believe it, the way she moved like a phantom. I just could not believe it. It was Manya Krakowski."

He said, "I held her close in my arms, she was slight as a shadow. The sound of her voice when she spoke was not even human. Manya Krakowski, she was a breathtaking beauty, she was only sixteen, she was barely a woman, she was picking *poziomki* when the Germans stormed in. She ran toward her house. It was already burning. She found a tangle of bodies entwined in the hallway. She ran back to the woods with her hair all on fire. It burned and blistered her features, and they never healed fully. For three years she survived on mushrooms and lichen and nuts and *poziomki*. She hid for three years in the dark partisan forest. They were lush woods for hiding and tall woods for hanging."

He said, "That Manya Krakowski was a breathtaking beauty. I will always remember, she was the most beautiful girl from Krakow to Warsaw. It was the last time I saw her, there, in the ruins of the old Jewish graveyard. I remember her eyes, they were not merely empty. They were ash and bright ember still smoking with horror. I thought to cry, to put the cruel fire out. I thought to shed water, but not a single drop came out.

"I just could not believe it, the look of her like Medusa. I just could not believe it, that the world did not end. I just could not believe it, the way a life gets consumed."

She sat very still and her own deep shining dark Jewish eyes filled with stinging saltwater. She could not take away her father's deep pain so she just took his hand. They were knit together both into the very same scarred keloid thread of the warp.

That Saturday night she went out on her very first date and nothing much happened, at least nothing incendiary. Nothing much like a miracle anyway, that is to say, nothing near like falling in love.

Not even a spark.

PART TWO

Inheriting Parental Trauma

Introduction

The second generation are "guardians of an absent meaning." They seek to connect with and mourn the loss of an extended family whom they never knew but whose existence is a palpable presence in their lives. The *presence of this absence* shapes the boundaries of the interpsychic lives of second-generation witnesses. Furthermore, the Jewish future is informed in a fundamental way by "dialogues" with victims of the Holocaust.

Contributors to this section raise a variety of issues concerning the legacy of the Shoah. For example, can one resist writing about the Holocaust? Can one inherit suffering? Is memory of Auschwitz somehow genetically transmitted? Moreover, the question of gender arises. Mothers appear more likely to speak openly of the Shoah. Perhaps matrilineal transmission is a vital factor in helping offspring connect with their loss. Contributors also wonder about their own relationship to the Holocaust, fear of relationships, and a gradual awakening to the fact that their lives have been shadowed by the demons of Auschwitz.

Intersoul Flanking

Writing about the Holocaust

NAVA SEMEL

People ask in open amazement: "About the Holocaust? Why that?" Sometimes they lower their voice and add: "You couldn't pick a happier subject?"
I find myself in a position of apologizing, defending myself, or at least
feeling obligated to explain. Writing isn't a question of selecting. Maybe it's
more precise to compare it to forced labor, when you, the writer, don't
know who is the obstinate entity pushing your hand to the paper and
demanding that you rub shoulders with the materials of your life. An entity
that won't let you sink into whining, but will pinch you and press you to
the difficult, searing materials, the ones you grabbed with hidden fists; they
leak out of all the dams you toiled to build, spraying you and sweeping you
into the mouth of the river. Haven't I myself protested against it countless
times, and haven't I revolted? For four years when I wound the collection
of stories *The Glass Hat* around myself, I often shouted: "Enough! Why
me?" As if someone were pointing at me and forcing me. It wasn't a debt,
maybe a bill that came due. I wasn't even aware of the cunning process by
which the strange entity drew me into the trap. After all, I had protected
myself all the years and hadn't brought home a trace. I put on thick garments of ignorance. My childhood home was fortified against direct memories or their echoes that were restored in the public ritual. I naïvely brought
home Katzetnik's *House of Dolls,* my mother picked it up, slammed it shut
like a door, and ordered: "Tomorrow morning you take it back to the
school library!" And I obeyed, and didn't even sneak a peek at it. On
Holocaust Memorial Day, the radio stayed off, and when I grew up, the
television—only that day—and yet, I remember sharply how the siren would

pierce the walls. Yes, they taught me to respect, to stand at tense attention and not to move a muscle. Not even a muscle in the soul. Something I will never be able to understand. A wall of recoil built of hard bricks and quickly plastered. During the seconds the siren wailed, the body was taut and afterward it went slack. Repression like those old people who fill up the house with junk and rags, and hide old gold Napoleon coins in a few sacks. Only when they die is the "treasure" revealed in the house. Old person and child, it makes no difference. The task of hoarding is routine in their soul.

The field around the word Holocaust was very broad. It was possible to stand at the margins and remain protected. The word Auschwitz had no field at all, no scope, was without familiar laws of gravity. Only a black hole constantly indicating a danger zone. A sequence of terrifying feelings that shrivels into one word. A raven, clinging to the walls and floors of the house, touching even the children's toys.

At twenty-seven, a year after I myself became a mother, I went to the table and started putting down letters. Something bothers me. A single story she told me the night before my wedding. Titus's mosquito is stinging and won't leave me alone. A beautiful story. About grace within bestiality. About a woman she knew in the camp. Nothing shocking, just compassion. A kind of human splendor. From the backdoor, I enter unwittingly. And I write and put it aside, and later on, I grope for another memory and put it aside, and a third one also comes up, drawn to the same place. Just feeling my way, I let myself off the hook, and push everything into a remote drawer. But she beckons to me, and a few months later, I'm tempted and read what's written. What is this you've done? Where did you go? Have you gone out of your mind? You approached that word, and if you just dare to ask about it, that word, who knows what will happen. She'll weep, she'll explode, she'll collapse. It's all your fault. What will happen? Children have a secret task to protect mothers. Auschwitz is the code word of all the terrors, the open sesame of something with only absolute madness behind it. So don't do it, please don't write. This is me pleading, and this is me yielding. I won't write. The belly of the drawer swallows but doesn't digest, goes on lying in wait. The right moment will come.

In a foreign country I meet a respected doctor. In Heidelberg, he researches the mysteries of the nucleus, an enlightened man, his face wrapped in a scholarly expression that changes to righteousness: they say the Holocaust is Jewish propaganda. There were shootings, of course, and killing certainly, after all, it was a dreadful war. But systematic annihilation? Gas chambers? Really, that's exaggerated! A sweaty summertime café. There was a sea there that roared like an incited animal. On the table are beer and cheap wine, and I pull the nonexistent sleeve to the nonexistent number with an overly dramatic gesture. And when I return to Israel, there is no other way out. I was trapped. With a transparent rod in my back, I sit upright, there isn't yet a desk, and in the kitchen, when the baby is sleeping, I am compelled, tense, with pen at the ready for danger. After writing, I find the jaw muscles clamped in a grimace. In my sleep, ashes fall, sometimes I can't place the border between what is happening in reality and the twilight beneath the biological slackness.

I come to Mother. Wary as a doctor who is just starting out in practice, I place the word on the table. The body twitching and in pain. Before the thunder. But she doesn't explode and doesn't collapse and doesn't weep. Finally, she breaks the silence, and I recognize the relief. At long last, somebody asked. From the tight coil, she pulls a few thin threads, so she won't tear them, God forbid. In forty years, you learn to be careful with dangerous materials. As I listen, I feel how, with small dancer's steps, I am approaching the margins surrounding the word. I constantly calm myself, after all Mother's with me, I'm protected, I'm not alone. As I relax, as I let myself go, the voices rise around me. Harsh resistance. Little girls, it's better for her to stay behind protecting locks. It won't get you anywhere, only harm. What right do you have to come and peck around in other people's wounds? So what if she is your mother, think about other people too. It's not you, it's only your childhood resounding, and that's the scorched area of her soul. And there are other souls too sitting on the margins and not daring to get up. What is this yearning to write, sick, sick—but I can't respond to the pulling of the sleeve, that's a need of my existence, beneath the skin, you're in a game of cat-and-mouse and you can't control it.

Writing is now like cripples who paint. They tie your hands and you write with your mouth. The mouth is silenced but you hold a pencil in your little toe. If only it will fall, if only I won't fall. After all, as soon as the crack is found, you are flooded and rise. What to do with the floating of fragmented memories and fictions you want to unite. Mother—where did that black purse come from, the one embroidered with pearls, the one that was in the toy chest? You brought it from there, didn't you? The belonging and the affinity of materials to other materials that beat on its life. A thousand navels. My childhood is not only mine. Father and Mother are not only mine, they are also their own. What she got is poured out in wild doses and not calculated in every radius called home.

Don't read back what I wrote, don't cling, those aren't the rosy areas of childhood and aren't composed of pinches on the cheeks. In writing, Leonardo's mirror returns, embroidered with all the images created from me, a delicate tapestry of pearls. The little girl I was pulls the thin thread that ties them and scatters them in all the rooms. Uncle Berger, why are you chasing that ancient German, and if he did save your mother, he certainly demanded something from her in return. Did you think there are noble people? And Naomi, what is she hoarding in her storage room for an emergency? Her mother, who is starving herself to death, and Eitan Lieberman, despite his name, don't want to be loved. Anyone who makes children is obligated to them by bonds of concern all their lives. They're exiled, my people, twisting and turning restlessly, not knowing how to shout. I filled them with my own caution to get through the coming of experience. Even now, the first time I am trying to restore the crumbs they're created from, I pull a blanket with fears over myself and want to cover my head so they won't touch me, once again I write precisely on the lines of the cutting four years ago, and also on the marks of the seams. Writing tears them off and sews them at the same time. The memory of fear back then of being your own poor relation, even now I locate possible escape routes, after all, I've memorized the lesson well. But now I don't apologize. It's true, I wrote about the word steeped in symbols and the unattainable holiness. I wrote about the Holocaust. No need to be ashamed, just to be afraid. That belongs to me, too, genetically. Aside from biography, no operation will remove it, a private Holocaust. A literary professional shrugged and said: We don't know how to eat that. For lunch or dinner?

After the book appears, a few readers begin to make themselves known to me. Hesitant, somewhat scared. They say, "I'm like that too—you know—I grew up in a house like that." Someone who showed up before the publication said, "Write for me too, maybe at long last, I'll understand that indecipherable childhood." One real Uncle Berger found me and wept. There were those who said, "Forgive me, I couldn't read it. It hurts." My dear friend—with a similar childhood—put it aside. I could certainly understand her better than anyone. If someone had asked me to read a book about the children of Holocaust survivors, I would also have declined, No thanks.

"The child of the survivor cannot grow up under the aegis of heroism, like the child whose father fell in battle or risked his life for the land. Under the dome of humiliation I grew up, like a frightened weed. I tormented

myself for the shame of a loathsome father and mother. You don't understand that I was born to a man and a woman who, at a certain time in their
lives, stopped being human creatures, we are the children of creatures trapped
in disgrace." Eitan Lieberman says it better now in my name. I didn't stick
clinical labels on their foreheads, what is stuck to them is enough in any
case. There are altogether ten people in the stories, not shouting and not
loud, and when they are asked to stand up in front of the class and say
something, they are immediately covered with a sense of guilt. What can we
do, they're a bit grating, not exactly the image of the new Israeli, the sturdy
Sabra. Not heroes with developed biceps, not one of the gang who steals
a Palmach chicken for the get-together. Mother sometimes asks, now aloud,
Maybe I did you wrong. Why did you have to inherit suffering?

Us? Suffering? A bad joke. Good God, I can't cope with what she went
through and she pities me. I ran my fingernail over the line of her scar and
she even guided the wrist. I didn't learn to use the scar as experienced
politicians do. They shoot it, usable merchandise, from the hip. The sharp
pain of writing comes back to me. The stump sends transmissions long after
the amputation. I went to Auschwitz after I finished writing. Paralyzed with
ancient, illogical fear. The belief that you don't tempt fate twice. It doesn't
suffer from amnesia. A straight line stretched between two points. Israel-
Auschwitz. Not a line of pathos and counterfeit emotion with the idea that
justifies might, with the mocked slogan "like sheep to the slaughter." Instant Holocaust, crushed in the teeth of politicians, worn out with so much
cheapness. In Auschwitz, the designers placed the "exhibits" behind tall
glass partitions so the smell wouldn't pass, only the sight blocked from a
laboratory point of view. So it wouldn't crash in front of the glass. There
I saw the neat documents concerning insects and pests, turning humanity
into the essence of putrefaction. There I saw the word *Vernichtung*. Whoever translated it into the Hebrew word meaning destruction wasn't precise.
Destruction recognized the existence of the destroyed. *Vernichtung* lowers
the threshold below zero, in the area suddenly outside the existing plateau;
in recent years, a similar word flickers in Hebrew, a linguistic innovation.
Not-being. Is it by accident that on the day I flew to Warsaw, the chief of
staff of the Israeli army spoke about "drugged cockroaches" and such?

A bottle made of glass like the hat on my head, or perhaps now it's
changed to hard plastic. It too has wonderful properties, a material that
blocks part of the sights and sounds, filters them through a synthetic,
manufactured partition. History doesn't suffer from the disease of forgetting. Its people do. After all, the race has changed. How amazed the Poles

were at the sight of the Jews who returned, they were so different. Very strange. Perhaps that was an accelerated healing. So what if you see the contusions, every operation has a price. We've puffed up a bit here and there, and the cheeks have grown pink with health, and what happened there has turned into useful material here. And when I went to Poland three years ago, the symbolizations of the insects and the bottle seemed to me to be the sharpest and most racist expressions possible. An exception that cannot be. It will sink. There is no other way. Kahane is not yet born. The trash can has already moved on the earth but has not yet stopped, not yet been forged, not yet taken possession. Ultimately, something will always remain unsolved. In the annals of my mother, things will never be told from beginning to end. What has already sunk has sunk and not even my vision will pull them out. The objective truth has stopped existing by now, only the truth in memory rages. This memory is the yoke and has to be pulled. Sometimes the shoulders tremble with the effort, sometimes you weep and break down. The problem is not if to remember but how to remember. Out of hatred and vengeance or out of exaltation?

My childhood will forever remain unsolved. Maybe the notion of deciphered childhood doesn't even exist.

The unsolved I will carry to my old age, accepting the judgment that contains a measure of love. This imperfection is my end. There is also something completely final in understanding that what happened forty years ago—both individually and collectively—is stamped in the foundation of my life. A gloomy cornerstone I am chained to. Others are too. That's our common childhood, children of the persecuted. To be persecuted in the second generation means to mark possible paths of retreat from every place even before you enter. Children of sad people. They forgot the habits of joy. Repair—it's impossible to forget what you don't learn.

Someone wiser than I said, "For the truth to come to light, it requires two, one who speaks it and one who listens." The two conditions were filled in me at twenty-seven. Not young. I ran in the scorched field where a meteor had passed. Everything that had once grown here turned to ashes and was burned up. I sit at the margin of the crater left by the blow to the planet and ask how it came, from what corner in what orbit, and if in the next rotation, it will strike again, lying in wait behind us. How do you make an interplanetary flanking, an intersoul flanking?

Translated by Barbara Harshav

My Share of the Pain

DANIEL VOGELMANN

I was born in Florence, Italy, on May 28, 1948, three years after the end of the Second World War and fourteen days after the founding of the State of Israel. You might say I chose the right time to be born, but . . . there's a but. (My whole life is full of buts.) My father, Schulim Vogelmann, was a survivor of Auschwitz, where he had lost his wife, Anna Disegni, and their eight-year-old daughter, Sissel. In 1947, he married the woman who was to become my mother, Albana Mondolfi, the widow of Raffaello Passigli and mother of an eight-year-old boy, Guidobaldo. Her husband had died of an illness a few days before September 8, 1943, the tragic onset of the German invasion of Italy. My mother and brother were saved because they were sheltered by nuns in a convent. My father (who also was living in Florence where he had arrived in 1922 from his native Lemberg (L'viv) by way of Vienna and Palestine) instead tried to flee to Switzerland with his wife and child but they were stopped at the border by Fascist police and sent back to Florence. From there they were taken to Milan and then, in the transport of January 30, 1944, to Auschwitz. Mother and daughter were immediately sent to the gas chambers; my father was put in the camp and became number 173484.

"Why was I saved and not my dear ones, and not the six million?" my father would often ask himself, gnawed by an unjustified feeling of guilt, even though he knew there was no reason. Or rather there were many. My father, when he was interned, was forty, physically strong, knew German well and Polish fairly well, and, more important, was a *Facharbeiter,* a skilled worker, a typesetter (we all know how useless intellectuals ended up . . .). But the main reason—and well did he know it—had another name: great good luck, fate. . . .

So, when I was born, my father was already forty-five, with a great tragedy behind him and the compulsion to put his life together again. Small wonder, then, that almost all his time was given over to working, to rebuilding his printing shop, the old and glorious Tipografia Giuntina (where, in 1928, D. H. Lawrence had *Lady Chatterley's Lover* printed). Therefore, he didn't play with me, but not only because he was "old" and because he worked all day. . . . Today I think that he couldn't let himself grow as attached to me as he had been to Sissel: how could he have borne another such loss, ever a possibility? Nor did my mother play with me, though for other reasons (but she too had gone through rather dramatic experiences). And even my brother didn't play with me, because he was all of nine years older than me. Sometimes I still wonder: What could he have thought of this new father and of this unexpected baby brother? Luckily, there lived with us a beloved old housekeeper, the unforgettable Gilda.

When did I first realize that my father was not a normal father, but one of the few Holocaust survivors, and therefore a *hero*? Maybe when I saw the blue number tattooed on his left arm? More likely I discovered the truth when film clips of the camps were shown on television; then my father (also at my mother's insistence) would get up and leave because he couldn't stand seeing those scenes again.

My father said little about his camp experiences, perhaps to not upset me. And yet something entered silently within me: fear of others? a sense of the absurd? the capriciousness of fate? In a word: from the moment that, in the normal course of events, I should not have been born, what sense did my life make, what should I do to justify it, and, above all, what ought I do to live up to such a father?

So it's not surprising that at fourteen I "decided" to become a model student, the first in the class. After all, my father hadn't been able to study much, so through study I could perhaps "surpass" him. I accordingly spent my high school years studying like crazy, neglecting almost entirely all the carefree pleasures of youth, and graduated with top grades. Now I *merely* had to choose what to do with my life, and that's where the trouble began.

The old questions about the meaning of life returned, about what one should and could do other than survive, granted that surviving was really worthwhile. During this crisis, which grew worse by the day, I obviously thought of suicide but, beyond the instinct of self-preservation, the thought of causing my father another great sorrow made me put the idea aside. I didn't know what to make of my life and, having no pressing economic needs, I did nothing, plunging ever deeper into a severe depression and winding up in the hospital. My parents couldn't understand what had happened to me all of a sudden and why I was incapable of living normally, for "I had everything to be happy." The only explanation they could finally bring themselves to accept was that I was ill. And if, in a way, I doubtlessly was ill, what was the cure? It's difficult not to think that I should not have been born, that I, too, indirectly, suffered from the survivor's syndrome, and to make matters worse, I had not even been at Auschwitz, hence had no "right" to be hurting. Pharmacological treatment didn't help much; I even tried a kind of psychotherapy, but who in Italy could understand the anguish of the child of a survivor? My only solace came from writing poetry and reading the great pessimists, starting with Ecclesiastes. But writing poetry isn't a career. And novels, unfortunately, I wasn't up to writing.

Then, luckily, I met Vanna, my future wife, who through her love helped me to cope. Yet, in this case too there was a but. . . . Vanna wasn't Jewish—you can imagine my father's reaction. Even though Vanna was willing to convert, my father wouldn't hear of it, and this certainly didn't help me get over my depression either. Then, on the ninth of June, 1974, when I was only twenty-six, my father suddenly died: his sick old heart could hold out no longer. I won't tell you of my grief, which you can easily guess.

At this point my mother, brother, and especially Vanna (who, understandably, after having converted, wanted to get married) "made" me go into the family business, the printing shop. These were the worst years of my life: to have to deal all day with calling cards, stationery, or books about the Etruscans was a kind of cultural death. I confess that I seriously thought again about suicide but held back because of my mother, of Vanna and even of my brother. Then that despair of mine helped me find a compromise: If I couldn't be a writer, if I couldn't stand being a printer, I would become a publisher. And so, with my brother's moral and material support, I founded the Giuntina Publishing House, specializing from the start in works with Jewish themes. The first book in the Schulim Vogelmann Series (dedicated to my father's memory) was *Night* by Elie Wiesel, an author then unknown in Italy. And that was no accident, because it is one of the most harrowing eyewitness accounts of the inferno of the death camps. Besides publishing it, I also had the satisfaction of translating it into Italian myself. And so, book after book (from Wiesel to Yehoshua, from Werfel to Nissenson), I built up a catalog of more than 120 titles.

In the meantime, in 1977, I had married Vanna and, unexpectedly, a year later, we had a son, whom I named Shulim (like my father, but without the *c*). I say "unexpectedly" because consciously, I didn't feel ready to bring a child into the world (and who knows if I ever would have). Shulim's birth was a true blessing: at last someone demanded nothing of me, other than to be loved and to love me. Thus, with my marriage, the birth of Shulim, and the start of my publishing activity, my life began to resemble a normal life.

After *Night,* one of the first books I published was *Children of the Holocaust* by Helen Epstein. That's when I discovered, not without surprise, that I wasn't the only son of a survivor to suffer from serious psychological disorders, but that I had many brothers and sisters with the same problems, the so-called second generation. Unfortunately, they were far away, in the United States or Israel. And then, what would I have told them? How could they have helped me? The only thing we could have done was to burst out weeping together. Yes, because, even though my situation had greatly improved, every so often I was stricken by terrible fits of depression that left me stunned. Luckily, I never stopped working on my books even if, during the blackest periods, for only a few hours a day. I tried everything to get over my depression, from Jungian analysis to transcendental meditation, from Zen to rebirthing, but in vain. Right now I'm trying the famous Prozac. Fortunately, I also have my good periods, which are essential to keep going (otherwise I wouldn't be able to stand it). Recently, I've even been able to write five short poems for Sissel, the little sister I never knew. And I keep wondering if I will ever know her. At times, I think I ought to live a long time, to add to her eight years my eighty or ninety. And then? Who will remember Sissel and the six million? Will the books, the films, Spielberg's archive be enough?

And has mankind learned anything from the Holocaust? Primo Levi's disconsolate words spring to mind: "It has happened. Therefore it can happen again." Perhaps, this time, not to the Jews. The ethnic cleansing in the former Yugoslavia and countless other daily massacres certainly give us no cause for optimism.

And yet (as Wiesel would say), life goes on. While I'm writing these comments, my son, Shulim, who is now seventeen, is in Poland with six thousand other young Jews on the "march of the living" to the extermination sites. A new generation, the "third," is coming of age; we like to think that it will be a serener and stronger generation of Jews who will perhaps give meaning to the calamity of their grandparents and the unhappiness of their parents.

Rereading what I have written up to now, I realize that I have never spoken of God, even though He was always implicit. But, after Auschwitz, can we still believe in the God of Israel, just, omnipotent, and compassionate? And if not, can a Jew really live without his God? To these questions, too—as we know by now—there are no answers. At least not in this life.

I therefore end my brief witness with an illuminating sentence from I. B. Singer: "The truth will be known—not here, but in the hereafter, providing anything is left of our miserable souls."

Five Short Poems for Sissel

DANIEL VOGELMANN

Translated by Lynne Sharon Schwartz

1   Dear little sister,
     Killed so long ago
     In a concentration camp,
     Today I offer you
     These five little poems.

2   How can we help but long
     For the immortality of the soul?
     At last I could meet
     My little sister Sissel,
     Who flew up to heaven before I was born.
     She would come toward me smiling
     And softly say,
     "Ah, you must be Daniel."

          Those whom the gods love best die young.
               —Menander and Leopardi

3   God must have loved you dearly indeed
     If he wanted you near him so soon.
     Then tell me, if all things are known to you now,
     Doesn't he love us too?

4   Promise to take my hand
That day
When I come to join you,
For—I must tell you—
I still feel
A little bit frightened . . .

5   Now, little sister, I'll take my leave.
Help me, if you can, to live
As well as to die.
You know from my words
How I hope one day we'll meet.
I can even envision it:
I stand there thrilled and trembling.

The Lifelong Reporting Trip

JULIE SALAMON

I've lived in New York City for twenty years now. But I was born and bred in the American heartland and bear its imprint in both my speech and my behavior. I am nice in the Midwestern way. Sometimes I feel burdened by my own niceness, my reluctance to stir up a fuss. New York taxi drivers always ask me where I'm from. I still find myself saying Seaman, Ohio.

Seaman is just a little bit north of the Ohio River, dirt poor and incredibly beautiful. Its population, between eight hundred and a thousand, hasn't changed much since I grew up there. I had a Walt Disney childhood, I grew up on Mickey Mouse, the Beatles, and Elvis—had a dog named Poochie and a pet chicken named Penny. I was a Girl Scout and in 4-H and learned how to drive a tractor when I was twelve. My father was the town doctor, an old-fashioned general practitioner. He made house calls, treated anyone who walked in the door whether they could pay or not. We were all-American all the way.

But I also feel very comfortable when I hear Hungarian being spoken and I weep at the sound of Gypsy music. You see, my parents grew up in eastern Europe, the part where Hungary, Czechoslovakia, and the Ukraine have overlapped throughout history. I guess you could say I'm part Appalachian, part Carpathian.

I am the child of successful immigrants. My father was a professional, my mother is very clever. They raised my sister and me to believe devoutly in the American dream, and we did because it had certainly worked the way it was supposed to for us. As I read my six-year-old daughter the Laura Ingalls Wilder *Little House on the Prairie* series, I feel as if I'm reading about my own family—though my parents made their trek west in an Oldsmobile, not a covered wagon.

Often I have wished I could stop right there, to simply be the daughter of successful immigrants, a nice person from Ohio—strong, upright, happy. This is not an inaccurate picture and for that I am grateful. But the third influence is inescapable. I am something else as well. I am the child of Holocaust survivors. My mother was an inmate at Auschwitz-Birkenau; my father at Dachau. My grandparents all died in the camps, along with many aunts, uncles, cousins. My father's first wife was killed at Auschwitz with the two-year-old daughter they had together. My stepfather (my father died just after my eighteenth birthday) spent the war in hiding, sometimes fighting with the Czech partisans, sometimes working at his profession—he is an engineer—using false papers that identified him as a Christian.

There is horror in the heart of my happy family and it has affected me profoundly. My parents raised me to be optimistic, to believe in goodness, the future, the possibility of beauty and love. Yet, they didn't hide their background from us, so we were also well aware of evil, no hope for the future, the reality of ugliness and hate.

I am forty-two as I write this and have spent much of my adult life trying to understand what effect each of these powerful historic influences has had on me. To this day I wage an internal battle between Pollyanna and Cassandra. Sometimes I suspect my Midwestern "niceness" is nothing more than a shield. I don't want to forget but I don't want to be bitter either. Sometimes it is hard to maintain this position and consider myself a rational person. But I have a wonderful husband (whose family, also Jewish, has been ensconced in the American Midwest for several generations, with only a few exceptions) and two young children. So responsibility to the past is tempered by duty to the present and the future. I want my children to learn from me what I learned from my parents—that compassion is more valuable than hatred. I also want them to know there is a link between the present and the past, that our happiness has been hard won.

I have not gone out of my way to identify myself with other children of the Holocaust besides my sister and our cousins. I have joined no second-generation groups; none of my closest friends are the children of survivors. There were no Jews besides us in Seaman, Ohio, where I grew up. I have read all my childhood diaries and found only a handful of references to the Holocaust; almost all of these are oblique (there is one mention, for ex-ample, of my father's first wife. I talked about her with my mother when my father was sick with lung cancer). I didn't have much contact with Jews of my age who were not relatives until I went to college, at Tufts University in Boston. There I discovered that when I mentioned my parents were camp survivors, people seemed to pity me. Because my parents never seemed like victims to me—quite the contrary, they seemed much stronger than most people—I soon stopped telling anyone outside of my closest circle. I don't think I was ashamed. Rather, it was too complicated to explain something I couldn't begin to understand myself.

Besides, upon my graduation from high school, a sorrow much closer to home dominated my emotional life. My father's death overshadowed the Holocaust in my private grief. And yet, over time, I found the two were inextricably linked. As I searched for my father I began to realize how little I knew of him, how deeply he had been wounded by the death camps. I began to realize, too, that my happy childhood had been shadowed by many ghosts and many demons. I came to feel more and more like an unformed person. Indeed, I had succeeded too well in putting on a "good front." I had an exciting job, working as a reporter for a big newspaper. I had gotten married relatively young for my generation; my husband and I had fun together, exploring New York and the world. We thought of ourselves as perpetual tourists. I had it all, it seemed—except peace of mind.

Eventually, perhaps inevitably, the Holocaust began making an appearance in my professional work. I was hired by the *Wall Street Journal* to cover the commodities markets in 1978. When I heard Helen Epstein's book *Children of the Holocaust* was about to be published in 1979, I volunteered to review the book for the paper. In that review I made my first public declaration of being the child of survivors. The review began:

> When I was a college junior, I enrolled in a course entitled "Immigration Literature." The reading list ran from Jerzy Kosinski's "The Painted Bird" to Eugene O'Neill's "Long Day's Journey into Night." In the fashion of the time, the professor encouraged us to write journals about our backgrounds. (If we could squeeze in some reference to a book on the list, that was nice, too.)
>
> One recent day, possessed by springtime nostalgia, I began leafing through my journal from that class. I was jarred by my own long forgotten words, not for their great clarity or wisdom, but because I'd just finished reading Helen Epstein's "Children of the Holocaust."
>
> Back in 1974 I wrote: "when I was quite young I was obsessed with the notion of concentration camps. I read "Exodus" by Leon Uris for the first time when I was seven, lingering over his renditions of what happened to people in concentration camps. My dreams were filled with visions of

mangled and bloodied Jewish bodies. I substituted fictional victims with my mother and father and would cry out in the night for Mommy and Daddy. I never told my parents why I cried so often at night. I'm not sure why.

I'm still not sure about a lot of things which may have to do with my knowledge that my parents survived Auschwitz and Dachau. Helen Epstein, whose parents spent much of World War II in concentration camps, felt a similar uncertainty.

I received a number of letters in response to the review, including a few pieces of hate mail. (I would grow accustomed to the occasional anti-Semitic outburst in my work mailbox, including a diatribe from a man who insisted the *Wall Street Journal* was in the hands of evil Jews, including "that cunning little Jewess Julie Salamon." The writer also included on his hit list my very non-Jewish colleague Tim Carrington, among others.) A number of friends and coworkers expressed admiration for my willingness to write so personally and surprise about my background (As I said, I give the impression of perhaps excessive "niceness" and "perkiness.")

That seemed to be that. I didn't become deeply introspective. I kept my energy and my angst focused on my work—and my play. Like my mother and father before me, and my sister, too, I kept very, very busy. Was this a reaction to the Holocaust? Like so much in my life, I don't know.

In 1983, the *Wall Street Journal* began a daily Leisure and Arts page and hired me to be its regular movie critic. Though I had always been a movie fan, my new job catapulted me into a new world. I saw almost every new movie that was released, from the most obscure documentary to the big Hollywood blockbusters. As I wrote about film, I became more and more accustomed to revealing myself in print. I don't mean my movie columns were *about* me so much as they were subjective, overtly and deliberately informed by my sensibility in a way that my news reportage was not and could not be. I spent much of my time analyzing how filmmakers used narrative to express themselves, to find themselves. It occurred to me one day that perhaps I could do this.

In 1988, I published my first book, a novel called *White Lies*. It was a work of fiction, though its themes and many of its characters were unabashedly autobiographical. Its main character, Jamaica Just, is the child of Holocaust survivors who settled in the American heartland. Her father is a sainted country doctor; her mother an improbably energetic and optimistic—and somewhat exasperating—homemaker and businesswoman. In this book, for the first time in a systematic way, I grappled with the peculiar worldview that I'd developed. I gave Jamaica many of the characteristics I saw in myself. She is funny and neurotic and good-hearted on the one hand; consumed by grief and shame and confusion on the other:

> Almost everyone she knew besides Sammy was a victim of something, although none of them could top her. Who else had the glamour of the Holocaust? Why not be the best? The most victimized?
>
> At college she would sit back smugly during bull sessions, when scared, fresh-faced youngsters trying to prove just how interesting they were would reduce tragedy to headlines. The point was to startle, not inform. The litany was endless: parents who divorced the instant their youngest left the house; mothers who forced their sons to track down their fathers' love affairs and testify against them in court; wives left widowed by their husbands' suicides, leaving them no choice but to pack up their children and impose on relatives; fathers who died leaving their children in the hands of evil stepfathers; parents who hadn't talked in twenty years; mothers who slept around and felt compelled to "share" the information with their children.
>
> Jamaica would nod sympathetically. Because she seemed to listen so well, she became everybody's best friend; people mistook her silent glow of moral superiority for shyness. They didn't know what she was thinking: Had any of them, their parents, been tattooed and shaved, turned spooked and deranged? Were their grandparents murdered? Did their mothers talk cheerily about girlhood chums they went to camp with and mean Auschwitz? Go on. Top that.
>
> Jamaica couldn't. She couldn't even match it.

The "white lies" of the title refer to the countless fibs all parents tell their children to protect them.

> When Geneva (Jamaica's older sister) was fifteen, she took driver's education at school. "Don't tell Daddy, dear," Eva (their mother) advised. "Keep it a little secret." The Just children were used to keeping little secrets, like the one about the bottles of Mogen David wine hidden in the hall closet behind the good linens, or the one about the candles the family lit in the master bedroom on Friday nights. They kept secrets about trips to synagogues in Cincinnati on Yom Kippur and secrets about the Hebrew lessons they learned from Berlitz records. Jamaica figured their parents didn't want them to feel embarrassed in front of their friends, but later Geneva's shrink would say they were being prepared for another Holocaust. When Jamaica told Geneva she thought psychiatrists were full of shit, Geneva replied

sweetly: "It doesn't matter if you don't understand yourself if you're happy with things. It doesn't matter how sick you are if you're contented. It only matters if you're unhappy."

The response to *White Lies* was both smaller and bigger than I expected. It didn't become a literary phenomenon; I received a brief, mixed review in the *New York Times Book Review,* a snide review in the *Los Angeles Times,* an enthusiastic review in The *Christian Science Monitor,* and many favorable write-ups in the Jewish press. I learned a lot about writing a book. I received a surprisingly huge response from readers, considering the limited size of the book's printing. Most significantly for me, I felt calmer somehow. I was able to feel a compassion for Jamaica's angst that I hadn't been able to feel for myself. About Jamaica I had written:

> Hadn't she spent years anguishing over this pivotal event of her life, and the fact that it had taken place before she'd been born? Her alienation was complete, separated as she was even from other Jews who were made uncomfortable by the ugly scar on her past. Even from Sammy (her husband). Here was her chance to tell the world what had happened to her.
> But nothing had happened to her, really.

After *White Lies* I began to accept the notion that my life could be authentic even though I hadn't experienced Auschwitz. I felt a lessening of the guilt that had always nagged at me *for my very existence.*

Ironically, as I was achieving some distance from the Holocaust, the world was discovering it. The Holocaust Memorial Museum in Washington, D.C., was being built; the Holocaust was being taught in secular schools as well as in religious ones; conventions of Holocaust survivors and their children were becoming regular events, occurring with more and more frequency.

For my part, I was settling into the business of life. After eleven years of marriage, my husband and I had our first child, a daughter, in 1989. My older sister has a daughter a year older than mine and a son a few months younger. The present became very compelling—and joyful, as we watched our children enjoy their grandparents, a pleasure my sister and I never had. In 1991, my second book was published, *The Devil's Candy: The Bonfire of the Vanities Goes to Hollywood.* Perhaps symbolically, this book, a fly-on-the-wall account of big-budget Hollywood filmmaking, had nothing to do with the Holocaust or with me. It was the confident work of a professional observer. The reviews were overwhelmingly positive. It seemed I had left my past behind.

But that was not the case. I went on to write yet another book about my family, this time in nonfiction form. That wasn't my intent. I had been trying for some time after *The Devil's Candy* to find a book subject that compelled me. On a visit to Seaman I was struck by how the town had changed. A highway near town had sapped the downtown of life; instead of bringing jobs in, the highway took people out. My remote village had met the modern world and it wasn't a happy marriage. I'd spent several months flying back and forth, trying to find a way to tell this story. Finally, I wrote a fifty-page proposal about the place, which included one paragraph about my family's background, by way of explaining my qualifications to write this book. Ann Godoff, who is now the editorial director at Random House, zeroed in on this one paragraph and said, "This sounds interesting. I'd like to read a book about *that*."

I was desolate. I liked this editor very much and wanted to work with her. But I thought I had moved on. The Holocaust had lost its grip on me.

Then I read in a magazine that Steven Spielberg was about to begin filming *Schindler's List* in Poland. To understand what happened next requires an understanding of my mother's philosophy of life. I decided to book a plane ticket to Poland, that it was *b'shert*, fate, that dictated it. What really set things in motion, however, was my mother's decision to come with me. I took a road trip with her and my stepfather to "Schindler's List," to Auschwitz, and then to Huzst, the eastern European town where she was from. That was the beginning of the book that became *The Net of Dreams: A Family's Search for a Rightful Place*.

In the book's prologue, I ask the question, why am I writing this book?

I often mention my upbringing in [Seaman] this "colorful" impoverished backwater to let people know I'm not just another Jewish girl from New York. I have watched myself deliberately bring my parents into conversation, often as comic foils for amusing stories about the adventures of eastern European Jews in the American heartland. If the talk went deeper, allowing for the revelation that they were not just immigrants but concentration camp survivors, I dreaded the inevitable expressions of sympathy. I developed a practiced response: "Oh, no, it wasn't like that at all. My parents were very unusual, very upbeat. We were very happy."

We were—and we weren't. Like every family, we had our own mythology, and I accepted it, more or less. When my mother told me how lucky she was, how happy we were, I felt I had no choice but to believe her. If she, with her history, was lucky, then I was obliged to be lucky and happy beyond belief.

But when my father died six weeks after I finished high school, I didn't feel lucky at all. I felt unbearably sad. My father's death cracked the notion that my parents were infallible, having been tested in the cruelest of history's laboratories. I came to realize how little I knew of what they had been before, when they had been unlucky and unhappy.

Thus began what has been a lifelong reporting trip, as I tried time and again to write my family's story. The more data I accumulated, the more I found fact and fiction laying equal claim to my imagination. No matter how hard I tried to find the "truth," I found I still didn't know what to make of the happy family [portraits sitting in pretty little frames all over my house]. Were we—were they—tragic or triumphant?

That is the question I tried to answer as I traveled across eastern Europe with my mother and stepfather—back to Auschwitz and to Huzst, the town my mother was from. I traveled back and forth to Ohio, talked to relatives and friends, acquaintances and patients of my father's. I tried to find out who my parents were before the war, how they came to be the people I knew, what their journey meant to me and to my children.

"Was it cathartic?" someone asked me after she read my book.

"Cathartic?" I mumbled, not quite sure what she meant. Was that why I wrote the book? For catharsis? I looked up catharsis, to see the exact definition: "purification or purgation of the emotions (as pity and fear), primarily through art." Purgation? Had I purged myself? (Purge: "to clear of guilt or of moral or ceremonial defilement.") Was that the point?

Maybe in part. But I had another purpose. I had become a mother, an adult, finally. I was ready to see my parents as I never had before: as human beings. Their Holocaust experiences as well as their personalities had always made it difficult for me to see them in scale. They were always larger than life, part of a historic tragedy, epic. Their extraordinariness made ordinariness seem out of my grasp, inconsequential. They never said those awful words: How can you worry about pimples, boyfriends, tests, adolescence after we survived the camps? They didn't have to. I did it myself.

In *White Lies* I examined this absence of identity from a child's point of view (though I was thirty-one when I began writing the book). Perhaps belatedly, I was coming into my own as an adult and, for the first time, articulating the question: What has all *that* meant to me?

The questions I wanted answered had changed somewhat by the time I wrote *The Net of Dreams.* I had one child, I was pregnant with a second during most of the writing of the book. Now I wanted to know: Who were they? Who were my parents before the war and after? Certainly, the Holocaust was a devastating crucible for them, but it defined them only in part. I wanted to understand them and their lives apart from it and apart from me. Perhaps this was part of a "catharsis." But it was something else as well, part of an inquiry into human resourcefulness and adaptability. Somehow, I felt, learning who they were and how they redefined themselves after the war might help me raise my own children.

There was something else. Moved as I have been by any number of Holocaust stories, as diverse as Primo Levi's and Steven Spielberg's, none of them have spoken directly to me. When I have tried to place my family in these scenarios, I've found a gap. They haven't fit. I realized that, though I had a generalized sense of the evil, the horror, the sorrow, I needed to particularize it. I knew what had happened to the six million but I didn't know what had happened, exactly, to my grandparents. Why hadn't they fled? Why did my parents survive? What were they thinking during those weeks and months and years of the war? I had interpretations, including my own, but very few details. I was a reporter. I had developed the patience and the skill it takes to pull information and emotion out of people. Why not do this with my own family?

The book took me on an extraordinary journey, geographically and emotionally. The book turned out to be a story of the Holocaust, yes, but also the story of how our family became American.

Catharsis? No, not that. The Holocaust cannot be purged, erased, figured out, dealt with. It is with me every day, one way or the other. I rarely pass a homeless person on the street without stopping to give something, and when I don't I feel enormously guilty. I cannot bear to be identified as the oppressor in any way at all. My mother once said: "My life was more interesting because of the Holocaust." This may sound preposterous but it is true. Tragedy uprooted her and catapulted her into the world. Similarly, I have struggled to take some good away from it. My life in many ways is a reaction against the Holocaust. I am intolerant of bigotry, hatred, arrogance. ("Oversensitive," says my mother, who, unlike me, is a survivor.)

With *The Net of Dreams* I found something more valuable to me than catharsis. At the very end of the book I write about a family gathering with my sister and her husband and her children, my mother and stepfather, and my family. My sister and I hurried back from a long walk and talk, worried that everyone was worried about us. Instead, they were all lolling around watching television, reading the newspaper, playing:

> Only later did it occur to me that perhaps my search had culminated in that placid scene. Wasn't this ordinariness, this "miraculous" ordinariness what my parents had struggled so hard for. All my father had seemed to want was a wife and children and to do some good. Achieving this deceptively modest ambition—so much can go wrong!—must have taken heroic effort for this man who had lost everything.
>
> Yet instead of locking his heart he had opened it—as much as he had dared. He had tried again in a new country, with a new family and a new life. He told my mother before he died that he had no regrets about anything he did after the war. I like to think of this parting gift as assurance that, although part of him died with his first family, he still loved his second. I feel more grateful than ever for that love but no longer as burdened by it. I now believe my mother when she tells me, "Don't you know that all your Daddy and I ever wanted for you girls is for you to be happy."

The book concludes with a sense of peace that I feel—as much as it is possible to feel at peace in a world that hasn't learned the lessons of the Holocaust:

> One day I suspect my children will discover for themselves what has taken me so long to learn—that we are bound together by our family stories, which are written and revised every day. They will understand why, every night before they go to bed, we say the prayer that my father said with Suzy and me.

> Now I lay me down to sleep.
> I pray the Lord my soul to keep.
> Guard me through the starry night
> And wake me safe with sunshine bright.
> Amen.

PART THREE

The Journey to Parents' Birthplaces and to Death Camps

Introduction

As the Shoah occupies an increasingly important role in the saga of Jewish history, it acquires distinctive liturgy and rituals. Judaism has no more important imperative than remembrance. But remembering also means doing, as in the commandment "Remember the Sabbath day and keep it holy." Second-generation witnesses focus on appropriate rituals of remembrance. Among these rituals, pilgrimages to the birthplaces of their parents and to death camps assume primacy. For many in the second generation, this journey already began in their minds as children. The trip "back there" where life began and, for so many millions, ended is an entry into the landscape of Jewish history, a way of mourning their losses, and a means of better connecting with their parents.

Coming Full Circle

NAOMI BERGER

I Am

I am a child of Holocaust survivors.

I wonder could I have survived the horrors of Auschwitz.

I hear the screams of frightened women and children as they are led to
the gas chambers.

I see piles of naked bodies, their limbs spread, their eyes stare empty
with death.

I want to close my eyes and escape this nightmare.

I am a child of Holocaust survivors.

I pretend that my parents' trauma has no impact on me.

I feel the vulnerability of being a Jew in a Christian culture.

I touch my children and pray that they will not experience the horrors
of hatred.

I worry that evil and bigotry will touch my perfect world.

I cry for all of the innocent children in Tel Aviv, Gaza, New York,
Oklahoma, Bosnia, and Somalia.

I am a child of Holocaust survivors.

I understand that evil and hatred have existed from the beginning of
humanity.

I say that we can join together to ensure that goodness and love will
prevail in the end.

I dream of a world free of hatred, discrimination, and craziness.

I try to make a difference by helping to heal broken hearts and para-
lyzed souls.
I hope that history will not repeat itself.
I am a child of Holocaust survivors.

The year is 1973, the religion department at Syracuse University advertises
a position in Judaica. My husband was the first Jewish candidate to be
considered for a position in the department, which, at that time, consisted
primarily of professors from a Methodist background, many of whom were
ordained ministers. Fearing the possibility that a Jewish professor teaching
Judaism might use the podium to influence the students' religious beliefs,
rather than focus on Jewish studies as an academic discipline, one professor
on the search committee inquired, "How do you feel about your religion?"
Reflecting on this interview later, we wondered if a similar question would
be asked of a Christian candidate.

It is summer of 1973 in Oxford, Ohio. My husband has accepted the
teaching position in New York State and we began to make moving arrangements. We needed estimates from moving companies. The man who
came to look at our belongings was tall, well built, with light hair and blue
eyes. He was very friendly and talkative. As we went through the house he
admired some pictures and art objects, things he clearly had not seen before. He asked questions and commented on some of the items. Being in
a good mood and wanting to connect with his potential new customers, he
shared his observations about previous customers' homes. At this point he
commented that Jews bury their dead standing up. "They also hide their
money underneath the tiles in their homes," he said in an expert voice. We
hurried to end his visit and called a different moving company.

It is Syracuse in the late 1970s. "Holocaust," a made-for-television
miniseries, garners high ratings. We gather in front of the set for four
nights, following the story of the Weiss family as their comfortable lives are
slowly destroyed. One morning during that week, we stepped outside our
home and noticed that the sidewalk was marked with yellow arrows. We
walked around the neighborhood to see if these arrows were on other
sidewalks. Our home was the only one. We spent time speculating as to the
meaning of these arrows. No explanation made sense. We called some of
our friends and asked them what they thought. No one offered a reasonable
explanation. Aware of our increased anxiety and the need to reject some
"crazy" thoughts and images, we decided to act responsibly and called the

police. Two officers came to our door. We pointed to the arrows. The officers could not explain the mystery either, but promised to drive around our house for a few days as a preventive measure. Two days later, we awoke to the noise of the Public Works Department as they tore up the sidewalk. The arrows were to direct the workers in their task. We laughed at our anxiety and analyzed the impact of the miniseries on our perceptions.

It is Dewitt, 1987. Our oldest son is completing his freshman year at Jamesville DeWitt High School. He is very excited as he shows us his yearbook. We look through the pages recognizing the faces of his friends. We laugh at some of their remarks and look for his picture. We come to the page with the individual student pictures. Our son's photograph is at the bottom of the page. Someone has written a message on the photo. We look closely and read "Hitler had the right idea" accompanied by a swastika. Our hearts stop and our stomachs tighten. We read it again, making sure it is not a mistake. We call our son and question him. "Did you see this?" "Do you know who wrote this?" Our son is obviously uncomfortable. He does not want to draw attention to this. After all, he had a good year, he made many friends, he was involved in clubs and extracurricular activities. This ugliness did not fit his experience. What should we do? Should we draw more attention to this? How can we express our anger and disgust without hurting him? Maybe we should let it go, just ignore it. Finally, we decide that my husband should meet with the school principal and bring this to his attention.

A meeting is held. The principal and the chair of the social studies department are present. My husband shows them the yearbook page and expresses his concern. After all, kids learn to hate from their parents. More education is required, he stresses. Students need to learn to respect the differences between people and cultures, and to learn about the consequences of such hatred. "How does the school curriculum address the question of the Holocaust?" he asks. The principal does not want any trouble. This school system has an excellent reputation. Certain problems do not exist in the district. "This is most likely a joke not intended to hurt anybody," he says. Proudly, he announces that the school definitely does not support hatred or discrimination. The Holocaust is addressed in social studies classes. The social studies chair triumphantly shows my husband a textbook where the subject is discussed—in half a page. My husband points out that the information is minimal and does not address cultural sensitivity. The principal explains that the curriculum is very crowded; there is not enough time to study this subject in depth. My husband leaves, feeling angry, after first suggesting additional reading material and films to help sensitize students to anti-Semitism and hatred. He offers to lecture to the class. The principal thanks him. There is no follow-up.

A couple of years later, my son is involved with a Jewish youth group. He is excited and eager to participate. His peers reach out to him with great affection. A weekend retreat is organized, focusing on heightening the participants' sense of Jewish identity, helping them commit to a Jewish lifestyle. My son is eager to make this commitment. Coming home, he declares that he bet that he will wear a yarmulke (head covering Jews wear during prayer) for six weeks. He also suggests that we keep kosher. "No way!" I snap. "I am not going to change my cooking habits, this is nonnegotiable." "Let me try," he asks, "I want to see what it is like." I continue to be unreasonable. Unexpectedly, and deep from inside my body, I feel an intense energy of rage. I cannot allow him to do this. He should not draw attention to his Jewishness in a public school. After all, we live in a Christian society.

The energy intensifies, I am like a lioness who feels the threat of losing her cubs. I tell myself to relax. "You are being irrational," I say to myself, but the energy will not subside. "I will join the Unitarian church if I have to," I exclaim. "My son is asking for trouble" is my argument. Seeking to calm down, I go for a ride in the car. The rage continues to grow inside my chest. "Who am I angry at?" I ask myself as I look around sensing that these strong feelings are not organized or focused. "You are crazy," I tell myself. "Stop it." My son is determined to win this bet and wears the yarmulke for a full six weeks. I refuse to entertain any possibility of changing our eating habits and thus fail to be supportive of his wish to explore his religious heritage.

A few weeks later, as my rational self is restored, I experience deep sadness at the position I took. I wonder about the origin of my intense emotions and conclude that my parents' Holocaust experiences must have had more of an impact on me than I am willing to acknowledge. The wounds of this trauma must have passed to the second generation. I push these insights out of my mind and focus on my feelings toward my son. I become aware of my deep appreciation of his strength and determination to stand tall and win the bet. My heart fills with warm, loving feelings toward him. My son is confident. His sense of identity is solid.

Habib Davanloo, in his analysis of the metapsychology of the unconscious, points out the importance of experiencing one's unconscious sadistic impulses as a prerequisite to working through grief-laden feelings and successfully resolving separation and individuation issues. Children of survivors experience their parents' intense focus. They often feel strong expectations to be their parents' source of vicarious gratification of lost dreams and destroyed ambitions. This pressure invokes intense conflicted feelings toward the parents. Further, children of survivors often report the need to protect and please their parents, not to add any pain or disappointment to the wounds that they suffered. This, in turn, evokes strong unconscious guilt feelings against the experience of any normal developmental aggression toward the parents, aggression that is part of maturation. Any sadistic impulses dealing with separation, loss, or death are thus suppressed and denied. Any aggression toward the parents' victimized and helpless status in the concentration camps is defended against, by the child's feeling protective, and by identifying with the part the child cannot reject for fear of raising the sadistic impulses to consciousness.

The year is 1995. We are sitting in a country club in Boca Raton, Florida, with our friend Erna, a Holocaust survivor, who has lectured extensively both in Syracuse and in Florida about her wartime experiences. She believes very strongly in the need to educate about the Holocaust as a measure of insuring that it will not reoccur. Her efforts were instrumental in bringing about legislation that requires the teaching of the Holocaust in all levels of the Florida school system. She was recently honored by receiving the Woman of the Year award at a formal dinner party in an exclusive country club. She is visibly excited as she shares with us the experience of that evening. She tells us that twenty years ago, when she and her husband moved to Boca Raton, this club did not accept Jews as members, nor would they rent a conference room to a Jewish organization of which she was a member. "Well," she said triumphantly, "we have won! Look around you. All these people are members, and most of them are Jewish."

I always knew that my parents survived concentration camps. I have no recollection when I found this out, nor did we ever talk about their Holocaust experience. Yet, that horrible past was hovering over our family like a cloud. There were times that the cloud became darker, threatening to burst; at other times it eased off, moving further from our reach, but it was always there.

I was born in Topolchany, a small town in Slovakia, as were both my parents. My family emigrated to Israel when I was a year old. Besides my one uncle, my father's brother, who escaped Europe in the late thirties, I have no extended family. After World War II, Czechoslovakia was under Communist domination until the fall of the Berlin wall. Situated behind the infamous Iron Curtain, the country was difficult to enter and, for me, mysterious and very distant. The fact that my parents rarely discussed their prewar lives in Europe only increased, in my childhood mind, the mystery of that part of my roots. Thus, I resolved the issue by concluding that my family's history began shortly before I was born. My parents made sure that my growing up experience was protected, safe, and happy. I was not to have any frustrated wants, nor was I supposed to experience any hardship. "We want you to have a different life than we have, we do not want you to suffer like we suffered" was my mother's frequent comment. "Don't worry," she would say. "As long as I am behind you nothing bad will happen to you," she would reassure me while assuring herself of our bond. Although I never responded to these statements, I recall feeling the presence of the dark cloud reaching down as if to reveal the deep terror underlying this pseudoconfident statement. She had not been able to protect any of her extended family from the Nazis. My mother carries the guilt of being the sole survivor of her entire family.

Then there was the picture album. A handful of extant pictures was the sole validation that my family had a history. Our family album contains a picture of my father weighing less than a hundred pounds, his head shaven, his face gaunt. There is a photo of his sister leaning against a tree branch dressed in a bathing suit smiling into the camera. There is a shot of my father with a group of men sitting around a table in what looks like a resort site. There is the picture of my father's four children, two girls and two boys. They are his first family. The girls look to be ten and eight. They look serious, not very happy about having to pose for the camera. Looking at them, I can see the facial resemblance. The two boys appear to be five and three. The oldest of the two resembles his two sisters. He, too, looks into the camera with wide, serious eyes. His younger brother looks as if he is ready to participate in some mischief. As I look at the picture, I realize that I do not know their names. There is also a photo of my father's first wife holding one of the children. This was taken while the family was on a vacation. Finally, there is a lock of hair curl kept in a small china dish. This hair, I was told, belonged to one of the children. It was the family custom to cut a curl of the child's hair on their birthday and keep it in the family album. There is no trace of my father's seven brothers, his mother, or any other extended family members.

On my mother's side there are no pictures of any family members. They vanished without leaving any remnant. Neither is there a trace of her first husband of whom she speaks lovingly. No picture of her father in-law. Nor are there any photos of her parents, grandparents, three sisters, and two nephews. No trace either of uncles or cousins. There is no other memento to prove that indeed there was a rich family life before the cloud descended. The next page of the album contains the picture of my parents shortly after their wedding. They are sitting with their heads touching, their faces are smiling, they took young and relaxed. It is impossible to tell from this snapshot that my father was fifteen years older than my mother. He looks handsome with his light hair and blue eyes. My mother looks young. Her dark hair is combed back and her dark brown eyes are smiling. There is no cloud in that picture. There are two other pieces of evidence of the past: the number tattooed on my father's arm and packages of stationery with the title Alterax. Somehow, I knew that the number was tattooed on his arm in the concentration camp. I never looked to see what the numbers were and do not remember which arm was tattooed. I recall a blue tattoo as part of the cloud not to be talked about. The stationery, I was told, was from my father's textile business. My mother told me that he had a thriving business before the war, and that he was the most successful businessman in his town. These stories did not match my father as I knew him; thus, I did not know how to integrate this historical information into my perception of him.

Although my father was committed to his vow of silence about the past, my mother occasionally mentioned her previous life. She spoke of her first husband, her father-in-law with whom they shared a home, and the hotel they owned and that she helped manage at the young age of twenty. But for me, growing up in Israel, these stories seemed like fairy tales in the children's books I loved to read. All the characters mentioned in these stories were gone. Thus, I locked any images I might have constructed about these persons, and any feelings I might have had, somewhere between my unconscious and subconscious. Further, I determined that none of it had anything to do with me and thus had no impact on me whatsoever.

The state of Israel in the 1950s and 1960s supported this denial on a national level. The country was established after the brutal murder of six million European Jews. Thus, the whole nation vowed "never again." Never again will Jews be led to the slaughter, helpless and powerless. Following this commitment was a conscious effort to reject what the Israelis saw as fearfulness and powerlessness. Jews living in the Diaspora (any country outside of Israel) were seen as living at the mercy of those countries' governments and, thus, vulnerable. The Israelis could not tolerate any reminder of Jewish vulnerability. Thus Diaspora Jews were viewed contemptuously, while the image of the omnipotent Israeli soldier, with his Uzi machine gun, was fostered and admired. Religion was also rejected by most of the Israeli population, who adopted a cynical attitude toward anything spiritual. Religion, they argued, provided only a false sense of security.

History proved that only political independence and sophisticated arms guarantee the survival of the Jewish people. God did not answer the prayers of His people during the Holocaust. Quite the contrary was the case. He let them be tortured and gassed. Putting one's faith in God was considered foolish and a reminder of the Diaspora Jew. Ironically, it was as if the country partly adopted the anti-Semitic images of the Jews, which blamed the victims for their fate as a means of differentiating from that traumatic history. The history curriculum at school focused on periods before the twentieth century. The Holocaust was not taught. Furthermore, mental health professionals treating survivors did not connect their symptoms to the traumas they survived. Those experiences had *nothing to do* with the patients' presenting complaints. It was as if the entire country united in a conspiracy of denial and suppression. The American-Jewish community reacted similarly to the survivors, who began pouring into the United States. The presence of these survivors brought to consciousness the vulnerability of American-Jews as a minority culture. The Jewish community distanced itself from the new immigrants, often turning their own fear into a sense of superiority.

Among my peers, no one discussed the past either. Although we knew that there was a great deal of pain in many of our homes it was never articulated. Talking about the war would confirm that it happened. The idea that my mother and my father were taken out of their homes and transported in cattle cars to extermination camps where they were treated worse than animals was too painful, too threatening, and too shameful to face. Thus, the Second World War, like the biblical story of the flood, marked a complete turning point in the survivors' lives. It took the dramatic military victory of 1967, when the Israeli army single-handedly, and within twenty-four hours, inflicted a decisive and humiliating defeat on the armies of five Arab countries who united in an attempt to destroy the state of Israel and annihilate its people, to begin the healing process caused by the trauma of the Holocaust. That victory was the healing force that provided the confidence that Jews are no longer defenseless against powers of discrimination and hatred that threaten to exterminate them. This renewed confidence and the assertion of strength projected to the entire world enabled Israelis—and Jews worldwide—to begin the slow process of dealing with the devastating trauma of the Holocaust.

I hated my father. He was old, distant, and angry. He could not tolerate the noise of children's play. Nor was he interested in socializing and reaching out. Instead, he demanded to be left alone, not to be disturbed behind his wall of distancing. I recall hearing him leave the house at dawn riding his bike for more than an hour to reach the factory where he worked. He came home about five in the afternoon. My mother, eager to please him and needing to manage his unpredictable outbursts of rage, waited for him, his dinner prepared just as he liked it, ensuring his comfort as he sat at the kitchen table. She would serve him his food and urge me to be quiet and not disturb him. My father would say very little. Hiding behind the newspaper, he ignored our presence. When he finished his dinner and the paper he would go to bed. There was no laughter when he was present. I was careful to avoid him, not to upset him, and to stay out of his way. As my mother worked in the kitchen urging me to eat, he would complain about her spoiling me, his voice irritable. My mother would remind him not to get upset. My father would respond with a disgusted look and return to his paper. At other times he was unable to contain his rage. On those occasions he would come after me roaring, his hands gripping a rug beater. While he swung at me I would run in terror, crying and hiding behind my mother. She in turn, would plead with him to calm down. She would then tell me to behave. On other occasions, however, she would send him after me either because I neglected to clean my room or was late coming home. At those times, his rage was unshielded.

On rare occasions I recall my parents visiting friends, or friends coming to our house. Mostly, however, my parents chose to isolate. My father expressed anger at people, saying that they cannot be trusted and that he was not interested spending time chatting with them. When I would ask my mother why they rarely went out or invited people over, as my friends' parents did, she would explain that my father earned very little money and they could not afford to entertain. Thus, their socialization consisted of taking long Saturday morning and evening walks on the town's main street. Every few years, when this isolation became unbearable for my mother, she would pack her bags and leave for Europe, where she would stay for a few months shopping and going out with friends or spending time relaxing at a mountain resort.

Psychiatric literature describes survivor syndrome as consisting of characteristics such as chronic depression, anxiety reactions, tendency to isolate, and to withdraw. It explains that survivors display tremendous fear of loving someone because of having lost most, if not all, family members. The fear of another loss and reliving the pain, especially because they were not able to work through their feelings about their losses, threatened them with depression. The survivors lost their world. They lost the fundamental psychological markers on which their world was based, on which civilization was founded, the basic trust in human worth, basic confidence, and hope. Those who survived had neither the opportunity to bury their dead nor the luxury of time to mourn their loses. Furthermore, it makes sense that experiencing affect at the camps was dangerous. To survive, one needed to defend against feelings. Experiencing the daily horrors of camp existence coupled with the constant threat and uncertainty of staying alive made emotional numbness a necessary defense, freeing one to focus on surviving. However, many survivors failed to shed these defenses when the war was over and these defenses were no longer necessary. My father was one of these individuals. Although he survived labor camps and death camps, he stayed closed off and emotionally unavailable for the rest of his life. While he physically survived the war, his "emotional life" ended in September 1944 when the Germans rounded up the Jews of Topolchany and sent them to Auschwitz.

My father was the oldest of eight children in his family of origin. His father died when he was sixteen. As the oldest child, he was left with the responsibility of helping his mother support his siblings. My father went to work and established a flourishing textile business. He became a pillar of the local Jewish community and was involved in philanthropic activities. Owing to his business and community standing, he received protected citizenship status after the Germans conquered Slovakia. Thus, he was able to stay in his house while other, less fortunate Jews were relocated to ghettos. The promulgation of rules prohibiting Jews from owning businesses forced him to nominate a local Christian as figurehead owner of his company while he continued to run it behind the scenes. When the rumors about Jews being deported to death camps reached Topolchany, my father and his wife considered escaping with the children to the mountains. However, because of the young age of the children and the fear of not having access to milk and other supplies, they opted to stay.

One day in September 1944, my father was at the barbershop having a shave and a haircut; his children were playing, barefoot, in the courtyard. The Germans came and took them away. My father's wife and his four children were sent to Auschwitz where they were gassed, while my father was sent to forced labor camps. This period of his life is shrouded in silence. There are no stories about his experience. His life story picks up again after his liberation, when he returned to Topolchany, resumed control over his business, and married my mother. Owing to great postwar demand for goods and services, he soon flourished and rebuilt his life. However, within two years after the end of the war, the Communist regime took over and nationalized all private businesses. Thus, my father suffered another loss. Resisting helplessness, and trying to gain control over his destiny, he decided to leave Europe and immigrate to Israel. He never set foot in Europe again.

After our arrival in Israel, my father became seriously ill with a liver disease, which kept him bedridden for one year. Despite doctors' pessimistic prognoses, he managed to pull through. He continued experiencing severe periodic attacks of anemia throughout his life. Recovering from this illness seemed to be his last struggle to live. The person that I knew did not want to fight, to dream, or to follow any personal ambitions. My father, as I knew him, resigned himself to merely existing. Although there were many opportunities for entrepreneurs in the newly established state, my father was satisfied with a menial clerical position. He lost all interest or will to assume any responsibility or face pressures. His productive life was over.

My father was forty-seven when I was born. It was the same year that, deprived of his business, he decided to leave Europe. Once again my parents faced the trauma of packing their belongings, and complying with authorities' rules as to which things they were allowed to take. My mother told me that before their departure, my father went to a toy store and bought one of every toy in the store's inventory. I love this story, as it is one of the very few times that my father overtly expressed love and caring toward me. However, this place in his heart shut down, locked behind an iron wall, as he began a new life in Israel. A crack in this wall occurred shortly before his death. As he lay in his hospital bed hooked up to machines, tubes coming out of his nose, an IV in his arm, and knowing that he had very little time left, he instructed my mother not to allow me to see him, as I might be frightened by his condition. In his last hours my father tried to protect me from the pain of seeing death's ugly face.

I was sixteen when my father died of liver complications after a prostate operation. I recall being angry, hating him for dying, for his distance, his meanness, and his refusal to participate in life. Following his example of how to manage painful feelings, I insisted on suppressing all memory of him. As far as I was concerned he did not exist. His death would not have any impact on me, I declared to myself in a defiant voice. Despite my mother's protests, I refused to mourn him. I remember tearing down the posters pasted on the fence around our house, announcing his death, declaring in teenage defiance, "He did not love me so why should I care?" and went to the movies with my friends (Jewish mourning customs forbid attendance at entertainment places for one year after the death of a family member).

Years later, in conversations with me, my mother attempts to resolve her own mixed feelings toward my father, saying, "We never understood him. The poor man lost four children and a prosperous business, how can one digest such losses, losses like that are beyond a human being's comprehension. Your father was not normal, these losses broke his spirit." Only many years after that, I finally let go of my anger and experienced forgiveness and warm feelings toward him.

At the annual community *yom hashoah* commemoration, I was invited to participate in a Jewish program aired on local television. Before the program, the moderator asked if I would be willing to light a candle commemorating the victims' memory and say a few words at the opening of the show. I agreed. As the camera turned toward me, I lit the candle and heard myself say that I was lighting this candle in memory of all my extended family who perished at the hands of the Nazis, including my two half sisters and two half brothers. Driving home from the studio, I recall experiencing feelings of excitement in my chest, a sense of amazement at what I had said. For the first time, I had allowed myself to connect with that past. My own defense wall was beginning to crack as I acknowledged my connection to those brothers, sisters, grandparents, aunts, and uncles. Although I had not met them nor did I know their names, they did exist and I could mourn their loss.

It is 1992. My husband and I are in Berlin, where he is giving a paper at an international Holocaust conference. It is Saturday and we decide to go to synagogue. It is a pleasant day and the half-hour walk affords us an opportunity to learn about the former Jewish neighborhood. We arrive at the synagogue entrance and are greeted by an armed guard. He asks us to identify ourselves and scans our bodies with a metal detector. We are instantly reminded that practicing Judaism in Germany continues to be potentially fatal. We feel a mixture of hurt, anger, and relief for the protection provided by the German government. We are cleared and allowed to proceed into the temple. Inside, the cantor's beautiful tenor voice chants the prayers. We look around the sanctuary and notice that there are very few people. A number of worshipers are Russian Jews who immigrated to Germany after the collapse of the Soviet Union and the easing of its immigration laws. After the service, the entire congregation is invited to the temple's social hall for kiddush. We introduce ourselves to the rabbi and ask him to tell us about the Jewish community in Berlin. He is delighted to share his thoughts. He talks at length, recalling how the once-thriving Jewish community has been practically destroyed. Hardly any Jews are left in Berlin. Those who are here, he says, are mainly elderly. The young generation went either to Israel or to America. He adds that the new immigrants from the Soviet Union are revitalizing the community; however, many of them have very little knowledge of Jewish tradition, as religious expression was forbidden in the USSR. We walk back to the hotel in silence. Hitler succeeded in destroying a whole community. Berlin is practically Judenrein (free of Jews).

As we reach our hotel, we come upon a demonstration. Hundreds of people carry placards declaring the end of hatred and discrimination. Many of the participants are of Turkish background who have been brutally attacked by skinhead groups protesting Germany's liberal immigration laws. There is also a group of Jewish marchers carrying banners in English and in Hebrew. I recognize some people from the conference and rush to join them. Someone hands me a banner with the words "No More Hatred." I join the protesters and march with them toward the Berlin wall. As I march with the crowd, I can hardly feel my feet touching the ground. My excitement is very high. I feel strong, I feel alive. The route passes by a train station in front of which stands a memorial for Holocaust victims. It is designed as a road sign, with arrows pointing toward different concentration camps. At this spot Jews were packed into cattle trains and taken to their death. I think about my family members who were murdered in these camps and I hear my voice rise as I join the other group members chanting "Never Again."

The next morning we join Mel Mermelstein, a survivor of Buchenwald, to visit that camp. Mel, a resident of California, tells us that since his liberation he has made numerous trips to Buchenwald, bringing his children and other relatives to this place of agony. He seems to have a compulsive need to talk about his experience. Unlike my father, this man deals with his trauma by constantly telling and retelling the horrors he endured. Many survivors avoid participating in their present lives by focusing on the past. Our driver is a young German who lives in California and makes his living as a newspaper photographer. He volunteered to drive because of his need to face the Holocaust as a descendant of the perpetrators. He tells us that both his father and grandfather were active in the Nazi movement. He left Germany because he needed to reject his people who perpetrated such horrors. He returns now in an attempt to understand his father and grand-father. I become aware of the wounding of the second generation of Germans as they struggle to cope with the truth about their parents. This awareness is heightened as we visit the camp.

Buchenwald was a labor camp. Medical "experiments" were among the atrocities conducted there. Thus, for example, I saw an exhibit of shrunken heads, and lamp shades made of human skin, and soap made of human fat. Prisoners were ordered to undergo physical examinations. Because Buchenwald was not an extermination camp, the Germans murdered their victims by means other than gassing. They forced them to do hard labor and deprived them of food. In the examination room prisoners were asked to stand on a scale on the pretext of recording their weight and height. As prisoners stood erect with their back to the wall, they did not notice the narrow slit, behind which stood an SS man who shot the unsuspecting prisoner in the neck. The body was then placed on a chute leading to a room underneath where it was burned in the crematorium. The Germans conducted their killing most efficiently. My mind wanders, I try to imagine the murderer killing unsuspecting prisoners. What kind of person can do this? I imagine an average family man who kisses his wife and children good-bye and goes to his job where he shoots people in the back of the neck. The same man must have come home after a day's work and played with his children and made love to his wife. My thoughts return to our driver. I wonder what his father did during the war. How many innocent people did he murder? I wonder what is going on in this young man's mind and what his feelings are as he sees for the first time the nightmare of a concentration camp. Back in our hotel room we take a long hot bath, trying to wash away the horrors of the day.

It is 1994, and we are once again in Berlin. I enjoy walking in the now familiar downtown of what used to be West Berlin. As I wander on Kudamstrasse, West Berlin's main street, my thoughts return to my experience the previous night. After a reception, I had befriended a German woman who participated in the conference we are attending. The woman was a reporter for a Polish newspaper. Her father had been a soldier in the German army during the war, and her grandfather had been a Nazi war criminal. She talked about the difficulty that children of Nazis confront in attempting to deal with their parents' crimes.

My informant explained the rationalization that she and many of her peers adopted in dealing with their feelings about the Holocaust. Performing good deeds, volunteering as guides in concentration camps, traveling to

Israel and working on kibbutzim would successfully differentiate them from the crimes of their parents. She spent two years as a volunteer in the Auschwitz archives. She disclosed that presently she is separated from her husband, who is hospitalized with a psychotic disorder. He felt tremendous guilt and shame over his parents' deeds during the war and coped with this guilt by compulsively focusing on avoiding doing anything wrong, not causing anyone the slightest discomfort, being honest to perfection. His anger toward his parents was internalized, transferred into intense self-criticism and self-hatred, which then manifested itself through voices blaming him for being evil and not deserving to live.

"You know," my companion said, "I always believed that to deal with my parents' past I needed to be different, I needed to devote myself to helping others and educating others about the dangers of hatred. However, what I came to realize is that the real work to be done is to confront my father and my feelings toward him. Working through the legacy of my family requires facing the whole truth about my parents, my love, and the intense contempt I feel toward them." How interesting, I thought; here we were, two women, one a child of survivors, the other a child of perpetrators, both impacted by events that happened before our birth, both trying to face our feelings toward our parents and their experiences during the war.

The pilot announces that we will be landing in Budapest within ten minutes. I look out of the plane's window and see the green hills surrounding the city. I feel happy, like the feelings one has anticipating returning home after a long absence. I smile to myself; after all I have no allegiance to Hungary or its people, many of whom were Nazi collaborators. Nevertheless, I cannot suppress this excitement. Within minutes of our landing I feel at home. Speaking the language, I am able to communicate like a native. The hotel receptionist greets my husband and me with a friendly smile. We fill out the required papers and inquire how to get to the Jewish temple and the cemetery. The desk clerk responds in Hebrew. Our mouths drop. We do not expect to meet Jews, let alone someone who speaks Hebrew.

The following day we have an interview with the local rabbi and ask about the Jewish community in Budapest, and in Hungary. He explains that, after the collapse of communism, the new political situation permits more religious affiliation. However, he stresses that the once-thriving Jewish community is gone. Very few Jews are left in Hungary and many of them are old. Nevertheless, he explains, anti-Semitism remains. He mentions the racial and anti-Jewish speeches in the Hungarian parliament. Politicians once again employ the old technique of scapegoating to explain Hungary's economic hardships. He also reports that many of Budapest's main synagogue's precious religious artifacts have disappeared. Back on the street we meet an elderly woman who, in response to our questions, shares more stories about hatred and discrimination. She is pessimistic about the future of Budapest's few thousand remaining Jews. As we walk away, I no longer feel at home and am ready to leave. It is obvious that Hungary is far from confronting its past. We walk toward our hotel and pass a movie theater where the upcoming attraction is *Schindler's List.*

Next morning we pack our bags and drive to Slovakia. I am going to visit Topolchany, a three-hour drive from Budapest. At the border I hand the guard my American passport. He opens the passport to the first page with the identification information. I look for his reaction as he notes that Topolchany is my birthplace. I want him to ask me questions: Are you coming back to find your roots? When did you leave Slovakia? Why did you leave? I wonder if he will recognize that I am a descendant of Slovakian citizens who were driven out of homes, where they and their ancestors lived for generations; their only "crime" was having been born Jews. The guard smiles as he returns my passport. He says nothing as he motions us to drive through.

We finally arrive at our destination. Topolchany is a medium-size city inhabited primarily by blue-collar workers. We stop near the center of town and look for a restaurant. The waiter, a young man in his late teens or early twenties, is intrigued by the two foreigners. It is rare to meet Americans here. We order a dish of blintzes. Eager to please, the waiter is curious about where we came from and about what brought us to Topolchany. We show him a piece of paper with the address of my father's house. We communicate with our hands, facial expressions, and a mixture of German and Hungarian words. Pointing to the address, we ask, "Can you tell us how to get there?" He does not recognize the address. We explain that it is in the center of town, where there used to be a community bathhouse and not far from a kindergarten. The landmarks do not help him recognize the address. "There is no such street," he says. "Yes, there is," I insist. "My father used to live there." "When was that?" he asks. "This was before the war," I explain, writing 1945 on a piece of paper to help him understand. "Oh," he says, "history." He begins to comprehend the purpose of our visit.

The waiter is now committed to helping us in our detective mission. He is very excited, offering to confer with other employees more familiar with Topolchany's past. He returns to our table, a disappointed expression on his face. "The names of the streets were changed when the Communists took over, and were recently changed again after the overthrow of communism," he explains. "No one remembers where the street by this name was." Continuing his efforts to be helpful, he suggests that we go to the city's municipal office, where there are maps of old Topolchany. As we leave the restaurant, we remark on the thoroughness of the extermination of the Jews. Not only did the *people* disappear, the names of the streets where they lived have also been changed, as if to deny that the community ever existed. We are aware that we are witnessing the politicization of history.

The clerks at the city archives are impatient; they do not want to help. A young high school student, witnessing our efforts, interrupts. She speaks some English and offers to help, telling us about the existence of a Jewish temple and a cemetery. Further, she has some idea of the location of the street we are looking for. As we follow her to the town center, she points to a certain house; it is the one in the address. We stop in front of the two-story home behind whose gate we see a courtyard. The picture of my two half brothers and my two half sisters flashes in my mind; I imagine them barefoot, and playing when the Gestapo pull up in front of the house and take them away. We take pictures from different angles, quietly absorbed in our thoughts and feelings.

We leave the courtyard and follow the young woman toward the temple. As we walk she shares that she knows of the existence of Topolchany's prewar Jewish community. "There are no Jews here today," she says. "You are the first Jewish people that I have ever met." Once again we are reminded of the devastating impact of the Holocaust. Topolchany is truly Judenrein.

The temple is a small, decrepit building. Its weather-beaten doors are locked. Behind the temple's high walls, connected to both sides of the building, are the remains of the Jewish cemetery. Here some of my family's loved ones were buried before 1945. Next to the temple are small houses with backyards. We can see chickens and ducks roaming around behind the fence. We discover that the only one with a key to the building is an elderly caretaker who comes here daily at different hours. No one knows his name or how we could contact him. The cemetery is walled off to protect against vandalism.

We stand in front of the temple for a long time. I feel like I am standing in a sacred place. I look at this modest building that was once the center of Jewish community life in Topolchany, and realize that it stands in silent defiance against the cruel historical reality, insisting in its present uselessness that the people of Topolchany can change their street names but the history of the Jewish presence cannot be denied. I feel a strong urge to enter the cemetery, to walk by the graves, find the gravestones with my family's name, touch the silent stones that validate my ancestors' existence. But the gate is locked. We make several attempts to climb the wall and decide to let go. We walk quietly to our parked car. My husband suggests that we stay the night and attempt next morning to locate the guard. "No," I reply. "Topolchany rejected its Jews. I want to leave." Leaving Topolchany, I feel peace, having resolved an important internal conflict. I experience the wave of these feelings breaking through the walled-off areas deep in my being and a sweet sadness beginning to take over as I realize that I have come full circle.

Returning

HELEN EPSTEIN

There is a tourism peculiar to our time—the visit to an estranged family past. My destination is Prague. There are no border hassles now, no questions, no lines. A stamp in my passport and I am face-to-face with my Aunt Kitty.

At sixty-eight, Kitty colors her hair blonde and pampers her skin. The two giant jars of Pond's face cream in my suitcase are for her. But Kitty's days begin at six-thirty and end at nine or ten at night, and her face has the haggard look that makes everyone in Prague look older than in the West. Her husband died twenty years ago, and for the past decade, she has shared her small Old City flat with her boyfriend, Jaroslav.

Jaroslav is four years younger than Kitty, a Protestant, and a "good old boy," who walks around at home in his underwear. During "victorious February" of 1948, when the Communists took over Czechoslovakia, he was one of the workers who marched with a rifle on his shoulder in Wenceslas Square. My father always said that the sight of that armed workers' militia was what finally persuaded him to emigrate. Within a year, Jaroslav became disillusioned with the kind of people who had taken over the party— "capitalists in Communist clothing" he calls them—and, like most Czechoslovaks, turned inward, concentrating on his family, trying not to grow bitter as he saw party hacks with no experience in his field being promoted over his head. He is, like Kitty, divorced—about half of Czech marriages now end in divorce—and is a grandfather.

We drive toward Prague, Kitty chattering away in Czech, and the city unfolds before us like a fairy tale: spires, towers, statues, lilacs, the river— *zlatà Praha*, golden Prague.

Kitty takes me to lunch, at the *Obec,* the pink Jewish community build-ing next to the oldest functioning synagogue in Europe. There are about eight thousand Jews left in Prague and, at the *Obec,* you see that they are divided between old people who survived the war, their children, and grand-children. Most of the grandchildren, including the chief rabbi, are the children of mixed marriages who have formally converted to Judaism and are engaged in self-education. Becoming an observant Catholic, Jew, or Protestant is today in part a political statement. There is one rosy-faced Czech at the *Obec* eating lunch in black Hasidic garb as well as a family whose men are wearing yarmulkas.

Kitty thinks there is something medieval about practicing Jews. But because she is an Auschwitz survivor and multilingual, and lives only five minutes away, she works at the *Obec* part-time. Now she takes me out for a walk through the neighborhood where she and my mother grew up, pointing out the buildings where she and my mother lived, one block apart, in the 1920s, in apartments with nine rooms accommodating not only the family but also a cook, a governess, and a maid. Kitty and my mother climbed on the roofs, and threw things down onto the crowded boulevard below. Kitty once got so angry at my mother that she told her that their children would not be allowed to play together. Alas, Kitty says now, that's exactly what happened. I ask whether we can go into the apartments but everything has been converted to offices and she will not even try to ne-gotiate entry. She just says this is not America and we go home.

Jaroslav, Kitty, and I now sit down to a dinner of bread, deviled eggs, salami, and beer, all of which will become redundant over the next ten days.

We watch a large color TV as we eat. The seven-thirty news, once generally ignored, is now the highlight of the day, showing a parade of events that, even after six months, have not lost their exoticism. We watch Václav Havel addressing the European Parliament, saying, as he has been saying in almost every speech, that his country has to learn everything, build everything, from scratch—including a democracy. Jaroslav, who is drinking his second liter of beer, talks back to the TV set. He is a great fan of Václav Havel because "he's a man of the people." But he's getting impatient with speeches. He would like to revolutionize the Czech attitude toward work, which is a legacy of communism of doing a job poorly and then sitting in a tavern for five hours, or using company materials and time to do private jobs for personal profit. People have no sense of the personal responsibility democracy entails.

When the news is over, Kitty cleans up in her tiny kitchen. She runs a bath for me in the bathroom that manages to pack a tub, a sink, and washing machine into another closet-sized space. They unfold the couch, and produce an old-fashioned duvet. I go to sleep feeling constricted, as though the boundaries of my world have shrunk. The velvet revolution is real but, after forty years of communism, few citizens know how it feels to stretch or reach. There is a police station across the street; Kitty used to worry about an informer in the house next door. Every few hours, a car pulls up. It's hard to get to sleep.

Day Two

It's May 9, the national holiday that marks the end of World War II in Czechoslovakia. For the first time since 1948, the Czech flag flies alone, without its Soviet counterpart. Until this year, the end of the war was celebrated as the "Soviet victory over fascism"; this year, not only were American former GIs welcomed in Plzeň, but many Czechs are wearing lapel pins showing twin American and Czechoslovak flags.

Kitty's son, Micki, his wife, Jarka, and their two children are taking me to Kolin, the small town on the Elbe where our ancestors lived. They are intrigued by my foray into what is, for them, totally unknown history, and curious what an American journalist will do to uncover it.

Jarka is thirty-three. She dislikes living in Prague and seizes any opportunity to head back into the country and do some gardening. She keeps close watch on the children and their diet, particularly because her son has severe eczema, which, she is convinced, is a result of Czechoslovakia's polluted environment. Jarka won't buy produce not grown in a private garden, because she thinks it is poisoned by pesticides. She distrusts doctors as well as grocers, uses a metal pendulum to check out anything she or her children eat, and attends lectures about *psychotronika*, which, since the velvet revolution, has come up from underground in Prague. When I arrived, Jarka held her pendulum over the bubblegum I brought for her children, much to the dismay of Kitty who thinks *psychotronika* is as medieval as Orthodox Judaism, and the pendulum found the bubblegum safe.

Micki is forty-two, a middle manager, and an avid driver. In the car, he turns on Europe II, a Western radio station that has only recently become available in Prague, and starts weaving in and out between the other Skodas on the two-lane highway. "What, exactly, is the situation in Israel?" he asks, and suddenly I am faced with the full impact of totalitarianism. Though born to two Jews, Micki does not know Hanukkah from Passover (his wife doesn't know much more about Catholicism). He was born in the year Israel was established, and because he discounts all he has been told officially about the Middle East as Soviet propaganda, he knows nothing at all about Jews and Arabs. I try to provide a capsule history but it is so complicated that Micki himself changes the subject.

We park the car in Kolin's central square, and take photographs. My relatives stare as I approach elderly people to ask whether they knew my grandmother's family. Before the velvet revolution, no one dared ask a stranger more than the most necessary question. Questions recalled interrogations; interrogators were totalitarian forms of control. I am asking questions, such as how long have you lived here? Did you know Jews? After a few false starts, we come upon an eighty-four-year-old man whose granddaughter is a writer in Austria. He tells us what the square looked like seventy-five years ago, how on Sundays, the whole town promenaded under a covered *corso,* and how much better things were then. There is a Jewish quarter with a synagogue, he says, but no Jews. In the 1890s, it contained the largest Czech-speaking Jewish community outside of Prague. The Nazis destroyed the records. He remembers our family name, Sachsel—there was a bookseller named Sachsel, he says—then wishes us a pleasant stay.

The *Židovna* (Jewish area) is a ghost town. The cobblestoned streets are narrow here, the houses small, dilapidated, and abandoned. Outside one of them is a pile of debris and inside, two young men in jeans are working. One emerges through the low doorway and, when he finds out I'm American and Jewish, starts smiling. He had a girlfriend who went to Israel a few years ago and, as it happens, he is invested in this neighborhood. After the velvet revolution, he and a few friends bought one of the houses from the city of Kolin and they are building a four-room hotel. His guess is that the basement dates to the fourteenth century. The city plans to gentrify the old Jewish section, even turn the synagogue into a concert hall. Although reconstruction is his hobby, he says, he hopes to make some money. Would we like to see the synagogue? He'll show us.

We walk down the "Jewish street" and stop before a building.

"Take a deep breath and hold it!" he says, as we walk through a dark, stinking alleyway. A small dog inside the courtyard starts barking, an empty can comes flying out the window at us. I look up and I am standing six feet away from Kolin's synagogue, which looks like an abandoned building in the South Bronx. "Gypsies," my guide says, indicating upstairs. "The city will move them out when all the renovation is done."

I stand in the trash-strewn courtyard of my grandmother's synagogue and feel no trace of her world. Perhaps I feel nothing because these two empty, dilapidated streets are my first direct experience of the physical reality of extinction and it is so painful that it simply blows all my fuses; perhaps she didn't even live here where I am standing, and without a living link to the past, it is impossible to connect. My guide looks at me questioningly. I nod, and we go back out into the empty street.

In the Mayakovsky conference hall back in Prague, several hundred people have been attending the first meeting of the newly formed Israel-Czechoslovak Friendship Society. The usher hands me a pin depicting the Israeli and Czechoslovak flags, joined together.

My friend Jiří Tichý is sitting up on the dais. Unlike my relatives, he is a veteran dissident who once had a group of Amnesty International members campaigning to get him out of jail. He has just returned from Israel, where, in the company of Václav Havel, he attended an international convention of Czechoslovak Jews. He is tanned, and with his longish hair, beard, and short-sleeved sports shirt, looks much as he did when I last saw him twenty years ago.

I first met Jiří in Israel when we were both students. We used to walk all over Jerusalem together like Mutt and Jeff, I nearly six feet tall, he barely over five feet. Jiří was born in 1945, the son of a Jewish father who emigrated to Israel and a Christian mother who remained in Prague. He fled to Israel after the Russian invasion, but he returned to Prague because he could not imagine living out his life anywhere else. Jiří was never a good correspondent; we lost touch. Now as I try vainly to catch his eye I realize how this meeting, bureaucratic for me, is important for him. The last time Czechoslovakia and Israel had cordial relations was in 1948, when Czechoslovakia provided Israel with weapons for the War of Independence. Now people—Christians as well as Jews—have come from all over the country to try to re-create that bond.

Micki and I decided to wait in the café downstairs. He is curious about Jiří, a man our age, and more or less from his own background, who has been imprisoned for his political beliefs and who now is on first-name terms with the people who are running the country. I am impatient to see an old friend, amazed that he has wound up a political activist. The meeting finally ends and we meet in a great bear hug.

When, in 1970, Jiří decided to return to Prague despite the Russian occupation, he was determined to do all he could to end Communist rule. He was twenty-four then, reckless and passionate. "It was clear to me," he says, "that I'd never get to do anything I really wanted to do, so my life was my family, the underground, and I drank." At first, he worked in a print shop but there came a time when he refused to print "some piece of nonsense," and he was thrown out. Then he worked for a theater, which, in 1972, the government closed down for political impropriety. Until 1977, he worked at the National Gallery installing exhibits, but after becoming involved with Charta 77, he moved to the archeology department of another museum. He worked there for three years, writing and printing *samizdat* before his underground activities were discovered and he was thrown out in 1980. He married, fathered a son, got divorced, then moved in with Marcella, the art historian with whom he shared a home and three children.

Jiří spent the eighties, performing menial labor. The first four years, he worked in construction—"boots, mud, cold"—and the last five as a laborer for Prague's parks department, "planting tulips, mowing lawns," sometimes driving a tractor right outside the windows of his eleven-year-old daughter's school. Adelka's teachers were wonderful, he says. When he was jailed for hiding Charta 77 files in his country cottage, they let Adelka know that her father was a responsible citizen and not a criminal as the television news had it. When the velvet revolution began, he had only to ask and the teachers would provide him with chairs, desks, paper—anything the Civic Forum needed. Jail was not so bad, at least not as bad as he had expected.

Micki is quiet during Jiří's recitation. Now I hear him say, apologetically, the words that my parents used to mock when they were said by Germans describing the Nazi period, "I feel I have to tell you this, Jiří: *We did not know.*"

I watch Jiří as he listens to Micki. They are both sons of survivors. Jiří wants to understand that almost all of the citizens remained silent while he was in prison, to bear them no grudge, and to enlist them in his campaign for a democratic Czechoslovakia. Jiří is an uncommonly forgiving man. But I can sense the chasm between my cousin and my friend. Their difference is written on their faces as well as on their clothes, on Micki's son's Lego sets and Jiří's stepson's political activities. I feel a twinge of contempt for Micki and a swell of admiration for Jiří, then a question for myself. What would I have done had my parents and I remained in Prague? I would like to think I would have acted like Jiří. But sitting across a table from him, examining his lined face, older than his years, I wonder: How would I have weighed the needs of my husband and children against our need for a free society? I am accustomed to these kinds of questions being raised in art films about South Africa or Argentina—not in my own life. As I do several times when I am in Czechoslovakia, I am thankful that my parents immigrated to the United States.

Day Three: Helena

I wake up to hear Kitty insisting that I must register at the Central Police Station. This procedure is a relic of the Nazis, institutionalized by the Communists. I argue that surely registration has become obsolete. She is adamant, and it is clear to me that she is scared. Yes, I will go register with the police. Afterward, I head for Wencelas Square and sit down in an outdoor café set up just under the windows of the apartment in which my parents and I lived in 1948.

Wenceslas Square is now a crowded pedestrian mall. A few feet away from me, a statue of Tomáš G. Masaryk, president of the First Republic of Czechoslovakia begins the huge exhibition, *Kde domov můj?* (Where is my home?), which stretches down a chain of giant kiosks to a large exhibition hall. The show is named after the Czech national anthem and is part of a campaign to fill in the hole that, for most citizens, is twentieth-century Czechoslovak history. The kiosks are pasted over with documents that, for the past forty years, were banned from TV and school curricula and extirpated from libraries, bookstores, and films. They include newspaper articles and photographs from World War II, from the infamous Slánský trial in 1952, from the Prague Spring of 1968. The excitement they evoke is audible. People of all ages crowd around to read a record of loss: lost lives, lost years, a lost country. I look up at the first-story apartment where I spent the first eight months of my life, an apartment inhabited first by Czechs, then by Nazis, then my Jewish parents, and I wonder who lives there now.

Then I take the train to the suburb where Helena, my mother's friend when she lived in that apartment, lives. My mother said that Helena was so beautiful that the famous painter Jan Slavíček, as well as many Nazis, became obsessed with her. I never understood exactly what Helena, a Christian, did during the six years that the Nazis occupied Czechoslovakia, but I noted that my mother spoke of Helena with unusual respect. She agreed to naming me after my paternal grandmother because it was her friend's name as well. I wanted to interview Helena about both my mother and grandmother.

Helena is a frail woman with eyes of steel. Raised by a literary, politically active father, she was thrown out of school for participating in an anti-Nazi demonstration. That's why, she explains, she was sent to the English gymnasium where she met my mother. At eighteen, she was trained as a "Czech connection" for the Resistance in a basement near my grandmother's salon. She still could send a man flying halfway across the room, she says with some pride. During the war, she transmitted information, hid and moved documents and people. When the war was over, she repatriated survivors, divorced her husband, and chose to be a single mother. She spent most of the past three decades on the Communist blacklist, looking for work.

She takes me for a tour of the house, hung with Jan Slavíček's paintings downstairs, and magazine centerfolds of naked women upstairs. I ask what that's about and Helena sighs. She says anything that was forbidden these past forty years is now the latest rage. Pornography is not viewed as sexist; it's another form of anticommunism, like religious affiliation. She views the velvet revolution with a jaundiced eye. Like Jaroslav, she is worried that the Civic Forum has already been infiltrated by wolves in sheep's clothing and that Havel has been too soft on the secret police. She thinks that Havel, whom she first knew as an actor, has a fine sense of the absurd and will not be corrupted, but she worries about his lack of political acumen, his lack of practical experience, and the similar deficits of those who surround him.

Our conversation moves from details of my mother's adolescence ("You won't believe this, but your mother danced a *fantastic* tango") to Masaryk's First Republic ("Not the fairy tale they're now making it out to be") to the story of a night during the war when her husband got drunk, beat her up, and then called the Gestapo to help him find her. She gives me a photograph of her first wedding, for which my grandmother designed the bridal gown. Six hours go by in what seems an instant. Helena tells me, almost as an afterthought, that she needs to take very expensive medication and is looking for work. Couldn't I find her an American book to translate? She has never joined any organization; she has never belonged to any clique. She's older than the people now running things in Prague, and competition for translations is fierce. I promise to do what I can.

The Weekend

We drive past the swimming club where my parents first met and where my father played water polo in the 1920s, past the restaurant where Kitty and my mother went to tea dances when they were teenagers, past the racetrack where my grandfather took his mistress, Mrs. Hirsch, in the 1930s. Kitty likes to talk about her childhood and her perceptions of my mother's home, which always appeared decadent, chaotic, and unhappy beside her own.

After about an hour, we arrive at a cluster of cottages. Kitty and Jaroslav have just traded in their old *chata* for a larger one that looks like a Swiss chalet. "After everything we lost, it means a lot to me," she says. The *chata* is deceptive. While it looks sumptuous outside, there is only partial plumbing. Drinking water must be hand pumped from a murky well, and the elaborate "American-ever-burning" Lincoln stove is fueled by the low-grade coal briquets that are responsible for so much of Prague's air pollution.

Before we are unpacked, the neighbors start dropping in. Kitty busies herself unpacking, preparing food, cleaning up, postponing our scheduled time for talking about my mother and grandmother. It's becoming clear to me that she, unlike my mother, does not often talk about the past. When I ask her questions, she answers in a perfunctory way, grows impatient, and either gets up or changes the subject.

When the visitors clear out, I try again to interview Kitty but there are many things she can't remember, questions she answers in one or two words. About an hour into the interview, as we reach 1939, Kitty gets up and disappears into the bathroom. When she comes back, she says, "My father wanted to send me to England, but I kept telling him that the Czechs wouldn't let the Germans do anything to us."

"Enough!" says Jaroslav. "Leave something for tomorrow," and I go to the kitchen with Kitty to make *knedliky* for supper.

I, who have trouble finishing a half glass of white wine, down two glasses of slivovitz, straight. But despite the crickets and the clean air, I can't get to sleep. These questions have occurred to me before, but they never possessed me as they do now. How can Kitty live in a city where other people inhabit what was once her home? How can she walk down the same streets she walked when she was deported? How can she trust Jaroslav? How can she go to work every day at the Obec? What happens to all the stuff she is blocking out? I decide to jump from 1939 to 1948 in our interview and keep questions closely focused on my mother.

Day Seven: Roudnice

Monday, my seventh day in Prague, begins in a courtroom. My friend Jiří is driving me to the town where my father's family lived for several hundred years before 1939. But first, we are going to Jiří's hearing. Jiří was arrested and imprisoned last fall for his political activities. Now, with former dissidents governing the country, it has become necessary to bend the law and declare the prior conviction an error. He explains all this as his Skoda stands overheating in a traffic jam. We arrive in court fifteen minutes late.

After an hour of Czech legalese, Jiří's prior conviction is declared an error and we are off to Roudnice, a small town on the Elbe River. My father was born there in 1904, when Franz Josef was still emperor of Austria-Hungary. The house my great-grandfather built in 1830—reportedly the first Jewish-owned house allowed to be built outside the ghetto—is still standing. Several generations of my ancestors are buried there. Like so many others in this century of dislocation, I have never been able to visit their graves.

By chance, Jiří was in Roudnice a few weeks earlier for his newspaper, reporting on Roudnice's Jewish cemeteries, which the Nazis left alone but which are now being vandalized. Jiří found that the new Jewish cemetery, dating to 1890, was being used as a dump by an auto mechanic and other tradespeople. In both the new and the old cemetery, which dates to 1611, some tombstones have been carted away for use as building material, and some graves pried open, possibly by thieves in search of jewelry. With no gates and no Jews left to care for them, the cemeteries are overgrown as well as littered, and have become a playground for Roudnice's bored teenagers.

Jiří is holding onto a tape recorder as he drives. He is interviewing me for *Respekt*. For him, I am not only an American writer come back to see where she was born, but also the daughter of two *bona fide* former Czech Jews. My father, Kurt Epstein, was a second lieutenant in the Czechoslovak army and an athlete who played for Czechoslovakia's water polo team in two Olympic games. My mother was a dress designer in Prague. Jiří speaks into the microphone, emphasizing that my parents were both fervent Czech patriots who resettled in Prague after their return from the concentration camps and left the country only in 1948. Through my own excitement of finally seeing the place where my father grew up, I become aware of Jiří's excitement at finally being able to publicly document our common history, the Jewish history that has been suppressed for forty years.

We drive through flat farm country, broken only by the Říp, where the leader Čech, looking over the picturesque countryside, decided to settle his people. For as long as I can remember, my family had a watercolor of this odd geological formation hanging in our kitchen in Manhattan. Now, as I see it rising up out of the fields, my chest tightens and my eyes start to burn. My father went back to his hometown just once after World War II. The sole survivor of his family, he found the return so painful that he never even brought my mother to see the house in which he grew up. After 1948, my father decided never to return to Europe. The European chapter of his life, he sometimes said, was closed.

We pull up in Roudnice's town square and ring the bell of a retired high school teacher whom Jiří met here last time. He is a bluff, friendly man—the prototype of a teacher—who seats us in his living room to talk. Of course he knew Kurt Epstein, the swimmer. He played water polo in the Olympics. He also remembers my father's younger brother, Bruno, Roudnice's village idiot, who was brain damaged at birth and walked around muttering to himself. Without a pause, the teacher confesses that, as a kid, he threw stones at my uncle, and looks at me ruefully. I nod. I know Bruno was retarded. In my father's account, my uncle was the reason my family did not leave Czechoslovakia before 1939. All the other family members obtained visas for what was then Palestine. Bruno was declared ineligible, my grandmother Helena refused to emigrate without him, and all the Epsteins except for my father were gassed to death by the Nazis.

Jiří and the teacher sigh. Then the teacher pulls out a telephone directory. The Epsteins lived on Jan Hus street, he says. He himself doesn't know the number of the house but he will call up someone Jewish, who is sure to know.

When my father was growing up, before World War I, there were about three hundred Jews in Roudnice; now there are only two or three. The schoolteacher finds a widow who lives with her son—she came back from Terezin, she's about sixty-two, she will know for sure where the Epsteins lived—and offers to walk us over there.

We stop at a stone building surrounded by a fence. Jiří rings the bell and, elated, we watch a slim, dark-haired woman in slacks walk toward us. She has beautiful, sparkling eyes. Jiří asks if it's true that she was born in Roudnice and has lived here all her life. She says yes; how might she help us? I tell her I am the daughter of Kurt Epstein. She smiles at me, but blankly. Jiří asks if she knew the Epstein family. She thinks for a moment, still smiling. Then she says she's so sorry but she doesn't remember them.

The high school teacher presses her: The Epsteins . . . he was a water polo player . . . they had the tannery down by the railroad tracks. The woman's smile is gone now and her eyes are blank. She says softly, "You know, after I came back, I forgot the way it was before. I don't remember anything. I would like to help you. I'm sorry."

Her words hit me so hard I have to turn away. Jiří has lost his customary ebullience and is staring at the ground. We walk back toward the town square in silence. Of course. How could she possibly continue living in a town as small as Roudnice and remember? The teacher, too, is subdued. He begins to recount stories of the deportations and tells us in detail about a local Christian woman married to a Jewish man who killed her children and herself rather than risk life under the Nazi occupation.

The teacher leaves us to eat lunch in a noisy tavern and hurries off. Like almost everyone else I met in Czechoslovakia, he is taking English lessons. A ragged woman turns on the television set but it barely makes a dent in the noise level. The young men swilling down their beer look us over without subtlety and I tell Jiří that I don't like anything I've seen in this town. Just then, the schoolteacher hurries back in with a new idea. "Mr. Paudera!" he exclaims. Vladimir Paudera is eighty-five. He lives on Husova. He's sure to be home. We should just walk down to the river, past the school, and ask for him. Jiří and I note the name, but our last meeting has taken the wind out of our sails. We have our goulash and beer and agree not to expect much.

The street that my father grew up on was once a bustling stretch of fancy buildings just opposite the railroad station. Now it is gray and lackluster, marked by empty lots. We ring Mr. Paudera's bell, and Jiří asks him if he could come down to chat. In what seems an instant, he is downstairs in his slippers: a dapper man, who walks four kilometers every day. When I extend my hand and tell him I am Kurt Epstein's daughter, he beams and shakes it vigorously.

"I'll show you everything!" he announces. "The house, the river, the tannery. You know, we had a club when we were little, even before the Swimming Club of Roudnice. We met every week, each time at a different house, so I knew your father's house very well. There were two brothers, two Jews and two 'Aryans'—well, one of those was me!"

With his Czech pronunciation of the word Aryan still resounding in my ears, Vladimir Paudera launches into an account of how he was born into a Roman Catholic family in this gray house in which he has lived without interruption since 1905. His father was a goldsmith who had always lived surrounded by Jews, and Mr. Paudera himself grew up the same way. We do not ask him about the years 1930 to 1990. Now, of course, he is just about the only person still living on Jan Hus Street who lived here before the war.

"Have you been inside your father's house?" he asks. "Well, what are we waiting for?"

We hurry to keep up with him as he opens a double door and stops before a dusty three-foot-high marble plaque, inscribed in Latin, mounted onto the wall: This House Was Built by Aloisio J. Samohrdo in the Year 1900 for the Brothers Maximilian and Gustav Epstein. Maximilian was my grandfather. We start taking pictures but Mr. Paudera intervenes. He goes into the restaurant that now occupies the ground floor of my father's house and where Mr. Paudera eats lunch every day. He comes back with a waiter, a pail, and a dishrag. We take turns cleaning the plaque while office workers and other waiters stop to take a look at me, an American, granddaughter of the man who once owned this house.

"Don't you want to take it back with you?" the waiter asks, indicating the plaque.

I can't tell whether he's joking or serious but I shake my head, then walk back outside to look at the house. It is a three-story salmon-colored structure, with the rococco detail—cherubs, fruit bowls, the ornamental letter E beneath each of the first story windows—popular at the turn of the century. By some miracle, it is by far the best-maintained building I have seen in Roudnice and it is easy to imagine the solid, bourgeois routines of my father's childhood that transpired within.

"Shall we go upstairs?" asks Mr. Paudera. He bounds up the stone steps, the way he must have as a small boy, knocks on a closed office door, and announces that the granddaughter of the man who built this house has come to take a look. The rooms are well kept with the linoleum floors, bare white walls, and the enormous fluorescent light fixtures characteristic of Czechoslovak offices.

"Look up!" commands Mr. Paudera.

We all look up and are astonished to see a frescoed ceiling bordered by an intricately carved wood moulding, perfectly preserved except for one hole where an electrician has chosen to thread his wiring.

"This was the dining room," says Mr. Paudera to two women who have risen from behind their desks.

The Epstein family in Roudnice in 1910, I think, as I gaze up at the painted ceiling, was not unlike its upper-middle-class Victorian counterpart. My father occasionally mentioned the cook and the parlor maid, his violin lessons, the Jewish National Fund box at the foot of the staircase. Grandfather Maximilian was a pillar of the community. Grandmother Helena supervised the household and baked exquisitely. Every summer, they took their vacation in Carlsbad. There was the sense that nothing could happen that had not already happened before, the surety of seasons, certainly no drama or mystery, just as there was no mystery to my father himself.

He was a tall, extroverted, uncomplicated man, with a classic swimmer's build—broad shoulders, slim hips—and features that have always seemed to me typical of his generation of central European Jews: high forehead, sharpset eyes under bushy brows, hair cropped close around an expressive face (my father viewed long hair as a symptom of lax discipline, and worried that if he let his grow more than an inch away from his scalp, someone might mistake him for a hippie). His life entailed great loss and upheaval, but the losses came when he was older, and his athlete's regimen helped him weather their effects. When he returned from the concentration camps, he rejoined his athlete friends and became a member of the Czechoslovak Olympic Committee. He was one of the rare people who, irrespective of history or personal calamity, are born with and retain a sense of entitlement to life.

"Do you want to see the living room?" asks Mr. Paudera.

We walk through my father's house, through the living room and kitchen, upstairs where my father slept, back downstairs to the ground floor, which, Mr. Paudera says, was a huge workroom where leather was prepared for shipping to customers. The tannery my grandfather owned was a few blocks down the "Jewish street," next to the synagogue.

Mr. Paudera leads us down the covered arcade from Husova Ulice to the river. "Our little paradise," he calls the Elbe, in which he and my father swam from spring until winter. My father liked to reminisce about swimming in the wide, unpolluted river that ran a stone's throw away from his home. Roudnice boys of my father's age often threw stones at him as he swam. My father explained to us that people in those days believed that Jews were physically stunted from so many years of ghetto life. He responded by founding, with friends, the Independent Swimming Club of Roudnice, becoming first a competitive swimmer and rower and then a water polo player.

My father told tales of underwater skirmishes where heads were held underwater, bathing trunks ripped off, and testicles squeezed. They all ended, bafflingly, with the moral: "The important thing is not to win but to have participated." We heard about the Berlin Olympics of 1936 and the controversy over whether to participate or to boycott. My father participated in much the same spirit as he had founded the Independent Swimming Club of Roudnice and, although his water polo team did not win a medal, made sure his children knew that Jesse Owens had won four.

Mr. Paudera is lost in recollections. He tells me about the tavern on the outskirts of town in the early 1920s where fathers would take their sons for dinner and then send them upstairs to be sexually initiated by the same girls who had served them their meal. Mr. Paudera clutches at his chest and insists that he himself was never inside but that he had once accompanied his friend Levy, who availed himself of the local services. Levy was among those who did not return.

Jiří is impatient to show me the cemeteries. They are, for him, not only a desecration, but also a symbol of everything wrong with the society created by forty years of communism. In the strongly humanitarian climate of Václav Havel's Czechoslovakia, this cemetery (and others like it throughout the country) are an embarrassment. Moreover, like many Czechs— some of them recent converts to Judaism—Jiří views strong support of Jews as a political act, an indication of an individual's values.

We walk up the cobblestoned street, through the now invisible gateway to the ghetto, past the building by the railroad tracks that was my grandfather's tannery, up the hill toward the cemeteries. The houses alongside us are all inhabited and well maintained; if you did not know this was the old Jewish Street you would not look twice. Then the houses on the left side stop, a wooded area begins, and we step into the old Jewish cemetery. It is everything you'd expect a vandalized cemetery to look like. Tombstones have been knocked over and are obscured by rusting pipes and torn plastic. Some graves have been dug up. There is junk everywhere. I take it in with my eyes but I have run out of emotion. I find myself explaining to my enraged journalist friend and an embarrassed Mr. Paudera that I am relieved to see no swastikas.

Mr. Paudera is shaking his head. In his opinion, the Catholics should tend the cemetery now that there are no Jews left. The Catholic cemetery is regularly visited and cared for—and there is a fence around it.

We drive to the new cemetery, whose graves date from 1890. My great-grandparents are buried here but I do not want to search through the junk for their tombstones. Mr. Paudera shows us where the cemetery wall bordering on an open field has been destroyed by trucks backing up so that pillagers can load the marble they then use or sell for building. Jiří shows me the tiny, empty grave of Hanička Katz, whose tombstone records a life of one year (1924–25). Her body has been dug up. In its place is a package of cigarettes and a few rusty cans. We walk around the small chapel and, with a cry, Jiří discovers that the Star of David, which had been in place three weeks earlier, is now gone. That does it for me.

"I have to lie down," I say, and we go to Mr. Paudera's house where I lie flat on my back, my eyes closed.

I understand why my father could never again set foot in Roudnice or even Europe. I also understand why I had been driven to return.

Jiří and I drive back to Prague in silence.

Day Eight

I decide to spend my last day in Černošice with Helena. Although we have not acknowledged it in words, both of us suspect she may not live until next summer. I want to soak up her presence, not only because she was my mother's best friend, but also because she is one of those real-life heroines whose lives are rarely recorded and made available to other women. As I take the commuter train out to the suburbs, I realize that there is an urgency about life in Prague now, a sense of a golden moment, that reminds me of Israel, where I lived just after the Six-Day War. Euphoria reigns. All things seem possible, and people talk earnestly about the future, about avoiding both the mistakes of the Communist past and the capitalist present.

On Sunday when I came back from the country and to Prague Castle, the streets and bridges were filled with people out for a stroll, artisans peddling their wares, bands of musicians, mimes, actors. On the Charles Bridge, under a statue of one of the saints, a guitarist was singing in English the Beatles song "Fool on the Hill," and, as happened so many times in Czechoslovakia, I found myself in tears. Prague is basking in the glow of a seemingly endless summer, but I'm old enough to know it will end.

Helena greets me in the garden, where she and her husband grow their own potatoes, onions, and cucumbers. We sit down and, once again, six hours go by in an instant. I explain to her that there are foundations in America and Israel for people like herself—Christians who helped Jews during the Nazi occupation—and that I will see what I can do about registering her, getting her the German-made medication she needs. Helena finds this possibility attractive but strange. She did what she had to do; she never asked whether the people she helped were Jews or Christians. When I suggest she write a book, she laughs. "My account of everything that's happened here in the past fifty years is so inconsistent with everybody else's—no one would believe it!"

We hold hands for a few moments. Helena's daughter Clara, who was born one year before me, committed suicide when she was eighteen, and

Helena, who shares her name with me, regards me as her goddaughter. We talk until I realize that if I don't leave, I will miss my train, and I run down the hill to the train station.

My family—Jaroslav, Kitty, Micki, Jarka, and the two children—and I are having our farewell dinner at one of Prague's exclusive restaurants. Jaroslav is uncomfortable with the deferential service—he is wearing a tan shirt and slacks and keeps repeating *hogel fogel,* Czech slang for fancy-shmancy, irritating Kitty for whom the white tablecloths, the grand piano, and fine view of the city are a nostalgic reminder of her youth. Jarka has left her metal pendulum at home; the kids can eat what they wish tonight. The hors d'oeuvres are a gussied-up version of what I've been eating all week: ham *rouladen,* herring, and deviled eggs (garnished with caviar). There are rolls instead of bread; beef as well as pork entrées, and, on every table, small bottles of Heinz ketchup!

The pianist eavesdrops on our conversation and launches into a heart-felt rendition of the themes from *Exodus,* then *Doctor Zhivago,* both out-lawed until recently. Jaroslav grows increasingly irritated as the waiters lounge around in the nearly empty dining room. After our main course, he says he's going for a walk. I jump up after him and we walk slowly in the park above the restaurant, where he played as a child. He tells me about his mother and father, the poverty in which he grew up during the First Re-public, how hopeful he had been about communism, and how fearful he is now. Not for himself—he's almost a pensioner now—but for his children and for this beautiful country, which in its long history has had so little freedom to be what it could be.

The Last Morning

I have given most of my clothing, including my nightgown, to Kitty, and my suitcase is packed with Czech sausage, Czech pottery, Czech children's books and toys. I pass through customs quickly, then sit down at the bar, where I order a cup of black coffee and two slices of peasant bread. The passage from Prague to Frankfurt is perhaps not as dramatic as that from mainland China to Hong Kong, but it is a passage nonetheless and I find myself lingering.

I wait until almost everyone has left the waiting area, where a large color TV set is suspended from the ceiling. There, alone, I watch a little girl wearing a gas mask, pushing her toy baby carriage through a Prague street, followed by shots of devastated forests. As I walk out onto the airfield, I am surprised to see Jarka waving from up on the balustrade. Kitty has gone on to the dentist—the last thing I remember her asking Jaroslav was if one hundred korun was enough of a "tip" for a tooth extraction. I wave back to Jarka, waiting for everyone to board. Then I wipe my eyes, and climb the stairs up to the plane. I'm going home.

July 1990

Memory Macht Frei

MELVIN JULES BUKIET

My father, myself, and eighteen men and three women of my father's age and background are going to Auschwitz. Visions of cattle cars and SS guards intrude over the kind attentions of our stewardess. I am sipping brandy, listening to Duke Ellington on the earphones, reclining. Soon the veal dinner will come and then a movie, a comedy starring Robert Redford and Jane Fonda. The plane will pass from night into day and touch gently down in the sunny Polish spring. After that—the Krematoria.

My father and every adult male I saw until I was ten were born in Poland between 1915 and 1925. Those born before were too old to survive; those born after, too young. Most boys of their age also died. Through will, strength, intelligence, and especially, luck they endured and came to America. None of them ever returned until now. My father has been asked a number of times to join groups traveling to Poland, but they were always the American-Jewish this or the American-Jewish that, for all of which he feels deeply, but with none of which he would venture back in time. This group, without a name, is only for those who were there before.

We will be there for a week, touring points of common interest, Auschwitz, Majdanek, Treblinka, the Warsaw ghetto. At some time, however, most plan to leave the group to return to Proszowice, Tishavitz, or Zaklakov, or whichever one of the thousands of Jewless towns of contemporary Poland they used to call "home."

We gathered at Kennedy Airport an hour before the flight. Already there seemed to be two distinct subgroups among us, the *machers* and the dreamers. The *machers* were pushing, bustling for tickets, and introducing themselves while the dreamers faded into the background. Sam Goldstein, a pugnacious ox of a man with a face like a jack-o'-lantern, is maybe the most

128

extreme representative of the first of the two groups. Sam (who owns a sweater factory in which he employs only Poles) organized the trip. He himself wanted to go but he didn't want to go alone, so he put an ad in the *Jewish Press,* took orders, made arrangements. Like Sam, my father and the men I grew up among are all *machers* who have made themselves American successes. Until this trip I hardly knew that the dreamers, soft-spoken, self-effacing men, existed. I thought that their type died. Unable to withstand the mental pains of the lager, they still have nightmares, but, miraculously, they are here to have those nightmares. A story is told to me of a village bully who died less than a month into his stay at Majdanek. Where tiny Noah Jaffe was used to tiny meals, the bully could not do without his daily dozen eggs and kielbasa. On this trip, I will discover that there is a bit of *macher* at work within every dreamer and a dreamer sleeping within every *macher.*

Padding to the plane bathroom, one of the men from the tour, a tired-looking man with a thin, drooping nose and large eyes, puts his hand on my shoulder and says that he thinks it is good that I am here. "My daughter didn't want to go," he says. "I don't blame her. I didn't want to go either."

When I ask why then he came, he shrugs with passive eloquence. "The same reason I did the first time. I had to."

Whether guns or nightmares drive one into the camps almost makes no difference. Coercion from without or from within is still coercion. These people with me have never had a choice. They are neither brave and noble volunteers nor idle curiosity seekers. They are not the members of the President's Holocaust Commission, who can sit on a dais and declare what lessons the world must learn, because thirty-five years after their liberation they are still unsure of what they have learned. *Machers* and dreamers both, they are on private, personal missions to confront demons called forth by them from a world that no longer exists.

To me, however, the world of the past seems more and more real every minute. The stolid Polish passport inspector could have spotted the large black J on my visa, and shifted our group off to the side, to a special van. The land we pass through is absolutely flat. That does not mean that it is good for farming, which it is, but that there is no place to hide. The rural medieval towns with their thatched-roof cottages with their cuckoo clock decorations are not picturesque, but foreign, and unwilling to accept foreigners. The old ladies working the fields in their brightly colored sweaters (manufactured by Goldstein) and the young couple picnicking by the side of the road are ironic counterparts to our hermetically sealed tourist bus, which follows the signs to Oświęcim. This word may be unfamiliar. It was to the Germans, who could not pronounce it, who changed it to Auschwitz. I cannot believe that this word is written so honestly, so straightforwardly it might as well read Scarsdale. Primitive tribes thought of word and substance as one, and thought that if they knew their enemy's secret name they could destroy him. Old Jews are afraid to utter the name of the Lord. I see the sign and feel cramps.

People have lived in this town for eight hundred years, but prosperity came only when people began dying here. First the operation of the camp and now its use as a tourist attraction have kept the local economy strong since 1940. Oświęcim has become a prosperous exurb of Kraków, perhaps because of its excellent rail connections. Again, it bears repetition, it is shocking, people live here.

I do not want to pass through the gate. I hesitate on the verge like a suicide contemplating a leap. Above me the famous words Arbeit Macht Frei (Work makes one free) are written in wrought iron fit into an arching metal border. Pictures are taken of the sign, and I briefly, nervously, think that I would like one of myself standing on my head beneath it, but I do not suggest it because my father does not understand sacrilege. He and all those who have been here before walk past me, under the sign. Does this mean that they accept the truth of its statement? Has it worked for them? I have the fantasy that my entire life until this moment has been a dream and that the second I pass the evil, mocking, sentiment, New York, and everything else that I think I have known since 1953 will disappear. The year 1953 itself will disappear. The year will be 1943 (only ten years difference!) and I will be back in the lager.

First impression—Auschwitz looks kinder than I expected. Beyond the gates are about twenty-five barracks. Two stories tall, made of brick, with windows, they look a little like garden apartments, which my father builds in New Jersey. Of course, it is the life within the barracks, the death within them and everywhere else here, the shooting wall, the portable gallows, the gas chamber, in which lies the horror, but my feeling of surprising benignity remains. Even as we pass the exhibits of maps, documents, photographs, bones, a roomful of hair meant to be sent to German textile factories, and one particularly chilling display in which hundreds of emptied canisters of Zyklon B (with the strange word "Giftgas!" on each) are heaped up like so many of the bodies they produced—it doesn't seem that bad. Something is missing—Jews.

The first camp was originally built by and for the Polish artillery. It was captured and expanded by the Germans early in 1940. It housed mostly Soviet prisoners of war.

Auschwitz II, or Birkenau, or Brzezinka (the Polish word so melodically tinkling, the German a howl), is where the Jews were kept and killed. If Auschwitz is a normal prison where one's vision is everywhere blocked by a wall, Birkenau is a world without end. On an infinite, open, emerald green, grass-covered expanse are barracks upon barracks upon barracks made of wood, without windows, on the model of stables. Of course, the grass was not here in 1943. It was trampled under millions of feet, and any individual blades that managed to poke through were eaten by the starving inmates, just as the ovens were meant to devour any stubborn enough to survive the sickness, filth, degradation, overwork, and tortures of this place. It is an unimaginably huge, nearly perfect rectangular grid surrounded and subdivided by double rows of electrified barbed wire hung on curving concrete pylons. In a prison one can imagine life on the other side of one's walls, but here, looking through the wires into the next section of the grid, there is only a suffocating geometric containment, as if one were trapped between opposing mirrors. I would not be surprised if each one of the hundreds of barracks were a perfect miniature of the entire camp, and if each space allotted each human being on the triple-tiered bunks that run the length of each barracks' wall was a complement to the barracks itself. Birkenau, and the pattern of the mind confronting it, is a set of Chinese boxes broken only by the single pair of railroad tracks that runs through the center of the camp and ends in the Krematoria.

Everyone in our group has a story about this place. His first day here, Abe Baumgartner saw an eight-year-old boy instructed to put a noose around the head of his father. The boy was then instructed to tilt over the box on which his father stood.

Leonard Berman, a retired contractor from Atlanta, was a dentist before the war. In the lager, however, masonry was a more valued skill, and so he said he was a mason. After mortaring exactly one brick he was found out. His hand was laid flat on the red-hot oven as punishment, and then they turned him into a mason after all. He helped build houses for the SS and every two weeks he helped rebuild the Krematoria chimneys, which kept catching fire from the excess of human creosote.

After the war, in the United States, Leonard Berman tried to resume his chosen profession, but without an American degree he could aid only other dentists. He realized that he had another skill. He became a mason, started his own company, expanded, made good.

The Krematoria were blown up by the Germans before they abandoned the camp, and are now massive ruins of buckled concrete and moss-covered brick, up from between which dainty purple flowers have grown. The parts of the installations that were built underground (the undressing and "shower" rooms) are gaping pits like exhumed graves, which is exactly what they are.

There is not much else to see here. Just another row of barracks and another krematorium, another row of barracks, another krematorium. A nation of men, women, and children, farmers, artists, merchants, scholars, and thieves, their only bond their belief in a silent God, lived in the barracks and died in the ovens. There was no need for more here, because nothing else happened here. Just life and death. Its simplicity, like its perfect geometry, is frightening.

Naomi Kesler, who came here after being locked into then let out of a burning synagogue, says, "I don't believe it. I was here and I still don't believe it, how it could happen like this. Such a fine people, the Germans, such a cultured people, how could they do this to us? Why should they want to?" Rabbi Elijah Greenberg says, "We always die, in every war. That's why we Jews are always against war and violence."

I think it is more than enlightened self-interest. Rabbi Greenberg should know. During the war he worked in "Canada," the storaging section of Birkenau so named because of the riches it held, the suitcases, the clothes, the watches, the jewels, the gold teeth, the artificial limbs of the martyrs. Rabbi Greenberg does not think highly of material wealth, but he knows that the spiritual did not count for more in the *lager.*

Nathan Kanoff is a little old man, always wearing the same clunky black shoes, thin white socks, baggy pants, beige sweater, and hat, always lagging behind, getting lost. He provides us with comic relief and something more, because he is the most deeply religious person among us. He was not here during the war, having emigrated to Palestine in the 1920s, but his wife, a cripple, was liberated from Birkenau, and he is here in her stead. No place familiar to other Jews is foreign to him. When we light candles (in the one undestroyed gas chamber, a terrible damp cavern), Nathan Kanoff mutters a hoarse, heartfelt Kaddish, then thinks it appropriate to say a few words. "The candle is the symbol of the soul. When we light candles we recall the souls of the past. We bear witness to the suffering of the Jewish people. May the Lord comfort us that we carry on."

It is the first mention of God since we landed on Polish soil, and coming from Nathan Kanoff's wise, awkward person, I am almost taken in by it until I realize that this is exactly what has been bothering me all along. Auschwitz remains very much alive in my mind. It is therefore surprising to see it as it never was, beneath a balmy blue sky, with flowers, but it is even more surprising to be here without the cries of pain and the crackling of the wires, without the pain itself as administered by bludgeon, whip, or shiny black jackboot, and without the smell of human smoke, without the sky on fire. Like the burning bush that betokened by its constancy the presence of God, the eternally burning Krematoria signified his absence. Unless silence is assent.

It seems to me that the holy places of mankind are those in which God shows himself, the black rock in Mecca from which Mohammed ascended, the Calvary Church on the site of Jesus' crucifixion, and, of course, the many holy land locations of the Hebrew Bible. It also seems to me that the only places where God has shown his true nature since the days of the Bible are Auschwitz, Treblinka, Majdanek, Sobibor, Chelmno, and Belzec, and that these are therefore the new holy places. I believe in God, but I do not like Him. I believe in Jewishness, not Judaism.

I think this out while pacing meditatively across the ruins of Krematoria #2. How many feet walked as slowly into the chamber beneath me? No one knows. How many walked out? None. Why?

Absentmindedly, I pick up a piece of brick, which I rub my fingers against like a good luck charm, and when it comes time to go I find that I cannot relinquish it. I slip it into my pocket, more as a relic than a souvenir, but I am observed by Saul Tumin, who arrived here shortly before the end of the war. By then no one knew what they were doing. No one knew he was here. No one bothered to kill him.

"You know," he tells me, "after the war I was in Germany. I went to see Hitler's house. I wanted to see the house he lived in." What he means, like the others, again, is "Why?" Why would a civilized human being, someone who lived in a house like anyone else, do such a thing?

"And there were other people there, Germans. And they were taking stones from Hitler's house."

Now, I do not know exactly what he means, how he means this to refer to me, if he means this to refer to me. Yes, I am taking stones from Hitler's house, or maybe from God's. Jews traditionally place a small pebble atop the headstone of a grave they visit. The exact meaning of this custom has been lost, but it may be to add to the memorial, and here I've taken from it. Still, I cannot let go this jagged piece of brick charred black with the ashes of my ancestors.

Two images will occur and recur to me throughout the trip. One is of light and flame, which cannot be held, which can symbolize either the soul or the torments so many souls went through in this cursed place, and the other is of stone, the first quality of which is palpability, which can symbolize any certainty or truth or the tomb, which amounts to the same thing in this cursed place.

First impression of Proszowice—I'd rather be in Auschwitz.

Most of the people on the tour were disappointed by their towns, some because the reality was different from their memory, and some because it was the same. Of course, there were elements of both similarity and difference everywhere. The land and the look of the people never change, but the twentieth century has finally made its way into the most isolated shtetl. The telephones have to be cranked, but the fact is that there are telephones. The television is primitive, but it will no doubt grow in scope and sophistication. Soviet influence is pervasive. Also, there are no Jews.

When Rabbi Greenberg returned to Siemiatycze he could not find his mother's house. Her name was not in the town archives, nor was his birth certificate on file. "I don't understand this," said the conscientous party clerk. "How long ago did your family leave?"

"In 1943."

A light dawned. The clerk asked, "Jew?"

The rabbi nodded.

The clerk was sympathetic but certain. "All documents pertaining to the native Hebraic population are gone."

"Gone? When, how, by who?" The rabbi wanted to know.

"Gone. Like the Jews themselves."

Ruth Kemmelman also failed to find the remembrance she sought. She had come with us to Poland specifically to visit her mother's headstone. She had contributed to its upkeep for years. "U.J.A. anyone will give to," she said, "but if your own cemetery you don't, who will?" Finally, about to view this precious piece of granite, she said, "You know, I wanted to do this as long as I live," as if she had not lived before the war.

Mrs. Kemmelman rejoined our group at Treblinka, where not a barracks, not a gate, not a trace is left of the camp that killed 750,000 people.

Instead there are seventeen thousand upended stones planted in an open field. It is an eerie, static memorial that evokes both garden and graveyard, and it seems more appropriate than the heroic statues or informative plaques or total disregard we have found elsewhere, but Mrs. Kemmelman does not notice. In shock, she maunders, "The cemetery is there. My grandmother is there. But my mother is gone. After all these years." It is clear that only now has her mother truly died for her.

Some people need something to hold onto. I think of my brick and Treblinka's stone forest and the magical rock that kept Mrs. Kemmelman's mother alive. For Manny Weiss it is his camera. He holds it between himself and the world like a cross before a vampire, but he hardly seems to realize the danger he is protecting himself from. The camera has turned him into a happy-go-lucky American tourist, capable of flirting with Polish schoolgirls in the shade of Majdanek's giant concrete urn with its fifteen hundred cubic meters of human ash.

Manny took the girls' picture, asked their names and where they were from. Then he nearly leaped for joy. "Radom! You're from Radom! That's my town. Maybe you can take me home?"

Manny spoke to the girls' matron, hitched a ride, and stayed in Radom until it was time to return to New York. He slept there. He talked, he joked, he took pictures. He told them about America and about Auschwitz, and as he does not seem much the better for the former, he does not seem much the worse for the latter.

Saul Tumin was not eager. To the contrary. His last memory of Zaklakov was of his forced march out while his childhood friends, his schoolmates, and the friends of his parents stood on the roofs and laughed and played the harmushka.

"Harmushka?" I asked.

At a momentary loss for the correct word amid the English, Yiddish, Polish, multilingual hodegpodge of the tour, he gestured in a slow motion, clapping. Then it came to him. "Accordion."

One of those musicians, a man who had converted before the war, now occupied his family's house. The man was drunk. He cursed and demanded money, and poor, ironic, terrified Mr. Tumin might have given it to him if not for his wife. Sarah Tumin was born the year the war broke out. Three years later, she witnessed her mother's murder by a German soldier. She spent the rest of the war in the woods with her grandmother and the partisans. Tears well spontaneously at the corners of her eyes when she thinks of the mother she hardly knew, but she is tough as steel and would not allow anyone to harm her frail mate. She and he walked proudly down the street he had last seen at gunpoint. They spoke to no one, but they found the town's ancient cemetery, which was rubble, and they dusted off whatever fragments they could find.

Harold Dan (shortened from Dannenberg) came from Warsaw. He was a resourceful young boy, who scampered easily over the ghetto walls to trade on the black market for food, but one day he was caught. He was put in the Pawianek prison, where he and the rest of those caught that day heard those caught the day before killed, and then cleared away the bodies. The next night they were taken out to the courtyard. When Harold heard the machine gun click he fell to the ground and got up only when a new group of prisoners came to drag him away. Every night for two weeks he was taken out to be shot, and every night he fell and later helped remove the bodies of those who had stood next to him. Finally he escaped from the prison and could have escaped from Warsaw, but chose to stay. When I asked him why, he answered simply. "There was no place else to go."

Just as nothing is left of Treblinka, where most of it perished, nothing is left of the Jewish community of Warsaw. Nothing of the largest Jewish community in the world outside of New York, half a million people. Where the ghetto stood and fought are ranks of Socialist realist high-rises and a token statue.

I wish that Proszowice was gone too. This quaint, innocuous village of maybe two thousand people, stretched out for a mile along a narrow main street with one bulge for a town square, scares me in a way that the endless death camp could not. If painful, and ultimately incomprehensible, Auschwitz is nonetheless familiar. From the people I've met, through the books I've read, through the thoughts I've had, Auschwitz has always been presupposed. To the extent that my father never would have come to America to meet my mother (whose parents ran away from the czar), my existence is directly contingent upon World War II. It is a terrible foundation to have to build on, but there it is. My world begins in 1943, on March 13, the liquidation of the Kraków ghetto. Before that is void. There is nothing here for me.

It is an odd, yellow-plastered house with an orange-tiled roof that appears almost Mediterranean. No one lives there anymore, but the door is open. Through gauzy curtains I can see a black-and-white checked floor leading up to a counter on which a sweet-looking red liquid and different kinds of cakes are displayed. It is a bakery. Beyond the counter and a young Polish counter girl, I can see into the back room where my dead aunt cooked, where my dead uncle studied, where my dead grandfather and my dead grandmother made love, where my father lived. The wide planked wood floor must be as it was and the dark beamed ceiling must be as it was, but instead of furniture there are enormous baker's ovens. Instantly, I think of the Krematoria.

I buy a piece of cake and eat it, separating the flavors of heavy cream, sour rye flour, crushed poppy seeds, and powdered sugar. I try to recapture the past in the tastes of the present. The girl behind the counter thinks I'm crazy. I stand there, gawking at everything, swirling the cake around my mouth. I think of Proust's Madeleine, but the effect of my too sweet, sticky, country pastry cannot compare, because the past I am attempting to rec-ollect did not exist. Something will not allow me, even in my mind, to cross the threshold of the glass-topped counter.

Next door is the blacksmith's, where my uncle used to work. It looks like a medieval torture chamber with tongs, grips, bellows, hot coals. My father points to a building and says that's where they killed Getzel and his five sons. He points to another and says that's where Yitzhak Weinberg was killed when he tried to leave town with a silver candelabra. Everywhere here is redolent of death. Only in "our" backyard is there something that does not fit. In a dozen stacked cages are about forty rabbits. Some are all gray and some are black and white, and they are doing what rabbits do. I am mesmerized by their sexual activity. It is so out of place in this place where everything reminds me of death. At least a remnant emerged from the lagers, but nothing is left here. Then, in a storeroom I am not supposed to enter, I see a rabbit skin, blood stained and stretched out to dry. That is more like it.

It is not that the evil is more personal here than at Auschwitz, but that it is unexpected. The camps were made to kill, and in so doing they merely fulfilled their purpose, but Proszowice market was made for the exchange of sugar beets and tobacco, not for the human roundup that took place there in 1942 (before the transfer to the Kraków ghetto, before the liqui-dation on March 13). The pleasant, rural calmness here today almost tempts one to listen to the vicious deniers who claim that the Holocaust never occurred. Certainly, the locals who hated and hounded us into the waiting German arms would agree. My father talks to them and they remember him and his parents, and they ask about him and his parents and they don't think for a second about World War II. Except for one old woman who crosses herself on seeing this ghost returned from the dead, they act as if he had taken a bus out of town thirty-five years ago and went to Atlantic

City. My father says that they still hate us, but the horror is that they don't. There is no malice in their gap-toothed smiling faces. Without Jews to hate, they do not remember what it was like to hate Jews. We are minor curiosities, minor celebrities, our taxi like a court carriage making a feed stop on the road from Moscow to Berlin. I feel not only that there are no Jews here now, but that there never were.

The cake has no taste.

My father and I took one more side trip, to Jawiszowice, the subcamp of Auschwitz in which he spent most of the war. It is about five kilometers south of Oświęcim, three kilometers from the coal mine at Brzeszcze, where he walked every morning and night. Next to the mine is an abandoned concrete skeleton that looks like the frame for launching a submarine. It was supposed to be an electrical plant, but the war ended before it was finished, and my father stopped working on it. He brought concrete there, one bag under his left arm, one bag under his right. He brought the dead bodies of those who could not do this back with him to Jawiszowice. They were much easier to carry. Sometimes the daily procession would meet another procession with another dead man, but the other had died of natural causes and was on his way to a decent Christian burial. "We used to see the mourners sobbing and crying," my father says now. "And we would laugh. I mean, so someone died, so what?"

One day the capo, a German criminal before the war, now foreman, approached my father. He had a cudgel in his hand. My father, all of eighty or ninety pounds, shoveling the concrete mix he had just carried, did not know what he had done wrong, but he knew that it didn't matter. Once this man started beating someone he didn't stop until his chosen victim was dead. My father said, "You're not going to hit me."

The capo laughed and came at him.

My father buried his shovel in the man's head. A crowd began to gather, but before the SS could see who had done what to whom a fog fell. My father says that in his entire life he has never seen a fog come so quickly, so totally. A whistle blew so that all the workers had to come together, so that none could escape, and no one ever found out. The war went on.

We pass farms and another coal mine, which was manned by a different subcamp, and then we enter a small town that was obviously built in the fifties to house the miners who would not live in barracks. My father says, "Here."

There is a small park outlined by a row of stunted bushes with shriveled berries on them. There is a shallow wading pool where dirt has drifted over the winter and formed an island on which a single weed has taken root. At the far end of the park a traveling carnival has temporarily encamped. The carnival consists of two children's rides, two imitation railroad cars (one for snacks, the other a shooting gallery), and one portable bandstand on which a singer performs pop tunes for a dozen children and three old men.

We skirt the festivities and walk over every inch of the *lager*/park. My father finds the spot where his barracks stood, where the gallows stood, where the guardtower stood, where now there are only gravel walkways, benches, and a few pretty flowers. Then we find four gray cement buildings that were there back then. One, the old kitchen, is now the town cinema. Another, now a storing place for park equipment, was a combination latrine and storing place for dead bodies. The two last administrative buildings still serve some governmental function, but the government has changed, and the sign between them has been removed. It used to read Arbeit Macht Frei.

I didn't know that this catchphrase was written anywhere other than over the entrance to the main camp, but apparently the Germans thought the joke funny enough to repeat. I think it's pretty funny myself. Certainly, this trip is work, and I feel anything but free. The more I see, the more imprisoned I am by the past.

My father says that this land is cursed. If so, it is also cursed everywhere that he walks and everywhere that I walk, because the curse is not only in the blood soaked into the earth, but also in the blood of those who know this. We are tainted by our knowledge.

The two sons of one of the other men on the tour were supposed to come with us, but they backed down at the last minute, claiming that with the tense world situation (Iran, Afghanistan) they were afraid of a war. I think that the war they were afraid of ended thirty-five years ago, but I don't blame them. Being here is an ugly, fearsome thing.

Any war, let alone World War II, let alone Lager Jawiszowice, seems alien when considered against the background of this park, this playground. Territory, commerce, and, worst of all, ideals become obscene when people kill for them. War is useless, stupid, wicked, so tell me, "Why?"

Western wisdom has it that something called freedom is worth fighting for, but if work doesn't make one free neither does war. Neither do memory or the imagination. Freedom does not exist. It is the illusion that has taken the place of religion as the source of dignity in the Western world, the acceptance of which signified the end of the age of Jewish faith. That is why the sign did not say Work Makes One Holy, which may be why the Jewish God saw fit to remain silent.

During a short rain at Majdanek, while we took shelter in one of the barracks, Rabbi Greenberg said to me, "Heaven is crying." Too little, too late. From now on if I want tears I cry for myself.

We are all under a life sentence. The only difference is that some sentences are imposed from without, like Auschwitz, while others, like this trip to Auschwitz, come from within. The deliberate remembrance of the vile past for the sake of a better future, the dedication of an uncertain future to a miserable past—or not—is the only free choice we have to make. We have to make it. If not, we are no better than God. God lives in an eternal present without past or future, while the human domain of time and mortality is all that entails the twin ungodlike qualities of morality and beauty. Freedom makes one work. We must pass through the gates.

Written circa 1981

The Journey to Poland

MICHAL GOVRIN

In late October 1975, when I was in my early twenties and completing my doctorate in Paris, I went to Poland. An almost impossible journey then for a young woman, alone, with an Israeli passport, at the time when there were no diplomatic relations between the Eastern Bloc and Israel. (Only because of a French-Jewish friend, who turned me into a "representative of France" at the International Theater Festival in Wroclaw [Breslau], did I receive a special visa for a week.)

The night before the trip, when everything was ready, I called my parents in Tel Aviv and told them. I asked my shocked mother for the exact address of her family home in Kraków. Only later that winter, when I visited Israel, did I understand what profound emotion took hold of my mother's few surviving friends and relatives from Kraków when they heard of the trip.

Traveling to Poland in 1975 was not part of the social phenomenon it is today. The group definition of "second-generation Holocaust survivors" hadn't yet been coined. You had to find everything by yourself. How to plan the trip and how to feel, how to talk about it. The letter to my parents began a long formulation. Even the choice of parents as the addressees of an intimate discourse was not the norm then.

Today, that trip seems like a geological rift that changed my emotional and intellectual landscape, and placed its seal on my writing. Yet, the "journey to Poland" didn't begin in 1975, but in early childhood, in Tel Aviv in the 1950s. Distant shocks preceded the rift.

The "journey to Poland" began in that journey "to there"—the journey every child makes to the regions of before he was born, to the unknown past of his parents, to the secret of his birth. My journey to Mother's world began long before I "understood" who my mother, Regina-Rina

141

Poser-Loeb-Govrin, was, before I "knew" that she survived the "Holocaust," that she once had another husband, that I had a half brother. But there was the other "knowledge," that knowledge of preknowledge and of prelanguage, transmitted in the thousand languages that connect a child and his parents without words. A knowledge that lay like a dark cloud on the horizon. Terrifying and seductive.

For years the journey proceeded on a double track. One outside the home and one inside it. And there was an almost complete separation between the two. As if everything that was said outside had nothing to do with Mother. Outside, incomprehensible, violent stories about the Holocaust were forced upon the little girl's consciousness. In school assemblies, in lessons for Holocaust Memorial Day, and later in lessons of "annals of the Jewish People," which were taught separately from "history" classes, and described events that happened in "another Jewish time and place," where Talmudists and small-town Jews strolled among the goats and railroad cars of the ghetto. Even the Eichmann trial, on the radio in school and at home, was an event you had to listen to, but had no real relation to Mother. (And even if things were said about it then at home, I succeeded in repressing them from consciousness.)

At home, there were bright stories about Kraków, the boulevards, the Hebrew High School, the cook, the maids, about skiing and summer holidays in the mountains, in Zakopane, and sometimes on Friday evening, Mother and I would dance a "Krakowiak" on the big rug in the living room. And there was Mother's compulsive forced-labor housecleaning, and her periods of rage and despair when I didn't straighten up my room (what I called "prophecies of rage" with self-defensive cunning), there was the everlasting, frightened struggle to make me eat, and there was the disconnected silence that enveloped her when she didn't get out of bed on Yom Kippur. And there was the photo album "from there" at the bottom of Mother's lingerie drawer, with unfamiliar images, and also pictures of a boy, Marek. And stories about him, joyful, a baby in a cradle on the balcony, a beautiful child on the boulevard. And a tender memory of the goggle-moggle with sugar he loved so much (and only years later did I understand the terrifying circumstances of that). And there were the weekly get-togethers at Aunt Tonka's house (who was never introduced as the widow of Mother's older brother who was murdered), get-togethers so different from the humorous, confident gatherings of Father's family (members of the Third Aliyah and the leadership of the Yishuv and the State). At night, in Aunt Tonka's modest apartment, I was the only little girl—"a blonde, she looks like a shiksa"—in the middle of the Polish conversation of "friends from there," who looked to me like impoverished patricians, because almost all of them had once been mayors, and had papers to prove it, "[M]aryan papers."[1] And every year there were also the visits of Schindler, when you could go all dressed up with Mother's cousin to greet him at the Dan Hotel. And once, when Mother and I were coming back from "the city" on bus number twenty-two, Mother stopped next to the driver and blurted a short sentence at him for no reason. The driver, a gray-haired man in a jacket, was silent and turned his head away. "He was a ca-po," she said when we got off, pronouncing the pair of incomprehensible syllables gravely. All that was part of the cloud that darkened the horizon, yes, but had nothing to do with what was mentioned at school or on the radio.

Poland and Kraków weren't "real" places either, no more than King Solomon's Temple, for instance. I remember how stunned I was when I went with Mother to the film *King Matthew the First,* based on the children's story by Janusz Korczak, which I had read in Hebrew. In the film, the children spoke Polish! And it didn't sound like the language of the friends at Aunt Tonka's house. "Nice Polish," Mother explained, "of Poles." Poles? They apparently do exist somewhere.

Yet, a few events did form a first bridge between outside and inside. One day, in a used-book store in south Tel Aviv, Mother bought an album of black-and-white photos of Kraków. "Because the photos are beautiful," she emphasized, "they have artistic value." And indeed, the sights of the Renaissance city in the four seasons flowed before my eyes. A beautiful, tranquil city, full of greenery and towers. Jews? No, there were no Jews in that album, maybe only a few alleys "on the way to Kazimierz."

When I was ten, my parents sent me for private lessons in English, because "it's important to know languages." And thus I came to Mrs. Spiro, a gentle woman from London, married to Dr. Spiro, Mother's classmate from the Hebrew high school in Kraków. One day, when the lesson was over, Mrs. Spiro accompanied me to the edge of the yard of their house on King Solomon Street. I recall the sidewalk with big paving stones as she talked with me. Maybe I had complained before about Mother's strict demands, or maybe she started talking on her own. "Of course, you know what your mother went through, she was in the Holocaust.

---

1. Translator's note: This is an English rendition of a pun in the original, based on the sound confluence of the Hebrew *arim* (cities) and Aryan, which leads the child to think that they all "owned cities" over "there."

You have to understand her, the tensions she has sometimes," she said to me directly.

That was an earthquake. A double one. The understanding that Mother was in "the Holocaust," that awful thing they talk about in school assemblies, with "the six million." And that I, a ten-year-old girl, had to or even could "understand Mother." That is, to leave the symbiosis of mother and daughter constituting one expanded body, to cut myself off from my child's view, and see Mother as a separate person, with her own fate and reasons for moods that didn't depend only on me, or on my certain guilt. I remember how, at that moment, facing the spotted paving stones, I understood both those things all at once. Like a blinding blow.

Then came high school in Tel Aviv. Because both the principal and the assistant principal were graduates of the Hebrew High School in Kraków, their former classmates in that high school, including my mother, sent their children to study there. At that school, influenced by the principal and his assistant principal, both of them historians, there was an intense awareness of the Jewish past and life in the Diaspora—a rare dimension in the Zionist-Israeli landscape of Diaspora denial, and Gideon Hausner, the prosecutor in the Eichmann trial, initiated a "club to immortalize the Jewish community of Kraków." A group of students met with members of the Kraków community, who taught them the history of the city and the Jewish community before the destruction. The club also heard testimony from the Holocaust, with a special emphasis on the activities of the Jewish underground. The women's revolt in the Gestapo prison, led by Justina, was also dramatized and performed for the community members on the annual memorial day ("Holocaust celebrations" as the memorials were called by members of the drama club).

I was a member of the "club to immortalize," and I also played a Polish cook in the performance of the history of the uprising. But a partition still remained between me and the others, a zone of silence so dense that, to this day, I don't know which of the children of the Kraków community members were children of Holocaust survivors and not of parents who immigrated to Palestine before the war. If there were any, no bond was formed between us. We didn't talk about it. We remained isolated, caged in the sealed biographies of our parents.

There were other bridges here, almost subterranean ones, which, as far as I recall, were not formulated explicitly. The bond with the literature teacher, the poet, Itamar Yaoz-Kest, who survived as a child with his mother in Bergen-Belsen. In high school, there were only his influence on my literary development and a sense of closeness, a sort of secret look between "others." (Only later did I read the poems of "The Double Root" about his childhood "there," and his story describing, as he put it, a little girl who looked like me, the daughter of survivors.) And there was the love affair with the boy in my class, whose delicate smile on his drooping lower lip looked like the "different" smile of the literature teacher. His father, the lawyer, submitted reparations claims from Germany in those days—close enough to the seductive-dangerous realm. My complicated relations with that boy paralleled the shock of discovery of Kafka; and along with the tempest of feelings of fifteen-year-olds, that forbidden, denied, inflamed relation also had a pungent mixture of eros and sadism, a tenderness and an attraction to death, and above all, metaphysical dimensions that pierced the abyss of dark feelings, which somehow was also part of "there."

In my childhood, when Mother was an omnipotent entity within the house, I couldn't "understand" her. Now that I have grown up and left home, when she was the authority to rebel against and that the enzyme necessary to cut the fruit off from the branch erected a dam of alienation and enmity between us, I couldn't identify with her, with her humanity. There had to be a real separation. I had to live by myself. To go through the trials alone. To listen slowly to what was concealed.[2]

Then came the move to Europe, to Paris. To study for the doctorate and to write literature intensively. I went to the Paris of culture, of Rilke, of Proust, of Edith Piaf. But in 1972, soon after I arrived, the film *The Sorrow and the Pity* by Marcel Ophuls was released. When the screening ended in the cinema on the Champs-Élysées, I emerged into a different Paris, into a place where that mythical war had gone on. "I understood" that here, on rue de Rivoli, beneath my garret room, German tanks had passed (ever since then they began to inhabit my dreams), "I understood" that the description of the French as a nation of bold underground fighters

2. An amazing example of the layers of memory and forgetting was revealed to me as I wrote *The Name*. The only detail I borrowed in the novel from things I had heard from Mother was a story of the heroism of a woman who succeeded in escaping from Auschwitz-Birkenau, and when she was caught and taken to the Appelplatz, she managed to commit suicide. I also borrowed the admiring tone in which Mother spoke of the event. (Only later did I discover how it had served her as a model.) I created a biographical-fictional character of a virtuoso pianist, and "invented" a name for her—Mala—immortalized in the name of the heroine, Amalia. Years later, as I was finishing the book, I came across a written description of the event in Birkenau and discovered in a daze that the name of the woman was the same as the name I had "invented," "Mala," Mala Zimetbaum.

and rescuers of Jews—a notion I had grown up with in the years of the military pact between Israel and de Gaulle's France—was very far from reality. The clear, comforting borders between good and bad were shattered for me, and so were the simple moral judgments mobilized for ideologies. Here, far from a post–Six-Day War Israel secure in her power, far from the official versions of Holocaust and heroism, a different time was in the streets, a time not completely cut off from the war years. Here, for the first time, I experienced the sense of the other. As a Jew, as an Israeli. Wary of revealing my identity at the university that served as a center of Fatah activities, trembling in the Metro once as I read the Israeli newspaper *Ma'ariv*, until someone called it to my attention: "Mademoiselle, somebody spat on your jacket."

Distance also allowed a different discourse with my parents, especially with Mother. In the weekly letters, without the daily tension of life at home, a new bond was opened, between people who were close, who were beginning to speak more openly with one another. Even my clothes in the European winter, in the "retro" style, began to look like the clothes in Mother's old pictures from Poland, like her hairdo in the photo next to the Jeep from Hanover, when she served after the war as a commander in Aliyah B, the Brikha, camouflaged in an UNRWA (United Nations Relief and Works Agency) uniform. Poland, Hanover suddenly turned into places that were much closer, more present than the little state on the shores of the Mediterranean.

On the first Holocaust Memorial Day in Paris, I decided to stay in my apartment all day and to cut myself off from the street that lived by its own dates (for example, Armistice Day of World War I, the "Great War" that took place at the same time of the year). I spent the day reading works on the sources of Nazism, on the roots of anti-Semitism, on the German nationalism of Wagner (rehearsals of whose opera *Parsifal*, I had attended at the Paris Opera).

That summer, on a tour of Europe, an accident forced me to stay unexpectedly in Munich for three weeks. And then the blank spot that filled the heart of the European map for me—Germany—the blank, untouchable spot that sucked up all the evil, also fell. Here, next to the beer hall of "the Nazi buds," where some Israelis had taken me, in what was obviously a sick gesture, there was also an opera, where Mozart was performed, and there were wonderful museums and parks.

The forced stay in Germany and the Yom Kippur War the following autumn, which I spent in Paris facing the brightly lit Champs-Élysées while my dear ones were in mortal danger, proved to me that there is no refuge in the soothing distinctions between "then" and "now," between "there" and "here." And I also understood that there is no racial difference, imprinted at birth between "them" and "us," nor can we hide behind the fences of the Chosen People. And that, in every person, the murderer and the victim potentially exist, blended into each other, constantly demanding separation, every single day, with full awareness. I understood that I could no longer hide behind the collective, ready-made definitions of memory. That there would be no choice but to embark on the journey that is obstinate, lonely, and full of contradictions.

Germany, France, Europe. What is in that culture, in its roots, mixed with the gold of the baroque and the flickering brasses of symphonies; what is in the squares, in the churches, in the ideologies that allowed what happened? Prepared it? Didn't prevent it? What inflamed the hatred? What repressed it under pious words of morality? What fostered it in the heart of religious belief? What prepared it in the tales of God that man told himself to justify the outbursts of his evil instincts under the disguise of *imitatio Dei*?

And what still exists right before my eyes? Keeps on happening?

How to shift the borders between good and bad with a thin scalpel under a microscope?

How to distinguish anew, here and now? All the time?

And what is the terrorizing persuasive force of tales and of their metamorphoses into theologies, ideologies? How to struggle with forgetting, with denial, without whitewashing, but also without reiterating the same stories, without inflaming the same evil instincts? How to tell responsibly?

Jarring questions that filled me, that nourished my research, my theatrical productions, my literary writing, but did not yet touch Mother's hidden place.

I spent the summer of 1975 between Princeton and New York, collecting material for my doctorate, reading the works of Rebbi Nahman of Bratzlav in the old Jewish Theological Seminary (JTS) library, and in the evenings, swallowing the plethora of fringe theater, jazz, and transvestite clubs, and the international bohemian life of Manhattan. And thus I met that young violinist from Kraków who had fled Poland, and was working as a cabdriver. A handsome young man from Kraków. Kraków? A place where people live? The summer romance was a way to confront the profound seduction of the depths of the past stamped in me, as well as the depths of my femininity.

One day that summer, my aunt, Mother's sister-in-law, came to my apartment in midtown Manhattan. I knew her vaguely from a visit she had made to Israel years before, and after the death of Aunt Tonka in Tel Aviv, my aunt from Queens, the widow of Mother's second brother, who perished in the camps, was her last living close relative. She had survived Auschwitz and her young son was hidden by a Christian woman. After the war, my aunt and her son immigrated to New York.

That day, on the balcony on the thirtieth floor, facing the roofs of midtown Manhattan, my aunt spoke in broken English only about "then" and "there," as if here and now didn't exist, as if we had never left there. She and the Polish pop music at night melted the last wall of resistance. Now I had no excuse not to translate my preoccupation with the subject into action, no excuse not to go to Poland.

In late October, after the administrative alibi was concocted in Paris, I left. Ready. And not ready at all.

I was not ready for what I would find or for what I wouldn't find. I was not ready for the fear. The fear of returning to the strange hotel room at night, the primal fear that I would starve to death, which impelled me to eat nonstop, completely violating the rules of Kashrut, which I had observed ever since I came to Paris to study, eating with the dispensation "allowed during an emergency" that I granted myself (insolently?). Not ready for the fear that rushed me in a panic straight from the visit to Auschwitz-Birkenau to meetings with Polish artists and bohemian parties. I was especially not ready for the complexity of my responses, for their force. For what was revealed to me in "the living laboratory" I had poured by myself. The contradictory burst of fascination and revulsion, alienation and belonging, shame and vengeance, of helplessness, of complete denial. . . .

When I returned, the letter to my parents was a first attempt to look at what was revealed, to talk. The restrained language of the letter reflects the difficulty in going beyond the taboo, hoping they would understand through the silence. That different, new discourse with my parents accompanied us throughout the years until their death. A discourse of closeness, of belonging, of acceptance, beyond the generational differences.

The sense of belonging—along with my parents—to the "other, Jewish story" revealed in the depths of the journey only intensified in the following years, as the doors to the centers of European culture opened to me, as I devoted myself to writing. But at the same time, the understanding that it is impossible to go on telling as if nothing had happened also grew.

Understanding that, after Auschwitz, there are no more stories that didn't betray, there are no more innocent stories.

And what about Mother's shrouded "story"? Details continued to join together in fragments. For years, here and there, she mentioned events, some in conversations with me, some in conversations with others that I chanced upon. I listened when she spoke, and she spoke little. Never did I "interview" her, never did I ask. I respected her way of speaking, as well as her way of being silent. Even after I returned from Auschwitz, I didn't think she had to report or that I had to (or could) "know." I learned from her the lesson of the story in silence.

I heard the first fragment of a chronological description from my mother under extraordinary circumstances. In the autumn of 1977, she was summoned to give testimony in a German court in Hanover. I accompanied my parents to the trial, sitting with Father in the gallery and seeing Mother, with her special erect posture, surrounded by the black robes of the attorneys. In her fluent German, she described the Płaszów camp, where Jews from the Kraków ghetto were removed, she pointed authoritatively at the maps. Her voice trembled only a moment when she came to the description of the Kinderheim, the children's home in Płaszów, where children were taken from their parents. In a few words, she dealt with the *Aktsia*, told how all the inmates of the camp were taken out to the square while an orchestra played lullabies, to see how the SS loaded the children onto the trucks that took them to the gas chambers. She was asked what was the name of her son, and how old was he at the time of the *Aktsia*. She replied with an effort, "Marek. Eight years old." The prosecutor asked for a momentary recess, and then the questions resumed. (That prosecutor accompanied us when we left, apologizing in shame for the accused, the deputy of Amon Goeth, the commander of Płaszów, who was absent from the courtroom, "for medical reasons.")

A few years later, Mother tried to dramatize the story of the revolt of the women in Kraków at the vocational high school where she taught, wanting to bring the subject close to her women students. She worked with Father on the script, and developed original ideas of staging designed to increase audience participation. But, during the rehearsals, she developed such a serious skin disease, clearly as a rejection, that the doctor advised her to stop the production.

The presence of the Holocaust receded completely in her last months, as she struggled with the fatal cancer that was discovered in her. Death was too close to think about its old dread—at any rate, that was my feeling as I stood at her side, admiring her yearning for life, the audacity, the amazing black humor, which restored the dimensions of human absurdity even in the most difficult situations. The day before she lost consciousness, she spoke a lot, in a stupor, in Polish. What did she say? What was she still living there? I couldn't go with her. I remained alone, at her bedside. Then, as I was massaging her feet, those feet that had marched in the death march through frozen Europe, I was struck with the simple knowledge that it was to Mother's struggle, there, that I owed my birth.

I heard Mother's "story" only after her death—death that always turns a loved one into a "story" with a beginning and an end. During the *Shiva*, Rivka Horowitz came to Jerusalem from Bnei-Brak. A woman with bold blue eyes, whom I knew only by name. She was one of nine women, all of them graduates of Beit Yakov, the ultraorthodox school for girls in Kraków, whom my mother joined in the ghetto, despite differences of education and ideology. The ten women, "the minyan," supported one another in the ghetto, during the years in the Płaszów camp, in Auschwitz-Birkenau, throughout the death march, and in the final weeks in Bergen-Belsen. For three years, they hadn't abandoned one another; together they fought exhaustion, disease, had lived through the selections, until all of them survived. "There was strength in them. Moral strength," Mother explained when she and Father, both of them members of the liberal secular Mapai, assiduously attended the celebrations of the friends in Bnei Brak. At the *Shiva*, I heard from Rivka Horowitz for the first time about that period. She spoke for a few hours—out of a responsibility to tell me—and left. And I never saw her again. Later on, when I was almost finished writing *The Name, HaShem* (and after Mother's death, it seemed to me that, more than ever, the novel spoke of a "there" that was lost forever), came the first information about the family property in Kraków. Apartment houses, a button factory . . . Property? There? "In the regions of delusion?" And then, the name that had been common at home, Schindler, which suddenly became a book and then a film, and turned into a general legacy the story of the rescue of Mother's cousin and his wife, Mother's refusal to join the list of workers in the enamel factory in order to stay with Marek.

And then, one evening, the telephone rings in Jerusalem, and on the other end of the line, in English with a thick Polish accent, another member of that "minyan" introduces herself, Pearl Benisch, who published a book, *To Vanquish the Dragon*, with the full story of the group (from the author's religious perspective).[3] A copy arrived on Friday. On the Sabbath eve, I sat with my two little daughters in the living room and picked up the book. I leafed through it distractedly, until I came to the description of the destruction of the Kinderheim. And then I fled to the other room so the children wouldn't see me, and there I burst into sobs I didn't know were hidden inside me. A weeping that arose from there. Mine? Hers?

Until dawn that Sabbath, I read for the first time the story of Mother, in chronological order, dated, revealing the few facts I knew situated in their context. Even the description of the goggle-moggle with sugar that she had secretly made for Marek in the sewing workshop, where the women from Płaszów worked, smuggling the treat to the child when she came back. And how one day the Jewish supervisor discovered her stealing the egg, and threatened to turn her in. And how she stood before him then in mortal danger, and accused him in front of all the workers of the sewing shop of being a traitor to his people. I read how in the *Aktsia* of the destruction of the children's home, against the horrifying background of lullabies, Mother burst into the square toward the SS men who were pushing the weeping children onto the trucks. She shouted to them to take her with the child. And how her friends, the women of "the minyan," held her with all their might, pulled her back. I read about the sisterhood between the women in the group, about the pride, the unbelievable humor, how with astonishing freedom, they maintained their humanity in the *lagers* of Auschwitz-Birkenau. They, and many other women and men, were described in their humanity facing the crematoria. How they succeeded in putting on makeup to get through the selections, how they sneaked the weak women out of the line of the condemned, how they secretly lit candles at Hanukkah and held a Passover seder, and how, after the death march from Auschwitz to Bergen-Belsen, they still managed to laugh together when they got the wrong size prison uniforms. I read, frozen stiff, how, in Bergen-Belsen, Mother dared to be insolent to the female SS officer with the pride she still had left, surviving the public whipping, which few survived, without shouting, "so as not to give the SS the pleasure." Between the pages, the figure of Mother returned to me, cheering the women in Auschwitz with stories of her visit to the Land of Israel, singing them songs of the homeland on their muddy beds where they fell exhausted with typhus and teeming with lice, in Bergen-Belsen. Suddenly I understood one of the few stories Mother had told me about the camps, how she would

3. Pearl Benisch, *To Vanquish the Dragon* (Jerusalem: Feldheim Publisher, 1991).

sing to herself Tshemikhovski's poem: "You may laugh, laugh at the dreams, I the dreamer am telling you, I believe in Man, and in his spirit, his powerful spirit," emphasizing with her off-key voice the words: "I believe in Man, and in his spirit, his powerful spirit." . . .

Mother's "story." Discovering it in the heart of the journey to what was stamped inside me. Discovering it now in the middle of life, when I myself am a mother, and older than she—the young woman and mother who was there.

"Mother's story," or maybe only milestones around what remains hidden.

Translated from the Hebrew by Barbara Harshav

PART FOUR

Issues of Faith and Religion

Introduction

This section sheds light on how many in the second generation come to terms with being Jewish after Auschwitz. Questions are raised about the image of God and the continuing validity of the Sinai Covenant. The contributors reflect on the issue of what type of Jewish faith has emerged from the crucible of the death camps. For example, may Kaddish, the mourner's prayer that extols God's mighty name, be recited after the Shoah? For some, recitation of Kaddish opens the possibility of speaking about a complex family history. Those who maintain their belief in the traditional, pre-Holocaust God command great respect, even from second-generation theological skeptics, who themselves are no longer able to believe.

A prominent theme in these reflections and interviews is the second-generation mission to seek *tikkun olam,* a repair or restoration of the world insofar as this is possible after Auschwitz. This undertaking is a type of practical theology of deeds that assumes a commitment to social justice, and echoes the admonition of the prophet Amos: "Let justice roll down as waters, and righteousness as a mighty stream" (Amos 5:24). This legacy manifests itself in various forms: struggling for human rights, bringing Nazis to justice, fighting against anti-Semitism, bigotry, and racial hatred.

Faith after the Holocaust

For One Person, It Doesn't Pay to Cook

BARBARA FINKELSTEIN

> When I loved Him who was overall, as when I thanked
> Him on my knees for guiding me to where I had heard so
> sweet and mysterious melody, or hated and defied Him as
> now, it all came from Him—love and hate, good and evil.
> —W. H. Hudson, *Green Mansions*

Here is a joke about good people and bad people: A good man dies. In heaven an angel leads him to a little table and gives him some bread and water. The good man begins to eat when he notices hundreds of people in another part of the sky dining on steak and wine. The good man asks, "What's going on over there?" The angel says, "Oh, that's hell." The good man is taken aback. He asks, "If you please, why can't I have what they're having?" The angel replies, "You know for one person, it doesn't pay to cook."

Abraham the Patriarch took a different view of the matter. In *Genesis* he pleads with God to save a city of sinners for the sake of one righteous soul. To its credit, Jewish culture tolerates contradiction, and thus my father, an observant Jew, can appreciate the joke and the biblical text. His willingness to embrace paradox, and to do so with no apparent bitterness, is all the more stunning because he is a Holocaust survivor. In 1942, at seventeen, he watched his Polish neighbors cart his father off to the woods where they beat him to death. He last saw his mother and four younger sisters on a Nazi transport to the Sobibor death camp. His only remaining

156

family, a half brother, died after other Polish neighbors fed him rat poison. My father, Jake, as people call him now, escaped from a slave labor camp, was caught, was sentenced to die, and escaped again. Now, as always, he prays to God three times a day, strictly observes the Jewish dietary laws, and, every Friday morning, checks the *eruv*, a symbolic marker that lets Orthodox Jews honor the spirit of Sabbath while performing tasks such as carrying house keys and pushing baby strollers. My father's observance, punctilious in degree and fervor, is a reminder that God is in the details.

Every so often, my father and I have a conversation that goes like this:

ME: Why do you believe in God?

FATHER: (*With disbelief at my naïvete*) Because my father believed in God, his father believed in God, and his father believed in God.

ME: Do you ever wonder why God allowed the Holocaust to happen?

FATHER: A person can't ask himself that question.

ME: Aren't you ever angry at God?

FATHER: What good does anger do? Anger isn't going to change His nature.

ME: What is His nature?

FATHER: (*Crossing his arms and smiling ironically*) I think that if I get to heaven, and God wants to beat me up, I'll bend my neck so He can take better aim.

ME: Is that what you expect to happen?

FATHER: (*He laughs*) Maybe I'll look across the skies and notice that my former tormenters are sitting at a banquet and feasting on steak and wine.

ME: Wouldn't that bother you?

FATHER: (*Shrugging, as if to say, "That's life."*) Look at Genesis. Cain kills Abel. We're all one big family and we all kill each other. It's in our blood.

In short, this Holocaust survivor reveres an omnipotent God who witnessed the murders of his three little sisters and let Josef Mengele, Auschwitz's Angel of Death, live until 1979. My father might say, with less malice than Shelley's Prometheus, who once told Jupiter, "Be thy swift mischiefs sent / To blast mankind, from yon ethereal tower. / Let thy malignant spirit move / In darkness over those I love."

Like my father, Rivka Shuster Finkelstein is an observant Jew. Every Sabbath my sixty-eight-year-old mother invites a dozen-odd lonely hearts to her suburban New Jersey home for lunch. If not for her, Congregation Sons of Israel's octogenarians and born-again Jews would spend the Sabbath alone eating canned gefilte fish and Meal Mart cholent. Unschooled in the Jewish texts, my mother relies on her ground chicken meatballs and kreplach to educate her flock in the ways of Yiddishkeyt, Yiddish for "Jewish tradition, culture, character, and religion." Only occasionally does she mention that, for her, being a Jew once meant hearing the screams of her father and two sisters as the Gestapo machine-gunned them to death.

Here is what one of our conversations sounds like:

ME: Do you ever wonder why God spared you and not your father and sisters? [Her mother died before the war.]

MOTHER: I think I was spared for a purpose.

ME: What purpose?

MOTHER: To help my two older brothers. In my life I was meant to take care of them.

ME: Why would God want to spare them?

MOTHER: (*Matter of factly*) I think somebody interceded on their behalf.

ME: Like your mother or father?

MOTHER: Or some other ancestor. Maybe one of my ancestors was a saint, and God rewarded him, or her, with a favor.

ME: Your own life wasn't worthy of being spared?

MOTHER: I think of myself as an agent.

ME: Of God?

MOTHER: Of my ancestors.

ME: Are you ever angry at God?

MOTHER: For what?

ME: For not stepping in and protecting your family.

MOTHER: (*Lightly*) I have a discussion with God.

ME: An angry discussion?

MOTHER: Just a talk, like the talk we're having now.

ME: What do you say to Him?

MOTHER: What I have always said: "Please, God, don't let anybody kill me. Let me spend the rest of my life in a cold barn, but let me live!"

Thus, my mother too refrains from rebuking God for His apparent malevolence. Wasn't it for her that Keats wrote, "What am I that should so be saved from death?"

More than once, I have wondered why my parents, who lost family and country, should be fervent in their faith while I, who have not seen war, famine, or persecution, am tentative. As a child, I believed that God, like Santa Claus, knew "if you've been bad or good," and would reward my parents with long, happy lives. Moreover, I thought that all the Jewish deaths in the 1930s and 1940s would serve as a moral escrow account from

which several post-Holocaust generations could borrow. Through my asso-
ciation with my mother and father, I would be rewarded with a long, happy
life too. This line of reasoning served me well until, one night at Hebrew
School, it occurred to me that God neither thwarts man-made evils such as
Nazis nor natural disasters such as earthquakes and floods. To my chagrin,
I realized that God had taken a decidedly un-Santalike approach to a
Holocaust survivor-friend of my parents. Instead of granting *her* long life,
He watched as she stuck her head in an oven and killed herself. If God was
really good and all-powerful, as the Hebrew prayerbook posited, He would
not let evil gain the upper hand time and time again. Adolescence rarely
being the province of subtle thought, I concluded that God could not
possibly exist.

Children of the Holocaust survivors have the dubious option of turning
the Holocaust into a TOE, a theory of everything. As the surrogate for
God, the Holocaust becomes a shadowy but pervasive force that coordi-
nates one's place of birth, family relations, capacity for emotional maturity,
choice of mate, and general outlook on life. I, for one, have seen the
Holocaust as a First Cause from which everything bad in my life flows.
Elevating the Holocaust in this way has been largely damaging. For one, it
does not account for the existence of goodness in life, without which children would grow up to be sadists and killers. For another, it paints the
world in such bleak colors that meaning and joy move into the realm of the
unattainable. A TOE that offers a reasonable but depressing calculus of life
is like the successful operation that kills the patient. In the short run, it may
provide a theoretical guide, but ultimately some psychic complication makes
the hypothesis harmful to body and soul.

As with all lives, mine began before I was born. My parents emigrated
to the United States in 1950 from Bindermichel, a displaced persons camp
in Linz, Austria. They lived in the Williamsburg section of Brooklyn with
my older sister and brother for several months and then moved to Camden
County, New Jersey. My father had bought twenty-three acres of farmland
sight unseen after reading in the Jewish *Forvertz* that other Jews had
made a living as chicken farmers in Jersey towns such as Vineland and
Lakewood. He and my mother planned to stay on the farm for a few years
and then come back to New York. My birth, and my younger sister's,
might have put a strain on my parents' finances, but it did not have to
keep Rivka and Jake on the farm until 1983. As I see it, virtually all
decisions in my family fell victim to economic necessity, happenstance, and
shortsightedness.

Living in rural south Jersey may have had several detractions—isolation from other Jews, to name the most obvious—but, according to my parents, it had one overriding selling point: My parents could observe the Sabbath. In Brooklyn they had worked seven days a week flipping burgers in a luncheonette. They believed that running a farm would let them rest on the seventh day as they had in Poland before World War II. The speciousness of this argument did not hit me until recently when I realized that, as owners of the luncheonette in a Jewish neighborhood, my parents also had the option of observing the Sabbath in New York among fellow Jews. Besides, chickens must eat seven days a week, and they are not dextrous enough to feed themselves. My parents' reason for leaving Brooklyn strikes me as irrational, and like their thirty-three-yearlong stay on the farm, the result of financial pressures and poor judgment. Perhaps their self-imposed exile from any Jewish community was a lot less logical, maybe more tragic, than they themselves have ever understood.

A road trip I took in the mid-1980s from Virginia to New York confirmed what I sensed as a kid in the late 1960s: Camden County is the northernmost outpost of the American South. Many of our neighbors, black and white, were originally from Virginia and the Carolinas. The rest of the local population consisted of Italian fruit farmers and Protestants with jobs as truck drivers, landscapers, and shipyard workers. The big events in my town included the crowning of the Memorial Day Poppy Queen, spaghetti dinners at the fire hall, and the Annual Citizenship Award by the American Legion. My parents viewed even these mundane activities as Christian and pronounced them off-limits. My forbidden entry into this world of community get-togethers puts me in mind of the Eddie Murphy routine in which Murphy, masquerading as a white man, gets on a bus full of white people and discovers that whites are one big happy family, eager to offer one another friendship and moral support. To me, the gentile world felt like Eddie Murphy's bus, a magical place from which I was excluded.

Our segregation from the Christian mainstream made Gentiles exotic, even when they were clearly *uncivilized*. According to my parents, goyim ate meatballs out of a can, wasted their time at the local dragstrip, and threw money away on excesses such as movies and vacations. Unlike my thrifty parents, who saved every penny for their children's college education, wastrel Gentiles blew money on bicycles, Barbie dolls, sports equipment, and all sorts of other entertainments that my parents derided as *Narishkeyt*, Yiddish for "nonsense." Being Jewish was a no-frills way of life that, if suffered with good cheer, promised a sensational payoff someday. It was also the moral ground. According to my parents, Gentiles might look like fine people, but besides hobbies such as fishing, they killed Jews. Nothing personal, but Christians took in bloodlust with their mother's milk. My mother reminded us about her Polish best friend, who stood on the street cheering as the Gestapo rounded up the Jews.

My parents hoped that an unflattering characterization of Gentiles would frighten me into preferring the Jewish world, a perplexing goal in my circumstances as I hardly knew any Jews. Their animus succeeded only in glamorizing the enemy. I would have sold my birthright—whatever that might have been—for a spaghetti dinner at the fire hall.

My parents attempted to undo the Christian influences in our lives by sending us to Hebrew School. The tactic backfired. As radio commentator Dennis Prager observed recently, "It is much easier to be the liberalizing and universalizing influence on a religious child than to be the religious influence on a secular child." To wit, I went to Hebrew School kicking and screaming all the way.

In social terms, the kids at Hebrew School were my superiors. They lived in affluent suburbs, had fathers with professional or white-collar jobs, and belonged to Conservative youth groups. (The Orthodox school in Camden, ten miles farther west, made four round-trips a week unrealistic for people trying to run a chicken business.) To enter this world of Jewish youth groups and mall-bought clothing, I took the Atlantic City–Philadelphia Cities Service bus to Haddon Heights, a trip I shared with south Jersey hairdressers, sewing machine operators, janitors, and hookers. Any one of them might have given me enlightening advice about the world outside the farm if I hadn't been so scared of talking to them. By the time I sat listening to stern old Mrs. Levin conjugate Hebrew verbs, I was too done in by a kind of psychic dysautonomia to learn anything.

Like most twelve-year-olds, I wanted to look, act, dress, live, and think like my friends. With my Christian peers, I did. They were part of my everyday life. They lived in rural towns like mine and went to my public school. They invited me to their homes during (Christian) holidays. They were my high school thespian pals and tennis partners. It's no wonder that the Hebrew School kids saw me as an outsider. To their mind, *I* was a foreigner like my parents, *too Jewish* to travel to a Conservative synagogue on Saturdays, *too Jewish* to eat the nonkosher food in their homes. Sadly, the circumstances of my family life prevented me from belonging in either camp. The occasional anti-Semitic insult from a Christian was upsetting, but it wasn't nearly as alienating to me as the baffled expressions I encountered in the faces at Hebrew School.

My parents themselves appeared to have little in common with any of the Jews we knew. The few in our town, all of them chicken farmers, were secular and participated in the town's life. The parents of my Hebrew School classmates were Americans, financially successful but, as my parents saw it, spiritually impoverished. My mother and father must have felt very alone in the American-Jewish world of Portnoys and Catskill bungalow colonies. Their loneliness accounts for the spontaneous, heartfelt conversations they used to have with observant Jews they met on the Boardwalk in Atlantic City, where we spent several Rosh Hashanas and Yom Kippurs. I still remember one elderly Jew, a man dressed in a tweed suit and white Hush Puppies, saying, with a sigh, "*Avec a velt!*" (Vanished—a world). He didn't even need a full sentence to express the vastness of his loss, and my parents'. My mother and father understood these Jews—total strangers—in an instant. All the others were just hollow Americans.

In the late 1960s, synagogues and Jewish community centers rarely organized Holocaust memorials. At Hebrew School and at the after-school Midrasha I attended in my junior year of high school, I thought I was the only descendant of Holocaust survivors. This misconception grew legs in the light of an incident that happened one afternoon at Hebrew School. A girl named Esther drew a swastika on the synagogue wall and joked that she, a Nazi, was desecrating a Jewish place of worship. You could have blown me over. I was so shocked by her—vulgarity? Sophistication? Self-hatred? When I came to New York after college, I met other Jews, especially children of Holocaust survivors, who might have seen Esther's swastika as an example of Jewish gallows humor. In fact, a son of survivors I knew told me that whenever he wanted to get his brother out of the bathroom, he would shout, like a Nazi, "*Juden, raus!*" I suppose my shyness and discomfort among Jews made me look pretty alien to the kids at Hebrew School. I was just *disconnected*.

It didn't help that whenever I misbehaved—a common response to my frustrating circumstances—my parents threatened to send me to Stern College, the women's division of Yeshiva University, in New York. I thought that meant living with truly pious girls, dressing in Amish-style frocks, and speaking in whispers. This picture corresponded more exactly to the personality of a Christian girl I knew whose parents were Rhodesian missionaries. Despite the kosher food I ate and the Hebrew prayers I recited at home on Saturdays, I was obdurately secular, and I quailed at the thought of living with religious Jews 'round the clock. The truth is, I was almost as ignorant about Judaism as my Christian friends who occasionally asked me if I liked being Jewish. I didn't, but I had too much pride to say so. One of my best moments as a kid came on a Sunday in 1966, when my Hebrew School teacher pointed to me, the blue-eyed, blonde-haired daughter of Polish Jews, and said I was an excellent example of the Aryan type. I went home and told my father. He was aghast. I felt honored.

By the end of my second week at Douglass College, I stopped observing the Sabbath. Holding a pencil on Saturday made me nearly as delirious as sneaking off to the movies with a gentile boy, which I did in my last days of high school. Toward the end of freshman year, I ate my first nonkosher food, an Oscar Meyer wiener that a Lutheran girl in my dorm dared me to eat. Every artifact of my parents' shtetl Judaism soon cracked under the tender pressure of secular Christian college life. I was not the only daughter of Orthodox parents who succumbed to some variety of religious truancy. One Orthodox girl I knew at the university Hillel, the kosher dining hall, averred that no woman should consider getting married until she had slept with at least twenty men. After achieving her quota, she got married and moved to one of Israel's religious West Bank towns.

As I see it now, the main impetus for my disaffection from Judaism was not public school, college, or Christmas with my Christian friends. It was my fractious relationship with my parents. My life with them was a battle royal. As ambitious Jewish kids in Poland, my parents had expected to better their circumstances, and probably would have but for the war. In America, they could not understand why their children weren't happy all the time and dedicated to making a million bucks. My parents wanted me to be a *voil*, modest, Jewish daughter who, while raising a family and practicing law, might also run for a seat in Congress. Yet, nothing in my life on the farm prepared me for this caste, and I felt like a cripple for not coming within spitting distance of it. Rivka and Jake knew how to survive, but they did not know how to live. Their Holocaust and their orthodoxy had brought us to a New Jersey backwater, and had set me at odds with Jewish and Christian society. I wasn't about to look for guidance in *their* Torah.

A great revelation hit me in July 1975. I had just graduated from college with a B.A. in literature. In my desperation to avoid the farm, I took a job with the Oppenheimer Management Corporation, a mutual funds company, as a typist. On my first day at work, I sat at a black IBM typewriter with a Dictaphone headset in my ears, transcribing letters to disgruntled holders of mutual fund portfolios. I was in a state of stupefaction. How had I gone from being the member of a chosen people to being a back-office secretary? In my misery, I sought an immediate explanation and, like my parents, found it in an easy-to-spot enemy. My foe was the capitalist system. It could not see past my youth, sex, or inexperience to the wondrous potential inside me. On Wall Street, I was nothing more than a pair of hands, paid just enough money to keep me from starvation. My crowning humiliation came when Oppenheimer's president asked me to bring him a pitcher of water. How could he? Couldn't he tell what stuff I was made of? In my ignorance of the workaday world, I did not see that this man had taken an interest in a green, unsophisticated twenty-one-year-old. If he was exploiting my labor, he was also watching to see how I responded to taking direction. By five o'clock that day, I believed that the Oppenheimer Management Corporation had done me a grievous wrong. I do not exaggerate when I say that I arrived at Wall Street the atheist daughter of Orthodox Jews and went home on the subway a damn socialist.

My nature tended to seek a simple, unifying explanation of the world. Now I had a new religion that satisfied all my questions and tied the answers up into a neat bundle:

Q: Why was I so miserable sitting at a desk for eight hours a day with a Dictaphone in my ears?

A: I was suffering under the yoke of capitalism, whose industry captains were buying my labor for $135 a week.

SUBTEXT: Capitalism, not my lack of vocational preparation, was the reason for my lousy job.

Q: Why had I always felt like a misfit among Jews?

A: I was the victim of class differences. What could a girl from a chicken farm possibly have in common with girls whose fathers were doctors, lawyers, and accountants?

SUBTEXT: All misfortune was rooted in external economic reality, not in personal character.

Q: Why did I have no lasting friendships with the girls from public school?

A: Because of their petty bourgeois prejudices, *my parents* had thwarted the natural solidarity that could have arisen between my Christian friends and me.

SUBTEXT: My parents knew nothing about human nature, which was fundamentally good if unimpeded by religious and class bigotry.

Q: Why did the Holocaust happen?

A: It was in the Fascists' interest to disunite the international working class. The Fascists appealed to the admittedly base nature of some human beings and told them that the international Jewish conspiracy was their true enemy.

SUBTEXT: Economic greed, not aggression, disfigured human relations.

In short, my socialism blamed systems and family for the bent of my personality. Like a child, I saw corporate presidents and parents as two-dimensional monoliths, hell-bent on maintaining their power through cruelly arbitrary institutions. Looking beyond the facade of my anger for some historical or psychological interpretation of life would have demanded my compassion—for my parents and for myself. I was not capable of that. Shaped by my parents' black-and-white view of life, I thought of my socialism as all good and my parents' orthodoxy as all bad. For the next two years, Judaism struck me as bleak, dead-end, negative. My own ideology expressed my faith in the corrigible side of humankind. If taught the tenets of socialism, every person had the potential to become good. Why shouldn't I have believed that? I saw what sort of life Torah, faith in God, and religious sequestration had brought me. My parents' Judaism bore no trace of buoyancy. I wasn't about to carry their mistakes into my generation.

In the late 1970s, I discovered another way of distancing myself from my parents and their Judaism. I moved to the Virgin Islands with my boyfriend, a scraggly haired Jewish socialist whose contempt for "money-grubbing rabbis" summed up his family's attitude toward the religion. Naturally, my parents couldn't stand him. But if he was my *besherter*, my destined love, they wouldn't stand in my way. All I had to do was marry the guy. The reasons why this fellow and I stayed together for six years could probably fill the rest of this essay, but suffice it to say, they had little to do with destined love. With his marxist cant, he was a suitable foil to my parents' dogmatism. He may have been my partner in my war against life-as-it-was, but he was not the love of my life. I refused to marry him. After we flew off to the Virgin Islands, my parents stopped talking to me.

Cut loose from my Jewish moorings, I became, paradoxically, sentimental and hostile toward Judaism. In the middle of the Caribbean, I read fiction by Isaac Bashevis Singer and got teary-eyed over Yiddish folk melodies sung by Natania Davrath, an opera soprano. At the same time, I looked to a slew of leftist periodicals, including *Mother Jones, In These Times*, and the *Guardian*, a New York-based marxist newspaper printed in hysterical orange and black ink, to hammer out a political perspective of life. Fueled additionally by C. Wright Mills's *The Power Elite*, I would get into a lather about the exploits of multinational corporations, and I attributed the financial policies of the American ruling class to the "underdevelopment" of the third world. About the Holocaust, and especially about Israel, I would read nary a word. As a testament to the self-serving, self-preserving circuitry of the human brain, those subjects bored me to death. They were my parents' preoccupations, not mine.

One night in St. Thomas, my boyfriend and I went to the movie theater and saw an all-star, made-for-TV movie called *Victory at Entebbe*. In the movie, the German Red Brigades hijack an Air France jet bound for Israel and isolate the Jewish passengers. Yakov, played by Theodore Bikel, fears for his life and hides his Jewish identity. At some point, possibly after Col. Yonatan Netanyahu leads the Israeli commando raid on the Entebbe airport, Yakov breaks down. He quotes from Psalm 137, King David's poem about the Babylonian exile: "If I forget thee, O Jerusalem, let my right hand forget her cunning./If I do not remember thee, let my tongue cleave to the roof of my mouth; if I prefer not Jerusalem above my chief joy." After hearing these lines, I was a wreck. I cannot attest to the quality of *Victory at Entebbe*, but I left that movie in tears. Yakov's shame struck at the heart of my tormented identity.

Soon after this, when Rosh Hashana and Yom Kippur rolled around, I had a hard time muting my petit bourgeois religious yearnings. I visited the St. Thomas synagogue, a picturesque landmark with a sand floor and an elaborate chandelier. Its raison d'être appeared to be cadging money from tourists to fix the ceiling. My secularism notwithstanding, I was a purist at heart—aren't all fundamentalists?—and the reform service, complete with organ music and English liturgy, made my stomach lurch. I may have strayed from the rabbinic teachings, but I expected them to remain intact until the time when I might need them again. In any case, that wasn't to be any time soon.

Every religion requires a church. My church became Liberation News Service, a left-of-center news collective I joined when I returned to New York. The writers there were all seasoned habitués of the anti-Vietnam War movement, and had grown up in middle- and upper-middle-class homes much like the kids from Hebrew School. Ironically, the only socialist I had ever known was my boyfriend. After a couple of weeks as an "LNSer," I quickly discovered that I was as untutored in leftist culture as I had been about the Jewish world. At LNS, I was met by a cabal that spoke a language I barely knew. "Homophobia" and "white skin privilege" spiced up the LNSers' speech like croutons in a salad. These graduates of Swarthmore and Harvard championed the presumed victims of capitalist and imperialist oppression, including blacks, Puerto Rican nationalists, Sandanistas, Eritreans, secular Iranians, gay people, women, the mentally ill, workers, the Teamsters for a Democratic Union, and the "third world" prisoners at the Green Haven Correctional Facility, whom the LNSers referred to as "the brothers." Several women in the news collective criticized me for doing too much research for each article; excessive intellectualism in a woman made her "male-identified" (a bad thing). To my mind, however, I was years behind these "movement activists," and if I spent nights and weekends reading about the class struggle, well, I was only playing catch-up.

During my twenty-two-month stint as a political writer, Jews and half Jews made up 50 percent of LNS. They could be relied on to pen the occasional vitriolic article about Zionist abuse of Palestinians. As my beat was the environment and Central America (two issues about which I, the girl from a south Jersey chicken farm, knew zip), I was spared the challenge of vilifying Israel. I had less hesitation, though, about taking up with a new boyfriend, the Irish-American son of a Fortune 500 CEO, whose main extracurricular activity was an entity called the Palestine Solidarity Committee. He said that Israel was as guilty of apartheid as South Africa, and that one of its biggest crimes was stealing "Arab" water for use in Israeli factories and swimming pools. As a Trotskyist, he was convinced that the permanent revolution was just around the corner, and he even managed to write about Khomeini as a latter-day Lenin, leading the masses in a crusade against the morally bankrupt capitalist West. He had punk tendencies and kept a poster of a crematorium over his bed.

Two gay women, one white, one black, were predictably platitudinous on gay issues, but they couldn't swallow the LNS line on Israel. They found the group's anti-Zionist rhetoric offensive. They knew my parents were Holocaust survivors—a category that one of the half Jews wrote off as an exaggeration—and told me that LNS's anti-Israel screeds were not merely anti-Zionist, they were anti-Jewish. Turns out that my former boyfriend, the Virgin Islands socialist, had contributed an article subtitled "Zionist Oppression of Palestinians" from his new digs in San Francisco. I think the two gay women looked to me, the daughter of survivors, for some moral compass. Thoroughly mystified as to where my loyalty lay, I said that the article was in keeping with LNS's policy of defending the oppressed, whoever they may be. For many years I thought the women disapproved of my heterosexuality, but in recalling this incident, I wonder now if they didn't see me as a coward. As I kept reminding myself, Israel was not my beat. It was my parents'. I had telephoned them several times, and they still refused to talk to me. Damned if I was going to speak out on their behalf.

In the end, LNS's narrow view of journalism wore me down. We writers could write about racism, black nationalism, gay rights, labor strikes, third world women, affirmative action, and occasionally the antinuclear movement, but subjects unamenable to leftist dogma were verboten. These included the Kool Aid massacre in Guyana, the Chinese invasion of Vietnam, the Soviet Union and the Eastern Bloc countries, the Mafia, Idi Amin, Entebbe, Legionnaire's Disease, Elvis Presley, Son of Sam, Russian Jews, and Ireland, which was nothing more than a bunch of white people killing one another. Personnel tensions escalated when two members left to join a Maoist group and my boyfriend, more and more enamored of Leon Trotsky, joined the Socialist Workers Party. The blacks resented the whites for not feeling black pain, the lesbians said straight women were male-identified homophobes, and one poor heterosexual chap, a virgin, felt that I, the only straight woman, should do the politically correct thing and make him a man (I declined the job). By 1980, when I was ready to defect, LNS was on its deathbed. In its postmortem, the group concluded that LNS began falling apart when the Vietnam War ended, but I think it hoisted itself on its own petard.

After I ditched my Trot boyfriend and made a mental jailbreak from my marxist prison, I wrote a letter in semiliterate Yiddish to my parents asking if I could interview them about their wartime experiences. Ever since my days in the Virgin Islands, when I was reading Bashevis Singer and getting moony over Netania Davrath, I wanted to write a book about the effects of the war on my family. Three years after issuing their decree of excommunication, my parents relented. I used to think that my rapprochement with my parents and my departure from Liberation News Service were coincidental events. I suspect, though, that with my disaffection from "the world of the brothers," I was ready to reenter "the world of my fathers."

Despite my prodigal return, I was still without a philosophy to guide me in my thoughts and behavior. Nature abhorring a vacuum, hedonism rushed in to fill the breach. I spent the next two years in a whirl of sybaritic activity that would have made the Hellenists blush. I applied all the passion of my previous political quest to my latest religion, whose sole purpose was anesthetic. Fun, my anodyne, prevented me from facing the pain of my parents' grief, their decades-long depression, and the losses that hung over our family at every meal, every holiday, every Sabbath. [As Keats wrote, "[T]he sharp anguish of my shriek/Stung my own ears—I strove hard to escape/The numbness." Or, to paraphrase General MacArthur, fun was hell.

Writing *Summer Long-a-coming*, a novel about the ripple effects of the Holocaust on a family like mine, had some therapeutic benefits for me. First, it taught me that to accomplish anything good, I had to sit still and focus my ideas. Second, it let me look over my shoulder at a subject that was too complicated and too painful to approach head-on. Third, it helped me see that the Holocaust, whatever else it was, was also a mindless cataclysm that did not necessarily have anything against me and my family personally. We were just little people that got in its way.

We leap over a decade to 1996. I live with my eight-year-old son in a Jewish section of New York City. I am not the weirdo I perceived myself to be in Hebrew School, or in public school, for that matter. Time and an anthropological bent of mind make it possible for me to see everybody as a bit of a misfit.

Still, my odyssey surely sets me apart from most of my neighborhood friends and acquaintances. I have passed through a range of ideologies and experiences to arrive at a destination they never seriously questioned; many of them went to yeshiva and spent time in Israel. I got married late and divorced early; nearly everyone I know is married to men they met in their twenties. I feel nervous and emotional in *shul;* they build their social life around *shul* activities. Yet, by this point in my life, I would find a wholly secular existence thin. It's the radical insufficiency of culture and community that turns my head toward the unseen and the unknowable. ("I always seek in what I see the likeness of something beyond the present and intangible object," said Shelley.) A life without faith would place a heavy burden on activities such as writing and work, which would necessarily become my main sources of meaning. And, perhaps most devastating of all, it would separate me further from my family.

In preparing to write this essay, I dug up a notebook I kept in the mid-1980s while I wrote *Summer Long-a-coming*. During that time, I attended a lecture series on Job given by Shlomo Riskin when he was the rabbi of Manhattan's Lincoln Square Synagogue. My notebook is full of his pithy comments, the most resonant among them being "The Torah says that wrongs are righted in historical time." If I had to cite one Jewish belief that frames all my questions about God, it would be this one. This axiom works only if I suppress a longing for balance in my life. But doing so would force me to assume a Panglossian—even a Joblike—belief that everything is as it should be in this not-so-perfect world. I can accept this way of thinking as it applies to my petty grudges, and I'll-show-'em state of mind in which I occasionally indulge. It does not stand up, however, against the colossal barbarisms, perpetrated in the name of one ideology or another, that disfigure human lives for generations. What exactly is historical time? Can we see signs of retribution within a span of fifty years? A thousand? Is retribution a desirable outcome? If it is, then Rabbi Riskin's statement may boil down to "What goes around, comes around." Like Voltaire's warring Bulgars and Avars, then, nations and peoples can expect to take turns killing, raping, torturing, maiming, and exiling one another. As Peggy Lee in a song once asked, "Is that all there is?"

Recently, I came across this gruesome description of Auschwitz in *Man's Search for Meaning* by Viktor E. Frankl, a psychiatrist and concentration camp survivor:

> "[A] twelve-year-old boy was carried in who had been forced to stand at attention for hours in the snow or to work outside with bare feet because there were no shoes for him in the [concentration] camp. His toes had become frostbitten, and the doctor on duty picked off the black gangrenous stumps with tweezers, one by one."

What if this twelve-year-old boy were my son? Would the rabbinic tenet that "wrongs will be righted in historical time" give me comfort during my seventy or eighty years on earth?

In Isaiah 51, Isaiah says that if the people harken to God's law, "the redeemed of the Lord shall return, and come with singing unto Zion." I'm sorry to say that exile, not redemption and return, appears to be the psychological emblem of my life. I feel closer to exile, not because I prefer it to glad tidings, or because I intentionally set out in childhood to flout the divine commandments, but because I came of age in a time and place devoid of community and sanctuary. It strikes me as miscreant of God to stack the deck against His people and then blame them for not measuring up to His standards. I'm reminded of the scene in *The Wizard of Oz* when Dorothy castigates the unseen wizard with, "You ought to be ashamed of yourself, frightening [Lion] when he came to you for help!" In the end, the main characters in Oz come to see that courage, heart, and intelligence lie within each one of us, and faith in the inherent goodness of life is our only hope for finding an authentic self. We keep coming back to God—to an ideal goodness—because, as my father says, we have no one else to turn to.

Which brings me back full circle to the conversations I have had with my father and mother. First, I can no longer blame my parents for imposing a crude facsimile of Orthodox Judaism on their children. They cannot be held responsible for making an irrational decision in a world of no fathers and mothers, a world that amounted to an ideological scrap of faith they were too uneducated to practice compassionately. ("How shall we sing the Lord's song in a strange land?") The Judaism they passed down to me had no social context; thanks to the Holocaust, the Judaism their parents passed down to them had no social context either. Maybe that's why my parents stayed on the farm for thirty-three years. *There was no familiar Jewish world to move back to.* The miracle is that, in choosing to live, work, and have faith, they have risen above their sufferings, which is the best each one of us can do.

Second, seeking an explanation for the Holocaust, and for the evil in the world, is a no-win proposition. I think this very quest sent me in every scattered direction, toward simplistic renderings of socialism and hedonism, neither of which brought me a moment's peace or illumination. The Holocaust falls under the category of *mysterium iniquitatis.* It is a crime beyond comprehension because it cannot be ascribed to biological, psychological, or sociological causes. Having faith in God, before Auschwitz and after, has little to do with the burdens history forces us to bear in our short lifetimes. Perhaps it is essential, as my father says, to have faith because our forebears did. I have to conclude that any person who has suffered this planet's worst indignities and who still believes in a divine plan is an extraordinary human being, and at the very least deserves our humble respect.

In my trek through rural Judaism, socialism, and hedonism, I have been forced to question who I am, what I believe, and what my purpose is. I have decided that for one person it does pay to cook. Goodness is not always apparent in our lives, but if it didn't exist, life would be unbearable. Loving goodness may be an obvious goal for a lot of people, but its preciousness lay hidden from me for a long time. Without goodness, and without the love that refines it, life *is* a cold barn. And while a cold barn will serve as a temporary refuge, it is no place to live a happy and meaningful life.

The Path to Kaddish

Prologue to a Son's Spiritual Autobiography

EUGENE L. POGANY

I continually return to sadness. From ignorance and unawareness, from emptiness and longing, from outrage and defiance, I come back to what has become a ripened sadness. It was once a sullen and groping sensitivity, a self-possessed but hollow rumination. There is as much clarity to it now as the still pool of unwept tears will allow. And there is strength and dignity, for it is no longer bent over onto itself; it is turned outward toward the world and it embraces it. It has always been there. I have spent my life fortifying myself against it, living in spite of it, suffering because of it, or stilling my awareness in an effort to see through it, or look beyond it. I wear my father's pain in the creased recesses of my eyes and my mother's losses in the cracking of my voice when I speak of them At times I try to hide it in my placid demeanor or transform it with whatever kindness and compassion I can conduct my affairs with people. I continually hide from it or digress from it. I have lately discovered a return to it. I stand closer to its forbidding sources, am coming to know its tributaries, and learning its black, gray, and white hues and its coarse, torn, and sometimes soothing textures. I fear it less; it is less toxic to me. And only lately am I finding words for it, to express it, to share it and to heal it—in my heart, and in our family's collective heart and soul.

A Jew by Birth and a Jew by Choice

I have come to believe that events and decisions in my parents' lives have made me a Jew not only by birth but also by fateful choice. I might not have been a Jew, or as much of a Jew, had it not been for my family's

172

persecution during the Holocaust and the transformative decisions that emerged from it.

My father, Nicholas, was born Jewish and was converted as a child to Catholicism. Like many Jews in his native Hungary toward the end of World War I, his family sought to avoid the shifting political, social, and economic forces that would severely limit their livelihoods. Ultimately those forces would crush the lives of many Jews in anti-Semitic violence in that nation after the First World War.

Although my father himself had been a practicing Catholic for most of his life, he always knew he was born a Jew; most of his relatives outside the immediate family continued to be Jewish, even if highly assimilated. During the Second World War, while he was conscripted into the Hungarian Labor Battalions, my father was in a special unit of "baptized Jews," who were forced to publicly display white, instead of yellow, stars of David to differentiate them from other Jews and from the gentile population. But for the Jewish battalionists who died brutal deaths in the Ukraine or Serbia, their duties were often not readily distinguishable from other Hungarian battalions. Those duties consisted of construction, road work, and sanitation details, both in the city and countryside. In reference to this time, my father has often referred to Aesop's tale of the bat who was neither beast nor bird as capturing his feelings about himself.

As successive stages of anti-Jewish legislation were putting an increasingly tighter stranglehold on the Jewish population, including assimilated and baptized Jews, even before the Hungarian deportations began in the spring of 1944, my father was coming to question his nearly lifelong identity as a Christian and felt more and more at one with his Jewish relatives and colleagues. Perhaps more than anything, he was astonished and disheartened by Christians who stood idly by and gave at least their tacit consent, if not their active complicity, to the imminent domestic slaughter and eventual deportation of almost all of Hungary's eight hundred thousand Jews.

Toward the end of 1944, like a number of other Jews and baptized Jews, my father received what ultimately amounted to a worthless letter of protection from the Hungarian Papal Nuncio, Angelo Rotta. Fearing that it would be used to identify him as a deserter from the labor battalion, my father anxiously and impulsively crumpled the wallet-size document, stuffed it in his mouth to crush it further, and swallowed it: *This is the body and blood of Christ* . . . The final sacrament, as it were, of his failed church must have weighed heavily on his tongue and palate sinking to his gut like a stone. It would be the only help he would receive from his Christian brethren. Might it have been at that moment that the spirit and hope of my father's heretofore Savior disappeared forever from his life?

My father's return to Judaism culminated in Bergen-Belsen. There he was deeply moved by Jewish fellow inmates observing Passover seder with matzahlike crackers supplied by the Swedish Red Cross. At that moment, with quiet grace and dignity, my father bore witness to the redeeming God of the Jews and transformed the destiny of the family he would one day create.

Ultimately, his love for my mother, who herself barely survived Bergen-Belsen and Theresienstadt, slave labor in a Dresden aircraft factory, and tuberculosis, and their mutual determination to raise Jewish children in the aftermath of their suffering, led my father shortly after the war to return to the religion of his birth. He was de facto excommunicated from the Mother Church when he reentered the synagogue and reembraced the Jews' covenant with the G-d of the Holocaust: *Blessed art Thou, Lord our G-d, King of the universe, who rejoices at His children's return to Zion.*

My father's father was a well-loved country veterinarian, who, as a practicing Catholic, died a relatively peaceful and timely death in 1943, a year before his own certain deportation. However, even escaping that fate, he did not find his final rest as a Catholic. Upon burial, his body was disinterred by a local Fascist official who did not want his wife buried next to someone with a Jewish past; he was reburied at the rear of the cemetery. In response, my father sent an angry letter to the Catholic primate of Hungary to protest the desecration of his father's grave. The letter was referred to the family's local diocese, where action was never taken.

My father's mother was a woman who, perhaps even more than her husband, was a believing and devout—albeit converted—Catholic, until she was deported and killed at Auschwitz. For the few weeks of her internment in the middle of May 1944, in the makeshift Jewish ghetto in her town of Szarvas, my grandmother was escorted regularly by Hungarian gendarmes to attend daily mass at her local church on the town's main street. By early June, she and the town's six hundred to seven hundred Jews were loaded onto farm carts, taken to the train station, and deported. Most of them would perish in Auschwitz. Hungary's obeisance to Hitler and its passionate hatred of Jews superseded their Lord's compassion to all God's children, Christian or not. From the country of her birth, clutching the crucifix of her Savior, my grandmother was spewed forth as a Jew, for her Lord's love was trampled under foot by the Magyar gendarmes who claimed to march in his name, or desecrated by her Christian neighbors who impassively looked on.

As these events were transpiring, my father's twin brother, George, had already been ordained in Vienna to the priesthood. Immediately before the war, my uncle traveled to Italy to receive medical treatment for kidney stones. The outbreak of the war prevented his return to conceivably the same fate my father and other family members suffered. George went from Rome to San Giovanni Rotondo, where for the next seventeen years he offered communion and the sacraments of the church to the sick in the local community, served mass, and worked as a correspondence secretary to the Capuchin friar Father Francesco Forgione Pio da Pietrelcina, known as Padre Pio, the stigmatic healer and miracle worker who received supplicants from all over the world.

Upon hearing of my father's reconversion after the war, my uncle was deeply pained at what he considered his brother's betrayal of the faith in which they had been lovingly raised. He came to the Unite States in 1956, several years after my parents settled there, having promised not to confuse his brother's three children by discussing religion with them. Until his death in 1993, he lived in the United States and served as parish priest and, eventually, papal prelate in the archdiocese of Newark, New Jersey. My father and uncle lived parallel lives in proximity to each other. But they never again discussed the deeply embedded spiritual rift between them. (These dramatic circumstances are discussed elsewhere in greater detail.)

Indeed, for many years, my father spoke only obliquely and abstractly about his life during the war, being careful not to betray too much of his raw grief. My mother's experiences have always been more accessible, sometimes painfully so. There are times when she can not stop talking about the Holocaust. Being a twenty-one-year-old newlywed in 1944—having spent her wedding night in a bomb shelter in Budapest during Allied bombing— she was deported later that year from the Budapest ghetto.

Many times, she has spoken of Budapest under the Fascists before deportation and life in the camps afterward. During one instance she continually relates, immediately before deportation in early December, in an apartment building near Budapest's train station, she was detained by a young Arrow Cross (Fascist) enlistee whose task it was to guard her group of detainees. From a room full of imminent deportees, he chose my mother to go shopping for groceries for the rest of the group. When she returned, he told her at the entrance to the building to flee because he knew she would be deported with the others. She knew this as well. A teenager, he pleaded with her not to go back in the building. He told her that Arrow Cross recruiters had come to his village in the countryside, promising him a fancy uniform, a rifle, and all sorts of special treatment and recognition. They had not delivered on their promises and neither had they told him what brutalities he would witness or be asked to commit. "I didn't know how terribly these poor people would suffer." He begged her to run away. But she stood there at the entrance to the building in her ragged clothes, with the Star of David sewn to her coat. "Where am I going to go? I have no place to go." Whereupon she walked back into the building.

The next day, my mother was put onto a cattle car and transported in the final, cold weeks of autumn to Bergen-Belsen, arriving about Christmas time. She remained there for several weeks before being transferred to Raguhn in eastern Germany, near Dresden, for forced labor in an airplane factory. Later, at the end of the war, she was taken to Theresienstadt, where she was liberated by the Russian army and was returned—again by cattle car—to Budapest.

From my mother's graphic descriptions, I have envisioned both the cruel and sometimes sympathetic guards, the camp inmates suffering and dying next to her or imploring her to keep a kosher home as a bargain with G-d to stay alive. There have been times when I could nearly taste the watery soup and morsels of bread, felt the blisters on my feet and the lice on my scalp, and gazed innumerable times in my mind's eye at the unrecognizable sixty-pound skeletal figure reflected in the ground floor factory window in Germany. Many times, I have imagined my mother's dead grandmother baking delicious pastries for her in her dreams at Bergen-Belsen and inmates ridiculing her for weeping when she awoke to find that the pastries were not real. Despite my mother's ongoing hunger, I believe that her grandmother came really to teach her of the survival value of tears, for weeping keeps the soul alive. As my mother herself recounted to me, the souls of those who had been in camp for too long and who could no longer weep would wither and die. Her grandmother's survival lesson completed, she came again to my mother years later in a dream, instructing her that her assistance would never again be as urgently needed.

In the House That Ruth Built

After the war, my mother spent almost a year and a half in tubercular sanitariums in Hungary and Slovakia. For three years after that, she and my father lived in Sweden, putting their lives back together with the help of an uncle who had escaped Czechoslovakia before the war. By war's end, my mother had lost her paternal grandfather, as well as numerous uncles, aunts, and cousins who were either killed in various death camps and SS *Aktionen*, or who died of starvation. Her mother had survived horrendous living conditions in the Budapest ghetto and would now accompany her daughter and son-in-law to Sweden. My father's parents were dead and his sister had barely survived brutal treatment in a concentration camp, partly for having attempted to escape. Only their brother was out of harm's way in the Italian monastic community that lovingly gave shelter to this Jewish-born priest. Various other relatives survived either the ghetto or the Serbian camp Bor.

After their three-year sojourn in Sweden, my parents replanted their lives in the urban, mostly Jewish environs in and around Newark, New Jersey. Their experience during the war and my early childhood environment were certainly not unique among Holocaust survivors settling in America's urban Jewish neighborhoods, even while my father's reconversion to Judaism was not typical.

I spent the better part of my childhood and youth energetically and aggressively fitting in to American culture. I pitched no-hitters and hit home runs, worshiped the New York Yankees, rejoicing at their victories and agonizing over their defeats. While other kids have imaginary playmates, I envisioned that the members of the Yankees were my extended family, so great was my need for idealized Americans in my life and so limited and virtually nonexistent was my actual, extended family.

My father proved to be not only a newcomer to the Jewish community but, as a recent immigrant, was unfamiliar with native American ways. At times, he spoke whimsically of his ignorance of baseball and how he nearly failed his U.S. citizenship test because of it. Though Yankee Stadium had become the naturalizing melting pot for many European greenhorn parents, my father, the quintessential newcomer, was never willing to take his kids to the "house that Ruth built." This cultured, well-educated, and somber European refugee never quite believed or accepted that Americans cared more about Babe Ruth and the dynasty he created in the Bronx than about any other—literary or biblical—Ruth, who, as a converted Jew in a foreign culture, may have been my father's spiritual forebear. Instead, he made fun of Americans' uncouth mentality, recited the Hungarian and German poetry of his youth to his children (or perhaps to others who were not present), or maybe he was secretly afraid of the large crowds at Yankee Stadium that might have conjured still recent, unspeakable memories. He saw me pitch in a few Little League games and remembers once overhearing a spectator in the stands comment, as one of my high fastballs hit the batter in the head, "Pogany really wants blood." I thought I did not mind his otherwise seeming indifference, not only to this most important of American rituals, but also to nearly the only way I had of expressing otherwise forbidden aggression, hostility, and defiance. Emotional life within our family was too muffled and restrained to endure and tolerate such displays of emotion. Quietly, away from the baseball field, I was becoming an angry, constricted, and sullen kid, alienated from my father's unfamiliar ways and opaque past. Neither my father nor my mother was aware of my very private, interior life, populated by anonymous victims and persecutors— "Jew" and "Nazis"—and fueled by hostility and outrage, fear, deep attachment, and love, and uncanny, undefinable longing.

Not unlike many children of survivors, I learned from a very young age to stifle and choke my anger and raw emotions because I did not want to inflict undue pain and suffering on my parents. The turmoil typical to various epochs of my life was overshadowed by the enormity of my parents' suffering, even when I was not consciously aware of the content and substance of it. The pain and awkwardness in my coming of age was not to be fully taken seriously by parents who had not entirely succeeded in stepping out from under the shadow of their infinitely more terrible traumas. I think I accurately perceived my parents as emotionally vulnerable, demanding, or needy of their ongoing connection to their children. Partly as a result, the boundaries between my parents' emotions and mine became vague and diffuse. I discovered sadness in myself and did not always know where it came from. And yet, I carried that sadness and remained loyal to it as if it were my own. Even when my parents were unable to speak of their experiences, I sensed their dim outlines and intuitively knew—the way children always seem to know—that it was too painful to ask about. So they didn't tell and I didn't ask. We unspokenly conspired with each other to remain silent: no questions, no answers. Like my brother and sister, and probably like many in our generation, I did not want to inflict any more sorrow or grief onto my parents' lives. In some ways, this gave meaning and purpose to our lives—to protect our parents from suffering—just as they desperately sought to make their children's lives safe and happy. Accordingly, we lived our lives as children, teenagers, and eventually adults, trying to find ways to make up for our mother's and father's obscure, lingering unhappiness.

My parents struggled, did the best they could to rebuild their lives, and tried to deny, or at least not dwell on, their abyss of pain and loss. More than anxiety, or pain, or anger—of each of which there existed plenty—I believe that silence preeminently pervaded our family life, especially the life of my father. That silence and his quiet stoical temperament created distance, confusion, and misunderstanding. For many reasons, my father did not become the strong and admired hero that little kids thrive on to become strong and admirable themselves. Instead, I found my heroes in American culture and a fragile sense of competence in academics and athletics. I remained disconnected from a diminutive immigrant who did not have very sharp elbows to make it in America and whose occasional outbursts of frustration and temper were confusing and bewildering to me and my siblings. I could not imagine the painful life events that may have given rise to the anger and infuriating shame of the sort that all fathers try to keep hidden from their children. I could only begin to think that he was deflated and discouraged by his cultural dislocation and self-conscious of his recent entry into the American and Jewish communities. Not until much later did I discern his sadness, outrage, and longing, and much later still did I realize their source.

I have come to see that part of the tragedy of the Holocaust for my brothers, sisters, and myself is that it represented all the stories and life experiences that were too painful for my parents to be able to share with us as children, or for us to be able to absorb. Shaming experiences and surviving while others have not survived do not make for vitalizing, heroic stories of good guys overcoming bad guys. It was years before their grief and shame had sufficiently subsided and before we were old enough to begin to hear dim, tolerable echoes of their experiences, at least those of my mother. For the longest time, my father spoke only abstractly of survivor's guilt and the treachery of a world that tacitly condoned the murder of so many Jews. It was left to my father's *Lager* mate from Bergen-Belsen to inform me years later in Israel of my father's gentleness, generosity, and humility during his internment. My deep regret is that as a child I could not well distinguish between muffled outrage, quiet humility, and distant melancholy.

Ever since I can remember, my mother has spoken, to those who would listen—if not to her young children—about her internment and the life and death of her family members. She still tells and continually retells her stories. Each time she does so, it is like surviving her experiences anew or recalling and memorializing her love for those who did not survive. Sometimes, when she feels sad or hurt, she will reflexively tell stories of submerged sadness and victimization from the war and the camps. Her stories at times fill the gaps of our visits these days, as if when we run out of things to talk about, she will go back to the ground of her identity: *she is a survivor*—the only child of a father who died before her birth and a mother whose hair turned white within days of her daughter's deportation, and the loving and adored granddaughter, niece, and cousin of all too many men, women, and children who perished. Her talking is reflexive, sad, and seemingly always cathartic. For my mother, it is as if her stories are her prayers of grief and mourning. For, indeed, they help her preserve and sanctify the memory of her loved ones and honor her legacy of suffering as a Jew.

There are times when my mother's talk connects me to her; although, at other times, I feel disconnected. When I was younger, during my adolescence and young adulthood, it was simply too difficult to tune in and remain focused. It was as if I had just heard an entire story but could not remember a single detail. I still have not entirely absorbed all of what my mother has repeated innumerable times. And neither has she exhausted her seemingly endless storehouse of recollections.

In listening and, at times, failing adequately to listen, I have come to realize now as a parent that even the things that are very dear to our hearts rarely fully command the attention of our children for very long—not because they may be insignificant but because they may be frighteningly significant. I believe that my mother's at times driven storytelling and my father's silence convinced me of the need to find gentle ways to ask many questions and to have the answers spoken, repeated, and recorded as permanent records—oral histories—so that children and family members can absorb messages in their own time and at their own pace. For otherwise, I hesitate to think that I would never be adequately able to recount to my children the most important, core memories that impart some degree of meaning to our family's and people's history.

A Jewish Heart and a Searching Soul

Before the war, though my mother was a nonobservant Jew, and my father a good Catholic, when they settled in America and raised their three children, they were quite committed to providing them a Jewish education. Their and our culture's survival was a miracle; our continued survival as Jews became their heartfelt responsibility.

I always felt Jewish in my heart. I loved being Jewish and feeling Jewish: being a Jew was always a defining property of who I was. Even before I learned explicitly of Jewish victimization, I seemed to identify with

Jewish suffering and with the sadness, gentleness, and vulnerability of my parents, which I associated with Jewish qualities. Perhaps despite my father having been Catholic for thirty years, or more precisely, because he was persecuted as a Jew, and ultimately went to great pains to be identified as one, I felt grateful and proud to be Jewish. It felt more than just my birthright; it was an affirming and inspiring legacy forged by the suffering and decisiveness of both my parents. More than the content of their terrible experiences during the war, what I mostly knew from the past was that being Jewish was very important to my parents and that it was very important for us now to continue to be Jews.

Throughout my childhood, I remained quite loyal to Judaism though, not untypically, was highly ambivalent about religious education. Our parents were immigrants to the American Jewish community and relatively isolated survivors of a catastrophe about which few people were yet equipped to even inquire. My mother and father could not help ease our self-conscious efforts to feel part of that community. Though I learned and wholeheartedly recited Jewish prayers, my family's underlying sorrow and grief taught me intuitively that prayers do not get heard, certainly not when it came to fixing whatever it was that made life so unhappy and disconnected. I fashioned my own childhood world in which G-d could and did matter. But I knew in my child's heart that the G-d to whom I prayed for the Yankees to win the World Series was out of His league when it came to fixing our unhappiness. I never abandoned Judaism; I studied it, lived in Israel for a year, and tried to move closer to more rigorous religious observance. But I realized only much later that the personal G-d of the Jews would not show His face and neither would His commandments be compelling until my family's grief became more comprehensible and tolerable.

"Sheldon, Come Home!"

Within my own remote and quietly driven temperament my spiritual longings took root. While I continued to struggle for personal connection to my family and others, as well as to a personally meaningful G-d, I nevertheless searched for openness of heart and clarity of mind in a more mystical and reflective path. While still a college student in the early 1970s, I began a contemplative meditation practice, meditating religiously for many years and with a more pragmatic zeal for many more.

Even here, I attempted to place an essentially nontheistic spiritual practice into a Jewish framework. I traveled to Israel in part to study Jewish mysticism, and discovered some important Kabbalistic parallels to my meditation practice. At times, I imagined meeting G-d or great teachers in my meditations just as the masters, the Baal Shem Tov or Isaac Luria, had met and communed with great sages during their mystical soul journeys. Even the dangers of an ambitious meditative practice I envisioned as getting isolated and lost in Rabbi Akiba's mystical *pardes,* where at least I could go mad in familiar company. It was as if my mystical, meditative path were a nonpersonal way of dissolving the uncanny, multigenerational sadness that emerged from events in others' lives and the memories—or maybe just the frightening fantasies—of those events that had barely begun to be shared.

Perhaps more than anything, meditation seemed a way of magically removing, or at least soothing, the distance and silence that had entered my relationship with my parents, family, and culture. It reaffirmed and made peaceful and pleasurable the familiar silence in which I grew up. My practice helped diffuse the repressed rage and anguish that had churned in my life for so long. It stilled and calmed the forever intangible sorrow, the source of which unfolded far below the surface dynamics of economic survival or academic success, parent-child dislocations, or sibling rivalry in the day-to-day life of our family. If, as Rabbi Abraham Joshua Heschel once suggested, prayer is the overflowing of silence, then I was cultivating a river of it should I one day become once again ready to pray.

According to a story I once heard from my synagogue's rabbi, a middle-age American-Jewish woman searches the entire world for a certain enlightened mystical master. When she finally finds the cave in which he lives in the foothills of the Himalayas, throngs of his devotees prohibit her from having an unannounced audience with their much-revered guru. Undaunted, she pushes her way through the mass of followers, enters the dimly lit inner chamber of the meditating master, and screams imperiously, "Sheldon, come home!"

My mother never had to retrieve me in an Himalayan ashram, unlike this archetypal Sheldon, that disaffected American-Jew who, like many others in the 1960s, left his family, history, and spiritual roots for a more reclusive and ethereal path. Even as I could not find my place in a more traditional Jewish stance, I was always quietly certain, though just as stubbornly unconvinced, that "enlightenment" could never dispel the pain of my family's losses or soften the brutality of the way that many of our people died. Nor could it lighten the questions that had never been asked or remove the unhappiness that had never been penetrated. Though I knew only the dim realities of my family's and culture's turmoil, I was coming to realize that this was largely the ground from which my parents' sadness, and in turn my own, had emerged. In my meditations I came to realize that I was quietly fooling myself into believing that my sadness would be "transcended." But as I learned more about my parents' and family's lives during the Holocaust, I recognized ever so privately that this path of transcendence was a betrayal of memory and, ultimately, an evasion of responsibility.

Cultivating a Listening Heart

Nor were my personal strivings entirely otherwordly, but quite normal—for marriage, family, a meaningful vocation, and personal connection to others. Throughout my childhood, my ear had always been practiced at plumbing the silence and gaps in speech and human interactions for clues and signals to their meaning and intention. And my heart had always been inclined to summon a person's story out of the dark, first simply to hear it, and then to understand and remember it. Perhaps like many children of Holocaust survivors, I sought from a very early age to become a professional helper in general and a professional listener in particular. Listening, hearing, and helping others remember and bear witness became my life's purposes as a psychotherapist. While I discovered how affirming it is for someone to be heard and understood, I was equally affirmed in helping access silence and bring forth and heal the pain that silence protected. In helping others access their stories and their families' narrative histories, I acquired the tools to begin to appropriate my own. But I learned most of all that one's connection to wider history needs to begin in the profoundly personal.

The Path to Mourning

I was now in my early forties and was facing decisions about what kind of Jewish education and level of observance I would expose my two young sons to. As perhaps most sons-become-fathers look to their own fathers' inner lives and religious practices as a standard and guidepost, I, too, looked to the precedent set by my father. But he was a practicing Catholic from early childhood throughout the formative years of his life, even while he subsequently kept his earlier spirituality and religious practices invisible from his children. Yet, I could not begin my family's religious life in a vacuum, totally disengaged from my father's inner life. To gain access to it and to discover the source of his remoteness, I had to begin by exploring the impact on him of turning away from the faith in which he was raised.

I am not certain if my father was ever a deeply religious man, although I had once learned that, during his youth, he had considered becoming a priest; his reconversion to Judaism seemed to emerge more out of his deep disillusionment in Christianity and his identification with fellow victims of persecution, by whose faith he was deeply impressed and humbled. He was born a Jew, raised a Catholic, had loved and married a Jewish woman, and ultimately was persecuted as a Jew with other well-loved Jewish relatives, friends, and colleagues. I believe that my father's grief for his family created the most difficult knots in his religious life. After the war, most Jewish survivors had neither the opportunity nor the capacity to mourn their monumental losses. How much less so could my father grieve, especially over the death of his devoutly Catholic mother in Auschwitz? He had lost his faith in the redemptive power of his former Savior, as well as the healing power of his church, and, as a recently reconverted Jew, had no access to Kaddish or its meaning. The loss of a familiar and embracing religious community and the unavailability of a religiously sanctioned way to mourn made my father's grief less accessible. It had remained embedded in his soul and in our family's soul since then. I had only to ask him about my grandmother's death to be greeted by withdrawal and silence, and then uncannily to feel his sadness swell in my throat. As well, as my father has noted to me, his mother might not have accepted her son's reconversion to the religion of his birth. It is painfully ironic that such a deeply personal decision by my father to reembrace Judaism, forged by betrayal and persecution, might have prevented his mother from accepting the words of his grief over her death.

Thus, throughout my childhood, my father never adequately mourned nor expressed much grief for this most important loss. Indeed, he even avoided speaking about his mother. He recently acknowledged in a long-awaited oral history I conducted with him that he carries his unexpressed tears with him every day of his life. And, as he spoke these words, his voice cracked, almost dislodging the long-repressed torrent of grief and sadness carried ever so privately in his heart. Though I had thought about it before that moment, it was precisely then that I offered to say Kaddish for the customary eleven months for his mother—my grandmother—almost fifty years after her death.

Saying Kaddish was mostly to acknowledge the sadness and grief that my father had silently carried, that had entered and permeated our home as children, and that had at times unwittingly choked each of our hearts and souls. Without denying or disrespecting the difference of my grandmother's spiritual and religious path, I said Kaddish really to bring the meaning of her loss into our family and community. It was, as with all mourning, to access and preserve memory—to lighten grief so that memory could be kept alive and carried on.

During this period of observing Kaddish, while on a week-long family trip to Hungary in the autumn of 1992, I would take a taxicab early every morning before sunrise from our hotel to the former Jewish ghetto to participate in morning prayer with barely a minyan of mostly elderly worshipers in a small shul in the former Jewish ghetto, near the grand Dohany Street synagogue, and facing a courtyard in which stood Hungary's first memorial to the Holocaust. Among this group of ghetto and camp survivors and some younger, pious Jews who been born after the war, I would say Kaddish for my grandmother who had perished in the spring of 1944. Where more fitting to speak the Jews' words of grief and longing than in the nation at whose hands she had perished, in the company of the remnant community that represented the very roots of my parents' lives, and the community to which my father had returned? Besides our family's personal healing, I privately and humbly sensed that by saying Kaddish in Hungary I was helping hallow the desecrated ground.

Redeeming Our Narrative

It is clear that my mother's stories of suffering and survival, and her subsequent commitment to raising a Jewish family, have affirmed me as a Jew. But it is more ironic that my father's and his family's painful and divisive excursion through Christian religious sensibilities have been equally affirming of my place among the Jewish people. Having said Kaddish for my grandmother for the sake of our collective grief, I have become more ready to face my life as a Jewish man—as the grandson of Christians and the son of Jews, as well as the father of two Jewish children who will come to know what our faith and sometimes convoluted history are about. Their grandfather's life as a Catholic will not be kept from them. But my father's reentry into Jewish life and Jewish history during and after Passover in Bergen-Belsen in 1945 will become our model for hallowing the everyday and imparting some small degree of religious meaning to our family's and people's turmoil. Though my father vociferously denies any heroism or exemplary virtue while in Bergen-Belsen, another fellow inmate, who was transported later to Theresienstadt, and who, by chance, met my mother there, said to her of my father, "He always acted like a mensch." Thus, my father taught me how to be a Jew by these two things: consciously embracing the fate and destiny of the Jewish people, and, even in extraordinary circumstances, striving to be a mensch. Though the form may vary, this would be part of the core content of my family's lives as Jews.

Though my formerly devout Catholic father never taught me, I am learning to teach my sons about welcoming the Sabbath with blessings and songs, creatively and lovingly coaxing and cajoling them to sit with me at Shabbat services, and beginning to inform them about their grandparents' lives during the Holocaust. I wish to teach without traumatizing them, to suggest to them—without misleading them into feeling like heroes or martyrs—that suffering and surviving great turmoil and continuing to live with dignity and hope are central to our collective narrative—as central as the simple joy and blessing of being Jews. Although my father had not been able to experience this simple joy during the formative years of his life, perhaps my children will.

"The Rest Is Commentary..."

My sadness has not disappeared nor has my father's or mother's, even in the midst of our lives' joys and attainments. Although I believe that we are slightly better able to talk about our feelings and experiences, to tell the difference between those feelings and whose sadness is whose, and to continue to speak the stories of rich and loving, sometimes painful and confusing, memory that is our history.

For me, videotaping conversations with my parents, traveling with them and our entire family to Hungary, and especially saying Kaddish to help heal our family's sadness have opened the door to reconnect with memories of their lives, and thereby begin to fill in the silence of many years. Indeed, in Budapest, I could finally hear and absorb my mother's stories when there were streets and buildings to which to connect her tales. And my father might have spoken more freely just by virtue of the very supportive and evocative family trip to the country of his youth. I am not certain who or exactly what helped ease open the door of memory for him. Perhaps it was not just ripened memory, but the overflowing longing of a now aged man to inform his children and family of his life, less impeded by the grief and survivor's guilt with which he left his familiar homeland almost fifty years earlier. For myself, I know it was only after my observing Kaddish for the death of my grandmother that I was, for the first time, able to ask the appropriate questions, without either choking on them or protectively stifling them for fear of treading into forbidden areas of my father's heart. Kaddish has helped to heal *my* sadness and *my* fear and has in that way created a safer mutually accessible relationship between my father and myself. Whatever the origin and spur to his liberated recollections, during our journey my father, at age eighty, began to introduce all of us to our grandmother's life and history and to entire epochs of his life earlier unknown to us. Though sadness persists, memory has been unlocked and shared, and longing has been eased. And we know our father and mother, and we know ourselves better for it. And life feels fuller.

I Was Born in Bergen-Belsen

MENACHEM Z. ROSENSAFT

I was born in Bergen-Belsen. That is the essence of my being. My cradle stood only a short distance from the mass graves in which Anne Frank and tens of thousands of other European Jews lie buried anonymously. My parents survived the horrors of Auschwitz; my grandparents did not. I am alive; my brother died in a gas chamber.

More than two thousand Jewish children were born in the displaced persons camp of Bergen-Belsen in Germany between 1945 and 1950. What had been one of the most notorious Nazi concentration camps became a sanctuary of life. Today, those children are adults, scattered throughout the world, with families and careers of their own. Most of us have never met, but we know one another intimately. Together with all the other Jews of our generation whose parents experienced Hitler's Europe, we belong to a special group: We are the children of the survivors of the Holocaust.

Sometimes when I am alone, I see, or imagine that I see, the fading image of a five-and-a-half-year-old boy named Benjamin. Once upon a time, in the spring and early summer of 1943, that little boy lived and laughed and played with his parents and grandparents in the ghetto of the Polish city of Sosnowiec. On August 1, 1943, the Germans began liquidating the various ghettos in that part of Poland, and three days later, upon arriving at Birkenau, the death camp of Auschwitz, my brother was separated from his—our—mother and murdered in a gas chamber together with his father and our grandparents. I am haunted by his face, his eyes, and I listen to a voice I never heard. But do I see him, or is it merely my reflection? Are my tears mine, or are they his? I do not know. I shall never know.

Still, other than in the limited sense that the designation is self-explanatory, it is difficult to define the children of Holocaust survivors as a

188

separate entity. We come from different European backgrounds, live in countries throughout the world, pursue a multitude of careers, and have diverse interests. Even our attitudes toward Judaism are vastly dissimilar. In brief, we are no more homogeneous than the survivors themselves. Mostly, all we have in common is our parents' experiences . . . but because of those experiences, we have everything in common.

As a group, the sons and daughters of the survivors are unique in that although we did not experience the Holocaust, we have, thanks to our parents, a particular knowledge of and sensitivity to its significance and consequences.

Confronting our collective identity has not been without cost. Far too often, it has resulted in an artificial and counterproductive separateness. We do not share in our parents' exclusivity. They went through the Holocaust. We did not. They saw their families and friends murdered. We grew up in comfort and security. We are not survivors in any sense of the term. They, and they alone, are entitled to that designation. Nor do we have any exclusive rights to the survivors' legacy or to the memory of the Holocaust. These belong to the Jewish people and to humankind.

However, while being children of survivors does not give us any privileges, it does impose a far-reaching responsibility. We were given life and placed on earth with a solemn obligation. Our parents survived to bear witness. We, in turn, must be their attestors. Our task is to remind the word of the Holocaust to prevent its recurrence. And to understand our parents and their experiences, we must first at least attempt to penetrate the darkness.

Kaddish after Auschwitz

"Yitgadal ve Yitkadash Shme Raba." "Hallowed and Exalted be His Great Name." Kaddish. The Jewish prayer of mourning in which the dead are remembered through the sanctification of God's name. How can one reconcile the murder of more than one million Jewish children with the existence of God? Their haunting memory is enough to dismiss in its entirety the obscenity uttered by certain ultra-Orthodox rabbis who say that the Holocaust was a punishment decreed by God. These children certainly never did anything to deserve or invoke God's wrath. Indeed, if God perpetrated or was to any degree responsible for the Holocaust, if He allowed it to happen, that would be the most compelling reason for us to question our belief in God.

Where was God during the Holocaust? Martin Buber wrote about the "eclipse of the light of heaven, eclipse of God" during "the historic hour through which the world is passing." How can we continue to praise a God who could have stopped the Holocaust but failed to do so?

One evening in the fall of 1943, after roll call, my father was sitting outside a Birkenau barracks with a group of fellow prisoners from Zawiercie, a town near my father's hometown of Bendin. As they listened to the cries and screams of Jews being forced into the gas chambers, the *Zawiercier Rav*, the town's aged rabbi, observed calmly but with no small measure of anguish that it was possible for God to be a liar. Asked to explain this apparent heresy, he replied: "If the Ribono shel Olam—the Master of the Universe—up in heaven were to open His window and look down on us now, He would avert His eyes and say that He had not done this, and that would be a lie."

About the same time, during the festival of Sukkot, 1943, my father smuggled a tiny apple into the barracks so that the *Zawiercier Rav* could make kiddush, the sanctification recited before Sabbath and festival meals. Throughout the clandestine prayer service, the old man contemplated the apple. At last, when it was time for kiddush, he picked it up. "And over this," he said softly, mostly to himself, "I would then have to say, '*ve-akhalta, ve-savata, uverakhta et Ha-Shem Elokeikha.*' " "And you will eat, and you will be satisfied, and you will praise the Lord, your God," the biblical verse that is recited during the blessing after a meal. "I will not eat," he exclaimed, "for I will not be satisfied, and I do not want to *bentsh*," that is, to say the benediction after a meal. And with that, he put down the apple, and turned away. The *Zawiercier Rav* had not stopped believing in God, even in Auschwitz. He still praised Him, every day three times a day. But he refused to be grateful for nonexisting nourishment. That was his act of defiance.

But what if God was not with the killers, with the forces that inflicted the Holocaust on humanity? Perhaps both Buber and the *Zawiercier Rav* looked for God in the wrong place. Think of the divine power, the spiritual strength, of a mother comforting a child on the way to a gas chamber. If God was present at Auschwitz, it was in that mother, in her words, in her emotions, in the instinct that kept her from abandoning her child. If God was at Treblinka, it was within the Polish-Jewish educator Janusz Korczak as he accompanied his orphans to their death.

Every Jew who shared his or her meager ration of food with a neighbor in a ghetto or camp sanctified God's name. God was within every Jew who told a story or a joke or sang a melody in a death camp barracks to alleviate a friend's agony. God permeated every Jew who held a dying parent, or a brother or sister, or a friend, or even a stranger. The mystical divine spark that characterizes true Jewish faith, the *shekhina*, was in every Jew who remained human to another fellow human being, and in every non-Jew who defied the forces of evil by risking his or her life to save a Jew. That divine spark was within my mother as she kept 149 Jewish children alive at Bergen-Belsen throughout the winter and early spring of 1945, just as it was within Raoul Wallenberg and within every Dane who rowed a Jewish neighbor to safety.

My Grandfather

Three photographs have survived of Reb Menachem Mendl Rosensaft of Bendin, Poland. They, and memories, are all that remain of a man whose entire being was symbolic of the best and purest there was in that destroyed Jewish world of eastern Europe. Steeped in Jewish learning and culture, his life reflected, above all, a deep love of the Jewish people and an unending concern for those in need.

Born in 1863 or 1864, the son of Moshe Shmuel Rosensaft, a disciple of Rabbi Yitzhak Meir Alter, the founder of the Hasidic dynasty of Ger, Reb Mendl was an *ilui*, an exceptionally brilliant student at a prestigious Polish yeshiva. After marrying at a young age the daughter of another highly respected Gerer Hasid, the wealthy Reb Yankel Szpiro of Bendin, Reb Mendl was able to dedicate all his time and energies to his religious studies and writings, and to his countless communal charities, while his wife, Devora, managed the family business. He belonged to every possible Jewish welfare committee in town, serving readily together with assimilated, Polish-speaking Jews as well as with profoundly religious Jews like himself. Most of his philanthropy was undertaken anonymously.

As a father, he was loving and tolerant. He knew that not all his children remained as religiously observant as he would have wished—my father, for instance, was active in the labor Zionist movement—but that did not affect his relationship with them. And they, in turn, never consciously offended him.

The coming of the war and the subsequent establishment of the ghetto did not change him. He was by then close to eighty. At one point, as the full dimensions of the impending catastrophe became increasingly evident, an attempt was made to rescue Reb Mendl from the ghetto. In 1942 or early 1943, my father arranged with a non-Jewish acquaintance of his, a Bendin barrel maker, to hide three members of the family. He suggested that a member of each generation be saved: Reb Mendl, one of my father's sisters, and one of the children. Reb Mendl firmly refused. He would not possibly save himself while any of his children or grandchildren remained in danger. My father's sisters reacted similarly, as did all the other members of the family. They either would live together or die together—and by that time the gas chambers of Auschwitz were no longer a secret.

On June 22, 1943, when my father was deported from Bendin, Reb Mendl announced that he would wait in his room until his son returned. That night, unbeknownst to him, my father did, in fact, escape from the Auschwitz-bound train, but he was severely wounded by German bullets. With great difficulty, he made his way back to the ghetto. The following morning, Reb Mendl waited patiently in his room. Only after his Yossel had come home, after he had hugged and blessed him, was Reb Mendl willing to go to the synagogue and pray. Less than six weeks later, on August 1, 1943, the first day of the final evacuation of the Jews from the ghetto of Bendin, Reb Mendl Rosensaft died a natural death in my father's arms.

Of the three existing photographs of my grandfather, the first is of a robust man in his late fifties or early sixties, with a dark but graying beard and sharp eyes. He is well dressed, wearing a velvet hat.

In the second photograph, Reb Mendl is much older, in his seventies. His carefully combed beard is completely white by now, the face is more wrinkled, and the eyes, though still bright and clear, are somehow softer. In both these pictures, he is posing for the photographer and looking straight ahead, not at anyone or anything in particular.

The third photograph is the most important. It shows Reb Mendl standing outside his house, near a window, wearing his hat and coat, as erect and dignified as in the two others, but on his sleeve there is a white armband. Shortly before the liquidation of the Bendin ghetto, the Germans decided to film it for their archives, and my grandfather happened to be on the street at that time.

After the war, the film was found by some Poles, non-Jews, in a cellar were the Germans had left it. One of them, a friend of my father's, recognized Reb Mendl, cut out the frame in which he appeared, and, when he learned that my father had survived, sent it to him in Bergen-Belsen. Eventually, my parents had that picture enlarged and framed, and it has been hanging on the wall of my room, now in my office, for as long as I can remember.

For me, this photograph represents the link between the grandfather I never knew and myself, between his generation and mine. When I look at it, I can see the deep pain and anxiety in his eyes. He seems to be looking not at the cameraman but into the lens, and beyond. As a child, I was convinced that he was staring directly at me, that his look was for me alone. And perhaps it was. Perhaps Reb Mendl realized that he was being filmed, and that this was his only chance to communicate with his as yet unborn grandchild, for he must have believed that his youngest son would someday have a son, too. And if he understood that this moment was of special significance, perhaps he attempted to put into his gaze at that one instant his entire life, his thoughts, his memories, his knowledge, his wisdom, his blessings, all the lullabies and stories, the teachings and explanations, all his emotions and his love: everything he would have wanted to convey to his grandson could he have held him and spoken to him.

My Father

After his father's death, my father found refuge for a few weeks in the nearby town of Zawiercie, but in late August 1943, he was deported to Auschwitz, where the blue number 140594 was tattooed on his arm. On September 30, he and two friends from Bendin snuck into the women's camp at Birkenau to look for members of their families. Caught by the SS guards, they were punished with a ten-day incarceration in Auschwitz's infamous Block 11, the death block that was commonly known as the Bunker.

In early 1944, my father was transferred from Birkenau to a labor camp at Lagisha, not far from Bendin. A few months later, he escaped from Lagisha, returned to Bendin, and was hidden there for the next six weeks by a Polish friend. In April 1944, while attempting to obtain false papers that would enable him to reach Hungary, he was recaptured by the Germans and taken back to Auschwitz.

He spent the next several months in Block 11, where he was tortured continually. For much of that time, he was imprisoned in one of three tiny standing cells in the most remote corner of the building's cellar. There, German journalist Bernd Naumann wrote in his 1966 book *Auschwitz*, "The condemned had to crawl in like dogs—at times four prisoners vegetated in these holes—and in complete darkness serve out their punishment, standing, in less than one square yard of space. . . . It is said that quite a few went mad here." The Germans wanted my father to disclose the identity of the friend who had hidden him, something he steadfastly refused to do. Incredibly, he survived the ordeal, his sanity and values intact.

On November 14, 1944, my father was taken from Auschwitz to the concentration camp of Langensalza in central Germany. Sometime during the winter of 1945, he was transferred to another camp in the Harz mountains, Dora-Mittelbau, where V-2 rockets were manufactured. In early April 1945, he was sent to Bergen-Belsen, where he was liberated by British troops on April 15.

A few days after the liberation, the then-34-year-old Josef Rosensaft, known as Yossel, was chosen by his fellow survivors to be their spokesman in dealing with the British. He was elected chairman of the Jewish committee of the Belsen DP camp, and for the next five and a half years he was the undisputed leader of its thousands of inhabitants. From September 1945 until 1950, he was also chairman of the Central Jewish Committee in the British zone of Germany.

The issues confronting the survivors of Belsen were complex. The British wanted the survivors to return to their homes; the Jewish survivors from Poland, and many of those from Hungary, did not want to go back. The British wanted the Jewish survivors to be classified by nationality together with non-Jewish refugees; the Jewish survivors wanted to be classified separately as Jews. The British wanted to relocate all the survivors to other DP camps; the Jewish survivors wanted to remain where they were. My father prevailed on all counts.

He simultaneously worked with and defied the British authorities. A representative of the American-Jewish Joint Distribution Committee stationed in Belsen reported to his superiors in New York in August 1945 that my father "is always incurring the wrath of the Army officials here. He is always threatened with arrest. . . . He thinks nothing of flaunting military regulations repeatedly. . . . " His goals were to achieve the physical and spiritual rehabilitation of the survivors; to provide them with a full Jewish religious, cultural, and political environment; to ensure that they lived as comfortably as possible while they were in Belsen; to protect and defend their rights; to see all the survivors resettled, whether in Israel or elsewhere; and to protect the memory of the victims of the Holocaust.

Samuel Goldsmith, a British journalist, recalled:

> As so often happens to people who accept a challenge and find their destiny in leadership, the stature of Yossel grew with his responsibilities.

When contacts between Jewish organizations and Belsen survivors were at last established, Yossel became a Jewish politician of international importance. He was recognized as the man who created, out of misery and chaos, the first Jewish autonomous community in modern times, a kind of miniature republic. In a way, it was an experiment in self-government three years before the establishment of the Jewish state. It was Yossel who—from Belsen!—organized help for the Haganah and dispatched large consignments of medical supplies, blankets, and more aggressive equipment, as well as the young men who, trained in Belsen, went to join the Israeli Army during the war of independence in 1948.

Many of my father's political activities during the first three years after liberation were rooted in the survivors' insistence on unrestricted immigration to Palestine and the establishment of a Jewish state there. Testifying before the Anglo-American Committee of Inquiry on Palestine in early 1946, he told its members that if the survivors would not be allowed to go to Palestine, "we shall go back to Belsen, Dachau, Buchenwald and Auschwitz, and you will bear the moral responsibility for it."

In December 1945, he was invited to the United States to attend the first postwar national conference of the United Jewish Appeal in Atlantic City, New Jersey. Years afterward, Philip Bernstein, the executive vice president of the Council of Jewish Federations, described my father's appearance there as follows:

When he was introduced and rose to speak, they saw a small man, hardly five feet tall and weighing not more than 110 or 120 pounds at most, with a gaunt pale face which itself conveyed the persecution and starvation he had been through. But his eyes seemed to pierce the audience with their fervor. . . .

He portrayed indelibly the brutality the inmates had suffered with incredible courage and perseverance. The community leaders understood the ingenious lengths the inmates had gone to in order to survive, with unrelenting devotion to Judaism and to the Jewish people.

He told the American Jewish leaders, in the strongest terms, the meaning of what had to be done urgently and with the utmost support to help the survivors rebuild their lives and their communities, to live in dignity and security.

He stunned the audience with his eloquence and with his power, with the depth of his passion and challenge, from that seemingly frail and tormented body

Several weeks after their liberation, my parents met. They were married on August 18, 1946, and I was born on May 1, 1948. Their devotion to their fellow survivors was such that despite numerous opportunities to leave, they remained in Belsen until 1950 when all but a few hundred of its inhabitants had found new homes. These remaining survivors were moved to another camp, Upjever, in northern Germany, where they lived for another year, and my father went with them. When the Belsen DP camp was closed in the summer of 1950, my father found a temporary home for our small family in Montreux, Switzerland, and for the next year, he divided his time between Upjever and Montreux. In 1958, we finally settled in New York.

Throughout the 1950s and 1960s, my father was one of the very few survivors to speak out publicly and continually about the Holocaust and its implications. In 1958, when the French government sought to exhume 139 French bodies from the mass graves of Bergen-Belsen, he initiated an eleven-year-long international political struggle and legal proceeding to preserve the sanctity of the dead. He was ultimately fully vindicated by an international arbitral commission, and the Belsen mass graves remained unopened.

He played an important, albeit unheralded, role in the intricate negotiations that resulted in the payment of reparations by the West German government to both Holocaust survivors and the State of Israel. Gottlieb Hammer, one of the senior Zionist officials of the postwar era, recalled in his memoirs that my father was one of the first to advocate that Germany should have to pay at least some measure of restitution to the survivors. In a letter dated October 12, 1952, after the reparations agreements had been signed, Dr. Nahum Goldmann, the president of the World Jewish Congress and of the Conference on Jewish Material Claims Against Germany, who had conducted the negotiations with the West German government, expressed his "gratitude and deep appreciation" for my father's contributions to this endeavor. "What you did and accomplished," Goldmann wrote, "was of the greatest significance for the successful conclusion of the negotiations. . . . The fact that your work took place behind the scenes increases it value. . . . "

My father founded the World Federation of Bergen-Belsen Survivors Associations, one of the earliest and most active of the organizations of Holocaust survivors, and was its president until his death. Together with my mother, Norbert Wollheim, who had been his vice chairman in the Central Committee, and Sam Bloch, who succeeded him as head of the World Federation, he organized pilgrimages to Belsen; established a major international award for Holocaust literature (Elie Wiesel was its first recipient); brought together Belsen survivors every year to mark the anniversary of their liberation; erected a monument to the dead of Belsen on Mount Zion in Jerusalem; published works in English, Yiddish, and Hebrew about the Holocaust in general and Belsen in particular; looked after *his* "Belseners," as they called themselves, throughout the world; and raised his fiery voice whenever the memory of the Holocaust was put into question. "He became our Ancient Mariner," wrote historian Lucy Dawidowicz, "who 'passed from land to land' with 'strange power of speech' to tell his tale to who-soever would listen."

He was also a doting father who taught me how to swim, told me bedtime stories, bought me toys, and took great pride in my academic and other accomplishments. I remember him looking out the window of my parents' bedroom as he watched me wait for the school bus. I remember the tears in his eyes when I became a Bar Mitzvah and when Jeanie and I were married. I remember him giving my American-born best friend, Rob-ert, a Yiddish nickname, and how he always treated him and my other friends as members of our family. I remember how he loved to spoil Jeanie's younger sister, Gloria. I remember his broad smile when I graduated from high school and from Johns Hopkins University. I remember him calling his friends whenever an article or poem of mine was published. I remember listening with him to recordings of hasidic melodies. I remember going to synagogue with him and listening to him recite the prayers by heart. We spoke every day, even when he was traveling.

He was a constant source of advice and encouragement when I started teaching at New York's City College as Elie Wiesel's assistant while doing graduate work in Modern Western European History at Columbia Univer-sity. My master's thesis was on my father's successful struggle to prevent the French government from desecrating the mass graves of Belsen. During the summer of 1975, when I was considering a change of careers, we spent countless hours discussing my options. He was enthusiastic when I told him that I had decided to study law, something he had always wanted, but had never pressured, me to do. Those were my last substantive conversations with him. On September 10, 1975, midway between Rosh Hashanah and Yom Kippur, he died in London of a massive stroke.

At his funeral, Elie Wiesel eulogized him in Yiddish: "I know countless souls, sanctified by fire, will soon greet you there, souls from Bendin and Belsen, Majdanek and Warsaw, the souls from thousands of destroyed Jew-ish communities in Europe. And they will embrace you as one of their own and bring you to the Heavenly Tribunal and, still higher, to the Celestial Throne, and they will say, 'Look, *he* did not forget us'.

"Day in, day out, from morning until late at night, everywhere and under all circumstances, even on *simchas,* his spirit glowed in our fire.

"Few sanctified the Holocaust as he did. Few suffered as he did. Few loved its holy martyrs as he did. So they will embrace him with love and gratitude, as though he were their defender."

Elie Wiesel

Beyond question, the person who has had the greatest impact on the second generation as a whole is Elie Wiesel. His memoir, *Night,* enabled us to relate to our parents' experiences through the eyes and heart of one who experienced the Holocaust as a teenager. His novels allowed us to identify with fictional characters who asked the very questions that were haunting us. And his commitment to human rights, his readiness to apply the lessons of the Holocaust to contemporary issues while at all times emphasizing its Jewish particularity, enabled us to synthesize past and present.

Elie was a friend of my parents and a frequent guest in our home. One evening at the beginning of my senior year of high school, he asked me how I liked my classes. I told him that I enjoyed all but the English Seminar, an advanced literature and writing course. I explained that I did not like the teacher's approach, and showed Elie the comments he had written on a paper of mine.

Elie agreed that the teacher's style was hopelessly antiquated, and that it would not in any way sharpen my writing or analytic skills. He then offered to meet with me every week or two and look over what I had written. I accepted eagerly. Throughout the next year, he not only greatly expanded my intellectual horizons, but he also taught me to appreciate the complex essence of language and words.

Our friendship continued after I finished high school and he remained very much my mentor. Whenever I was home from college, we would meet, he would critique whatever I had written, and we would discuss a whole range of subjects, from abstract philosophical issues to the latest political scandal in Washington or Israel.

In 1972, when Elie was appointed Distinguished Professor at New York's City College, he asked me to be his first teaching assistant. For the next three years, I worked closely with him in his lecture courses on Holocaust literature and seminars on Hasidism.

In June 1981, while we were in Israel for the World Gathering of Holocaust Survivors, Elie told me that he found the English translation of the powerful "Legacy" of the survivors, which he had written in Yiddish and French for the occasion, to be trite and unpoetic. He asked me if I would prepare a completely new translation that would express the sense of the original. I did so, and he was satisfied with that version. Ultimately, my translation was read at the closing ceremony at Jerusalem's Western Wall.

Elie has had a greater formative influence on me than anyone other than my parents. In many ways he and my father complemented each other. With respect to the remembrance of the Holocaust in particular, and to the Jewish political arena in general, Elie provided the intellectual, philosophical dimension to my father's action-oriented personality. On most issues, they were in complete accord.

Elie always emphasized the special relationship linking the survivors and the second generation. In May of 1984, at the First International Conference of Children of Holocaust Survivors, he told us:

> When I speak to others, surely you know that I mean you, all the time. You are my audience, because it is you who matter. . . . We have become partners now, united by the same lofty and urgent goal. We are no longer afraid of unshed tears or of unspoken words. Until now you have been our students, perhaps even our disciples. At times, to some of us, you have been our children, troubled and exalted by our desire to see in you more than our children. We saw in you our parents. You became our parents. But now we are closer than ever before because we have spoken and because you have spoken to one another.
>
> We look at one another with pride and gratitude and we think that whatever happened to Abraham and Isaac has happened to us too. The *Akedah,* after all, was not consummated. The testimony of our life and death will not vanish. Our memories will not die with us.

The Absence of Older Siblings

In my mind, my brother always remained the little boy who died in Birkenau. I never imagined him as a teenager or as an adult, but his absence from my life as an older sibling has left its mark. I did not realize how deeply this void had affected me until I met Rabbi David Lincoln in early 1987, shortly after he had become the spiritual leader of the Park Avenue synagogue in New York City. In our first conversation, he asked me if I was related to Yossel Rosensaft who, he said, was one of his heroes. It turned out that David was born in London in 1937, the same year as my brother, and he vividly remembers hearing and reading about my father during the immediate postwar years, before I was born. Thus, he has memories my brother might have had.

We discovered that we share many interests and soon became close friends. David is unusual among contemporary rabbis—or other Jews his age, for that matter—in that he speaks Yiddish fluently and is fascinated by everything connected to eastern and central European Jewry. There are echoes in our conversation that appear to have transcended time. When he teaches Talmud, when he gives advice, when we discuss politics, whether American, Israeli, or Jewish, when he talks about trips to Russia or the Ukraine, his perspective is somehow that of a member of my brother's annihilated generation. When he stood with me at my mother's hospital bed a few days before she died and she was able to joke with him in Yiddish, knowing that he understood the full bittersweet meaning of her words, I felt that he was there as more than a rabbi or even a friend. Through my friendship with David, I have begun to have a sense of what it might have been like to know my brother.

From Belsen Children to the International Network of Children of Jewish Holocaust Survivors

After leaving Belsen in 1950, my parents remained in close and constant contact with their fellow survivors, especially those who had been in the leadership of the DP camp's Jewish Committee. They met regularly, and held annual reunions on the anniversary of their liberation. They also included their children, many of whom had been born in Belsen, in their activities and events. By the time we were teenagers, many of us knew one another even though our parents lived in different parts of Israel, the United States, Canada, and Europe.

On July 1, 1962, my parents invited 145 Belsen children, as we were known, between twelve and sixteen, to our own gathering in Herzlia, Israel. That first meeting was followed by others at which we continued to discuss our shared identity, and in 1964, we undertook a project of our own. Our parents were about to celebrate the twentieth anniversary of their liberation, and we wanted to pay tribute to them in our own words. We contacted about three hundred Belsen children throughout the world and asked them to submit articles, short stories, and poems about the Holocaust, the postwar years, or any other appropriate related topic. Within a few months, we received more than seventy submissions, and in the spring of 1965 we published twenty-six of these in the *Bergen-Belsen Youth Magazine,* which I had the privilege to edit. "We, who call ourselves the children of Belsen," I wrote in the introduction, "believe that we are a part of Belsen."

In the mid-1970s, a number of second-generation groups came into existence in various parts of the United States. In Boston, Eva Fogelman started the first support group for children of survivors, and New York's second-generation group came into being as a junior auxiliary of the Warsaw Ghetto Resistance Organization. In 1976, I was invited to the first meeting of the New York group. I stayed away. At the time, my father had only recently passed away, and I was beginning my law studies. Moreover, I was not at all convinced that I wanted to belong to an organized body of children of Holocaust survivors. I believed that I could be more effective by continuing to lecture and write about the Holocaust and its impact.

I changed my mind in the fall of 1979 at a New York Conference *on* Children of Holocaust Survivors. Organized by a well-meaning Jewish organization, this conference featured psychologist after psychiatrist after psychoanalyst after an array of other mental health specialists who considered themselves authorities on survivors and their children. In turn, each of them publicly dissected our supposed pathology, trauma, guilt complexes, collective idiosyncrasies, and other alleged common characteristics. I was appalled. I did not recognize myself or any of my friends in the collective psychobabble to which we were subjected.

This is not to say that all children of survivors are free of psychological problems. There are those who are severely troubled by their parents' experiences, or who have been unable to come to terms with their identity. But that is true of society as a whole: a certain percentage is, for one reason or other, in need of psychological help. It was as if one were to determine the drinking habits of all adult Americans based on a study of Alcoholic Anonymous participants.

My wife, Jeanie, a few other friends of ours who had also attended the 1979 conference, and I decided to become active in the New York second-generation group. We wanted to make sure that we would henceforth speak for ourselves rather than be talked about, and to direct out collective energy into constructive, forward-looking channels.

In 1980–81, a number of us helped organize the World Gathering of Holocaust Survivors that took place in Israel in June of 1981. There, we had our sessions for a thousand sons and daughters of survivors. We concluded that although we wanted to continue helping the survivors with their commemorative activities, we needed our own organization.

In September 1981, we established the International Network of Children of Jewish Holocaust Survivors, and I was elected its first chairman. Over the Memorial Day weekend of 1984, we organized the first international second-generation conference in New York. More than sixteen hundred sons and daughters of survivors attended.

We undertook numerous projects. In 1982, we held the first New York citywide rally on behalf of Ethiopian Jewry; we organized second-generation programming for the survivor gatherings in Washington, D.C., in 1983 and in Philadelphia in 1985; we played a critical role in sparking international interest in the whereabouts of Josef Mengele, the SS doctor who had personally sent thousands upon thousands of Jews, including my mother's sister, to the gas chambers, and had performed terminal medical experiments on Auschwitz inmates; and in 1987, together with Brooklyn district attorney Elizabeth Holtzman and Eli Rosenbaum, general counsel of the World Jewish Congress, we persuaded the government of Panama not to give refuge to convicted Nazi war criminal Karl Linnas and helped ensure his deportation to the Soviet Union. In the spring of 1985, we were among the most outspoken critics of President Reagan's decision to lay a wreath at the German military cemetery at Bitburg, where members of Hitler's Waffen-SS are buried; and on May 5 of that year, we traveled to Bergen-Belsen to reconsecrate its mass graves after President Reagan and West German chancellor Helmut Kohl had stopped there on their way to Bitburg. More recently, we have been at the forefront of efforts to obtain comprehensive health insurance for Holocaust survivors. Individually, we remain active in all aspects of Holocaust commemoration on both the national and local levels. For example, Romana Primus, who was also born in the Belsen DP camp, Rositta Kenigsberg, and I were appointed by President Clinton to the United States Holocaust Memorial Council; and together with Jeanie and other children of survivors, we organized the United States Holocaust Memorial Museum's January 2000 Conference on the Post-Holocaust DP Camps.

Preserving the Intensity of Memory

During the first three decades after the Holocaust, a few isolated survivors, my father and Elie Wiesel among them, were virtually alone in their efforts to perpetuate its memory. They were largely ignored, reaching mostly other survivors and those among their children who took the time to listen.

Since then, the situation has changed dramatically. The Holocaust is today one of the most prominent themes on the Jewish community's agenda. In Israel, Yad Vashem in Jerusalem and the Ghetto Fighters' House at Kibbutz Lohamei Haghettaot are recognized as essential parts of our heritage. In Washington, D.C., the U.S. Holocaust Memorial Museum brings the full magnitude and complexity of the Holocaust into the consciousness of thousands upon thousands of Americans and other visitors every single week. Millions of visitors, most of them non-Jews, have been to the museum since its opening in April 1993. At the same time, leading universities offer courses in Holocaust studies; Holocaust centers have been and are being set up in cities throughout North America; and virtually every Jewish organization is sponsoring a number of different Holocaust-related projects.

Why, then, is there also a sense of unease? Why am I, for one, not altogether comfortable with the popular appeal that the Holocaust has acquired? Perhaps because the experience must not be allowed to lose its aura of mystery. Objective, cognitive analysis alone is insufficient. Elie Wiesel has written, "Auschwitz signifies not only the failure of two thousand years of Christian civilization, but also the defeat of the intellect that wants to find a Meaning—with a capital M—in history. What Auschwitz embodied had none."

Seen in its own oppressive light, the Holocaust stands alone in time as an absolute aberration of history. It is the unprecedented, the unfathomable, and, above all, the inexplicable. Sober chronologies of dates, events, and statistics are critical to our understanding but provide only one dimension. Histories of the Holocaust based exclusively or even primarily on German documents may convey the intent and actions of the perpetrators but do not adequately, if at all, reflect the experiences of the victims. Thus, ghetto diaries, underground newspapers, contemporaneous letters, and the survivors' recollections are essential to any comprehensive narrative. And no one can penetrate the nocturnal universe of Auschwitz and Bergen-Belsen without absorbing songs, poems, and prayers that defy all standards of historiographic methodology.

A barracks wall at Auschwitz contains the following phrase: "Andreas Rapaport—lived sixteen years." Try to imagine this boy, realizing that he was about to die, as he tried to leave a sign, a remembrance of his all too brief existence on earth. Andreas Rapaport was the author of his own eulogy: Andreas Rapaport—lived sixteen years. Andreas Rapaport—abandoned, alone, afraid. Andreas Rapaport—hungry, in pain. Andreas Rapaport—gas-filled lungs. Andreas Rapaport—burning flesh in the crematorium, black smoke, ashes.

In September 1945, my mother, then Dr. Hadassah Bimko, was one of the principal witnesses for the prosecution at the trial of the commandants, doctors, and guards of Auschwitz and Bergen-Belsen who had been arrested by the British at the liberation of Bergen-Belsen. Held in Lüneburg, Germany, this military tribunal was the first war crimes trial of the murderers of European Jewry. In her testimony, which was described in detail in the world press, my mother told the court how countless Jews, including her parents, husband, sister, and child, had been sent to the gas chambers, and she described the Nazis' brutality and sadism. For the first time, the world was faced with one who had been there, with a survivor.

On her second day on the witness stand, one of the court-appointed defense attorneys suggested, according to a report published in the *New York Times* on September 23, 1945, that my mother's statement that she had seen Josef Kramer, the commandant of Birkenau and Bergen-Belsen, kick and beat the camp inmates was "pure fabrication." "I would like to point out," my mother replied, "I was present and not the defending counsel during those conditions that I have described."

In other words, less than six months after the end of the Holocaust, attempts were already being made to deny that it had happened, and how it had happened. And only because of the eyewitness testimony of survivors such as my mother was the world forced to confront the horrifying reality of Auschwitz, Treblinka, Majdanek, and Bergen-Belsen.

With the passing of time, our mental pictures go out of focus, our collective memories become blurred. We all have memories, even we who were born afterward. And they were once fresh. When my father told me how he was shot by the Germans while escaping from a moving train bound for Auschwitz, when he told me how his father died in his arms, when he told me how he was tortured in Auschwitz, every one of his experiences was sharply recorded in my mind. He died a quarter of a century ago. And I no longer remember his words as clearly as I once did.

As our knowledge of the Holocaust steadily increases, we must be careful not to become desensitized. As we perpetuate memory, we must also prevent it from becoming commonplace. We must continue to be moved by the image of Andreas Rapaport, who knew that he would not live to celebrate his seventeenth birthday. We must continue to be awed by the defiance of the *Zawiercier Rav*. There are times when even scholars must abandon their dispassion. Remembrance without emotion is hollow, and the dead deserve our anguish.

Beyond Remembrance

After our daughter, Jodi, was born on January 24, 1978, I often wondered how I would be able to convey to her a realistic image of my father—her grandfather—after whom she is named. How could I convey to her his devotion to the Jewish people and his love for the Yiddish language and for Jewish culture, his unyielding integrity and courage, his sense of humor, his fierce loyalty to his friends, and his lifelong pride in his identity as a Jew from Bendin, Auschwitz, and Belsen? How would she ever hear the hasidic songs he sang with his beautiful clear voice, and the marvelous, sad, and humorous stories he told so well? But then I realized that it was through him that I was able to know my own grandfather, and it was only through me that Jodi would ever know my father, his values, and his world.

I emphasize the word "through" rather than "from." Our children must learn through us, as well as from us, just as we learned about the past—our past—both through and from our parents. In everything I have ever done, I have tried to be an extension of my father, to reflect his principles, values, and ideals; and I can only hope that Jodi has in turn absorbed them, too, through and from Jeanie and myself.

The essence of Jodi's personality demonstrated itself during the difficult months of my mother's final illness. At eighty-four, she started to succumb to the impact of the malaria and hepatitis she had contracted at Auschwitz. By then, Jodi had started her first year of college at Johns Hopkins. Repeatedly, sometimes weekly, Jodi came to New York to visit my mother. Once, she came by train in the morning, spent a few hours with her in the hospital, and returned to Baltimore the same evening. When my mother was taken to the hospital for the last time, Jodi immediately came from Baltimore and remained until the end, spending hours with Jeanie and me at her bedside during those terrifying weeks. On Friday evening, October 3, 1997, a few hours after the end of Rosh Hashanah, the three of us were with her. She was in a wonderful mood, talking about the publication of her memoirs that she had finished writing. And while I was holding one of her hands and Jodi the other, she left us.

My mother's funeral was on the anniversary of my father's death. As Jodi eulogized her and spoke about all she had learned from her, we realized how thoroughly she understands and appreciates her heritage. At Johns Hopkins, Jodi headed the Holocaust Remembrance committee and was active in campus Jewish life. She has returned home every year to lead the

Rosh Hashanah and Yom Kippur services for four- and five-year-old children at our synagogue. As she becomes an independent young woman, it becomes increasingly evident that she proudly identifies with, and reflects the values of, all four of her grandparents: my parents who survived Auschwitz and Belsen; Jeanie's mother, Lily Czaban Bloch, who was a hidden child; and Jeanie's father, Sam Bloch, who fought the Germans as a partisan in the forests of Lithuania and Belorus, and who is today one of the preeminent leaders of the survivors of the Holocaust.

Specifically, I am convinced that we must provide our children with a thorough Jewish education and give them the necessary tools to be knowledgeable and creative participants in our ongoing evolution as a people. This cannot be accomplished if the Holocaust is presented as the most significant event in Jewish history. The Jews, including survivors and children of survivors, who have made the remembrance of the Holocaust the focal point of their Jewish identity do not understand the significance of being a Jew.

As the heirs of the millions who perished during the Holocaust, every facet of the Jewish condition must be integral to our collective being. The reason for being Jewish, and for wanting to remain Jewish, is not and cannot be because the Germans wanted to annihilate us. If we want to instill a love of Judaism in our children, we must expose them to its beauty, to its moral teachings, and to all the complexities of its millennia-old religious and cultural tradition

Moreover, it is not enough for us to commemorate the past. Our place at all times must be at the forefront of the struggle against every form of racial, religious, and ethnic hatred of any kind. We must not forget that Jews are never the only victims of evil. The Armenian and Rwandan genocides, the mass murder of Gypsies by the Nazis, and ethnic cleansing in the former Yugoslavia are but four examples of civilization run amok in the twentieth century alone.

Accordingly, we do not have the right to spend our time talking to ourselves about ourselves. The critical dialogue that we must initiate and maintain is with others of our generation whose parents did not go through the Holocaust. Our role in the community is of primary importance. We must be active and bring our presence and our particular perspective to bear within our respective synagogues, within local and national Jewish organizations, and within society as a whole.

We have learned from our parents' experiences that indifference to the suffering of others is in itself a crime. Because of who we are, we constitute a moral force whose voice can have an impact on humankind. We must, both individually and collectively, raise this voice on behalf of all, Jews and non-Jews alike, who are subjected to discrimination and oppression, or who are threatened by annihilation, anywhere in the world. And we may never be passive, or allow others to be passive, in the face of oppression, for we know only too well that the ultimate consequence of apathy and silence was embodied forever in the flames of Auschwitz and the mass graves of Bergen-Belsen.

Adult Offspring of Holocaust Survivors as Moral Voices in the American-Jewish Community

EVA FOGELMAN

I am an adult child of Holocaust survivors born in a half bombed out hospital in Kassel, Germany. Without a doubt my parents' ordeals and how they transmitted them during my growing-up years inspired my professional endeavors, my worldview, and the moral responsibility I feel toward working on *tikkun olam* (repairing the world). It may seem odd, but my life has been enriched by what I do rather than weighed down or made burdensome.

Over the years I have gravitated toward other children of Holocaust survivors who share my outlook. One of these people is Bella Savran, a social worker, with whom I started short-term awareness groups for children of Holocaust survivors in 1976. While working with these groups, I was surprised to learn that on the one hand were young adults who were completely dysfunctional and who blamed everything that was wrong in their lives on their parents and the Holocaust. On the other hand were the offspring for whom the Holocaust was an impetus to make the world a better place and who understood that they were responsible for their own actions.

It was interesting to see how offspring of survivors integrated their parents' experiences into their lives in different ways. I discovered that among many members of the second generation, a sense of moral commitment came from confronting the injustice of the Holocaust and the complicity, silence, or indifference of the world. I became curious about how second-generation adults had become motivated to grapple with moral questions and become morally engaged.

208

What I discovered was that despite the heterogeneity of the offspring of survivors, their actions stem from an empathic response to their parents' suffering and a moral conviction of responsibility to the dead. To them, mourning was a powerful impetus to action.

Speaking up for moral causes is a constructive way to channel feelings of mourning that are aroused in members of the second generation and a way of resisting succumbing to despair. Although these members of the second generation did not experience direct losses themselves, they felt a powerful sense of empathy with the suffering of their parents and they mourned for the relatives who were murdered and for whom most of them are named.

For me, as a child of survivors, the moral questions raised by the annihilation of an entire group of people became the focus of my graduate work in social and personality psychology at the Graduate Center of City University of New York (CUNY). The central question I struggled with was how does one maintain moral integrity under extreme circumstances when the authority is malevolent? There I met others who were grappling with similar issues.

One of them was Stanley Milgram, whose groundbreaking book, *Obedience to Authority*, revealed that most people surrender personal responsibility if their actions are dictated by authority figures. Milgram's proof was based on his laboratory experiments: people were ordered by others in authority to give electrical shocks to others who could not remember word associations. In reality, this was a simulation. The shock machine was inoperative. In the following years, Milgram was criticized for carrying out an unethical form of research. In my view, this accusation is itself a form of denial and avoids confronting the "real" persecutors.

Being interested in moral capacity in human beings, I was intrigued by the minority in Milgram's study who disobeyed authority and refused to carry out the experiments. These subjects did not administer electrical shocks to the learner if he or she gave the wrong word association. Milgram did not answer the question I raised: What enabled these subjects to maintain their moral integrity?

My specific areas of concentration stem from my father's accounts of the German occupation. When the Germans rolled their tanks into Illya, a Byelorussian town a hundred miles east of Vilna, they issued an endless stream of restrictions and orders aimed at Jews. On Purim, March 20, 1942, the Germans intercepted Jews on their way to work and marched them all off to the village square. One thousand Illyan Jews, among them my father's aunt, uncle, cousins, and friends, were slaughtered. They inadvertently missed my father because he was already at work in the village bakery.

When the Gestapo burst into the bakery to search for Jews who had slipped through the roundup, the Russian supervisor confidently told them, "No Jews here." By the time they returned the following morning, the supervisor had helped my father escape into the woods where he met up with the few Jews who survived the massacre.

While my father hid in the woods, a poor farmer helped him. During the night, the farmer would send his children to my father with food and with ointment for his lice-infested hair. They would also take his clothes to be washed. When winter approached, the farmer, Ivan Safanov, arranged to have my father join the Byelorussian partisans. He survived the war and fought the enemy.

My understanding of morality under conditions of extreme terror became more complex when I learned that another colleague at CUNY, psychohistorian Robert Jay Lifton, did not discover any trace of guilt in the Nazi doctors he interviewed from the late 1970s until the early 1980s. The doctors were not just following orders or doing their duty. Lifton found that they strongly believed they were contributing to a biomedical ideology devoted to eliminating the "germ carrier" that prevented the development of an Aryan race. They felt justified in killing thousands and thousands of Jews.

In the early 1980s, I set out to discover what differentiated the Holocaust rescuers of Jews from most bystanders around them, and how their sense of morality was different from that of the Nazi doctors. I wanted to find out what the behavior of the rescuers could teach us about moral behavior in contemporary, everyday life.

When I began to voice an interest in these issues of courage and resistance, I discovered that most people were suspicious of altruistic behavior. They would say, "The rescuers must have had ulterior motives." Holocaust survivors would maintain, "Don't make such a big deal about the rescuers; there were so few." Psychoanalysts assert that altruism does not exist; unconscious motivation and narcissistic gratification are at the core of helping others.

They didn't convince me. It seemed to me that it took extraordinary courage to act to save a Jew when it meant death. I felt that if we could understand the rescuers, we could also comprehend the idle bystanders and the Nazi collaborators.

In 1981, I traveled throughout the United States, Israel, and Europe in search of rescuers. The details of my findings were recorded in my doctoral dissertation, and in my 1994 book, *Conscience and Courage: Rescuers of Jews During the Holocaust.*

When I present the results of my research to audiences, people inevitably ask, "What would I have done under similar circumstances?" We do not need life-and-death situations to speak up for tolerance and for the acceptance of people who are different from us. I ask my audiences to think about what each person does today, rather than ponder hypothetical questions such as "What would you have done fifty years ago?"

I began to search for the moral voices among the children of survivors who were taking moral action in their everyday life. And if they were, what form did the morality take? Did they need moral courage to act in a morally responsible way under normal conditions? Were risk and sacrifice necessary in the way it was during the Holocaust? I did not have to look very far to find these voices.

Menachem Rosensaft, a New York attorney, was the founding chairman of the International Network of Children of Jewish Holcocaust Survivors. He was among those who brought children of survivors together at the *Kotel* (Western Wall in Jerusalem) in 1981, to join the Holocaust survivors at the World Gathering of Holocaust Survivors. At that meeting, the second generation took a pledge to carry on commemoration, education, and Jewish continuity. Rosensaft and the others, myself among them, acted out of a sense of moral responsibility to the dead.

Through the network he and his colleagues created, children of survivors, as a group, became a moral voice in the American-Jewish community and in the international political arena. "One of my goals," Rosensaft told me, "was to make sure that the second generation not be introverted, but instead also be aware of human and social issues affecting the community as a whole. That's why we were the first group to organize a New York citywide rally on behalf of Ethiopian Jewry in 1982. He added, "We also were a leading factor in the opposition to President Reagan's decision to visit the German military cemetery at Bitburg in 1985, and were probably the one organized group that was consistently and vocally opposed to the president laying a wreath at the graves of the Waffen SS." On May 5, 1985, Rosensaft led a demonstration of second-generation members at Bergen-Belsen against what he called Reagan's "obscene package deal" of Bitburg and the Bergen-Belsen mass graves. More recently, Rosensaft has publicly criticized the German government for failing to provide Holocaust survivors with adequate medical coverage while paying generous pensions to veterans of the Waffen SS.

I found that the children of survivors were using their moral voices at different Jewish and secular institutions. From the World Jewish Congress to the halls of the United States Congress, they work at making the world a better place, while others express their moral convictions through their writing, research, and artistic enterprises.

As a social psychologist, I conducted in-depth interviews with some of these committed voices and leaders in the community. I wanted to find out if and how their parents' experiences under the Third Reich inspired their work and their actions. I did not directly ask questions about moral conviction. I derived my conclusions from a sequential analysis of their feelings and thoughts expressed during the interviews, and from their writings and speeches.

I chose these people because I think they act on the courage of their convictions, even when others criticize them. These individuals, all prominent in the American-Jewish community, have all had an impact on their local communities. Some have national and international reputations, and their voices make a difference in the lives of oppressed people, against injustice, bigotry, intolerance, and racism.

In some cases, they faced danger to help others in distress. Whether their motives were conscious or not, each person is carrying out a mission that was imbedded in his or her being. I found that the "moral self" was manifested in a variety of political and social arenas, from prosecuting Nazi war criminals to rescuing Jews from the former Soviet Union to resisting the rise of anti-Semitism in the world and in Germany today.

One person refused to be interviewed for the study. Although his public voice openly reflects a moral responsibility to the dead, he felt that if I grouped him with others who had similar convictions, it would somehow diminish the effectiveness of his unique voice. When one is pegged with an identifiable group all the stereotypes of this group—some positive but most negative—are attributed to him or her. By remaining separate, a person may feel he avoids being typecast and holds onto his uniqueness. I think this is a mistaken assumption.

Another interviewee wanted to remain anonymous because she felt that her work, which involves bringing Nazi war criminals to trial, would be labeled revenge if people knew that she was the child of survivors. She had already had this convoluted defense used against her in court, as have other lawyers with similar backgrounds. I respect her anonymity and have disguised her identity.

Some interviewees are very open about their family history; others are more private. I was not surprised to find that even among those who were generally knowledgeable about their parents, some did not know the details of their parents' ordeals. The interview process, in some cases, sent them back to their parents to ask more questions. Others live and breathe the murder of each relative.

How does this second-generation voice manifest itself? A case in point is the Middle East peace process. In the 1980s, efforts to bring about a genuine Israeli-Palestinian, or even Jewish-Palestinian, dialogue had come to a virtual standstill. Most Israeli and Jewish leaders, including the leadership of the American-Jewish community, refused to sit down with leaders of the Palestinian Liberation Organization (PLO), who had been responsible for the murder of Jews in Israel and elsewhere. Many in the peace movement believed that if a prominent Holocaust survivor sat down with Yasser Arafat, it would give a moral green light to a reenergized peace process. If those who were the most vulnerable would have the courage to sit and talk with the enemy, then perhaps others would be swayed to do so as well.

Although the survivor community on the whole opposed such a step, Menachem Rosensaft took the risk and traveled with four others to Sweden to meet with Arafat. He was at first shunned by the Holocaust survivor community and members of the organization he helped found, as well as by many American-Jewish organizations. It was clear the community was not ready to face the consequences of a failed effort toward peace.

Rosensaft's parents, the only survivors of their respective families, have been role models who prepared Menachem to be a spokesperson for the second generation. His father, Josef (Yosele), the leader of the Bergen-Belson Survivors' Association, also helped lead the non-Orthodox *she-erit ha-pletah*. This kind of *landsmanshaft* was a self-help group for European Jewish survivors who had no extended family with whom to celebrate holidays and life cycle events.

Yosele and his wife, Hadassah, were the last ones to leave the displaced persons camp in Bergen-Belsen, where for five and a half years he assisted and guided survivors to make the transition from victims to liberated people. Menachem was born there in May 1948.

Conversations about the war in Rosensaft's house did not focus on gruesome details. His mother, Dr. Hadassah Rosensaft, was a heroine. During her incarceration in Auschwitz, she lost her parents, first husband, and five-year-old son. Despite this personal tragedy, while working as a doctor in the inmates' infirmary, she risked her life to save hundreds of women from the gas chambers. She also took similar risks for some 150 children at Bergen-Belsen by bringing them extra milk, food rations, and scarce medication after she was transferred there. When the war was over, she accompanied these orphans to safety in Palestine, and then returned to war-torn Europe to help other survivors.

Rosensaft recalled his parents telling him about the Jewish ability to survive and reconstruction of Jewish life after the war. "In this spirit, my father's reading of the *haggadah* on Passover was interspersed with tales from Auschwitz and Bergen-Belsen, which had become part of our living, evolving family tradition. My parents put potato peels on the *seder* plate. 'These,' my father would explain at the beginning of the seder, 'remind us of Auschwitz where any inmate who was able to get hold of potato peels was fortunate. In the camps, potato peels were food'."

Menachem Rosensaft's moral voice has gone beyond the responsibility he felt as a child of survivors to remember and educate. He felt the need to promote peace and a tolerant State of Israel as well. He wanted to bring to justice Nazi war criminals, to fight racism and bigotry, and to work toward the continuity of the Jewish people. In recent years Rosensaft has begun to identify with his religious ancestry and has embraced a more traditional lifestyle. He sees this as a way of bridging the gap to his observant antecedents and as a way of identifying with his murdered relatives. If he keeps their memory alive, he feels, it as if they are somehow still with us.

"If we criticize the world for having been silent fifty years ago when Jews were being persecuted and murdered," Rosensaft told me, "we have no right to be silent when others are oppressed. In fact, any silence in the face of the suffering of others legitimizes those who fifty years ago were silent themselves." "Those Jews who refuse to recognize that Palestians are entitled to the same civil and human rights that we demand for ourselves are at best xenophobic," Rosensaft told me.

When the opportunity presented itself, Rosensaft was confronted with a moral choice: do the right thing or abide by the Jewish communitywide ban that forbade any meetings that would legitimize Arafat's leadership of the Palestinians. Rosensaft, who at that time was also the national president of the Labor Zionist Alliance, seized the opportunity to move the peace process forward without worrying about the impact on his leadership in the Jewish community.

Perhaps we can look back at Stockholm and remember that small voice that was trying to move the Jewish people toward a more optimistic future for Jews and non-Jews alike.

At a chance meeting between Menachem Rosensaft and Ronald Lauder, Lauder told Rosensaft that if he ever wanted to do something meaningful with his life, he should stop practicing international corporate litigation and come and see him. Shortly thereafter, Rosensaft took a break from practicing law and spent five years directing Lauder's Jewish Renaissance Foundation, which seeks to rebuild contemporary Jewish life in eastern and central Europe.

From Rosensaft's personal experiences, we can see that the moral voice is derived from critical images of the Holocaust as they are transmitted to the second generation. In each individual case, some salient memory, conscious or unconscious, takes on a life of its own. One of the attorneys in the office of Special Investigation I interviewed, who wishes to remain anonymous, remembered that the first time she ever heard the word "Nazis" was while watching the Three Stooges. "I couldn't have been more than six," she told me. "Mo had a moustache and a swastika on, and I thought it was very funny." She paused, then added: "But I didn't understand it. I knew from the way my mother reacted that it was very sad. I had a very loving, gentle mother."

Although most children of Holocaust survivors have a generalized feeling about how they learned about the war, the attorney has concrete memories of learning about the Nazi party. "I watched a trial on television." She does not remember if it was the Eichmann trial or a docudrama. What she does remember are the words of the victims who testified in court. She continued: "Women and men testified about the camps and medical experiments. I remember hearing the name Mengele."

On a Sunday outing with her father after seeing the program, she spontaneously asked him about his life under the Third Reich. "This is one very vivid memory of a conversation with my father." She was fourteen or fifteen and her brothers were not present. She recounted that her father told her he had been a refugee from Germany who managed to come to America in the late thirties and join the American armed forces. She continued, "My dad told me he dropped pamphlets behind enemy lines. I don't think he knew he would end up on the front lines, shouting into loudspeakers, doing dangerous things."

"While we were riding in the car," she recalled, "my father told me that he went into Dachau on April 30, the day after its liberation. He said,

'When I got there . . . ' and he stopped. I looked at him and he just stopped talking and I saw that he was trying very hard not to weep in front of me. But I didn't say anything and to this day he has not told me what he saw. It is very hard to know that my father could not tell me."

The attorney told me that the Holocaust was never seriously discussed in Hebrew School or in public school. But at home it was a different story. Although her parents did not go into specific details, discussion would focus on the ten members of her family who had died. "My mother had a big family and none of them survived. This one and this one and this one was killed. She would say, 'Your cousin . . . and so and so . . . was killed.' It became clear eventually that we were talking about a large number of people."

This young woman began to read about the Holocaust. Reading generated a feeling of wanting to right a terrible wrong. Then, in the 1970s, there were serious allegations about Nazi war criminals who had immigrated (or, even worse, had been recruited to come) to the United States. While in law school she read *Wanted*, Howard Blum's book about Nazis who came to live in the United States. She remembers thinking, My own government allowed these people to come here.

Documents were uncovered by the Justice Department, and in 1979, it established the Office of Special Investigations (OSI) at the behest of Congress—and under the leadership of Brooklyn congresswoman Elizabeth Holtzman, who represented a neighborhood filled with Holocaust survivors. The young attorney read an article about OSI, and knew immediately that this was her calling.

The evolution of a child's commitment to moral action stemming from the ordeal of his or her parents does not require detailed knowledge. For the woman at OSI, the critical images in childhood from television, the nonverbal communication from her father, and the indirect comments of her mother had an intense impact on her. In fact, not until her son did a school project on pilgrims did she learn how her father got out of Germany.

Another case in point is the Foundation for Ethnic Understanding that Rabbi Marc Schneier has established. The foundation exists primarily to improve relations between Jews and other minority groups. On the surface it may not appear as if Rabbi Schneier is acting out of dedication to his family history. His father, Arthur, is a child survivor from Austria who established his own organization, The Appeal Of Conscience Foundation, which recognizes world leaders who exert moral courage. But because racism was at the core of Nazi ideology, the foundation seeks to foster tolerance and understanding as a way of avoiding future holocausts to any group of people.

"As a second generation person," Rabbi Schneier explained,

> I see that the demographics are changing in this country. The Jewish people have a history of reaching out to others and trying to share our commonalities and recognize our differences. Within fifteen years, the present minorities will constitute the majority in America. That means that African Americans, Latinos, and Asians will be the dominant presence here. It is incumbent upon the American-Jewish community, which constitutes less than 2 percent of the American population, to reach out to them and try and look for lines of communication to further understanding.

Rabbi Schneier told me, "My commitment comes from having grown up in my father's home, from being the eighteenth generation of a line of rabbis and understanding that we, the second generation, have a historic responsibility. Our families could not save their own lives, but perhaps by remembering them, we can save and deepen our own. That to me is the challenge of the second and third generation: not to give Hitler a posthumous victory."

Marc founded and built the Hampton synagogue in Westhampton, New York. It was dedicated in August 1994 with a Torah from Hungary, the country in which his father hid during the war. Marc's father saw his synagogue go up in flames on Kristallnacht. "If there is any metaphor of my father's Holocaust experience that stands out in my mind, it is that. And perhaps subconsciously it caused me to commit to building a synagogue. It may also explain why I responded the way I did to the burning of the African-American churches." When black churches were burning, Marc's foundation established a "From the Ashes Fund" with the board of rabbis to raise necessary funds to rebuild the houses of worship that were burned down.

Another second-generation scholar who has emerged to confront the German past is Daniel Jonah Goldhagen, author of *Hitler's Willing Executioners*. Many historians have tackled the questions Goldhagen raises, but unlike the others, his narrative is driven by the atrocities that were committed by the Nazis. Each page is filled with documentation of the abominations that Jews suffered at the hands of the Germans. Goldhagen elevated the discourse to a level of direct confrontation that broke the psychological atmosphere of denial in Germany. For example, he cites the example of a policeman escorting a group of children to a pit where he will murder them. Goldhagen asks: what is the policeman thinking as he is leading the children to be murdered?

Unlike previous theorists, Goldhagen dogmatically concludes that there is only one explanation for the ability of ordinary Germans to engage in such inhumane behavior: annihilationist anti-Semitism.

Goldhagen attributes the success of his book to his "intellectual authority" on this subject, rather than his moral authority as a second-generation scholar. But when it comes to creative and intellectual pursuits that are so directly linked to one's family history, such endeavors derive their spirit from the core self. One cannot separate the person from the work.

In my interview with Goldhagen, he refused to discuss many details of his childhood, because he wanted his scholarly work to be judged on its merits, rather than on his background. Nevertheless, he grew up with a father who survived the German occupation in the Czernowitz ghetto with his nuclear family. He describes his father, a Harvard professor of German history, as a "detached and penetrating scholar" who often discussed the Holocaust at home. Goldhagen says that "it was part of the landscape." At age ten, Goldhagen lived in Munich with his family, and since then has spent a considerable amount of time living and doing research in Germany.

Goldhagen maintains with narrow certitude that scholars who had previously done research on the Holocaust had all missed the point of annihilationist anti-Semitism. His moral voice would have much more authority if he would be more generous to the work of scholars who came before him. He has in effect diminished the historic contributions of such eminent writers as Raul Hilberg, Yehudah Bauer, Michael Marrus, and Christopher Browning.

Goldhagen had easy access to the archival material after Browning struggled, with determination and tenacity, to have the archives opened to researchers by reluctant German bureaucrats still trying to conceal Germany's role in mass murder. Browning's analysis, based on retrospective interviews with some of the members of the battalion, is more nuanced than Goldhagen's in explaining the motivation of the killers.

Goldhagen takes little moral risk when answering questions about present-day German anti-Semitism. He maintains that Germany is a miracle story: the Germans have undergone a fundamental change of national character as a result of the reeducation they received from the allies. He denies that serious racism exists in Germany today, and states that there was no link between the dangerous currents of contemporary racism and German racism before 1945. Goldhagen views current examples of racism and anti-

Semitism as isolated remnants that are politically and socially irrelevant. His position essentially contradicts the basic premise of his book, in which he traced a direct connection between the Germanic anti-Semitism that existed a hundred years before the Holocaust period with the Nazi annihilation of the Jews that came later.

One does not have to fight Holocaust demons directly to function as a moral voice. Issues not directly related to the past occur every day, along with new issues directly derived from the past. And children of survivors take leading roles in shaping the debate.

In the Soviet Jewry movement, children of survivors were at the forefront in saving fellow Jews. Rabbi Israel Singer, secretary general of the World Jewish Congress, and Malcolm Hoenlein, now executive director of the Conference of Presidents of Major American Jewish Organizations, each played leadership roles, risking their own lives to save Jews in the former republics of the Soviet Union. Hundreds of other children of survivors seized the opportunity to act on their moral consciences. Many said to themselves, "No one was there for my parents when they needed rescuing. I don't want future generations to say to me, where were you when Jews needed a lifeline?"

Israel Singer's father sent one sister to America before the outbreak of World War II. Singer told me, "We had 113 immediate members of our family who were killed. They were murdered in one day by the *Einsatzgruppen* on the Polish-Russian border in 1941. They never made it to the concentration camp; they were just shot into the pit, on Hoshana Rabah (a Jewish holiday), 1941. We know of their deaths because one person survived. He was standing at the grave with a child. He was missed, and he then hid in one place after another. Later, he was reunited with the family by one of the Red Cross organizations.

One of Singer's earliest memories is as a three-year old, standing at a kitchen table with 113 *yahrzeit* (memorial) candles that his grandmother lit on Hoshana Rabah. The Brooklyn apartment was often filled with survivors who gravitated toward his home because they had nowhere to sleep. Everyone lived in harmony. No one had money; no one had anything. There was little food. They would sleep in the living room. Singer remembers asking what these candles were for. He was told they represented each of his murdered relatives. He learned that the patriarch of the family was dragged from the synagogue wearing his *tallis* (prayer shawl). Buczacz had been a town with a Jewish population of forty-five thousand, including Nobel laureate Shai Agnon and later Nazi hunter Simon Wiesenthal.

Singer told me,

> Later, I would have weddings for my three daughters, and the only rule
> my mother made was that every living relative should be invited to each
> wedding: every child, every *mechutin* [the relationship that the respective
> parents of the husband and wife have to each other] and every daughter
> and baby. We invited very few friends. We invited only those people who
> survived the war and reproduced. There are 348 indirect survivors of the
> five people who survived the war, children of great-grandchildren. We
> remain in constant contact.

The other critical image that was etched in Rabbi Singer's memory was
the day Israel was declared a State. "I was aware that we were living in an
ultra-Orthodox neighborhood," he related to me. "My grandfather, who
wore a *bekishe* [long black coat] and *payos* [ritual sidecurls], hired a seam-
stress to sew a giant Israeli flag that was five stories tall. It covered the entire
front of our house. We displayed it the day Israel was born and for some
time thereafter. Ours was the only house in Williamsburg with an Israeli
flag, and my classmates and the Hassidim would walk by the house and
insult and attack that flag.

"My grandfather did not care; it was vindication for the survivors." He
also remembers a speech made by the anti-Zionist rabbi who lived in
Williamsburg. "He said that Hakadosh-Baruch-Hu [God] had no right to
test the Jewish people twice in one generation: first, by killing us and then
by giving us the State. He said it shouldn't be granted to us until the day
of the Messiah."

Singer acknowledges that these early experiences left indelible memories that stayed with him all through his life and influenced his worldview
and political activities.

Singer was a student and later a professor of political science at Brooklyn College. He also taught English at Yeshiva Torah Vodaath and law at
Bar Ilan University in Ramat Gan. He told me,

> I was against the Vietnam War. I fought for human rights, and was in-
> volved in struggles to take over the college during the sit-ins in the sixties
> at Brooklyn College. I was the only *yarmulke* [skullcap] involved in civil
> rights struggles in those days—a right wing Yeshiva student involved in left
> wing causes. But that brought me into a kind of public life, and that's how
> I became involved in the struggle for Soviet Jewry. That latter struggle
> brought me to the World Jewish Congress.

As a representative of the WJC, I negotiated Yosef Mendolevitch's release and the release of the other prisoners of conscience in the former Soviet Union. The World Jewish Congress brought about all these prisoners' freedom. I had gone to Russia with my wife. Part of my motivation came from the Holocaust, the responsibility that I felt to do things for others that people had not done for my own parents. And later I became involved in such causes as restitution. It's all part of the same thing. It's not a negative struggle. It's a positive struggle for Jews to become aware of who they are.

I visited almost every country in which Jews lived, from Australia to Norway, from Sweden to South Africa. I have met every different kind of survivor, from Argentina to Russia. I met survivors who were blind, elderly, who spoke only Yiddish, and I met one Sephardic Jew who came from Salonika.

On my honeymoon, my wife and I were sitting on a bus in a faraway place. I slid over to a person who looked Jewish and began to speak with him. At this point my wife told me that if we visited one more cemetery, one more memorial, if I talked to one more old Jew, she would just go back to the States and let me finish the honeymoon by myself.

In 1980, two sons of survivors, Sam Gejdenson from Connecticut and Ron Wyden from Oregon, both thirty-one, were elected to Congress. Each uses the democratic process to promote human equality, to oppose abuse of the environment, to deter nuclear buildup, and to open our shores to refugees. Leaders such as Gejdenson and Wyden (who is now a senator) instill hope in the positive use of governmental power, as opposed to the perversion of that power in the Third Reich. From Rabbi Abie Ingber, who is the director of Hillel at the University of Cincinatti, to Sam Norich, who was a student leader in Madison, Wisconsin, the second-generation's moral voices are also heard in local communities.

Sam Norich, now general manager of the Forward Association, was a director of the Commission on Israel-Diaspora Relations established by the Israel Democracy Institute, a think tank founded by Israeli Yossi Beilin. Norich reconnects to his Jewish roots and the dreams that were destroyed in his parents' birthplace.

Israel rekindled Norich's passion for Judaism. His father had been an active Socialist Zionist in his youth in Lodz and could not go to Palestine after the liberation because his wife and son were ill. For Sam Norich, "politics was an actualization of community. That's what attracted me to Israel, the idea that the place had been built by 'us.' " Norich remembers walking in Tel Aviv with his father's friend, a party comrade who worked in a construction company for thirty years. "He said: 'We built that one in sixty-eight, and we worked on that one in sixty-five.' "

Norich could feel that it was part of a collective Jewish effort and that he was part of it. He felt reconnected with his parents when he became active in Jewish activities. He felt "it was an affirmation of my belonging to a liberal and Zionist political tradition that I had come to independently. Once I got to Israel I discovered it had also been my father's political tradition." Learning about his father's political traditions modified and shaped Norich's.

What solidified Norich's leadership were his day-in-day-out activities in Madison, Wisconsin. "During my graduate years," he related, "I spent a huge proportion of my time on political activities. It simply became a habit. And with several other people, we founded Kibbutz Langdon, a residential co-op for students at the University of Wisconsin, and I lived there for three years."

The Jewish environment Norich chose to live in was defined not so much in religious terms as in social, communal, and political terms. Yet, his religious consciousness developed while living in this unusual American kibbutz.

Although Norich and the other children of survivors pursue morally based activities through organizations or communities, others, such as the prominent writer of social and literary criticism Leon Wieseltier of *The New Republic*, carry on individually. Wieseltier's mother, Stella, a Polish survivor, worked in the mid-1970s at the first Holcocaust resource center established in the United States, the Brooklyn Center for Holocaust Studies, founded by Dr. Yaffa Eliach.

Wieseltier constantly speaks up for the dead and for the restoration of their dignity when their memory is desecrated. When the memory of murdered Jews was being profaned at Auschwitz by Carmelite nuns, Wieseltier spoke out in the op-ed pages of the *New York Times*. His eloquence, his penetrating words, and his candor caught the attention of the body politic: "It appears that Auschwitz has lost none of its power to derange. Nobody dies there anymore; but decency still does."

Israel Singer tracks the money stolen from the victims of the Holocaust wherever it leads, and some of those places turn out to be extremely surprising. Thanks to his efforts (and those of World Jewish Congress president Edgar Bronfman Sr. and executive director Elan Steinberg, also a child of survivors), elderly survivors may soon be treated for medical and psychological conditions that could not be dealt with previously because of lack of funds. Perhaps some of them will be able to die with dignity.

Members of the second generation who truly speak in a moral voice understand that the State of Israel, imperfect vessel that it is, must be included in the agenda. For most of the moral voices, the public and personal are intertwined. And so we have to set examples publicly and privately. When one becomes a moral voice that represents a movement or a generation, separating the sacred from the profane is difficult. Leaders are scrutinized more closely than average people.

Elan Steinberg keeps his family background private, but he clearly was motivated by his parents' fighting spirit when he relentlessly strove to make the world aware of Prime Minister Kurt Waldheim's Nazi past, or when he spoke on behalf of survivors' stolen property and Swiss bank accounts. Steinberg's eloquent words say it all: "One of the earliest ways I related to my parents' hiding and escaping in the woods of Tarnopol, Poland, was at the Passover Seder, where we all have to see ourselves as if we came out of Egypt." He paraphrased the Haggadah: "Whether we are learned, whether we know of the Torah, whether we have studied, makes no difference whether or not you survived the Holocaust." Steinberg says, "I am not sure where luck applies, I am not sure where circumstances apply, so in that sense I viewed myself as a miracle child and in a perverse kind of way our revenge against Hitler."

Our obligation as sons and daughters of survivors is to create a world in which the traditional Jewish imperative of *tikkun olam* is a paramount priority. Actively engaging in moral causes is one way of undoing the sense of helplessness one feels in learning about what happened to our parents. Although we cannot undo the pain and suffering they endured, we can overcome this defenselessness by speaking up against injustices today and helping oppressed people.

PART FIVE

Identity and the Yiddish Language

Introduction

Yiddish was the language of most of the victims and martyrs of the Holocaust. It was the *mameloshen* that united Jews from a variety of eastern European nations. They may have done business in the language of their respective countries. But at home, with their families, and with friends, they spoke Yiddish. After the war, at memorial services held in America, speakers were admonished to deliver their remarks in Yiddish—the language that defines a culture, a religion, and a people of whom two-thirds were exterminated.

For the second generation it is as if speaking the language itself becomes an act of commemoration and solidarity. Contributors to this section raise important questions about the relationship between Yiddish and the lost world of European Judaism. Reviving Yiddish is a way of remaining connected to a vanished past. Yiddish is the language that links the second generation to their survivor parents, to relatives whom they never knew.

A Yiddish Writer Who Writes in French

MYRIAM ANISSIMOV

I belong to that peculiar generation of Jews whose lot was the obligation to speak Yiddish, my mother tongue, in a tongue that is both familiar and "foreign"—French. If Yiddish is still used as a vernacular language by the Hasidim, mainly in New York, Meah Shearim, and Bnei Brak, it is disappearing outside of those purely religious groups. Yet, fifty years ago, Yiddish—Jewish speech—was spoken by ten million persons. Jewish civilization in eastern Europe thought the world in Yiddish, that fusion language born on the banks of the Rhine in a hostile environment.

Before the catastrophe, the Hurban, hundreds of Yiddish newspapers appeared every day, writers imagined modernity in that idiom, which the Germans considered an offense, a spit in the face of the great Goethe.

Yiddish disappeared in the ghettos, in the immense graves the *Einsatzgruppen* made the victims dig before slaughtering them, in the gas chambers of the extermination camps. The dead exchanged their last words in Yiddish. Facing the jovial murderers, mothers calmed their children, told them good-bye in Yiddish before being rushed with them into the hole full of men, women, children, and blood. Little ones separated from their parents in the "cloaca" of Treblinka howled "Mamele! Tateh!" That reality has invaded my consciousness ever since I was four years old and a bloated young man, my father's brother, who had survived Auschwitz, came to our house. He told the miracle of his survival and the murder of his whole family, of our whole family, of an entire people in Yiddish, which had become the language of the dead. The photos showing heaps of cadavers had inscriptions in Hebrew letters. It was in Yiddish that my father demanded that I not forget them: *Farges nicht!*

In my childish eyes, Yiddish had become an idiom we alone understood and which marked our horrible peculiarity: of a group destined to die that had survived—legitimately? I wondered. So, when my father and mother spoke Yiddish, when my father addressed me in Yiddish, it seemed likely that an imminent catastrophe was about to take place.

Every year, one Sunday morning in spring, we walked along a little path on the edge of a woods. That was the commemoration of the execution of Châtillon d'Azergues. There, in the woods, Jews rounded up in the streets of Lyons had been slaughtered. When we came, everything was peaceful. I saw some flags at the head of the procession. You heard only the birds' songs and the sound of our footsteps on the pavement. Then the mother of a fifteen-year-old boy who was among the victims suddenly started sobbing, yelling in Yiddish. People rushed to hold her up as her voice was gradually drowned out by the hymn of the Vilna Partisans: "*Zog nit kein mol az du geist dem leztn veg . . .*" (Never say that you are walking the last road).

The Yiddish writers who had lived on now addressed only a handful of survivors. As for us naturalized Jewish children, the state considered us future citizens of the Mosaic faith. Nothing of the sort! If my father, an adherent of the Enlightenment, a former Bundist, member of the Union of Jews for Resistance and Mutual Aid (UJRE) did not cross the threshold of the *shul*, even on Yom Kippur, he was not averse to wait for his sister on the sidewalk while smoking a cornpaper Boyard. But he didn't work on Yom Kippur and lit candles im memory of his parents. Yom Kippur was still the dead. But the living? My father had endless discussions in Yiddish on Sunday morning on Place des Terreaux, and in the afternoon in my grandfather's library over a glass of tea.

Today, Yiddish libraries are frequented by melancholic Jews, barely able to stumble through a few sentences with an immense effort, fleeting images scurrying through their mind. But there is not only the sound of Yiddish, there is also the "smell" of Yiddish. The smell of eastern European Jewish food seems closely linked to the sound of the Yiddish language. And there is not only the smell of the kitchen, but also of the Workshop. I write Workshop with a capital letter because the Workshop was a whole world. The strange country where I grew up and which no longer exists. The vast room where the sewing machines hummed and where the steam rose releasing the finished goods under the damp cloth and the weight of the gas iron pushed by the presser, the dry cutting of the scissors that slashed paths drawn in chalk in the thick pad of coats.

I cannot hear Yiddish spoken without feeling an immense emotion that is never bound to a feeling of joy. Around the scraps of Yiddish that inhabit my dreams and my defective memory is a dark gulf filled with ashes. A few rare photos show us the catastrophe taking place, hazy images in black and white where naked women are seen carrying their children in their arms at the entrance to the gas chamber, executions, naked bodies rushed into the graves.

Other images in color, taken by the Nazi Walter Genewein in the Lodz Ghetto (*Litzmannstadt die Stadt der Zukunft* [Litzmannstadt, the city of the future—for the Nazis]), and sold to an antique dealer in Salzburg in 1987, tell us how the Jews lived in the anteroom of death. Haim Rumkowski, the chairman of the Judenrat, had prophesied: *"Unzer einziger veg iz arbeyt"* (Our only way—of survival—is work).

Primo Levi tells that, when he arrived at Auschwitz, a Polish Jew, amazed to learn that he spoke Italian, abused him: "If you don't speak Yiddish, you are not a Jew." Perhaps it was to convince himself of his Judaism that, forty years later, agnostic that he was, he dedicated a year to learning to read the major language spoken in the extermination camps. Levi, the Enlightenment intellectual, thus joined the immense host of those swallowed up; in their memory, he learned a few rudiments of their language, and wrote a book, *If Not Now When,* to immortalize a part of what had been annihilated.[1]

The books I have written have their source in the sparks, the phrases, the words of the Yiddish language. Even poor, defective, and miserable, these Yiddish sources have assumed a considerable importance. So impressive that they sustain, crossbreed the edifice of French, which is now merely the support, the vehicle of an emotion born in another world, and developed with other materials from an immense imaginary structure: the charred walls of the shtetl houses, the walls of the ghettos, the walls of the synagogues, the greenish walls of the gas chambers, Yiddish. Each word of the Yiddish language is familiar to me, but it lies in me as at the bottom of a grave, where, rifling through the earth, one digs up bone fragments.

In this state of mind, still unconscious, I as a child had to learn to read and write French. It was not easy. My teachers scolded me for seasoning my written French with neologisms that were both foreign and horrible. "Are your parents French?" one teacher remarked. Those disgraced words, crossed

---

1. This meditation of Rabbi Hillel the Elder is taken from Pirkei Avot 1:14: "If I am not for myself, who will be for me? If I am only for myself, what am I? And if not now, when?"

out with red lines, were fragments from conversations heard in the Work-shop, for we also lived in the Workshop. Full of remorse and resentment, I had to remove them from the territory of my papers. I was proud to reintroduce them into the hybrid language of my books. No doubt, on the fertile compost of the conflict between French and Yiddish, my manner—can that be called style?—was formed. Nothing had been premeditated. I had made no theoretical decision to achieve that result.

If the Yiddish world that disappeared in the Shoah belongs to the realm of myth and fantasy, I have still kept alive in me the voice of my father and my grandfather, of my Aunt Sourale, of my mother. I still have the miracu-lous privilege of being able to hear Yiddish in Paris, to recognize the savory French mixed with Yiddish that excited Paul Morand when he ventured in search of strong emotions in the alleys of the Marais.

When the last Yiddish-speaking Jews disappear, the thousands of books in the Medem Library in Paris will have no more readers. The millions of volumes printed in Yiddish everywhere in the world will no longer be wanted, no longer held or read. Those who wrote them will be forgotten, except for the few lucky ones who were translated. They will become ob-jects of scholarship at best. This gap we feel inside us will grow wider. Then silence will come. Yiddish will no longer be heard. No author will be fertilized anymore by its music, its humor, its sensuality, its poetry. Yiddish will have the status of a dead language, but for some of us—types who are also disappearing—it will be like an amputated limb whose sensory memory is preserved. We will have finally lost the world of our origins.

My mother bequeathed me my grandfather's six hundred books. Often contemplating their canvas jackets, deciphering with a shudder the letters of the Hebrew alphabet in works printed in Lodz, Vilna, Warsaw, Paris, Buenos Aires, New York, and Moscow, before and after the Hurban, I draw strength to write in French. Close to the Yiddish flickering in the shadow like the flame of a candle, to my amazement, I hear sentences loom up in French. In all circumstances, they preserve a bond with the sunken world of my origins. So, indestructibly linked to a language marked by the scourge of destruction and death, I became "a Yiddish writer in French."

Translated from the French by Barbara Harshav

On the Yiddish Question

ANITA NORICH

Half my lifetime ago, I was studying for my Ph.D. in English literature when I embarrassed myself with the following thought: I was about to become, by the standards that were then familiar to me, a highly (over) educated (albeit unemployed) intellectual, and yet, I was illiterate in my native tongue. I, who would soon take comprehensive exams concentrating on the history of the English novel, had never read a newspaper— much less a poem—in Yiddish, could name not a single Yiddish novel, and, by dint of much concentrated thought, might have been able to name no more than three Yiddish writers. I decided I should address what I understood as this anomaly and so, having studied French and, with much resistance, German, I petitioned Columbia to recognize Yiddish as one of my required foreign languages. When they refused, I was offended. Offended that "they" would not recognize the language that I, most of my peers, and many of our parents had not acknowledged either. And so I claimed that I needed Yiddish for professional reasons to do comparative work in the history of the Yiddish novel. This time, Columbia approved the petition and I was stuck, having at least to pretend to make good on my word. I learned to read Yiddish by sitting with my father, in my parents' Bronx kitchen, as he read volume one of *Ale verk fun Sholem Aleykhem (The collected works of Sholem Aleichem)*, a volume I borrowed from a neighbor. I watched his finger move across the letters on the page. He read as I followed, then he followed as I read, and within a few weeks I was reading on my own.

My parents were bemused by this project, at times proud that I seemed to be reclaiming a language we spoke at home but that none of us had particularly valued, at times annoyed that I was wasting my time—first in

232

a Ph.D. program when I could be teaching, then learning Yiddish when I could be studying more important, or at least more useful, subjects. I think I was a bit bemused myself, first that my father was at long last helping me with my homework (the immigrant experience had reversed those roles long ago), then at the struggle I had learning to read a language in which I was fluent. The differences between my impeccable kitchen Yiddish and that of the literary world were striking. And, finally, the more I read, the more I became fascinated with the incredible opulence of that literature, the tone of the irreverence and love it combined, its social passion, its formal and thematic range. I completed my degree, specializing in the Victorian novel, but continued to read Yiddish as well. My parents continued to be puzzled. In their youth, in Poland, they had read the literature I was now reading, but they had found it stifling, too limited for the expansive promise of European literatures—of Polish, German, Russian, English, and French in the original or translation. Why was their American-educated daughter exhibiting these regressive proclivities?

I exaggerate a bit, both my parents' bafflement and my own. I have told this story many times and always with a similar tone of ironic distance, as if it were a story about someone close to me but not me, as if it were an intellectual quest on which I had embarked in my impressionable youth, as if it were all about the wonders of Yiddish literature. I try very hard to tell it, to myself as well as to others, as if it had little to do with my parents' experiences in the Lodz ghetto or in Auschwitz, Bergen-Belsen, and Dachau, or with my own birth in a DP camp in Germany, or growing up as a child of these survivors. I tell it as if "survivor" needed no translation in my lexicon. But I know better. Yiddish was all the things I was finding in it, but it was also Lodz and my grandparents and a world I could never know. It was the sounds of home and also the sounds of the dead. When my dead spoke to me, they always spoke Yiddish. They never spoke of how they had been murdered, but always of Lodz and Zakopane and family and cooking and the fur trade and, sometimes, of the subversive power of books. And they never thought it odd to meet the child born after their deaths. Nor did they ever ask how a happy, well-adjusted American girl had come to speak such a wonderfully rich, unaccented Yiddish. I was passing, I could tell them, passing as an American, a student, sometimes as an American Jew. But I had not deserted them, leaving them to their fates. I still looked like them, thought like them, spoke like them. It is no wonder that I never told Columbia these reasons for wanting to learn Yiddish. But it is disconcerting that I never admitted them to myself.

My mother worried that Yiddish would literally betray me in ways that my unremarkable name and American English accent never would. One could hide behind Shakespeare or the Victorian novel, but Yiddish offered no safe haven. No passing was possible for me in Yiddish. On the contrary, it called attention to the hiding places I might have sought. When I went to Michigan (*mit di mishigane/meshugane?* [With the mad?]) went the inescapable pun that my mother was the first of many to make), things got worse because I was then in unknown terrain, no longer close to family or to the relative familiarity of New York. I don't even remember if my mother ever said these things directly.

I knew she thought them, or I thought I knew, because everything in my life had prepared me to have those thoughts myself. I may not have spoken to the dead of anything but prewar life, but every response I had to my own life was conditioned by their deaths, as if I had been there with them and barely escaped. When I entered a movie theater, I looked for the exit doors. When I met people, I wondered what they would be like in a crisis, if they were the kinds of people whose attics (in New York!) would be safe. I was, in short, a fairly typical child of survivors according to much of the psychological literature and popular perceptions: highly functioning, successful, loving, with a good sense of humor and social responsibility, frightened much of the time, living in a past I could not bear to name.

I knew the past in the same visceral way I had known as a small child that I should not speak Yiddish on Munich buses, or that my being even fifteen minutes late would make my mother worry beyond endurance, or that calling attention to oneself was dangerous. I had what I imagined to be my parents' reactions to the world. Psychologists no doubt have terms for such things—"secondary posttraumatic stress" or some equally misshapen words—not quite euphemisms, not quite accurate, ugly in sound and sense. The early 1970s, when children of survivors began to speak about the extent to which we shared experiences and reactions, was a great period of liberation for many of us. We, too, were normal as we had hoped all along. Too soon I came to reject this shared identity, reject the categories that I feared would constrain me, reject the role of victim it seemed increasingly to imply. What right had we—or *I*, the part of speech so hard to claim—to take center stage in the story of the Holocaust? What right to be studied or explained or pitied? It was self-indulgent, and I questioned neither the belief that such self-indulgence was a bad thing nor that it was self-indulgent nor what it meant to call it bad.

My mother's voice spoke thus in my ear—again, always, in Yiddish, wittily, ironically, disparagingly. I thought it was my voice because, though I could not have articulated it at the time, I was accustomed to thinking like my parents although I had not had (thank God, I still add) their experiences. Years later, I came to call this a dysfunctional reaction formation, proof to me yet again of my ability to hide behind unpleasant language, as if those sober, detached words could reveal what it felt like to respond to experiences I had never had. I wonder, now, what it means to see experiences and feelings on a continuum, as if feelings needed to be justified by having an antecedent in personal experience. I understood that my parents' worries, their fears and ambitions emerged out of their lives before and during the war. (It was always "the war," no gloss or further information ever being required.) Mine, I thought, emerged out of theirs. That left very little room for my experiences or even for feelings that were not so causally grounded.

In every way imaginable, this myth about responding as if I were someone else—like myths of self-sufficiency and dependency it partly replaced—was all encompassing. That, of course, is the power of myth. It gave me a way of explaining to myself why I wanted to be surrounded with a wide circle of friends (because my parents had), although it was so hard for me to trust anyone (as it was for my parents); why I agonized over every decision (as though it meant deciding whether fleeing Russia or staying put was the better option) but was considered a take-charge kind of person by those who thought they knew me (one always had to be prepared to act); why I needed to know everything (because maybe there was some piece of information that could make sense of the decision to flee or stay) but would reveal little about myself (because it might be used against me); why I distrusted change (it could be for the worse) but was not satisfied with the status quo (it was already bad).

What can it mean to feel as if one must justify emotions, seeking to legitimate them against some cosmic scale on which they rarely even register? On one side of the scale is THE WAR. On the other, my life with its comparatively minor sorrows or depressions or pains. It is difficult to be a strong willed, self-reflexive individual and yet sustain that level of personal insignificance throughout a lifetime. I have managed to do so for a very long time, but at a cost I have not yet been able to assess adequately.

There was a moment in my life when the overwhelming poignancy of it all became clearest. It was a year after my mother's death, in the midst of fathomless mourning beyond utterance and imagining. I spoke more Yiddish than usual that year, because I spent part of the year abroad with Yiddish-speaking relatives and friends. When my father and brother and I were composing the words to place on her headstone, I wanted to follow a custom I had seen in Israel. There, when Holocaust survivors die, a memorial is erected for them and, symbolically, for their immediate family, dead in the war but without graves or markers. Millions are slowly given a place of remembrance, name by name. I wanted to do that for my mother, who had carried the memory of her mother, her sister, and brother with her throughout her life and for whom we could do no more or less) than this final gesture. (Her father had been ill and died—blessedly, as it turns out—young. It was something of a miracle to have had one grandparent who had died in some rather commonplace way.) I knew that the inscription we composed had to be in Yiddish and it had to name my mother's family. *"Tsum eybikn ondenk fun ir mame Khane, shvester Gitl, un bruder Moyshe, umgekumen in letstn khurbn"* it finally said. (In eternal memory of her mother, Khane, sister, Gitl, and brother, Moshe, who perished in the last Holocaust.) I am named for her mother, Khane; my niece is named for her sister, Gitl; no one carries Moshe's name yet. They all seemed more alive to me somehow, by being buried and etched in stone with my mother. The English resonates differently from the Yiddish. *Khurbn* is Holocaust, but also ruin, devastation; it invokes the destruction of the Temple in Jerusalem as well. *Umkum* is death, but it is associated with violence. *Letstn* means last, a gesture to history and all the previous destructions, as well as a hope that this would be the final one, succeeded by no others in Jewish history. The cemetery at first refused to allow us to write any names other than my mother's on her headstone, although they offered to let us purchase a separate plot and erect a memorial stone there. They had clearly missed the point. After much negotiation, they consented.

I had been unable to speak at my mother's funeral, but I was determined to speak at the unveiling. The opportunity to do so seemed like a final gift from her. In what language, I wondered. I chose comprehension over appropriateness. It seemed most appropriate, for her and for her friends, that I speak in Yiddish, but I knew that some people would not understand me and so I made the choice that Yiddish speakers are increasingly compelled to make. My brother and I, it turns out, responded similarly to the fact that we were able to stand next to her grave, know her *yortsayt* (anniversary of death), compose her memorial: *skhus-oves* (ancestral merit), we thought in Yiddish. Again, a concept that is difficult to translate. It conveys a sense of privilege, unearned except by virtue of one's ancestors. Because of them one is blessed. This was a *skhus* of which my mother had been deprived, but that she had given me. I could choose a language and appropriate words, honor her memory with them, and was privileged to know when and where to utter them. The simple, concrete certainty of place and time became my nostalgia. Instead of photographs, stories, memories, I had a place where names were written. To think of standing near my mother's grave as a *skhus* . . . It was a rare moment of perception about what it meant to me to be a child of survivors. We take our blessings where we can find them, unwilling to let go of the idea of blessings, but craving something a little less numinous too.

Often, then and at other times, I have reached for the tangible as if to reassure myself of the palpability of existence. I have found, instead, that my imagination is peopled by those whom I have never met and lives in places I have never been. I have no desire to return to Munich or to the DP camp of my early years. I have never been to Poland and it seems wrong to me to go there. To find what? I think of it as one vast cemetery, but there is not even an actual cemetery where I can find the graves of my dead. It is a kind of palimpsest or pentimento for me, a canvas over which new images have been drawn, not quite erasing the old but blurring them beyond recognition.

There is a poem by one of my favorite Yiddish poets, Malka Heifetz-Tussman, called *"keylers un beydemer"* (Cellars and attics), in which the speaker and her friend, another poet named Ted, tell each other of their parents' homes. Ted speaks of the objects his children will find in their grandparents' cellar and attic near Boston—the clothes, pots, jewelry, guns—that contain the history and traditions of his family. She tells him of the ritual garments, menorahs, shofars that her children will find in their ancestral home. And when he asks where this house is, she answers, *"yidishlekh—/A frage af a frage:/Vu iz/dos alte hoyz mayn zeydns?"* (Jewishy—a question with a question: where is that old house of my grandfather's?"). Homecoming is not a function of place. Nor, despite what I have tried to learn from my professional commitments to literary criticism and, particularly, to Jewish culture, do I find a homecoming primarily in texts. I come home *to* language, *in* Yiddish, not only as the language spoken in my childhood home, but also as the language spoken in those older homes to which none of us can return.

The first book I wrote had no title until it was completed, and a friend, reading my introduction, found the title for me there: "The Homeless

Imagination," he said. It was there all along, a refrain I could not see. Its working title had been a little too precious: "In/Fertile Ground" I thought of calling it, trying to evoke the tensions about the future of Yiddish in Europe and America, the question of whether America could offer fertile soil for Yiddish, or whether it was, instead, fated to remain barren, incapable of new generation. Like Israel Joshua Singer, the subject of my book, I sought a location in which Yiddish, the imagination, culture, the future could all coexist.

The metaphor of homelessness seemed more apt than that of fertility, perhaps because it was less fraught. I have never, in fact, been homeless. Nor was Singer. Nor was Yiddish. I have a beautiful house, complete with a cellar and attic and antique furniture I have acquired in the last decade or so. (My parents' grandchildren, I thought with each new purchase, will have somewhere to go, to rummage through old things and discover the past.) I am perfectly at home in America, in its landscape and idiom, and I recognize that any alienation or estrangement from which I may suffer is only symbolic. It has never had any serious literal or material consequences. But my imagination continues to live elsewhere. That is something else I share with Yiddish. It can't go home again either, and while it may be welcomed elsewhere, its roots can't quite dig deeply enough.

I resist the impulse to anthropomorphize and psychoanalyze Yiddish, although I know that I am sometimes guilty of doing exactly that. I do not want my students or my readers to see it as another victim of the Holocaust, a precious remnant to be enshrined and guarded. I refuse to make an icon or an idol out of Yiddish, although now and then I cannot help sentimentalizing it a bit. It belongs everywhere and nowhere. It speaks to all Jews whose ancestors ever set foot in eastern Europe, but few of them can understand it. It occasions a great deal of mawkish nonsense as well as rigorous scholarship. It has a fantastic literature, but few can name its writers. It is full of pithy, witty, ironic idioms and, in Anglicized form, some of the worst, most degrading jokes I know. I love these contradictions. Often, I find them frustrating, but I love the range and energy they embody. Still, I worry that in casting my lot so firmly—personally and professionally—with Yiddish I may separate myself from the living, emerging cultures around me. There is a terrible kind of narcissism in thinking that one lives as the embodiment of the past, speaking the language the dead might have used, perhaps even speaking for them.

I have language nightmares. I walk into a classroom and begin lecturing, but no one understands me. It is an advanced Yiddish class, but everyone has signed up for something else and they think I am mad, speaking in tongues. (The *michigane/meshugene* [mad] again.) Or I am at a border crossing, nervously handing over my precious American passport, but unable to answer simple questions in English. I am in Germany, but when I speak German, croaking animal noises are all that emerge. These are transparent images, too easy to tell and to interpret, but nonetheless true. Then there are the daydreams. I am running out of people to talk to and it scares me to think of using words that no one around me will understand. I imagine myself, decades hence, a senile, old woman reverting to her first language, seeming to babble nonsense. I imagine myself after a stroke, after some horrible accident, stricken with some form of aphasia, having forgotten every language but the incomprehensible one. I imagine hospital staff solicitously worrying about what language most resembles mine and bringing in some German-speaking doctor to help. That's as far as my imagination is willing to go.

Usually (fortunately for me and those around me), my days and nights are not spent at such a pitch of anxiety. I have learned not to take myself so seriously, partly because it would make me insufferable, partly because nothing is as serious as the defining events of my life—events I did not, in fact, live. I rarely write or speak publicly about being a child of survivors. I worry that I ran out of new things to say more than twenty years ago and I am reluctant (even in this essay) to offer autobiographical insights that seem inevitably conventional and even self-congratulatory. ("See how I have managed to overcome these obstacles" is what I fear implying.) The very form of the memoir raises expectations that make me uncomfortable when I am the writing subject. Again, Malka Heifetz-Tussman gives me the language to express my hesitation. In a poem entitled "Tselokhes" (For spite), she answers the critics who expect that as a Jew and a Yiddish poet, she must write a poem about *khurbn*. Despite the destroyers of her people, to spite them she will live in the world, see her children marry and procreate new generations, and refrain from putting her grief into words. *"(A bushe oyftsushraybn/'troyer' af papir)"* [(A shame to write 'sorrow' on paper)], she exclaims, containing the vehemence of this outburst within the parentheses, as if it were an aside rather than the revelation she must convey to others who write such words too facilely.

(A bushe oyftsushraybn/'troyer' af papir). Much of what is most important to me is contained within my own parentheses in this essay: the explanations that seek to make comprehensible what may not be as clear even to me as I would like; those explanations that are utterly clear to me and yet

so difficult to convey; translations from Yiddish; even transliterations. *"Oyftsushraybn"* is a small rebellion. Should I write *"aftsushraybn"* as standard principles of transliteration dictate, or *"oyftsushrabyn,"* as my Polish-Yiddish accent would encourage? More than a comment about standardization, this question contains within it a range of cultural battles and the recognition that no one is learning my parents' Yiddish and no one will. The accent in which I teach Yiddish language is not the accent in which I speak to my father, so that, even in Yiddish, I seem to be always translating. *Troyer* is sorrow and sadness and grief and mourning. I cannot get all that into one English word. Translators always lament what is lost in the translation, and Yiddish should be considered no more or less difficult to translate than any other language. But, in the case of Yiddish, one of the things I fear losing in the translation is me. It is a *troyer*—a source of sorrow and sadness and grief and mourning—to be compelled to translate and yet I know that if I am to speak to the communities in which I live, I must translate although I am not—by training, inclination, or talent—a translator. My primary materials are almost always in Yiddish whether they are stories or poems or essays or, as in this case, me. The language in which I form and present these analyses is almost always English. My subject's language is foreign to most of my readers; the language and idiom in which I write are foreign to the cultural landscape that is my primary subject. Everyone who has experienced bilingual life will recognize some version of this dilemma. But in Yiddish it can assume epic proportions as speaking populations diminish and we recall their histories in this century.

The stakes in this are extraordinarily high. Sometimes, I feel translation as an act of violence, of betrayal. I want others to know "my" culture as it lived before the war. Translation seems to complete the work of obliteration carried out in Europe. It seems to call into question the viability of the still-living language. But I also think of it as a loving resistance, a defiance that preserves a culture whose transformation should not be met with silence. Much of my professional and personal life is spent trying to negotiate between these two extremes. My scholarly work has often demanded a dispassionate and objective tone, but there are times in the classroom when all such claims disappear and I exult in the decision I made twenty years ago to learn more Yiddish. A Yiddish sentence newly formed by a student from the Detroit suburbs, a Yiddish poem "discovered" by an American who never saw a Yiddish book, a conference in which colleagues my age speak to one another in a richly nuanced Yiddish, Yiddish E-mail (even in transliteration)—these are not the stuff of which revolutions or redemption are made. The delight they give me, though, should require no translation at all. These are among the moments that bring me as close as I will come to Lodz and to the grandparents whose name I bear.

(What is most haunting about the dead is that they always have the last word.)

Shards

MIRIAM TABAK GOTTDANK ISAACS

Yortseit

Pale moths behind
The wallboards, the
House bursts into flame
Rotting, decaying
I've lost something
Missed connections
I can't get where
I'm going
People fade in and out

The people fading in and out are members of my family. I will introduce
them to you as they have appeared to me. Because none of them are here
to tell, you must read here what I have learned from them.

Songs

When I was a child I wanted to learn as much as I could from my mother
but all she could teach me were fragments, like pottery shards, parts of
songs, stories and prayers. Most of these were in Yiddish, which was after
all what we spoke, but many of her bits and pieces were in other languages: Hebrew, Hungarian, Rumanian, even German. Now I realize
that one of the tasks of my life has been to piece these shards together;
to learn the rest of the lyrics, to know where they came from and what
they mean.

There was, for instance, a bit of a lullaby that was part of a Yiddish fairy tale. I desperately wanted to know how it continued once we got past the beginning:

"Once there was a king,
The king had a queen,
The queen had a vineyard,
The most beautiful one in the world."

It was a lullaby with a standard refrain: Lyulinke, my little bird, my child.

Amol iz geven a meylekh.
Der meylekh hot gehat a malke,
Di malke hot gehat a vayngurtn
Di shenste of der velt

What a tantalizing story for a child, though my mother could not explain how such a story, so sad and evocative, came to her in her native Hungarian-Rumanian-Czech village of Solotvina. Much later, I learned the whole song from books and teachers and it was even more beautiful than I ever dreamed.

My mother's name was Peki, a little package her mother brought home from Budapest. It was also variably Pnina, Paula, Yosephina, depending on who was calling her and what country was in charge in Transcarpathia as she was growing up. Her songs were often a reflection of her mood as she cooked or cleaned, and when she was upbeat she often sang a lilting German march. From the words, so close to Yiddish, I understood that this must have been a song she learned from the Nazi soldiers, a song bragging of their exploits with the ladies.

"Ven di Soldaten
Auf di Strass marchieren,
öfnen di Mädchen
Di Fenster un di Türen—ya, ya."
. . . boom sa

At a certain point I realized that this song must have been sung by the same German guards who starved and tortured her. This same song energized them to do their hateful work and, ironically, their victims, my mother among them, must have heard it again and again like an advertising jingle, and it stuck.

Now I am stuck with it and with the dreadful knowledge of what it meant. Many years later, when I was a mother myself, I heard that same song again in a toy shop in Paris. I was reaching for a jigsaw puzzle for my children when I heard that tune over the radio, and then, aghast, I saw that the company that made the puzzle was in Germany and named Ravensbruck. Ravensbruck was the name of the labor camp my mother was sent to after Auschwitz, where she labored until the final death march. Another piece to my puzzle. I dropped the picture puzzle from Ravensbruck and left the shop trembling. For me, Europe, unlike America, still reverberates with the echoes of disaster.

Jewels in the Shards

Most of the shards my mother passed on had jewels tucked away in them. Such a one is the song-prayer: *"Ikh dank dir, mamenyu, vayl ikh bin a Yid. Dokh dem iz mir tomid azoy git."* It translates roughly to "I thank you, Mother, because I am a Jew. It is the reason that things are so good for me." At first, I wondered about this. Given the suffering of my family, what could be so good about being Jewish? My father, good Socialist, Bundist that he was, usually derided such sentiments. "Where was God when all this was happening to you?" he would ask. "How can you still believe in anything?" But my mother's response was ultimately the more powerful. It was her simple, unquestioning faith. She could not hate anyone, Germans included. Her upbringing had bound her to God with utter devotion.

A tiny shard, a little proverb could have a great effect. *"Afile a vorim inter a shtayn vil lebn."* "Even a worm under a stone wants to live." I could not kill, not even a fly. I viewed all life as sacred, too perfect to be destroyed. I railed against Vietnam with vigor for the same reason. Now my children will not eat meat.

And a shard for comfort. When I was afraid at night she would begin with the genealogy of genealogies, *Gott fin Avrom, fin Yitskhak, fin Yankev, behit dayn folk Yisroel,* a women's prayer in a mix of Hebrew and Yiddish. But she could not continue beyond where it says the beloved Sabbath leaves us. In fact, my mother could only mumble the last lines as she did when she was a schoolgirl in Beis Yakov, pretending to know them. But many years later, when I was doing research on Hasidic women in Jerusalem, I found that same prayer on mock parchment in a gift shop and from there to my wall at home. It is still a source of comfort.

Genealogy

And so we carry our elders with us and we speak with ancestral voices. After Troy is sacked, the survivor, Aeneas, carries his ancient father on his back to find a new home. In Exodus, as the Hebrews flee in so much haste that even the bread cannot rise, they must still carry Joseph's bones to the Promised Land. Children of Holocaust survivors have no bones to carry but we do speak with ancestral voices. The voices are fragmented, tormented. It remains for us to piece them together, to retrieve their meanings, and to enrich them again.

My own genealogy is shallow. Our history did not allow for enough stability to keep records, and to go back and visit an old home is dangerous. But miraculously, through a distant relative in Israel whom I have only met through E-mail, I found out only recently the name of one of my great grandfathers, Abraham Schwartz, and that he was born in 1830, in Sziged. That is as far back as I can go unless I add in *Avrom, Yitzkak, and Yankev.*

The Gynecologist

I sat on the gynecologist's table, his fingertips circling my breasts. I was exposed, vulnerable, when he asked me his routine question, had anyone in my family had breast cancer. I thought for a moment and to my shock realized that every single woman in my family, excepting my mother, had been killed in war. That was my answer. I was susceptible to war. Later, in Israel, when soldiers were handing out gas masks before the Iraqi scud attacks I trembled with a deeply rooted fear, like so many in Israel at the time. It was too close.

How I Met My Mother's Sisters

My mother had three sisters and a brother but my only image of them is from a glimpse of a photograph of her sisters. They must have been about eighteen or nineteen, lovely young women with satin skin and warm eyes. Their names were Chanye, Mindl, and Maryim (I was named for the youngest). The two oldest girls had been Zionists and had gone to Palestine but, sadly, returned home to Solotvina. In Solotvina they married and had children and together they were sent off to Auschwitz in 1944 to line up before the deadly Mengele beast who selected "left-right, death-life". Maryim was a heroine, for though she was childless she chose to hold on to her sister's child and so died with them. Of their brother, Moishe, all I know of him is that he was a tease and scamp. The sisters used to chase him with a broom for trekking in dirt. Moishe survived the war only to be shot by Hungarian Fascists in Budapest, Fascists who wanted his boots.

But I really met my mother's family in my therapist's office. I was sitting in a lone chair facing an empty couch. He was using the "gestalt" method on me, invoking my all-too-vivid imagination to conjure up the family for whom I wept. My mother's family was large if one added in all the five half brothers and sisters, uncles and aunts, cousins. Bit by bit they all crept onto that couch so that there were too many for the couch to hold. Their faces were miserable and I cried but, fortunately, the therapist intervened. He told me I was not to see them, not in their hour of torture and death but as they were before, happy and cohesive. I spoke to them, there, and told them the following: "I would so have loved to know you, for you to have been with my mother. I am so sorry for what happened to you." *"Ikh volt aykh azoy fil gevolt kenen. Mayn mame hot azoy getroyert nokh aykh. Vos iz geshen mit aykh iz shreklikh. Zi hot aykh azoy lib gehat."* I said good-bye, keeping an image of them as they were when they were together and well.

Disposable People

What does it mean to be born in a displaced person's camp? My birthplace, Ginsburg, Germany, could never be where I was from. So I have learned to duck that simple question. I do not want people to say, "Oh, you're German" or, worse yet, "How did you get to survive?" No country wanted us in 1946, 1947, or 1948. And even then getting out of Germany was a challenge.

"Vu'achin zol ikh geyn
Az ikh hob keyn heym"

So sang the survivors. "Where can I go, when I have no home" went the mournful survivors' song. We moved from country to country, no nation really wanting us. The sense of displacement continues as a political reality.

At a certain point in my life I realized the grim fact that what happened to my mother and her family was not a historical aberration. It was because they were of a time and place that the world did not want any longer. Who wanted us, Yiddish-speaking, religious people? And so, when I think about these sisters and their little children for whom my mother wept so often I wonder at the world. These women were intelligent, talented, beautiful, hard working, and responsible. They were feminine and liked to rub their lips with red paper. They sang tunes from the local Yiddish theater. They kept an inn, baked bread, and kept a clean house. Why were they thrown away?

I still look for my family. Recently, at the Holocaust Memorial Museum, I felt all my old defense mechanisms kick in. My inner voice said, "Shield yourself, walk quickly, don't look too closely, don't let yourself feel anything. But my eyes betrayed me, scanning the photographs, looking, looking for what? They looked for pictures of Hungarian Jews, for my young mother in striped prisoner uniform, shaved head, trembling with hunger and fear. For my little cousins in somber march at the train stations. They were all there in Auschwitz, in the Kraców ghetto, in the round-ups. I did not really know their faces, so searching was difficult. I finally could not take it anymore and sobbed away the pain as soon as I was outside.

My Ghost Brother

My father, Israel, often spoke about the fact that he had a wife and son before the war. In 1939, my father suddenly found himself in and out of the Polish army. Accident took him to the Soviet Union and when he tried to get back to Kraców, where his wife and child were, he was arrested. He never saw them again nor found out what happened to them. Throughout my childhood I longed for a brother, that brother. I often looked at strangers, dark men about ten years older than myself, with dark eyes like mine. Here is my poem to him in English and Yiddish.

> You are lost in the shadows
> My little ghost brother.
> Somewhere in a ghetto
> Crushed in your mother's arms in a ditch.

Di bahaltst zikh in di shotns
Avremele, main briderl.
Ikh dershpir dikh amol
Du tsiterst in main neshome.

Though we've never met
I saw you once, on a train in Belgium.
You stood there, a pale boy
Just beyond my sight,
Then you vanished as I turned.
You are four years old, in sailor suit
Smiling impishly from a tattered photo
That our father cherished through the war.

Dayn shmaykhele kikt aroys fin an alt bildl
Shvartze krayzelekh
Amotroz antzugl.
Long years our father searched for you
Through lists of the living and the dead
Asking every little boy his name, his town.
Did you too look for us?

Es blaibn nor unentfertlekhe frages,
Vos iz mit dir geshen?
Ver hot dikh
Umgebrengt, vi azoy, var vos?

You play hide and seek in the shadows
My ghost brother, forever a child.
Es benkt zich mir nokh dir
Main nisht gevesener briderl
Un dain neshomele is shtendig mit mir.
So now I must live out both our lives
So rest in your Kraców cradle grave.

Grandparents

My grandparents were of another era, and though I never met any of them
I know that echoes of the century in which they were born have tendrils.

For instance, I was never to walk backward as a child. Which is what I often wanted to do. Why? I was told, because when you do so you are cursing your parents—*men shelt tate-mame*. Now I know, walking backward symbolizes in a very literal way contrariness. One is to walk in one's parents footsteps quite literally.

Unfortunately, all I have from my parents about their parents is their childhood perspectives and not a sense of them as individuals. But later, as I reached ages comparable to theirs, I began to put together facts and achieve a greater understanding, especially of my grandmothers, Gitl and Miriam, who were strong women. I was recently asked to talk about Jewish women to a group of African-American high school students who were learning about different cultures. I began by describing my grandmothers, telling them that my grandmothers had many children, lived in poverty, were mostly on their own, having to both work and take care of children without much help or money. These inner-city students related to them, probably more than suburban Jewish children would have. My grandmothers were deeply religious women, who wore wigs, who bore many children, and worked hard all their lives. I will never know who killed them or how they died after Hitler came, but the old—more than fifty—were the first to die.

My father's mother (the name Miriam came from both sides) was a midwife. Despite all her medical knowledge, she lost most of her nine children to illness and malnutrition. She struggled to keep the family alive and fed. My strongest image of her, from my father's account, is of a woman with several small children and a wagonload of furniture drawn by a horse, fleeing from Isterik in Galicia when the Russians advanced during the First World War. She hitched up the wagon and forded a river to get to safety in Hungary. The river swept all her possessions away and then they wandered on with nothing, not even her midwife certificate, which was swept away, to find the Jewish community in Papo, Hungary.

On my mother's side, my grandmother, Gitl, was the oldest of fifteen children. My grandfather, Favish, was much her senior, a widower with five children of his own. They had a large inn to keep with many windows to polish, floors to scrub, bread to bake, children to rear. My mother told me she nursed Maryim till she was old enough to come to her with a stool and help herself—all so she would not get pregnant again. When salesmen came they all had to crowd in together to free up rooms for the guests.

My grandfathers, both Orthodox Jews, are bearded mysteries to me. My mother's father, Favish, was the head of the Tabak clan. I had this confirmed by none other than Elie Wiesel, who also came from Marmoresh

Sziged as did the notorious Robert Maxwell. I have a snapshot of Favish, looking a bit dapper with a trim beard and mischievous blue eyes under a brimmed hat. He was an Orthodox Jew. Clearly music flowed from him too, for every Saturday morning he sang the weekly Bible portion so loudly that he woke up the whole household. He also enjoyed his food, relishing a piece of goose liver. Besides the inn for traveling salesmen, one of his several livelihoods was as a "mosgiakh," a meat inspector, but my mother admitted that in taking the exam he was not exactly kosher. Another family occupation was smuggling goods across the border over the Tisca. This was work for the children.

It would be tempting to romanticize my grandfather Abraham, who earned a living by keeping horses in Uschiki Dolne, Poland. This was a low-level profession among Jews but it encouraged an outdoors life. When World War I broke out, he had to leave his family to fight in the Austrian cavalry. By the time he returned from the war, my father was already a rebellious little hellion with a mind of his own and quick to defy Abraham and his fierce religious ways. Abraham threw out my father's books whenever he could get his hands on them, but that did not stop my father from reading *treyf*, that is, unholy books such as Jack London's *White Fang*. My father never liked or forgave my grandfather for their clash of values. But I think he and I might have gotten along.

Music as Medium

I met a person from Solotvina in a most unlikely way. Petro, a Ukrainian folk musician, was performing at Buffalo Gap, a music and dance camp in the hills of West Virginia. It was a special camp organized to bring together Yiddish and eastern European music. My first introduction to Petro was in the camp sauna, where he was happiest when he was flogging fellow steam bathers with oak leaf whips. Once I walked in with a fellow Yiddish speaker whose immediate reaction was, jokingly, *"Oy, a pogrom, a pogrom."*

By an odd coincidence this Petro came from remote Solotvina only the year before and was able to echo my mother's love for the place, for the plum trees, for the dance and music, for the natural beauty of the region. He even confirmed the Chelmlike story my mother had told me, that the town once built a bridge over the Ticza River, but then the river changed its course, leaving a bridge over dry land and a river without a bridge. From Petro's window I heard a recording of haunting music one morning. I followed the sound and walked in where he and a fellow musician, Sasha, played for me music from that exact region. It was a field recording of an old Gypsy, Mishka Baran, who used to play with the Jews. As I sat on the floor, cross-legged, through the music, I was flung down and drawn back in time and space. I had no choice but to allow myself to feel the full impact of the tragic reality, and the pain was so great it was unbearable and I fought back the tears while the gentle musicians softly left me to myself. They told me that music was part of me and could heal me.

Victim or Fighter

Imagine an eight-year-old girl pulling herself along on the kitchen linoleum, being taught Polish military skills by her father. In remembering his past, we reenacted basic skills on our kitchen floor with a broom handle bayonet in my hand. My father was certainly the most influential of all my family members but I have avoided focusing on him so far. Because I knew him best, perhaps I understand him least. Perhaps, too, I see in him the dark side of myself.

I once heard some psychiatrists holding forth on Holocaust survivors and the effects on us, their children. They said that we would fall into two approaches to the world, either as victims or as fighters. I agree. My mother saw herself as victim and acted as such, weeping and pleading with *der Oybester.* My father, who had been in the Polish army and later in the Soviet army, saw himself as a fighter. He hated Germans, Poles, Ukrainians, Christians, anti-Semites. He saw the world as a dangerous place, where safe places could always turn evil, where history did and would repeat itself. So I had to be vigilant, alert, and sober.

I have characterized him accurately but also unfairly. This man was a remarkable product of the *shtetl,* a loving family man, a devoted father, friend, and husband. Through him we remained in a world of the *shtetl.* Every evening we walked to the park benches, first in Montreal and then in Crown Heights, to debate the world's problems with the other survivors. He took my proper education upon himself and made sure that I continued to know my Yiddish language and culture.

About his and other Jews' experiences, he spared me nothing. I was to be mature and responsible. If Jews were disposable people on the refuse heap, then he was not about to let such things be done to him by any means and he would teach me how to know the world in his way. And survive in it. Such lessons are difficult lessons but important ones, not allowing for the comfort of security or stability. The world becomes like a mirage, changeable and unpredictable as are the people who inhabit it. How can one not admire his courage?

He was heroic in the historic way of the Yidl, the small Jew. His stature at 5'2" was a result of malnutrition. He even made fun of his own baldness, telling me that when he was young all the hair had fallen from his head and landed all over his hairy body. When people asked where he was from, he told them, *"Ikh bin a geshtrofener, a Galitsianer."* I have been punished, I speak a Galician Yiddish, the kind that was less erudite.

But he was proud. Proud of his worker origins and life. Of peasant, plebeian roots. He had neither respect nor longing for the life of the middle or upper classes. The Bundist-Socialist in him never left him ideologically compromised. So he worked for bosses all his life, using his hands and his skills as a trained craftsman in upholstery. He was once offered a better-paying job in a furniture factory, which he turned down. They made cheap furniture with staples and particle board, each person doing only one piece. He knew he would be bored and his skills would be lost, so he stayed to repair beautiful old furniture instead. His hands were like leather and his shoes always full of tacks. But when it came to education and writing, I, too, always refused to do the equivalent of piecework.

Lessons

There are those who dismiss the Holocaust. It is all too easy and tempting to avert one's gaze from ugliness, to refuse to believe that humans could be so cruel. Stories of the Holocaust are painful. The difficult path is often the only right one. But we underestimate our young and we need to teach them what humans are capable of and that civilization hides a beast within it. They already suspect this anyhow. So, I devise answers for the wise, the wicked, the foolish, and those who don't even know how to ask. In speaking about the Holocaust, we are speaking about the present as well as the past. No matter how many deny reality, the ghosts will not go away.

Children of survivors have to mourn in a different way. At an ordinary funeral one has the memories of family or friends lost. We don't have these either. We never knew most of the people we mourn. I learned to feel for my family through my mother's screams at night when dreams came unbidden.

The only material objects I have that connect me to my family are a few photographs that I have lovingly placed in albums. Much as I have stared into them, I realize that they are mirages, only the surface of a deeper reality. That deeper reality contains languages, awareness of tradition, of place and time.

I have become an odd blend of both my parents, loving but weak, angry and feisty. It is perhaps the gluing process, as I mature, that helps me reconcile those two parts so that the vessel can become whole again. I was drilled to be strong, self-sufficient, on guard, protective, ready, to be a survivor, for our people had to continue, we Jews. I begin to understand, as I learn and teach, how much of my intellectual and emotional life has been an effort to come to grips with the past—as much by distancing myself from it as by clinging. I have lived with fears of war, fascism, totalitarianism, Christian fundamentalism, of hostile aliens with evil intent. Intellectually and emotionally, I have searched for the vanished Yiddish world in which I was raised. I had only begun to resolve my parents difference and come to terms with an understanding that my parents' views were not really mutually contradictory. That I could question, could allow myself anger and still love. That I could revel in my Jewishness.

In my search I have indeed found my family but not my relatives. I have learned about my Jewish roots, about the way the world has potential for good as well as evil, sympathy and empathy for those other displaced persons like me. I was once teaching a little Vietnamese youth, who shyly told me that he was born in a refugee camp. I looked at him and told him that I too was born in a refugee camp and I saw his jaw drop and his eyes light up. Someone born in camp could also become a teacher. The vessel is more holes than shards and will always be so. I am left with more questions. Searching is now a collective project and there I am finding my family.

PART SIX

Confronting a Repressed Past

Introduction

For the offspring of perpetrators, the issue is how to break the wall of silence that all of them report experiencing growing up in Germany. While the children of survivors eventually reach out in compassion to their parents as victims, the offspring of perpetrators have the task of coming to grips with their parents as murderers. Here, one sees the notion of choice at work; descendants of the perpetrators may elect *not* to pursue the impact of the Holocaust on their interpsychic lives. Some try but are unable to overcome their sense of loyalty to family of origin even though their parents remain convinced National Socialists. But the impact nevertheless remains. For example, Bar On reports that "children of perpetrators have married less and are more often childless than children of survivors in the same age group."[1] On the theological level, why is it that Christianity's message of compassion and love was heard so rarely during the Shoah, and what is the responsibility of second-generation German pastors? One implicit question looms over the discussion in this part. Why has there not been an outpouring of literature of second-generation perpetrators akin to that written by second-generation Holocaust witnesses? Perhaps the contributions in this part will stimulate others to respond.

Attempting to confront the repressed past is the unifying theme of the contributors to this part, each of whose authors reports growing up without ever having met a Jewish person.

1. Dan Bar-On, *Legacy of Silence* (Cambridge: Harvard Univ. Press, 1989), 321.

Ratner's Kosher Restaurant

BJÖRN KRONDORFER

It was a hot and humid summer evening when I picked up my parents at New York's JFK airport. We took the subway to the city and chatted about the usual things—the fatigue after traveling, the weather, some politics—anything that would not show our anxiety about meeting each other in an unfamiliar setting. When we emerged from Grand Central Station, it was raining heavily. Dark clouds had unexpectedly converged on the city and left the streets in a foreboding light. I suggested taking a cab, but my parents insisted on walking and carrying the luggage they had brought from Germany to the nearby YMCA.

In letters I had tried to alert my parents to the dilapidated conditions at the YMCA, but they had brushed off my warnings, confident that even simple accommodations in New York would offer sufficient comfort for three nights. Now, wet and tired, they were taken aback by the graffiti, the dimly lit hallways, and their small room devoid of all luxuries. The air was sticky, the windows looked out into a smelly, lightless courtyard, and the mattresses were worn, and the communal showers crowded with young people. They tried to put a good face on the situation, brushed the dust off the night table, and worried about their luggage.

My father and I went across the street to grab some beer and pizza. The small take-out place was run by an Afghan, which my father noted with some excitement because our family had lived in Kabul back in the mid-1960s. My parents always recalled those years in Afghanistan as one of their happiest times. There, my father had taught economics to Afghan students and sometimes daydreamed about being an English officer in nineteenth-century India. My mother had provided a secure home for the three chil-

258

dren with the help of a servant, and had socialized with the staff of foreign aid agencies and European embassies. In such an environment, my parents regained a sense of worthiness that they had lost after the war.

My parents belong to a generation that came of age under the Nazi regime and, at the end of the war, was drafted, like my father, into the army, or, as in the case of my mother, left to her own devices in the crumbling empire at seventeen. They had experienced the defeat of the Third Reich primarily as a series of personal catastrophes. My father and grandfather were interned in prisoner-of-war camps; my father's only brother died at sixteen in the last month of the war, blowing himself up when mishandling an antitank gun; and his mother had to abandon their home in the Sudetenland, in the northwestern region of the former Czechoslovakia that had been annexed by the Nazis in 1938. My mother lost her father, an officer in the Wehrmacht, to an incurable stomach cancer before the German invasion of the Soviet Union; he left his wife with an infant, their fourth and last child, who later became my godfather. In January of 1945, my grandmother sent my mother alone on the *Flucht*, westward, and grabbing her two smallest children, fled the Russen, the Soviet army, a few days before they swept through her village in East Prussia.

These war memories must have faded away in Afghanistan, this remote country of intoxicating beauty. Only twenty years after the Shoah, a recovered economy had put West Germany into the position of offering foreign aid to nonindustrialized countries. My parents thrived in this situation. Their work in Afghanistan made them feel good, kindling a few postcolonial reveries. The Nazi era seemed far away.

I felt bad about the welcome my parents received on their first day in New York. They had not been in America before, and it was important to me to show them why I was intrigued by this country, where I was working on my doctorate at the time. My parents had never considered America a prime destination for their vacation, despite their passion for traveling. "What should we do there?" my mother often asked warily, as if, when imagining a trip to this country, she would get lost in a landscape emptied of cultural attractions and saturated with commercials and crimes. In her mind, Americans consisted mainly of elderly men wearing short-sleeved shirts and striped pants, and of their better halves in cream-colored costumes and lipstick too red and vibrant for their aged skin.

So we sat on the edges of their beds in a drab room, drank beer from bottles, and balanced napkins with slices of pizza on our laps. We cracked a few jokes and reminisced about those years in Afghanistan. When I left for the night to stay at a friend's place, my parents were in good spirits again. Afghanistan had played its magic trick.

Earlier that year, I had attended the American Gathering of Holocaust Survivors in Philadelphia, a meeting that affected me profoundly. Before coming to the United States, I had never interacted with Jews. Like most of my postwar generation, I knew Jews primarily from documentary photographs of the Holocaust rather than as a living people. When I was growing up, the small Jewish community that remained in West Germany was invisible to me, and it did not occur to me that I, a German born fourteen years after the collapse of the Nazi regime, was intimately tied to that history. Had I been asked then about my identity, I would have renounced any identification with the German nation, thinking this a conservative stance, and, instead, described myself in more progressive terms as an "internationalist." Now, at twenty-four, I met American Jews as fellow students, teachers, colleagues, and survivors. Only through these encounters did I fathom the extent of my ignorance about contemporary Jewish life. I also realized that the need to distance myself from my country was exactly what characterized me as a postwar German. Rejecting my "Germanness" for a more fashionable internationalism enabled me, with a good conscience, to evade the confrontation with my family's and country's past.

At the Philadelphia gathering of survivors, speaker after speaker had decried President Ronald Reagan's impending trip to Germany, where he and Chancellor Helmut Kohl were to pay tribute to "all victims of war and tyranny" at Bitburg, a military cemetery that included graves of members of the SS. Survivors were aggravated by Reagan's insensitivity and by Germany's attempt to normalize the past. They considered the American-German gesture of political reconciliation a betrayal of the memory of the Jewish victims of Nazism. Amidst their moral outcry, I felt waves of shame rushing through my body—and was awed by the kindness with which survivors treated me.

Shortly after the survivor gathering in Philadelphia, I returned briefly to Germany, primarily to visit friends and family. But I also had felt a great need to see sites connected to the Holocaust to try to comprehend the magnitude of the loss of Jewish lives and culture in my country. So I went to the Dachau concentration camp near Munich, on the very day that Reagan and Kohl solemnly walked through Bitburg's cemetery. Before Dachau, I had been in only one other concentration camp, Stutthof, to which my parents had taken their teenage children when vacationing in Poland. I had also learned basic facts about the Holocaust in German schools and the media, but no one taught this history in such a way as to enable my generation to relate to it personally. Certainly, no one taught us about Judaism or prepared us for the possibility of meeting Jewish people. When I first met Jews, I felt abashed—guilty, confused, and angry. It compelled me to study and explore the fragile post-Shoah relations between Jews and Germans.

Before my parents arrived in New York, they knew about my efforts to reach out to the Jewish community. I had tried to talk to them about it without eliciting much of a response. They reacted evasively and defensively. Perhaps they believed that my new-found fervor on behalf of Jewish-German relations was part of a general rebellion against older German generations that would pass before it affected them. Whenever the subject came up, they displayed a certain nonchalance, an attitude they kept up for most of the three days in New York.

They had come to New York as tourists, prepared to see the city's attractions rather than getting to know *my* America. Erroneously, I acted under the assumption that my parents were open to participating in *my* ways of seeing this country, particularly Jewish-American culture. I thought of them as open to new experiences because of their many travels and because they embraced the ideals of the *Bildungsbürgertum,* seeking to turn all experiences, including vacations, into opportunities to broaden their intellectual horizon. Indeed, they had read about New York's history, architecture, social problems, and even Jewish immigration, but they did not want to interact with the people. Rather, they looked at the American way of life from the outside. Wherever I took them, they consulted their guidebook, and from whatever they observed, they drew conclusions quite apart from what I wanted to tell them about the America I knew. I had to continually listen to their running commentary on American life, which, unfortunately, often verged on rehashing some of the anti-American clichés so widespread among Europeans.

I was not mature and strong enough to confront my parents directly. The more they chatted, the more passive I became. I was pained by the lack of meaningful conversation, a lack that I attributed to the general phenomenon of silence that characterizes intergenerational relations in postwar Germany. Although the Holocaust is not necessarily blotted out of Germany's political and historical awareness, the phenomenon I am referring to in this context is the silence within families about Jews and one's own family history. In the few war stories that circulated in my family, retold with little variation, the themes of childhood and postwar poverty figured prominently, but Jews never appeared.

As it so often happens in families where emotions are not expressed and vital things left unsaid, the amount of small talk proportionally increased with the level of frustration—until, on the last day in New York, something unexpected happened. I suggested having lunch at Ratner's Kosher Restaurant, and, to my surprise, my parents agreed. The plan was to go to the Lower East Side, get a taste of Jewish east European cuisine, and leave. I think my parents consented because they sensed some of my unhappiness and were willing to do me a favor. But they did not expect to be jolted out of their role of observing tourists. They simply assumed that going to a kosher restaurant was not essentially different from visiting any other ethnic food place.

We entered the restaurant and were seated at a center table. It seemed that we were the only Gentiles among mostly Orthodox Jews, something I noted with a trace of unflattering satisfaction, for it put me in an advantageous position. I had already experienced what it was like to feel "exposed" as a German, of worrying what others might think about me in a place frequented mostly by Jews. If, up to this point, my motivations were not entirely clear to me, they now became apparent. I wanted my parents to get a visceral feeling for being German in a Jewish environment, hoping they would begin to grasp some of my reality. Perhaps it would improve the ways we talked to each other. Perhaps they would listen to what I wanted to tell them.

Sure enough, my parents felt timid, and they buried their heads in the menus, studying them fastidiously. I suggested to order soup and knishes, dough stuffed with potato and cheese, and they eagerly complied.

My parents were not alone in feeling uncomfortable. In their presence, I began to feel uneasy, too. The last time I had been to Ratner's was with two Jewish friends, whose familiarity with the place made it easy to feel less inhibited. But in the company of my parents, I was just a "German," the three of us indistinguishable from any other German tourists. I feared that the regular patrons would look at us with suspicion, wondering why Germans wanted to eat at a kosher restaurant. Did we come for the food? Or did we come to observe them, the people my country had tried to annihilate a few decades ago?

Encouraged by my parents' general compliance, I broached again the issue of Jews and Germans. When the food was served, I started the conversation by telling them about Joanna and Jeff, the two Jewish friends with whom I had been at Ratner's before. I had met Joanna and Jeff first at a university in Philadelphia. Joanna had spent a semester in northern Germany and was somewhat familiar with the emotional and political blind spots of young Germans, which certainly helped our initial contact. At the same time, Joanna also needed to come to terms with her experience of staying in a country that had murdered her people. We looked for answers in each other that our families and communities did not, or could not, provide.

At one time, I had shown Joanna photographs of my trip to Dachau: of the nicely kept campgrounds, once the site of primitive barracks, now empty and covered with gravel, and of the flowers and trees planted around the crematory and ditches, where the Nazis had executed the inmates. When she came upon a picture of an oven, she spontaneously exclaimed: "That is obscene!" I felt immediately embarrassed, as if being caught in an indecency. Was it the oven itself that Joanna found obscene? Or did she accuse *me* of obscenity because I had dared to show this photo to her? Why would a German take a picture of something that negated her presence as a Jew? I never asked her for an explanation but was, silently, chagrined.

I did not tell my parents all these details but started to describe a more recent get-together with Joanna and Jeff. I had been invited to their commitment ceremony, a festive occasion for pledging their love to each other in company of family and friends. It was a kind of nonconventional celebration of a Jewish wedding, a self-designed ritual steeped in Jewish traditions.

What I wanted to convey to my parents was how special it felt to be invited as a German to such an event. I wanted them to realize how difficult it was to establish a trusting relationship between second-generation Jews and Germans. I wanted them to acknowledge that they and their parents' generation have left young Germans with a heavy weight on their shoulders. I wanted them to take their share of the responsibility. I wanted my parents to feel proud of their son's courage to tackle a burdensome task. Instead, they interrupted before I could even finish half of the story.

"Why do you always have to be something special?" they inquired, visibly distressed. "Why can't it be just a normal wedding?"

I was baffled by their questions. Whom did they address? Did they complain about me because they thought I considered myself "special," or about my friends because they would not celebrate a "normal wedding," or generally the younger generation, which they no longer understood? Contrary to my expectations, my parents did not seem to be upset about the Jewishness of my friends' ceremony. Rather, they objected to their choice to celebrate an unconventional wedding. Did they perceive the mistrust between the younger and older generations larger than the friction between Jews and Germans? Or was their peculiar question an attempt at diverting attention from the more troublesome issue of Jewish-German relations?

Not knowing how to respond to their ambiguous questions, I defended my friends' decision, and my parents argued about the general importance of holding on to traditions. I had wanted to introduce them to a piece of contemporary Jewish life. Instead, we entered into an absurd debate over the value of traditional customs.

We argued, of course, in German, and because we disagreed vehemently the volume of our voices slowly increased. Every so often my father and mother, conscious of the environment, hushed their voices. They did not want to attract attention but did not want to give up their side of the argument either.

We were interrupted when our waiter came to clear the table. We had not really noticed him earlier. He was a little older than my parents, going about his tasks cordially and unobtrusively, with a kind of noble modesty that one might expect from British butlers. He offered us desserts but we declined and asked for the check. He nodded his head, was about to turn, hesitated, looked at his hands, then turned around again to face my parents.

"*Wo kommen Sie her?*" he inquired in perfect German. "Where are you from?" My parents grew instantly pale and tense.

"*Ach, Sie sprechen ja deutch?*" my mother responded, friendly, but noticeably keeping her composure.

"*Ja,*" the waiter said, continuing the conversation in German. "I escaped from a small village in Hesse in 1938."

My father replied that they currently lived in Hesse, near Frankfurt, whereupon the waiter began to tell them about his deportation and escape. He never looked at me but was entirely focused on my parents when he recounted, in broad strokes, his years of survival. There was no anger in his voice. He was calm, almost subdued, yet conveyed a certain resoluteness: he would tell about his life, in German, to my parents, no matter what they thought.

His story could not have lasted longer than five minutes but it seemed endless. I was unable to listen for I was bathed in my parents' anxiety and nervousness. If the waiter had any doubt about who we were—after all, we could have been German-Jews—my parents' embarrassment made it clear with whom they identified: they felt guilty and perhaps even personally accused.

"How terrible!" my parents sighed repeatedly. "*Ach wie schrecklich!* Those were terrible times."

Undistracted by my parents' sparse interjections and sorrowful expressions, the waiter ended his story, then returned to his work without waiting for a response. He had made his point: summoning the courage to address us in German, the language of his childhood and of his persecutors, he had not remained silent. But he left my parents without a voice.

We sat in silence, staring at our plates. Eventually, my father handed me his wallet. Because he always paid the bills, I was surprised that he wanted me to pay this time. Putting me in charge of the situation was a sign of how deeply my parents were shaken up, even paralyzed.

I followed a spontaneous impulse and added, under my parents' eyes, a very generous tip, much more than was required. My parents did not complain, even though we had a running argument over the necessity of leaving tips, not a custom in Germany, and many New York waiters before had made little at our table. I suppose that my impulsive gesture was motivated by some feelings of guilt toward the waiter and vindictiveness against my parents. At the time, however, it simply felt good. Putting the dollar bills on the table revealed a changed relationship: our roles had reversed. No longer being mere observers, my parents struggled with the burden of history. What I had been unable to communicate about my life in America, they now experienced directly. They were confused, speechless, perhaps ashamed.

We got up, ready to leave. I had already reached the door when I noticed my mother staying behind. She looked around, and when she spotted the waiter, approached him and shook his hand.

As we walked to the nearest subway station, we remained silent. My parents have never since mentioned this incident.

More than ten years have passed since we stepped into Ratner's restaurant, years in which my parents and I have learned to better accept each other. They have come to realize that my quest for answers about the Holocaust did not evaporate like the steam of an adolescent rebellion. I have learned that their silence cannot be read simply as ill will but also as an indication of their emotional helplessness, to which, of course, they would not admit.

It had not occurred to me that my parents could feel overwhelmed when being confronted with a past over which they had little control as teenagers. When they unexpectedly became witness to the survivor's testimony, they lost their confidence and voice. They did not know what to say. But something else was set in motion. Already at the restaurant, my mother tried to establish some kind of contact to the survivor when she shook, at the end, the waiter's hand. I admired her for that—for her compassion and courage. But there was something pathetic about it, too. It felt wrong, like an inappropriate generosity. But what did I expect from by parents? Should they have tried to talk to the waiter? Ask for his name? Apologize? Make excuses? Admit their complicity?

I found their silence afterward difficult to accept. Yet, even today I have a hard time imagining a different ending. Perhaps my mother's gesture was all that was possible at the time. She and the waiter may have shared a moment of regret, trying to transcend the constraints of a hostile past.

The greatest similarity between the "children of persecuted and of persecutors . . . [is] a mission to rehabilitate their parents and undo the past," psychoanalyst Judith Kestenberg remarked in a comparative study of the second generation.[1] Taking my parents to Ratner's restaurant could be interpreted as my instinctive effort to rehabilitate them. Ten years ago, I interpreted their persistent silence as evidence that they resisted the challenge. Today, I am able to discern small changes since their encounter with a survivor. In subtle and indirect ways, they express their support of my concerns, such as sending me clipped newspaper articles on subjects related to the Holocaust or telling me on the phone about Jewish cultural events and lectures on Judaism they have attended in Germany.

But I am especially pleased about their cautious efforts of expanding the safe and rehearsed inventory of family narratives, revealing new aspects of their lives during the war. On one occasion, my mother talked about a train passing by behind her house in the countryside near Königsberg in East Prussia, now Kaliningrad. Prisoners behind barbed wire begged for water. In her recollection, these were Russian soldiers and she and her siblings apparently managed to get water to them. This story is, of course, still relatively "safe" because it centers on a small countering of the evils

---

1. Judith Kestenberg, "Introduction," in *Generations of the Holocaust,* ed. Martin S. Bergmann and Milton E. Jucovy (New York: Basic Books, 1982), 165. Kestenberg, however, rightly distinguishes between the two missions. She writes that "Nazi children must solve the problem of their parents' moral degradation; survivors' children's concerns about their parents' guilt is in great part an illusion."

of Nazi ideology. It is not a story about her family's complicity. On another occasion, however, my mother took a greater risk, leaving me dumbfounded. She showed me a photograph of a group of young girls at a birthday party. She first pointed out herself, a smiling child with long plaits so fashionable during the 1930s, and then called my attention to another sweet-faced girl, and said, "She was Jewish." At first, I could not react. Never before had my mother admitted that she knew Jewish people as a child.

"Do you know what happened to her?" I inquired after a moment of silence.

"Oh, I am sure she got out," she quickly responded and left the room.

The conversation was over. She had shown me the picture, revealed a part of her life hitherto kept hidden, but did not intend to discuss it with me. It was too frightening to entertain the thought of the girl's most likely fate.

I was similarly surprised when my father, years after the episode at Ratner's, volunteered to tell me more about the time when he was drafted into the German army. During our conversation, we stumbled across a period of several months in 1944 where he had been stationed in an anti-aircraft battalion at Blechhammer. I was familiar with the name Blechhammer because I had earlier met a Jewish survivor who had been imprisoned there. It was a satellite camp of Auschwitz that used Jews and POWs as slave laborers for its nearby chemical factory. At first, my father mentioned the name in passing. When I told him what I knew about the camp, he grew pale and said that he was unaware of the Jewish slave labor camp, but admitted to having once driven by a group of emaciated prisoners in striped uniforms marching along a street.

I was stunned. I was angry. I felt betrayed. Why had my father never before told me? My suspicion that Jews had been edited out of German family narratives finally confirmed—but at what price! I had not antici-pated that my own father had been near the cruelest aspect of Nazi genocidal policy.

Paradoxically, we did not experience this talk as a rupture of our rela-tionship but regained some intimacy. This was a strange occurrence that calls for explanation. When we talked, I was not really angry that my father had been in Blechhammer. Rather, I was upset that he had not mentioned it in all those years after the war or made an effort to learn more about the camp. Yet, my father also reacted with such anguish over the discovery of having been stationed next to a Jewish slave labor camp that I felt compassionate. What would I have done as a seventeen-year-old at an outpost of the German military?

I felt closer to my father, though this new-found closeness threw me into a dilemma. I did not want to be part of a reconciliation in which German fathers and sons mend their relationships on the backs of Holocaust victims and Jewish survivors. The danger of instrumentalizing the past was ever so near. Something else would have to happen. . . . A day later I asked my father whether he would write a letter to the Jewish survivor of Blechhammer. This, however, he could not bring himself to do.

I have written elsewhere and in more detail about Blechhammer, a story that continues to unfold to this day.[2] What is important in this context is my father's unexpected emotionality. He made himself vulnerable in the presence of his son with respect to the past, something that had not happened between us before—and may not have happened without my father's earlier anxiety at Ratner's restaurant.

It would be too much to say that my parents and I have reached a stage where we can freely and without suspicion talk to each other. My parents have never fully approved of my life in the United States or my continual interest in the Shoah. My father has not written the letter to the survivor of Blechhammer. And my mother, who opens up occasionally, is still strongly invested in presenting her family without blemish. "You're only interested in the dark aspect of our family and German culture," she recently complained with bitterness and regret. When I alluded to the fact that some aspects in my maternal grandfather's biography seem to point to his possible involvement in the Nazi Party, she vehemently denied it and accused me of disrespecting her parents. Again, I had overstepped my boundaries, causing a rift between my mother and me that has not healed until today.

The episode tells us how cautious a listener I have to be when bringing up the past with my parents, never knowing what questions can be asked and when to ask them. I still do not have a clear picture of my maternal grandfather, who fought in the First World War, crushed a rebellion of German Communists and revolutionary sailors in Königsberg in 1918, left—

2. I wrote about the initial discovery of my father's stay near this slave labor camp in *Rembrance and Reconciliation: Encounters Between Young Jews and Germans* (New Haven: Yale Univ. Press, 1995). In the afterword to the book by Edward Gastfriend, *My Father's Testament: Memoirs of a Jewish Teenager, 1938–1945* (Philadelphia: Temple Univ. Press, 2000), I wrote about a journey my father and I took together to places of his past, including Blechhammer.

according to my mother—a secure municipal position to escape the Nazi ideology of his young superior, rejoined the Wehrmacht as an officer during the military occupation of Poland, and died of cancer in February of 1941.

In 1996, I still live in the United States. The year before, my wife was pregnant with our second daughter. On December 5, when she was due, my father called and wanted to know whether his granddaughter was born yet. But our daughter Tabitha stayed for another two weeks in her safe place. My father was terribly disappointed. On December 5, he said, his brother had been born. I hadn't even known that.

I called him back later and told him that next time we get together I would like to learn more about his brother, this sixteen-year-old boy who had blown himself to pieces in defense of the Nazi regime.

A Troublemaker in a Skirt

ANNA E. ROSMUS

The first time I thought about my feelings toward Germany was in 1980, when I was twenty. At that time I took part in an international essay competition. My essay dealt with aspects of Germany that I liked and that were typically German. I called my contribution "Dates of Internal and External Freedoms Taken from History and Politics of Europe." To my mind, then, individual freedom was nowhere as extensively realized as in our own country. The contribution gained me the status of Germany's best young writer.

Six months later a different truth began to dawn on me. My father brought home the paperwork for another essay contest: "German History Prize of the Federal President," with the topic "Everyday Life in My Hometown During the Third Reich." I was already married and I had enrolled at the local university to study history. But I decided to participate in the contest, focusing on Passau's resistance and persecution. Whatever that might be.

To my amazement, I encountered tremendous obstacles in conducting my historical work. The Passauers' way of dealing with their past was quite simple: Everything was the fault of the leader of the district, all the others were basically opponents of the regime! Now—after fifty years—this so-called reality was to be questioned by me, a young woman. Suddenly, many people became anxious about their image as "opponents," and they sabotaged my work. My essay for the second contest exposed me to an unprecedented campaign of hatred and danger. I was confronted by terrifying experiences.

On the fiftieth anniversary of Hitler's seizure of power my problems became extreme. I introduced my very first book to the University of

270

Passau. In the discussion that followed, I was asked whether Dr. Emil Janik, who at the time was the editor of the *Journal of the Passau Bishopric,* had indeed been as "brown" (a Nazi, that is) as he was reputed to have been. I defended him, rejecting such rumors as unfounded, although I would not have been able to defend every one of his articles or his behavior, nor would I have wished to do so. For instance, he wrote: "It is not our fault if Europe spends its second Christmas at war." The Second World War is "a struggle for justice ordained by God," and "only victory by the Germans will guarantee peace." Therefore, "the will to victory, hard as steel" is required. He asked the readers to pray: "Lord, make us strong! Lord, give us strength! So that our just cause may create peace!" He published anti-Jewish propaganda, without ever repudiating it later or distancing himself from it. After the war, he had been awarded the Meritorious Service Cross of the Federal Republic besides a papal order. His brother Erwin, who lived in our immediate neighborhood, sued me for defamation of his brother's character. To me, all this came as a shock.

Overnight, friends of my family turned into malicious enemies. I was subjected to an overt hate campaign. Rumors were spread, witnesses were pressured. I had great difficulty finding a lawyer to represent my case. Nobody wanted to assume a "political" case in this town. And the attorney who at first took on my "defense" resigned before the start of the hearing. Because legal representation is compulsory, however, I began my search once again. After a while, an attorney was prepared to defend me. She came from another town, and was not fully aware of our social mechanisms.

All of my research about Emil Janik was confirmed by the court as factual and to the embarrassment of Janik, a citizen of Passau signed a declaration under oath that the name "brown Emil" had indeed been used for Dr. Janik. A highly respected Catholic priest confirmed this and said that he and other opponents of the regime suffered greatly from him during the Nazi period. Even with all this support, the hearing was horrible. For about two hours the three judges pressured me to sign an agreement not to use the epithet "brown Emil" again. After all, they said, Dr. Emil Janik had received the Bundesverdienstkreuz and the Bayerischer Verdienstorden, besides a title from the pope himself. Not a single one of my witnesses got a chance to testify. They all were sent home unheard. "In exchange," I was promised I would not have to apologize or to retract anything, nor would I have to pay damages—the plaintiff had demanded up to five hundred thousand German marks, about $300,000.

Martin Hirsch, a retired supreme court judge, suggested I give in, as I would not be given a fair trial here. At the appeals court, he was convinced, I would have even less of a chance, as the judges there are older and probably even less willing to hear arguments. Only at Germany's supreme court, he said, would I win right away. There was too much public attention and too much at stake to ignore the evidence. Unlike the colleagues in Passau, these judges are also experienced in handling delicate political cases. But by the time the case could be judged there, he estimated costs of $60,000 and at least five years. I had neither that much money nor did I want to wait. I wanted to go on with my research, so I signed the agreement.

Only a few people understood why a young woman would want to know what happened under the Nazis. Only a few people understood why I, a non-Jew, had an interest in the fate of Jews. And hardly anyone understood why I felt solidarity with minorities, for I belonged to the establishment by birth and upbringing. Both the example of the Nazi regime and the experience I have had in documenting it have taught me how easy it is to violate human dignity and to curtail freedom. Writing for the essay contest, the price of nonconformity and of Holocaust denial emerged as themes. Although my efforts were highly honored in Germany, locally they were vilified. My first two lawsuits compelled me to repeatedly ask myself: Am I living in a state where the rule of law is respected? What could happen to people in a similar situation, who did not have influential friends and who could not help themselves? Is this what is meant by freedom?

Occasionally, I had the impression that the whole town was conspiring against me. Repeatedly, files had been declared "lost," or had ostensibly "disappeared." In my own *Heimat* (hometown) I was tormented, slandered, and harassed solely because of my inquiry. I asked myself: Is it possible to love a country whose inhabitants want no truck with their past? Can I possibly feel at home in a nation in which the criminal police must provide security at numerous public meetings because my mere presence now provokes bomb threats? Is it possible for me to feel safe when night after night my telephone brings death threats? All of this because I wrote a book about the Nazi past, including the Jews of Passau? Many of these calls were made by well-known citizens. Some letters were written on official stationery. Some in this town regret that I did not live in medieval times, when, as they write, I would have been drowned or burned at the stake. One woman regrets that my mother didn't get an abortion when she was pregnant with me. Others preferred that I would have been gassed in a concentration camp, torn limb from limb, so that I would finally keep my "stinking Jewish trap" shut.

I was twenty-four and had never had an occasion to meet a Jew, as there were none left. I was born into a gentile world, and had not the faintest idea what it meant to be Jewish. But never before had I been confronted with prejudice or injustice. I was raised as a democrat, with an appreciation for foreigners, with tolerance and respect for all life. What I heard was beyond imagination.

I asked myself over and over again: What kind of human beings are these who call me "Jew-whore" and "dirty sow" because I am researching the whereabouts of some Passau Jews? What kind of country is it where I am asked whether I have programmed my daughter for the concentration camp because her name is Salome? What kind of mentality do people have who reproach me for occupying my time with "such unsavory rabble," "such disgusting miscreants"? Their mentality is evident from remarks such as: "For the Israelis getting the reparations was well worth the sacrifice of those Jews." After I had spent two weeks in a work camp at Neuengamme near Hamburg in 1984, I asked myself: What species of human beings could so easily threaten to murder me for the simple reason that together with other young people all over the world I have helped document the history of a concentration camp? My own "group" wanted to isolate me so radically, because I had tried to reach out to the Jewish experience.

At that time, I became aware that I would love to live among people who neither feared nor suppressed the truth and who acknowledge the mistakes in their past. I wanted to live among a people that regard those with different opinions as opponents but not as enemies. I knew I wanted to live among people who could bear to be criticized, among people who would attempt to correct their mistakes instead of denying them. I would like to live in a nation-state whose representatives are frank about dangers and do something about them, rather than pretend that they don't exist.

Born into a Devout Catholic Family

My grandmother was somehow different. Her nature was soft-hearted, her life was tough. Politics did not matter to her, and I believe they never did. What counted was everybody's happiness. The more I knew about her, the more I was convinced her parents had passed that on to her. They all were devout Catholics. My grandmother was almost 100 years old when she passed in September 1996. Over the past fifteen years, she frequently talked about Passau and the Nazi period.

The public did not care much about the few local people who had resisted the Nazis. One of the rare major actions reported by the Gestapo was organized by my grandmother. In 1941, she led an open protest march to City Hall—in defiance of the local Nazi authorities, who had ordered the removal of all crucifixes from the schools. Today, we know that this was just another order and that far worse ones were on the horizon. But then it caused a huge public outcry. A policeman threatened to arrest her. She was about to be deported to Dachau. But at the last minute, the lord mayor intervened, arguing that in this case her four children would require welfare. To save that money, she was freed.

One year later, in 1942, in Catholic regions such as Passau, priests were among the main targets; they were especially vulnerable to denunciation by women. For example, during a short film in a regular eighth-grade class, the windows were covered, darkening the room. Erika, one of the girls, was kidding around, deliberately disturbing the class. The priest asked her to behave. But she went on. He yelled at her. The girl finally became so wild that the priest slapped her. At home, she told her mother that he had "touched" her. The mother suggested that she talk to the vice principal, who, in turn, complained to the district leader, Max Moosbauer. Moosbauer could not stand that priest. For years he had been trying to remove him. He could never find evidence that this man was a subversive. Now, however, with a sexual accusation, he could be rid of him. He requested the priest's deportation to Dachau.

My mother was a seventh-grader at the same school. She heard about the episode, and she and her family lived in the same house as the priest. Before the dreaded black Gestapo car arrived in front of the house, the priest ran to the first floor, where my grandmother lived. He knocked at her door and asked for a place to hide. My grandmother let the priest come in, and locked the door. She was aware that the Gestapo would search for him and acted immediately. She asked Hermann, the tallest and most sociable of her sons, to run to Erika's house and get her mother to sign a confession that the girl had lied. My uncle Hermann got other parents to sign a petition. As soon as he returned, my grandmother took the list to the office of the district leader, who respected her and warned her not to aid the priest. But she insisted on rescuing him. He complained about her son's action and requested that the principal impose a proper punishment, such as suspension. My grandmother went to see him, too, and pleaded "guilty" for herself in her son's place. He had only done what she made him do, she said. She offered to accept any punishment herself, but she would tolerate no action against the priest or against her son. Next, my grandmother was ordered to report at the police station. She was interrogated and intimidated again, but she persevered, and the priest was spared. All it took was the deed of one woman.

For the citizens of Passau, this episode represented the maximum of stress and fear. For the minority, this was the most heroic gesture anyone could make. For the majority this was as outrageous as it was evil and dumb. But far worse things were yet to come. Soon, Passau maintained not only various labor camps but its third concentration subcamp opened. Every morning, prisoners were marched through streets to do forced labor. Every evening, they were marched back. They were kicked and hit. Nobody knew them, but many people saw them. They were foreign men, and most people didn't care. The Nazis told the locals that these were criminals and had to be punished.

My grandmother was one of the few people who didn't close her eyes: She looked at the scared, walking skeletons in their striped suits. She saw them pointing at their mouths and begging for food in a language she could not understand. She was a widow herself; two of her sons had died in Hitler's army. The third was at the front. She couldn't help him. But she helped those men from Russia. Every evening after work, she left with a big bowl under her coat and begged for leftovers, bread crumbs, potatoes, and vegetables. Every evening she walked one hour to a camp at the edge of the town and threw the food over the fence. Every evening, she made the two-hour trip, until the camp was forcefully evacuated late in April 1945. Twice she got caught, and was told she would be arrested. But she went on. Some other women did the same thing, although not traveling that far, and less often. They were determined to help these men survive. Further, they were hoping and praying that some day, other people might help their sons in Russia.

After my uncle Walter was released from a prisoner-of-war internment camp in Belgium in 1947, he studied in Passau, graduated, and became a Catholic priest. My mother was sixteen when the war ended. She was still at school studying, and wanted to teach. She was the first woman in Bavaria to teach Catholic religion. My father, among all kinds of other honorary positions, was soon appointed honorary judge at the Regensburg administrative court. He became one of the closest consultants of Bavaria's minister for cultural affairs, and was elected president of Passau's rather large Roman

Catholic diocese. This position made him not only one of the bishop's closest coworkers, but also a top representative of German Catholics. When Pope John Paul II came to Altoetting in 1982, my father welcomed him and read the lessons in the papal mass. There was no reason for me to struggle with my immediate family's past, nor was there a reason to suffer from it.

Crossing the Lines

But my curiosity had been aroused and I continued to ask questions. I wanted to know the facts about our recent past and the reasons for all these strange reactions. I wrote a few hundred letters and mailed them to many executives, public representatives, and private persons. But the results were almost exclusively negative. One part of the population told me they were too old to remember those times. Another part told me they were too young to remember them. Others told me that they had come from elsewhere after the war. And, of course, there were those who didn't answer at all.

To some extent I was ready to believe the excuses, but it was hard to imagine that *nobody* was able to answer *anything*. I had become very suspicious. I requested access to some of the old files. But what I encountered instead was another big denial. At first, I was told there were no files. Requesting old archival registers, I found lists and serial numbers; I was assured that these files were now lost.

My uncle recommended that I ask for the files of Passau's former lord mayor Max Moosbauer, who, it was said, gave the orders to execute Russian prisoners of war, and had tortured many local residents. But there were also rumors that, in reality, others were also involved. My uncle didn't know the details. He knew, however, that the lord mayor saved my granny's life twice. If I could get hold of his denazification papers, I would probably come across several other incidents that might be interesting. I was excited about this idea, and requested the two files immediately. But it took four years to compel my hometown to release them. I first was told I could not see them, as the city council had to respect Germany's privacy laws. After all, the former lord mayor had been dead for many years, and his family would probably suffer from a new discussion about his misdeeds. That was not right, I was told.

Both my uncle and my mother encouraged me to visit Moosbauer's two daughters, who were still living in his house, and ask for permission to read the files. I was very nervous about that but I was so desperate that I went. To my surprise, both still talked about "the good old days," when they were young and were members of the League of German Girls. There was nothing wrong about that, they told me, the girls did knitting, and singing, and babysitting. . . . Nobody was hanging out in the streets, there were no crimes committed by teenagers. And their father helped so many people. In the end, he had been kicked out of the Nazi Party, because others had taken over, and these others committed horrible crimes. But after the war, they explained, a lot of Passauers denied their participation and made him the scapegoat for their guilt.

Moosbauer's grandson held all the private photographs and papers. He admitted immediately that he had been among the founders of Passau's neo-Nazi movement in 1971. He also told me that he had quit after a few years, because the group had turned to violence. He willingly signed a paper granting me permission to read and to publish his grandfather's denazification files. On one hand, I was horrified, because this support was coming from an obvious Nazi family. But on the other hand, I would know the facts. With the permission paper in hand, I went back to the city administration. But I still did not get the files. This time, I was not denied access, but it wasn't granted either. Obviously, the administrator had decided to stonewall.

I was so upset that I filed a lawsuit against my hometown for unresponsiveness. I was the very first person in Germany to do so, and I did get access. This brought respect from many people in Germany, but in Passau it engendered primarily anger and hate. Moreover, the city did not give in right away. The files were now declared "lost in transit." I told the bureaucrats that if they wanted to keep their jobs, they'd have to "find" the files soon. After a while, I received the documents. At first, I could hardly believe what I read: there was evidence that huge massacres had taken place in my hometown. There were accusations of boycotts and Aryanization, there was talk about shootings, about executions and concentration camps . . . and, as if that were not enough, I recognized names of respected citizens who had been involved. After a four-year effort to wrest the records from city officials, it turned out they had had good reason to resist my research. By now, I was determined they wouldn't get away with it. But I knew it wouldn't be easy for me to reach my goal: I needed much more information.

I requested about five hundred more files at the city archives. With very few exceptions, they were again not forthcoming until I filed another lawsuit. There must have been thousands of victims and hundreds of crimes.

None of this had been made public. In addition nobody had cared about the few surviving emigrés. Probably, I could get in touch with some of them, and possibly they would tell me about their families. I was determined to search for them right away and to learn as much as possible about them. I wanted to know everything. I wanted to look at "our" past through their eyes. I wondered what I would "see" then. I wondered how I would manage to trace them and whether I could ever come close enough to them.

If I wanted to proceed beyond the private past of my family, I had to look for people I didn't know. I had to interview them to find out what happened to them. I had to know what "my" people had done to them, when and why. I wanted also to hear about their dreams, about their fears, and about their hopes. I was curious about their personalities. Who would they be? And how might they react if I approached them? Would they allow me a look "behind the scenes"? I could hardly picture taking such a first step, knowing it could be seen as inappropriate and probably a kind of assault as well. After all, I am German, not Jewish. I was torn between my historical interest and a moral conflict: I was just an individual, but carried a tremendous historical burden. I was too young to be guilty myself, and I was fortunate enough not to live with the personal guilt of a relative. But still, those I wanted to work with might consider my investigation too provocative and unjustified. What "right" did I have to do so? And why should any Jew ever trust anyone of "us" again?

But soon after I placed an advertisement in the New York–based German-Jewish newspaper *Aufbau*, it was obvious that only a few of "our" emigrés hesitated to correspond with me. Some *wondered* about me, and some *asked* a lot of questions. Some *hesitated,* and some were *not* ready to "forgive." Some were angry, and some were bitter. Many were disappointed and many demanding. In theory, I understood all that, and I was willing to put up with it. After all, they had good reason to react in this way. On the other hand, some trusted me with even their most private thoughts. For several of them I became a confidante, a symbolic figure of courage, strength, energy, and even a fighter of successful battles. Be that as it may—I had never intended to play at revolution.

But the more information I got, the more I was upset. All of these people had grown up in Bavaria, much the way I did. But while I had had a marvelous childhood, had grown up in harmony and privilege, offered a bright future, with a good education, close and powerful friends and an embracing family who lived a respected public life, the people who now gave me their trust had all had wrenching experiences. Most of them had been threatened by "our" local authorities, some had been tormented by prominent citizens, and some had been expelled by local politicians. Most of them had left Germany decades before my birth to survive. And almost all of them had lost relatives and friends in "our" concentration camps. "Their" people had suffered indescribably, while "my" people had committed these unspeakable crimes. All my sympathy and feeling of solidarity were on their "side."

But my fellow citizens did not want to remember the years of the "brown" dictatorship; above all, they did not want to remember their part in it. They liked Passau to be portrayed as a very old, beautiful, small German city, a tourist shop nestled among its three rivers. Nobody wanted to talk.

I was amazed to find that Hitler and some of the worst Nazis had been raised in or near Passau. Yet, nobody had ever encountered any Nazis. The more I delved into the past, the more agitated, even violent, people became. My crime: I was revealing Passau's hidden past and thus violating a taboo. The past when the town—touted as the seat of Nazi resistance—was in reality a stronghold of Nazi terror. The atrocities I uncovered have tainted the history of picture-book pretty Passau. Soon I was dubbed *schrecklich,* the terrible one, the terrifying one. A biographical account of my life is titled *Anna Rosmus—The Witch of Passau,* and a movie about the first years of research is called *The Nasty Girl.*

A Divorce

During my research, I learned that some of my husband's relatives had been active in the Nazi movement. His grandfather, for instance, "Aryanized" Jewish money without paying it back, and Richard, my husband's favorite uncle, was an SS man. If it is only that he has politically "wrong" relatives, I thought, we still could make it. He and I are Germans of another generation. I assured him that it wasn't his fault. But after a while, our marriage suffered. He could not come to terms with the changes in me. He understood the situation intellectually but he could not separate himself from his family emotionally. He made increasingly xenophobic and anti-Semitic remarks, commenting on my work and my new friends. His collection of Nazi literature grew steadily. The bizarre sound of "The Jews are our misfortune!" kept recurring. I could never have imagined a real person doing this, certainly not the possibility that I could be married to somebody like this. When Dolores Nadine was two years old, we agreed on a divorce. My daughter Beatrice Salome Kassandra was not yet born. He walked out of our lives, unable to cope with his different upbringing, while I tried to move on.

As I pushed harder and requested the aid of out-of-town newspaper reporters, the town turned against me: "with a venom that betrayed Passau's placid storybook facade," as Marc Fisher wrote in his book *Germany, the Germans, and the Burdens of History.* Over the years, my research would take me to the United States, Canada, Israel, and all over Europe. What I found shook the very foundation of my life. But I went on. Even Marc Fisher conceded:

> The country might not be ready for collective grief, but in the Bavarian town of Passau, Hitler and Himmler's boyhood home, one nasty girl made damn certain that no one could escape the past. From a head full of frosted curls to her fluffy pink bunny slippers, Anna Rosmus looked anything but a nosy, know-it-all Nazi hunter. . . . It was hard to imagine that she could inspire her own mother-in-law to say that because of people like Anna, Germany needed another Hitler. Hard to imagine Passau's Mayor, the local priests and many of her family's friends deciding that Rosmus was so evil she deserved to be "gassed, chopped up and pulverized." With the distance of time, the whole campaign against Anna seems impossible: She is unremittingly cheerful, optimistic beyond all cause, trusting despite years of betrayal.

With my fourth book, *Wintergreen: Suppressed Murders,* I returned to Passau's past. The book caused an outcry throughout Europe, and far beyond. Hundreds of articles were written about it, and dozens of TV reports were broadcast. On an international level, the crimes committed in Passau were of burning interest. The cold-blooded manner that snuffed out thousands of innocent lives, especially toward the end of the war, made headlines. In Passau there was an outcry because a few families "defended" their guilty relatives despite the evidence. Some individuals still alive and still in power had "forgotten" to mention their former roles and activities. Furthermore, the local newspaper distorted the results of my research beyond belief. More lawsuits ensued. Once again, the perpetrators were defended, I was maligned, and the many innocent victims were ignored.

The evidence I needed to report about the crimes was denied me "at home," in Passau. With the help of Bob Kesting from the United States Holocaust Memorial Museum, however, I was able to locate the relevant files at the National Archives in Washington, D.C. Nonetheless, most of the people in the area did not yet confront their guilt. Instead, they felt insulted by the Americans, calling them not "liberators" but "occupiers" and "enemies." I felt very different. I was endlessly grateful for another chance, given graciously to "my" nation after the war. I was deeply ashamed about the reaction of "my" people.

Confronting Bigotry

In 1954, Germany signed a treaty with France ensuring that all memorials to the victims of the Holocaust, and all of the Jewish cemeteries, would be maintained. In flagrant violation, a few months later Bavaria's ministry ordered the removal of most of the memorials. But the memorial site in Pocking, a small town near Passau, was too large and too famous to be destroyed. Instead, the government erased all the engraved names and other inscriptions. I was so upset that for years, I brought all available TV crews to this place. Even Morley Safer showed the blank walls twice on *60 Minutes*, in 1994. More than 100 million people saw them, before the Bavarian government finally restored the memorial. Now, at least, the names are back on the memorial. This was not done in public, however, but very secretly, without even a brief notice in the local newspaper. The public, it seems, is not supposed to know. Do they ever ask?

Whom does Passau honor? Among others, there is brewery owner Franz Stockbauer, one of Adolf Hitler's earliest financial patrons, who sent him gold as long as he was alive. He became an honorary citizen of Passau. He has a street dedicated to him. None of my protests was ever "heard." Another is Franz Schroenghamer-Heimdal, who composed anti-Semitic texts: "The primary characteristic of the eternal Jew is his complete lack of creative power. He is unable to work like the Aryan does, instead he merely exploits the work of others commercially. . . . We must dejewify ourselves. . . . A people that allows itself to be sucked dry in this manner by aliens from elsewhere has truly the patience of a sheep." He accused the Jews of "overthrowing the crown and the altar," and he claimed that Jews would declare women to be "common property." After the war, the city of Passau named a street after him, in my neighborhood, and made him an honorary citizen. The Federal Republic awarded him the Meritorious Service Cross, First Class. (He himself adopted the name Heimdal, 'guardian.') My petition to have his honorary citizen status revoked and the street renamed was rejected.

I felt the same way about a valuable collection of paintings that the Nazis stole from Jewish owners. Stored in the Oberhaus in Passau in 1945, this collection has still not been returned to the Jewish community. When the Jewish community inquired in writing in 1948 whether such assets had been preserved and where they were, a representative of the city maintained that nothing of this kind existed. The family of the famous senior rabbi of Kraców and Warsaw, Dov Ben Meisels, is still waiting for his manuscripts. I told them that these valuables were stolen by the Nazis and stored in Passau at the end of 1944. They were a component of the "Research Division for the Jewish Question," along with some fifteen thousand other volumes. My inquiries with respect to both of these collections have met with no response to date. Passau keeps quiet about the assets it holds. As a German of the second generation, I am ashamed.

At commemorations of All Saints, the bishop, the mayor, and many other leading citizens of Passau have always met at the so-called Heroes' Cemetery. This is the burial site of several hundred SS soldiers, including General von Hassenstein. Every year, Passau's mayor lays wreaths there, highly respected priests say mass there, and many citizens attend. My protests were to no avail. In November 1988, the fiftieth anniversary of the Pogrom Night, Passau refused my request to extend an invitation to the sole concentration camp survivor among its former victims. Instead, the citizens "commemorated" this night by themselves. The Cultural Affairs Office stuck a wooden Star of David among the SS graves to commemorate the Jewish victims. As a German of the second generation, I was emotionally unable to participate. As part of my protest, I demanded a memorial for Jewish victims and some of the rescuers instead. After several years this demand was heard.

In 1990, Passau officials destroyed the grave of Lydia Aaron and her gentile husband as nobody was paying the maintenance fees, I considered this an outrageous assault. The Nazis had killed all the relatives who might have cared for this grave! I published the whole story, and publicly demanded that the grave be restored and dedicated to all the Jews in Passau and to all those who had assisted them. Five years later, the memorial was finally paid for and dedicated by the city of Passau. Another memorial that I repeatedly demanded was for all the victims of National Socialism. It had already been requested and approved by Passau's city council in 1947, but it was never built. I couldn't accept that. In November 1996, it was finally dedicated at a very popular place—between the two houses where Adolf Hitler once lived.

Sepp Eder, until recently a mayor of Passau and chairman of the Social Democratic Party delegation, denounced people to the Gestapo as a young man. For years afterward he lived close to one of the victims who, thanks to him, had spent two and a half years in the penitentiary. But he never told his victim he was sorry for what he had done. My massive protest had no success. But I should not be surprised. In 1995, the community of Plattling, to the west of Passau, still listed Adolf Hitler and Heinrich Himmler as honorary citizens in its new town book. On the other hand, when Lazar Salzberg, once a millionaire, and survivor of various concentration camps, sued for symbolic "compensation" in 1961 and asked the Free State of Bavaria to award 1 DM for his wife, who was gassed in Auschwitz in 1943, and 1 DM for each of his gassed sons, both petitions were denied for reasons of state. After all, his wife had not been his source of support back then, they said. Further, he had married again after the war. As a second-generation German I felt not only terribly ashamed, but also guilty. All this took place not very long ago, but it is still part of Germany's present. I considered it my responsibility to stand up and speak out against it.

When the time came to celebrate the fiftieth anniversary of our libera-tion from National Socialism, I learned there was nothing planned. I envi-sioned an interfaith service at the cathedral where so many years ago Adolf Hitler's swastika flag had been blessed. I pictured a winning, conservative rabbi at the altar, and this time I wanted Jewish survivors welcomed as well. And I wanted the public to notice the change. I asked the city to invite fifty liberators together with fifty survivors as guests of honor. I wanted them all to be received as guests of honor. I wanted their fate to be known. I wanted them to bear witness. And I wanted the local people and the media to pay attention. As a German from the next generation, this meant a lot to me. It is not simply that we all owe them a lot; we also need their testimonies to teach future generations. We'll need the evidence to confront deniers, too. But there was hardly any reaction to all my plans. The only things I could do were to bring them back myself and to celebrate with them on my own. That's what I did.

By August 1994, I had moved to the United States to organize a series of events. I traced and invited about two hundred Americans who had helped liberate "us," and I invited all the survivors I could find. I asked the lord mayor and the city council of Passau to sponsor one night in a hotel for our guests; the officials declined. I begged and, after a while, started to push. As time went by, I became impatient and angry. I felt terribly sorry for those who longed for such an opportunity, and such a small gesture.

The local media was uninterested. As I myself did not have the money, I decided to go on a lecture tour. With the fees I got, I was able to realize at least part of my plan. After a few months, the bishop gave in. I had also arranged commemorations for murdered Jewish children, for tortured and murdered concentration camp inmates, and for two local priests who had sacrificed their lives to save others.

But the city of Passau celebrated very differently. They celebrated alone, in the midst of SS graves, without the victims. This time a Star of David was cemented in place—directly in front of the graves of the SS. The Jewish community of Lower Bavaria was formally called upon to participate "ecumenically" in the celebration. It was outrageous. I was so disgusted that I again asked a TV crew for help. When asked in an interview whether he considered an SS general a "victim of the Holocaust," our lord mayor stated that "details like these" will have to be discussed by historians. The local newspaper did not report the reception I had arranged at the city hall, nor about the interfaith service that was finally permitted. This was the very first interfaith service in two thousand years, but it was "buried" as if nothing had ever taken place. We still have a long way to go.

Standing Up and Speaking Out

For the past twenty-nine years, the DVU (German People's Union, a right wing political party) has held its meetings in my hometown, and up to six thousand radical right-wingers attend. Nazi emblems flash on shoulders again, the swastika war flag is displayed publicly, the forbidden Hitler salute is used. David Irving, who has been bragging for a few years that he is not officially allowed to enter Germany, has nonetheless been the star guest and speaker for several years. As a German of the second generation, I asked myself whether we can afford to stand by.

The hall where they gather had been built under the Nazis. It had been a symbol for racism and is still called Nibelung Hall. The Nibelungen meant a lot to Adolf Hitler and other racists then: they symbolized the pure "Aryans." I don't want such a tradition and I would like to remove this name. As a German of the second generation I'd like to name this building Ludwig-Winkler Hall or Ludwig Mitterer Hall. Ludwig Mitterer was a local priest who spoke out in public for human rights. He spoke out in public for Jews and handicapped people; he refused to use the heil Hitler salute. He was a decent person without arrogance, but with a lot of civil courage. He was killed by the Nazis in Berlin. Winkler was a local priest who did everything he could to stop the child murders in Hutthurm. He was shot by the SS as the Americans marched in. I would like to remember what they did by renaming the hall. But my hometown still rejects this. Civil courage seems not yet in high demand, and I am ashamed of that.

By the summer of 1987, addressing some one thousand demonstrators against the DVU, I portrayed in detail the moral obligation for Passau to confront xenophobia and intolerance and bigotry. I was disturbed by a constellation I had not noticed before: hundreds of policemen surrounding us, the demonstrators. They brought water sprinklers, directed against me. They wore helmets and carried billy clubs and guns. All my life, I had never seen anything like that. Police, to me, were for traffic control only. And there, they wore no helmets. . . . But more and more of them showed up in front of the city hall. It was frightening. But over at the Hall of the Nibelungs, where the right-wing extremists were meeting, nothing like that occurred.

After we walked peacefully up to them, the situation became worse. Both sides were mad at each other; some firecrackers were thrown. Violence was not what I wanted. With my high heels I stood rather lost and alone between a neo-Nazi crowd on one side, yelling Nazi songs and saluting with the Hitler salute, and a group of angry leftists, calling me a traitor and firing firecrackers on the other side. I silenced the leftists; the police intervened brutally. Within minutes, it was quiet again. But that event made it Germany's most controversial and most viewed news. There were reports all over Europe. The DVU was now definitively "on the map," and so was Passau.

I thought it would be a good idea to show an Anne Frank exhibit in Passau and to talk about racism and hatred using that example. Cornelis Suijk, the international director of the Anne Frank Foundation, agreed to talk to Willy Schmoeller, the lord mayor, about such an exhibition while the DVU was there. From my viewpoint, that would have been some kind of "balance" if one is at all possible. Suijk flew in from New York, but he stood in front of closed doors. Schmoeller refused to meet him, arguing that he did not need my assistance. I pushed for the exhibit anyway, and it was shown there a few months later. When Beate Klarsfeld, the Nazi hunter from Paris, offered to speak in public, Schmoeller declined to invite her or to pay for her travel expenses. he also declined to "offer" the city hall, where she could speak, claiming that the room "will be closed"on March 14. It did not count that her husband, Serge Klarsfeld, a Jewish lawyer, had been nearly beaten to death when he attended a DVU meting. The city didn't want her. As a young German, just like her, I asked her to come anyway, and arranged two talks for her. Together with local artists, we spoke about the dangers of xenophobia, hate, and bigotry.

Among the participants in the Beate Klarsfeld events were many women and men in their twenties, including many Austrians. To prohibit him from spewing out hatred again, Canada and Italy long ago banned David Irving, "our" star guest and speaker. Canada deported him twice. Germany was less stringent. For eleven years, I have been struggling against David Irving and Germany's organized right-wing extremists. I helped establish counterprotests for several years. I repeatedly demanded that the state must act. In due course I was sued by the DVU for slander; they claimed that I falsified evidence. They did not succeed. At the appeals level they claimed that I had bribed the reporters to write false reports. In court, however, I offered too much evidence. The DVU lost.

I also wondered what I could do for survivors and their relatives. The survivors cannot be forgotten and neither can those who died. I wanted at least some justice for them. There was still a big hole in the cultural fabric of my hometown. Because neither the city administration nor the churches nor other organizations were ready to do anything about it, I was determined to make up for this on my own. I won't rest until I see at least some of the people responsible for these atrocities apologize to their victims. Until that happens, I want to continue writing and teaching about it. "Our" memory still proves to be full of holes, in a shamefully guilty way.

Fulfilling Some Dreams

Collecting evidence of a few hundred incidents, half a century after they had taken place, I decided that what I could do was take as many people behind the scenes of our society as possible. For almost eighteen years, that is the course I have followed, hoping it is not too late. There have been six books, so far, and a series of cultural initiatives.

I asked some of the survivors: What would you like to see? What must be taken care of? What would you like me to do first? Some of their answers were amazing. Quite a few of them admitted, for instance, that they were homesick! That they still loved Germany and that they would love to return. After all they had gone through? After all the misery and all their losses? Not in my wildest dreams would I have pictured that. But how could I possibly say no? I went to Hans Hoesl, the lord mayor, and to Max Brunner, the cultural adviser, to the newspaper, and to many others as well. It was a disaster. There were cheap excuses such as "there's just no money in our budget for invitations like that." Millions of German marks are spent to illuminate a few buildings of my hometown, but fifty marks for a hotel room was not available! I tried to explain human need, and I started to beg for an invitation, for lodging, and for a program for these homesick survivors.

When I realized there was no way to convince anybody of the symbolic value, I was determined to make it happen anyway. I arranged for each of our emigrés to return. As a welcome, my mother gave Trudl Burian a big doll in 1988. It was meant as a replacement for the doll the SS man took away from her when she was forced to leave Germany decades ago. Trudl Burian was eighty now, but she cried about this gift like a little child. Her son informed me that she named the doll after me and it still sat on her sofa when she died in 1996. Dozens of hurtful memories were brought back by each of these emigrés. Despite our differences in age, we became so close that they trusted me with their most private thoughts. Sometimes we laughed together, and we cried together a lot more, especially when they left once again. But the program has been a big success. I realized also that a private person like me can achieve at least some things. Compared with what I wanted, it was not enough, of course. I was determined to go much further.

To establish a closer relationship between my hometown and Jews and Israel, I made numerous proposals over the years. The last one was to donate three thousand trees to congratulate Jerusalem on its three thousand-year anniversary. Now I want the curriculum in Bavaria changed. The first step was reached in 1988, when the schools were finally mandated to teach about the Holocaust, including local events.

But I also want another section of our history to be included: the history of "our" Jewry in general. I demand this, because for centuries, Jews have been part of our nation and part of our culture. Germany would not be what it is without the impact of "our" Jewry. At school, one never learns about any of this.

A Better Understanding

The more I learned about "our" history, the more I noticed personal changes. Getting in closer touch with Jews and foreigners abroad led to a very different lifestyle and new family values. My whole life had changed since I started the research in 1980. Survivors, emigrants, and their relatives have helped me gain a better understanding of Jews and Judaism. They welcomed me and my family to their congregations and their families. I didn't expect any of that. I'm still very much aware of what it means for a Jew to enter Germany—after Auschwitz. And I can only imagine how hard it must be for a Jew, whose own relatives perished during the Holocaust, to walk up to German Gentiles and engage in a cultural dialogue. Some of the survivors did; they went much further. They offered their friendship, which I happily accepted. Ever since I met them, years ago, they have been in my thoughts and have been a part of my projects on both sides of the Atlantic.

Creating a Symbol

In 1990, a movie about my struggle became a symbol. From the beginning, Michael Verhoeven, the film's director, understood that my story was not necessarily to be seen as the story of Passau. He did not intend to portray people who oppose my work intellectually or brutally. These characters are not proud of the Third Reich. He told a story of people who refuse to look at what happened. His main message is that young people must confront what their own country did. Only then will they be able to create a better society. On October 29, 1990, Richard Corliss wrote in *Time* magazine: "German films aren't funny. German films lack charm. German films avoid the Nazi past like the plague it was." Then he warned the readers: "Be prepared to junk preconceptions with *The Nasty Girl*, Michael Verhoeven's exhilarating true-life adventure about a Nazi hunter in modern Bavaria." The film and the research I have done both break a taboo. You can only change what happens now or in the future if you understand what happened then. We could not prevent Nazism; maybe we cannot prevent the next war. All we can probably do is to make people more sensitive. As a second-generation German, I view this not as a chance; I consider it much more an obligation.

Facing a Wall of Silence

BARBARA ROGERS

They charge us with indifference toward the laws of humanity. This charge we take seriously. In our enterprise man was always more important than money. My whole education taught me to make our enterprise serve the men who worked in it. This spirit filled the entire plant. Can you believe that something that took a century to grow can suddenly disappear? We all, defendants and our tens of thousands of workers and employees, do not believe it. We worried and toiled under conditions that are very difficult to understand and judge in retrospect. Indifference toward the fate of our workers is a charge that we do not deserve. Gentlemen of the tribunal, the defendants before you did their duty in the war and are conscious of no violation of the laws of humanity that form the basis for a united and peaceful world (from the final statement of Alfried Krupp. Trials of War Criminals Before Nuremberg Military Tribunals 1325).

The camp inmates were mostly Jewish women and girls from Hungary and Rumania who were put to work at Krupp's at the beginning of 1944. The conditions they suffered were beneath all dignity: they were wakened at 5 A.M.; they could not wash, as there was no water; there was no drink or food served in the morning; they marched for three-quarters of an hour, barely clothed or shod, in rain or snow, to reach their factory. They worked ten to eleven hours from 6 A.M. (Document 288, an affidavit on conditions at Krupp's by Dr. Jäger, Sereny 569).

The next document Mr. Justice Jackson turned to, D-313 (USA 901), was the testimony of a Polish camp doctor:

"As I understand it," Jackson said, "this was a POW and labor camp for Polish, French and later also Russian POW workers, also serving Krupp

289

at Essen. . . . I admit the distinction [between camps] is a little thin at times:

The camp was under the direction of the SS and Gestapo. Every day at least ten people were brought to me whose bodies were covered with bruises from the continual beatings with rubber tubes, steel switches or sticks. They writhed in agony and I had no medicines to help them. . . . The food consisted of a watery soup which was dirty and sandy, and sometimes foul cabbage which stank. The dishes out of which they ate were also used as toilets because they were too tired or weak to go outside. People died daily of hunger or ill-treatment. . . . There, as well as in the nearby camp for Russian women, beating was the order of the day. The conditions lasted from the very beginning until the day the Americans arrived. (Sereny, 569)

According to the firm's wartime records, the family-owned concern believed that automatic weapons are the weapons of the future and used the great prestige of Krupp's name to conscript Auschwitz prisoners—men, women, and children—for heavy labor in its shops. Setting an example of vigor and enterprise, the Essen Konzern refused to be turned back when the army, uneasy about the camp's proximity to the fluid eastern front, vetoed automatic weapons manufactured there. The firm's own records show that:

Krupp proposed that the factory building, which already stood complete in Auschwitz, be used for the manufacture of aircraft parts and shell fuses, since, in the meantime, the Essen fuse factory had been bombed out. The essential point that influences the decision is, once again, the availability of labor in the concentration camp. For this very reason, Krupp opposed a proposal to employ German workmen. When the army wanted to give the fuse contract to another firm . . . Krupp objected violently, laying particular stress on the firm's close connection with the Auschwitz concentration camp.

To an outsider the implications of all this are clear, and are reflected in Krupp's dreadful reputation abroad. Inside Germany the image is quite different (Manchester 5).

Alfried Krupp was my grandmother's nephew. In 1903, at seventeen, Alfried's mother, Bertha Krupp, "was designated owner and leader of the family business, the Fried, Krupp A.G. (Inc.)" in Essen, Germany, also called "the Armory of the Empire (*Waffenschmiede des Reiches*)" (Manchester 244). My grandmother, Barbara von Wilmowsky, was Bertha Krupp's younger and only sister.

The Krupp name was, and is to this day, admired and idealized. It conveys power, influence, and social welfare to its workers. Furthermore, the corporation was and is known and appreciated as the major provider of work for many people. Born in 1950, I grew up in Essen, where the Krupp company's home and headquarters had always been, not knowing anything about the past and what happened during the war.

The company and the name Krupp were very much part of my life, because my maternal grandparents, the Wilmowskys, had fled their home in the eastern part of Germany after the Russian occupation, and were given the opportunity to live on the main Krupp estate, only minutes away from my parents' house. Often, I would visit them, entering the huge, beautiful park with a majestic, castlelike house, called Villa Hügel, in which my grandmother had grown up. After the war, nobody lived in it; instead, it was used from then on only for social occasions, or as a meeting place for cultural events, such as concerts and exhibits. My grandparents were the last members of this family to live here during their final years—in a more simple way "in the tan brick house beside Villa Hügel, once a gatekeepers home" (Manchester 801). I liked and respected my grandfather, for whom I enjoyed playing the piano and with whom I loved to talk, very much.

Despite the continued presence of my grandparents, their background, the Krupp name, and everything it entailed in our lives, my mother enforced a strict taboo about mentioning our connection to the Krupp family. For about thirty-three years, I did not discuss this part of my family, life, and background with anyone.

When I was twenty-eight, my first husband and I and our children moved from Essen to Chicago. Toward the end of a six-year stay, while in therapy, I experienced the need to find out and learn more about my past and that of my family. In the Spertus College library, I found and dared to read, for the first time, Alfried's final statement in his Nuremberg trial. I was shocked, horrified, and appalled by its repulsive tone, arrogance, and unrepentance. Later, I encountered the same arrogance in other documents and statements by Alfried Krupp. For example, here is his affidavit of 1945:

> We Kruppians are no idealists, but realists. We had the impression that Hitler would give us a healthy development. And in fact he did this. The party system before was wild. . . . There are no ideals. Life is a fight "to-stay-alive," for bread and power. . . . In this hard fight, we needed a hard

and strong leadership. Hitler gave us both. After the years of his leadership, we all felt much better. I said that all Germans were standing behind
Hitler. The majority of the country stood behind its government. Maybe,
this was our weakness. A short while ago, I have read Churchill's speeches
and noticed how he constantly had to defend his policies against the
criticism of the parties and even had to change them. There was no such
thing with us. But, basically, it did not make much of a difference. The
whole nation supported the main lines which Hitler pursued. We Kruppians
have never cared much about life. We only wanted a system which func-
tions well and which would give us an opportunity to work without being
disturbed. (Poliakov 36)

After that experience, I became very much interested in learning more
about the Holocaust. Thus, in 1983–84, during my final months before I
had to return to Germany, I enrolled in a class called Encountering the
Holocaust. It marked the decisive moment that launched my journey of
learning about my family's past.

When the professor began to talk about Auschwitz, one of the first
things he mentioned was about its builders. He got up and wrote two
names on the blackboard: I. G. Farben and—Krupp. When the name Krupp
appeared on the blackboard, I felt as if the earth were opening under me.
I was overwhelmed by shock, disbelief, and shame. Although I certainly
knew about the Nuremberg trials and that my uncle had been prosecuted
and sentenced there, I had no idea why he had had to stand trial, what he
had been accused of, or anything else about his wartime history and the
culpability of the Krupp company.

The complete post-1945 silence about what happened, and about the
role of parents or other family members during Hitler's regime and the war,
was and remains a common tragedy in many German homes. Fortunately, in
my case, I could study and learn through books about this part of my family
history. The atmosphere of family silence was conspiratorial; it lay like a
heavy, thick blanket over most postwar children and teenagers. Being taught
not to ask, never to question, many of my generation became as blind,
uninformed, and ignorant as I recognized myself to be that day in class.

When Alfried Krupp appeared at family gatherings, I could feel and
sense the respect, pity, awe, and reverence with which he was met. As a
child, I had been taught that he was a victim: he was sentenced in Nuremberg
in his father's place, owing to his father's illness. In my family and elsewhere, he was regarded as a martyr. As William Manchester writes in "The

Arms of Krupp," "it persuaded millions of Germans that Nuremberg's most celebrated defendant of 1948 . . . was a martyr to the fatherland" (*652*).

I believed that my uncle bore no responsibility for the wartime decisions and actions of the company. The more I read and learned, however, the clearer it became to me that he had been involved in the company's management decisions since the war's onset. After March 31, 1942, Alfried Krupp "became the firm's *Vorsitzender des Vorstandes*, Director of Directors. As such, according to his own files, he . . . assigned Jewish prisoners from concentration camps to many different places"(Manchester 10).

Finally, in 1943, Alfried became the sole owner. From then on, he bore full responsibility. His involvement in a horrendous, unscrupulous exploitation of human beings through slave work, including occupied countries—using tens of thousands of foreign civilian workmen, prisoners of war, and concentration camp prisoners—was justified after the war by claiming that he would have lost his life if he had not followed orders. But also this was untrue:

> Auschwitz has been mentioned. Krupp's role there is indefensible by any civilized standards; it was, among other things, in flagrant violation of German labor laws. Alfried could not afterwards argue, as uniformed guards did, that he had been given the option of either obeying the commands of superior officers or perishing himself. The Führer had not asked him to take advantage of the victims of Auschwitz. He exploited them voluntarily. (Manchester, 450)

In 1950, my grandfather, Thilo von Wilmowsky, who as a young man had studied law—and who was angered, as Manchester observed, by "any implied criticism of the family name" (*802*), be it his or his wife's—wrote a book, *Warum wurde Krupp verurteilt?* (Why was Krupp condemned?), in which he passionately defended the Krupp company and Alfried for their World War II actions. My grandparents' fate had been very different and difficult—they were arrested after the July 20, 1944, assassination attempt on Hitler, in which they had not been involved. While my grandmother spent about two months in jail and was released after her trial, my grandfather was imprisoned in Sachsenhausen concentration camp during the final months of the war. His "crime" lay in writing critical letters about the SS and in trying to help a Jewish person.

My grandfather survived. His tragic fate during the end of the war raised him above all criticism. As a child, everything I heard and experienced about him made me feel a strong idealization and reverence for him. I shared the feelings deeply, as I genuinely loved my grandfather because of his patient, kind, thoughtful, friendly, gentle nature. Furthermore, he was always interested in what I was doing and took me seriously. I was sixteen when he died, and I had not questioned, thought, or asked about the past.

But why should the employment of KZ-prisoners (konzentrationslager) be regarded as a criminal offense at all? The prisoners had been robbed of their freedom, no matter if they were working in a factory or not. The judges could not have been in the dark about what the efforts of the Silesian Krupp works meant for the Jews in question, namely, that their lives were saved in the case of success. For many prisoners the alternative was being used in industrial production or extermination camps. And yet, the judgment found the industrialists, who provided the chance of survival for prisoners, guilty of a crime (Wilmowsky 192, my translation).

When, as a thirty-five year-old woman, I finally read my grandfather's book for the first time, I was filled with great disappointment, disbelief, and indignation. How could he passionately defend unspeakable crimes? I was in shock and deeply saddened. I could not believe the deceitful and mislead-ing "argument"—distorting reality—that the Berthawerke in Auschwitz saved human lives. Further, he presented Hitler's madness and crime of a "total war" as a simple matter of modern reality:

> The judgment in the Krupp-trial has . . . used the conception of 'plun-dering' in such a way as if the world, during the years of war from 1939 until 1945, was still in the state of 1907, as if the Second World War had been led in the style of the war of 1870/71. It obviously implies that 'total war' is a National Socialist propaganda phrase and not an elementary, hard fact of reality, aside from all ideologies. (Wilmowsky 108, my translation).

My grandfather also untruthfully regarded the Second World War, which was started by Hitler's and Germany's aggression, supported only all too willingly and submissively by enthusiastic, obedient Germans, as a war waged, as he put it, out of the "necessity of naked existence" (Wilmowsky 109).

The Holocaust class enabled me to see with my own eyes, to learn facts, to ask any questions I had, and—in writing papers—to find and express the feelings, questions, and thoughts I had buried completely inside of me. Learning the truth about the Holocaust enabled me to unearth these ques-tions. Consequently, I embarked on a continuing journey of learning about the Holocaust.

The Holocaust class had a profound impact on my life. I truly looked inside to find out what I felt and thought about the Holocaust, what effect it had on me; and, for the first time in my life, I could, through writing freely, express my very own thoughts and feelings. Where I had carried nothing but confusion and fear—something that felt like a sticky, black mass of tar inside of me and my brain—I began to bring about some clarity, honesty, and truth.

Over time, I was able to grasp more and more about my family's involvement, and to deal with the historical facts, overcoming familial imposed blindness and silence. Moreover, I learned to deal with the strong, emotional responses that at times overwhelmed me. These reactions resulted from my discovering shocking truths, from unresolved feelings, and from my indignation and despair about an environment that did not want me to ask, think, feel, learn, and speak freely.

In the beginning, confused by fear and conflicting emotions, I could hardly read, much less comprehend, information about my family's history. First, I needed to get to know and deal with my feelings, and it took years to let them come back alive within me, to understand and accept, work through, and live with them—learning why they were there, where they came from, what they meant—before I could intellectually comprehend and deal with what I was learning.

Within me, feelings of fundamental, basic trust, loyalty, and love were challenged by feelings of disbelief, shock, protest, rage, and despair. Strong fear and anxiety were my companions throughout learning, changing, and beginning to break my silence—only internally at first—then by writing, and later, publishing. Feelings about what I treasured in, and what had made me proud of, family members, my culture, and my country struggled with and often succumbed to feelings of shame, pain, disappointment, sadness, and loss.

Loyalty and love blinded me again and again. So did prejudices and patterns of thinking and feeling that had been programmed into me, some from generation to generation. Discovering them filled me with sadness and shame. I could only overcome these patterns by looking at them truthfully, questioning and judging them, and mourning and protesting my blindness and submission to them. Thus, very slowly, only step by step, could I analyze arguments, see through distortions, rationalizations, defenses, and lies, and try to find the truth and my own point of view. Eventually, I discovered that the truth, and even life and reality, were very, very different from what I had been taught.

I have come to realize that, having grown up in this postwar German atmosphere, certain viewpoints will always be very painful and confusing for me. The shock, sadness, and mourning that I feel and experience for the victims, and over the crimes committed by Germans, including members of my own family, during World War II, are overwhelming. The experience of growing up among Germans who buried their past without facing it is also a part of me. It left a legacy of silence, which became a terrible burden for the next generation.

Hardly any psychological literature exists about this German generation. While working on my own past with a Jewish psychoanalyst for about eighteen months during 1983 and 1984, the burden that my family's and country's Nazi past had caused me came up again and again. My therapist could find no information about my generation and its problems at that time.

In 1989, the Israeli psychologist Dan Bar-On explored the psychological impact of this silence in interviews with "the middle-aged children of the Nazi generation" (*Legacy of Silence*). He observed that "the psychological literature was loaded with research findings and reports about the children, even the grandchildren, of survivors. But I could uncover hardly a word about the perpetrators and their children" (9). Reading his book, I realized that by confronting and mourning my family's history, and thus an important part of my identity, I could break the *Legacy of Silence*. A door to more honest contact with myself, a door to my thoughts and feelings (which had to be repressed to not shake my parents' equilibrium), and a door to self-authenticity had been opened.

This process has transformed my life over the past fifteen years. I have developed and grown in a way that reflects increasingly what I have found to be truly important. Values and priorities formerly hidden within me exert more and more influence, enabling me to honor life, whether it is my own or another person's. This journey first forced me to honestly face my first marriage, my family, and my country after I returned to Essen from Chicago. I realized with pain that, within those bonds, I could not find or fulfill what I found meaningful, important, and treasured about life. Chicago represented the experience of being able to breathe freely with my mind, heart, and soul. After eight years back in Germany, when my youngest child left for college, I returned to Chicago on my own, where I am still building a completely different life for myself.

One of the deeply moving moments of my therapy occurred when my therapist returned from a trip to Israel. He told me about his visit to Yad

Vashem, Israel's Holocaust memorial. He described how, in a large, rectangular hall, accessible to visitors by walking on a path around it, the names of Auschwitz, Bergen-Belsen, Treblinka, and the other extermination camps are inscribed in the floor. He told me that he also thought about me when he stood there, realizing, "You have suffered too."

About five years later, I traveled to Israel and stood in the same place, thinking about how therapy opened the door to my path to regain the ability to mourn, to feel, to remember, to learn facts, and to change. Therapy finally—not only in a literal, but also metaphorical sense—led me to the same place: to Yad Vashem and the human capacity and basic, fundamental right, duty, and responsibility to look at and deal with my past.

In her book *The Great Silence,* Gabriele von Armin writes about the silence burdening the next German generation:

> I know only by looking back, that it was exactly my intention to deliver the great silence to emotional upset and to feel pain in order to live alive instead of being numbed and petrified.
>
> How do you deal with the past? A wise man told me, "by dealing with it." This is what I have tried. . . . There is no recipe, no result, no catharsis. There is no end. It never ends. One cannot be freed from it, one cannot be delivered from it, but in spite of it one can live and, all the more, love. In this year of reading, listening, and silence I have not gotten rid of the past. On the contrary: it has become an added gain." (Armin 7–8, my translation)

This has also been my experience during my journey over the past fifteen years.

My search for my family's past is continuous. For the Krupp part of my family, I could learn and find out all the facts through books, but there are other parts of my parents' past, which, to this day, remain buried under a thick blanket of silence. For example, I don't know any facts about the three war winters my father spent as a German soldier in Russia. All his life, and devastatingly into his old age, this time, his experiences, and, I suspect, his guilt haunted him. The sad reality that he never dealt with his past destroyed his life, and became a burden for his children. When I think of my father—a man who once had a passionate love for life—the image I recall is that of a bent man, broken in spirit, endlessly brooding in silence.

Although any open sympathy for Hitler or National Socialism was not part of my family experience after the war, and history could be discussed quite safely in general terms, any attempt I ever made to talk truthfully and openly with my parents about their personal experiences during this time was either met with silence or ended in escape and evasion, or even in critical, harsh comments, attacks, or judgments. They completely discouraged further questions. My parents erected an insurmountable wall between us and around themselves.

For many years, I struggled with the disappointment of not being able to have honest or open conversations or relationships with my parents. They chose not to be honest with themselves. In vain do I deeply and strongly wish that life had granted me the chance to have a different relationship and find another form of communication with my parents. Only some Germans of my generation were granted this chance, and for me, their accounts are very moving.

Despite many severe problems that I have observed in many Germans stemming from the inability to look honestly at their family and personal history, I have noticed hopeful and encouraging changes in the third generation. In Essen, for example, the "old synagogue," which was severely destroyed during Kristallnacht and which was used after the war as a museum for industrial design, including Krupp products, was restored and rebuilt during the 1980s. It has become a cultural and research center dealing with the part of Essen's past that, until then, was covered by a blanket of silence.

Following my therapy, I returned to and lived in Essen for four years and participated in some work and research. A continuing project at the old synagogue is to write formal historical memorials, which are collected in special boxes, about Jewish families who had lived in Essen. Thus, the Jews' destroyed lives and tragic fates are being recorded. In 1986, I met Beth Ellen Rosenbaum, the daughter of Holocaust survivor Kurt Rosenbaum. She had come from New York to find out what had happened to her grandparents. I worked with her, and independently, to research her grandparents' fate. Finally, a formal history of her family was written and added to the synagogue's growing collection. I also was able to persuade the Krupp Foundation to sponsor the catalogue of an exhibit for the old synagogue with unique dolls from the doll maker Edith Samuel, who was able to emigrate in time from Essen to Israel. Her father, Rabbi Salomon Samuel, had been a major contributor in the planning and building of the old synagogue.

With a feeling of relief and liberation I especially remember one exhibit in the old synagogue, done by a high school class. The students had tried to discover how many foreign and slave prisoner camps there had been in

Essen. The class had written about them, drawn maps, sharing and showing all the information they had been able to find. I think that only the third generation will be able to look at and deal with the Nazi past. This generation is much less inhibited than its two predecessor generations, and is far more honest and open in confronting the past.

The wall of silence that I and so many of the second generation encountered was a deeply formative—and in my case, for a long time, completely invisible and unconscious—part of our personal past. In the movie *Dark Lullabies,* a young German woman, Susanne Holman, talks about what changed within her when she discovered her village's war past. She observes: "I felt I had been cheated out of my history. I had lived here for twenty years, but I was missing part of the history that belonged to the place. I was never told about this, and that's why I never learned to ask questions about it. This was a very important discovery for me. It, to some extent, destroyed the feelings for the place which had been my home."

What hurts me about my parents' generation is not that they should have been better or different people. Faced with unimaginable life circumstances, I know that they made the choices that, at that point of their lives, their character, their background, culture, family, and national training brought them to. But I wish that after the war I could have witnessed indications of sincere self-doubts, of a rising self-awareness, of subsequent change, some expression of mourning, regret, remorse, an effort to effect change and improve the chances to learn and see, and for the development of the next generation.

Independent of the different views people held regarding what contributed to Hitler's and National Socialism's rise, I wish I had seen attempts to make amends and to ensure that certain attitudes and behaviors were not only questioned but also discarded. Growing up, I wish I had heard the words NEVER AGAIN.

Upon my return to Germany, I found it confusing and painful to realize that communication broke down and walls came up—even with people who sincerely condemned and criticized National Socialism and tyranny—where their personal or family history was involved, when the conversation touched areas where they carried burdens from the past. I also found that people, despite outwardly liberal views, were unable to escape the emotional and behavioral patterns established and programmed into minds and souls not only for generations before Hitler, but which were exploited, strongly reinforced, even deepened under Nazism and its propaganda. In her book *Albert Speer: His Battle with Truth,* Gitta Sereny writes about him: "There was a dimension missing in him, a capacity to feel which his childhood had blotted out, allowing him not to experience love but only romanticized substitutes for love. Pity, compassion, sympathy and empathy were not part of his emotional vocabulary" (719). I found this to be true in painful personal encounters with the first and second generation in Germany, especially after my awakening in the United States.

Under Hitler, people were deeply formed and programmed through an ideology of merciless hardness and cruelty that was to be applied toward oneself and others—Hitler's legacy. These attitudes and behavior patterns remained a dominant influence and strong undercurrent in peoples' psyches after 1945, and are, all too often, well hidden behind an outwardly liberal, democratic facade that falsely seems to deal openly with the past. I found out that an intellectual critique of National Socialism did not come along with emotional honesty and growth.

Anti-Semitism, which had already been before Hitler a very accepted form of prejudice and hatred, could not be voiced openly after 1945. But I could later sense and understand that in many people the basic attitude had not changed; it was just hidden, because after the Holocaust most people did not dare be openly anti-Semitic. It was a silence that did not signal the true absence of anti-Semitism and was not a result of learning and growth. I heard new scapegoats, such as the United States, being blamed and put down, and sometimes even associated with "Jewish influence."

During the Nazi regime, wrong, even criminal, behavior had become the accepted, established norm. Even after the war, inhuman or criminal behavior often would be excused, defended, belittled, ignored, or gently ridiculed. People rarely took a stance, clearly and unmistakably stating what is good or what is wrong in human interactions. I grew up and lived among people who often condoned behavior or actions that are wrong or even evil. Eventually, I realized that this atmosphere, among other things, had created a hole inside of me where I should have had a moral code or a conscience.

When I felt something was a wrong thing to do, I often would have conflicting opinions inside of me that would question what I saw, thought, and felt. These deliberations weakened my inner voice, created confusion in my mind, and not only caused insecurity within me, but also convinced me that there was something wrong with my true self's expression, with my inner voice, with how I saw and experienced, thought, and felt about right and wrong, good and evil. By now, I am more able to form and express opinions reflecting my inner convictions, and to act upon them.

When I came to Chicago at twenty-eight, I became alive, and I could more and more connect with life and people around me. It made me realize how isolated I had been in Germany, where I had felt like a stranger in my family while growing up. In the United States, I had begun to live in a culture where the silence I had been part of did not exist. Not only was I asked questions about the past, but the uninhibited, free environment brought up questions and feelings within me, not just about the past, but also about how I lived, and had lived, my life. Eventually, my journey into life began when I recognized and confronted the emotional silence within me with the help of another human being.

I needed support to overcome the walls of silence within me, to conquer my fears, prejudices, the internal programs and burdens that I unknowingly had breathed like air until then. With sadness I had to realize that the most important relationships of my life had been based upon my internal fears, which in turn had brought about my silence, compliance, and submission. But the end of my inner silence, and trying to speak up, brought about immense conflict in those relationships. Eventually, I had to come to terms with the fact that I could not change these relationships unilaterally.

I nurtured those friendships and relationships where I could be free, honest, open, and was appreciated—not for my silence, submission, or pleasantness, but for my spirit and truthfulness. Those friendships became my source of life and made it possible for me to become increasingly true to myself, and to look for, find, and follow my very own path into life. It has also given me great joy and deep satisfaction to support my wonderful children in their quest to listen to and follow their inner voices and remarkable true selves.

I view my responsibility and duty toward the gift of my life as using it to grow, mature, and learn. To ensure this development, I had to leave places and distance myself from relationships where silence was expected of me. It has been at times a painful and lonely journey. But it opened the door to life-affirming experiences that I would have never even thought possible only a few years ago.

I need to be with people who are interested in listening, where my voice can be heard and my experiences can help. Yet, my sense of loyalty toward my family still can fill me with fear, and sometimes conflicts with my desire for openness and enlightenment. I still struggle with the reproachful silence—which paralyzed me when I lived in Germany during those eight years between my America years—from my family, above all from my parents, toward what I wrote and could publish, and toward the things I did in trying to make a small difference.

The question that was so often put, defiantly and reproachfully, to my generation by our parents' generation—What would you have done?—I can only answer with my life. I see my life as being in the service of overcoming silences, within me and around me. So I deeply appreciate this chance to breach the wall of silence I encountered growing up. It is a moving experience for me to become part of *Second Generation Voices* so that my journey can be shared with others.

Works Cited

Arnim, Gabriele von. *Das grosse Schweigen.* Von der Schwierigkeit, mit den Schatten der Vergangenheit zu leben. München: Knaur, 1991.

Bar-On, Dan. *Legacy of Silence.* Encounters with Children of the Third Reich. Cambridge: Harvard Univ. Press, 1989.

Batty, Peter. *The House of Krupp.* New York: Stein and Day, 1966.

Dark Lullabies. Dir. Irene Lilienheim Angelico. National Film Board of Canada. 1985.

Manchester, William. *The Arms of Krupp.* Boston: Little, Brown and Company, 1964.

Poliakov, Leon, and Wulf, Josef. *Das dritte Reich und die Juden.* Dokumente und Aufsätze. Berlin: Arami, 1955.

Sereny, Gitta. *Albert Speer, His Battle with Truth.* New York: Vintage Books, 1996.

Trials of War Criminals Before the Nuremberg Military Tribunals under Council Law No. 10, Oct. 1946–Apr. 1949. English language edition (the "green" series). Washington: Microcard ed., 1971 reprint. Set of 15 vols., 186 cards total volume 9.

Wilmowsky, Thilo von. *Warum wurde Krupp verurteilt?* Legende und Justizirrtum. Düsseldorf: Econ Verlag, 1962.

Honor Thy Mother

Reflections on Being the Daughter of Nazis

LIESEL APPEL

"Am I going to see my daughter again before I die? Where is she? Why is she not coming home? Am I going to see my child again before I die?"

These were, I am told, my mother's last haunting words, as she lay dying, broken in body and spirit. She fought so hard and long to stay alive, but finally succumbed on March 19, 1988, before I could get back to Germany to see her. Her last wish was to be laid out in the white night-gown I had sent her many years ago, the garment she had kept just for her final journey. Her head rested on the pillow I had embroidered with a rose as a five-year-old.

She died in a sterile hospital room at the Dietrich Boenhofer Institute, a retirement home, in the small town of Ludenscheid/Sauerland, surrounded by strangers, except for one niece. At this moment, my quest to return to my homeland in time to make peace with her ended. I had not honored my mother for the better part of my life; I did not attend her funeral.

I was now an orphan, standing at the gateway to a new life, new knowledge, new understanding. But I had already become orphaned thirty-seven years before, on that horrible day when I learned that my beloved parents were Nazis. With the crystal-clear vision of a child's knowledge of right from wrong, I turned against my parents, basing my decision on the morality I had been taught by them. I had discovered that their moral code, "take care of your neighbors and one German is as good as another," had been empty words; they did not include all Germans and all neighbors and applied only to the chosen Aryan race, of which I was created to be one. Hitler wrote in *Mein Kampf*:

303

In my fortress of the Teutonic order
a young generation will grow up
before which the world will tremble.
I want the young to be violent,
domineering, undismayed, cruel.
The young must be all these things.
There must be nothing weak or gentle about them.
The splendid beast of prey
must once again flash from their eyes.
That way I can create something new.

I was nine when I felt for the first time the pain that is even greater than the pain of physically losing someone. This is the pain experienced when betrayed and misunderstood, and when we stop loving someone. To stop loving one's parents is to stop loving oneself. Until the moment in life, that is, when we realize that all we needed from our parents was life and that everything else is up to us. We have choices and we can re-create ourselves to whatever image we choose; while we cannot change another human being, we can change ourselves.

Father, who was my hero and idol, had died six months before that early spring day in 1951 when I encountered my first Jew. Love for my mother came to an end on this day; I never kissed her again, called her Mother, or talked to her about anything important. I became a self-destructive child and woman, unrelenting and unforgiving. I tried to kill myself by swallowing a handful of rat poison.

The past made me who I was, bounded in fear, pain, and loneliness with the shadow of guilt hanging over me. I did not believe that I deserved happiness or love.

The turning point did come, however, when I was forty-five. I had to begin my journey home, realizing that I have no right to judge anyone.

I am alone.
A wanderer on a spiritual quest
With a lifelong feeling of statelessness.
No home for my soul
No rest
Till the end of my quest.
Misunderstood and betrayed
Is it too late.

To walk the meadows and hills
Of my childhood again?
Is it too late?
To hold on
Is to die myself
And mutilate my soul.
Has my country finally changed?
Nothing stays the same.
I should make the journey home.
I am who I am.

For the past twelve years, I have spoken to many different groups, from sisterhoods, temple, and church congregations to groups of Holocaust survivors and *Kindertransport* members. Every time I have been open about my life and my family legacy, a little more light has penetrated the dark corners of my soul, and healing has occurred. I found in some of the men and women who listened a similar letting go of emotions, several of them sharing their own tragic stories for the first time. We are all interconnected and contain within our being something that may help and heal another person. Facing the truth sets us free. We are our brothers' and sisters' keepers and in this time and space together for a divine purpose and reason. One of the Jewish sages said: "If I am not for myself, who will be for me? If I am only for myself, who am I? If not now, when?"

For the better part of my adult life, I fabricated stories about my family. I lived a lie. Every time I encountered a Jew, I told a lie.

I was born late in my parents' life as a special gift to Adolf Hitler. This legacy was embedded into me from my earliest days. "You are a *Wunschkind,* a wished-for child. You owe a debt to the *Vaterland.* Your very existence has been a gift to your country."

When Germany lost the war and the Allied forces were everywhere, instead of the goose-stepping soldiers, which I had saluted as a small girl from our balcony, I was told again that my country would be restored to splendor as soon as these foreigners would leave and that it was up to me to see to it.

It was part of my charmed childhood, where loving parents and a large extended family made me feel special. In our beautiful, spacious home, concerts were held regularly. I was nurtured and read to, learned to recite poetry and play the piano from an early age, and because "in a healthy body lives a healthy mind," I could swim at two and keep up with Father on our long walks into the forest.

He brought beggars home from the street to eat at our table and, much to my mother's dismay, sit in our finest chairs. He wrote poems for me and about me, the little blonde, blue-eyed Aryan child that the sun and moon looked lovingly upon.

The German word *Heimat* is more encompassing than just "home." It includes spirit and soul. It meant so much to my father; he wrote: "Your home can be the world to you, but never the world your home." His beloved daughter would "make the world her home."

This wholesome image and way of living had, however, another side. My Father was fighting what he thought to be a holy war, wanting to destroy inhuman, non-German forces, and believing that "even a plant can be more German and pure than some people and have more substance and soul." "Look at the lily over there," he would tell visitors. "It stands proud and pure. A white daughter of a slender mother, raised with tenderness and the morning dew, like my own daughter, Liesel."

The family man, who was my father, had to leave for a while in 1944. I was told he had gone to Poland with his best friend, Erich Koch, who had been appointed governor of Poland. Father was put in charge of the Polish education system; the educator and committed teacher promptly closed schools in the invaded land: "Jewish, Gypsy, and Polish children are not entitled to learning."

When Father returned to us, the formerly victorious German armies had been defeated. My only sibling, brother Fritz, was twenty when I was born, and fighting on a navy submarine in the Nordic Sea. His ship was lost, and Mother cried a lot, not knowing that he had escaped and become a prisoner of war in England. And now, to make things worse, Father had to go into hiding. He left by night on his bicycle for my grandparents' house in Bottrop. He made the two hundred-mile journey traveling by night and sleeping in cornfields by day. But the American officers, ready to arrest him, were not far behind. When the knock on the door came, Grand-mother hid him in the attic. Grandmother lied. I have always thought it significant that she developed throat cancer soon after this incident and succumbed very quickly to the disease.

Father left her house and, on the way back to us, was caught and taken to a camp. I heard KZ, concentration camp, for the first time, when mother and neighbors whispered about the KZs. Father had been taken to a de-nazification camp, I found out later. When he returned, he was just a shell of his former self. There was going to be a trial in Nuremberg, and Koch's trial was to be in Poland.

On an early-morning walk along the seashore, where we had gone for a short vacation to help restore father's strength, he and I talked again about Germany's greatness and my legacy to my homeland, when suddenly he went on his knees. He moved to get up, but could not. I tried to help him, but my father, my idol, died in front of me of a heart attack. The tide was coming in as I tried desperately to keep his head out of the water. Finally, help came and pulled the dead man, with the child clinging to his corpse, out of the sea.

Six months later, my childhood came to an abrupt end. Still grieving after Father's death, I was playing alone outside of our house when a stranger walked toward me. I was not frightened of this man; he looked very kind. He carried a briefcase and wore a strange little cap at the back of his head. He was unaware that within a few minutes he would be destroying a family bond and turning a young girl into a lonely child, ready and willing to die from guilt and shame.

This man, an almost mystical figure in my life, came back in a spirit of forgiveness soon after the war. He came back to the country of his torment, his unbearable memories and tragedy still fresh. Yet, I sensed no hate or bitterness about him.

His name is Willi Meyer; he and his family had been our immediate neighbors. He told me quietly on this early spring day of 1951 that he and his family had lived in the house next to ours and that during Kristallnacht thugs had broken into his home and destroyed everything. Furniture and glass had been thrown from the second-floor balcony and one of the men had grabbed him and thrown him from the balcony. He was sure that he was going to die, but a miracle had happened. A man, one of the neighbors, had stepped forward and caught him in his arms. A special man had taken pity on the small Jewish boy. After hiding in the bushes, he had been rushed away to his German nanny, Johanna Banner, and was later smuggled to England. He now lived in Israel. I had no idea what or where Israel was, but immediately connected the story the man was telling me to my father, the great humanitarian. I took him by the hand and pulled him into our house to meet my mother, thinking she would be as proud of Father as I was.

The living room was dark as we entered. The stranger froze by the door. Mother and he looked at each other. I was taken out of the room and locked in my bedroom. I don't know what transpired between them, but when I was let out, Mother was red with rage. She demanded that I never do anything like this again. "Never bring people like that into our house again." I asked: "People like what? Mother, did we not save this boy?" She shouted: "Why should we have saved a Jew? Your father was a good man."

My bewilderment turned to rage. I pushed her away, called her "murderer," and told her never to touch me again. This was the dramatic end to my childhood.

I never forgave my mother until her death in 1988. As soon as I could, I moved away and became the perpetual immigrant, not settling anywhere for long. I departed for England at seventeen with just twenty marks in my pocket and clutching one small suitcase. I felt compelled to get as far away from my people as possible. I changed my identity, name, and religion. A black musician became my first husband and spiritual guru. I traveled to Africa, living in the bush with different tribes, worshiping their ancestors. I became committed to civil rights and the striving of the emerging black nations to achieve independence. Abolishing apartheid in South Africa was my passion as now is the Animal Rights Movement.

The few times I came to visit Mother, it was mostly to humiliate and hurt her. Her Aryan daughter now had two black children and a black husband. I made sure to tell her that I wanted nothing to do with Germany and my heritage. I had found nirvana in England and, later, the United States.

I did not realize then that we become what we can't forgive. I hated all intolerance, but I had become intolerant. I thought of myself as a free-spirited human being with no prejudice whatsoever, but I was holding onto prejudice with a bitter heart. I turned away from every German I met, believing that I had nothing in common with them.

I am not alone. When I finally went public with my story, I discovered that there are other Germans of my generation who feel the same way. We all lived in isolation and in foreign countries, from England to Canada to the United States and Israel. I was residing in Los Angeles when during a seminar, I encountered a young woman by the name of Rachel. She is the daughter of Auschwitz survivors, and shared with the large group that her parents had taught her never to forget or forgive. At that moment, I don't know what possessed me but I got out of my chair, stood next to her, and told the stunned audience that my parents were Nazis.

What did I expect? Certainly not what happened! After a period of silence, the room erupted. Men and women, many of them Jewish, rushed to Rachel and me. They hugged us, admonishing us to let go. This was the beginning of coming out from the shadows of guilt, and for the first time tell my story and the encounter with Willi Meyer. Even my children and former husband did not know of my past.

We have a very limited time on this earth. We are our brothers' and sisters' keepers. We should live life to the fullest without allowing ourselves to be burdened by negatives. When we learn to love unconditionally, at all times, and under all circumstances, we can finally live a serene life. We choose if we want to continue as victims and have the need for revenge or if we allow our tragedies to help us grow to love unconditionally. The best way to make sure that there never ever will be another Hitler is to teach the next generation to love and be responsible for their choices. To show them by our example that we are not looking to be understood but to understand and to help our fellow man—the strong taking care of the weak, unlike Nazism's credo of the strong murdering the weak and the different. We must never forget what the human mind and heart is capable of, and always be vigilant and speak up when and where we see any injustice committed against any fellow man or creature. We cannot serve life, which is the true meaning of our being here on this planet, when we have an unforgiving heart. "Let's all walk gently on this planet in sandals of love."

I converted to Judaism in 1990 at the University synagogue in Los Angeles. Following the Jewish teachings came natural to me; it is what I have always believed. An enlightened Christian minister told me once: "A Jew is a seeker of truth." I have always been a seeker of truth and I equate truth with love. Faith is a private matter and although my present husband, Don, is Jewish, I was already converting before I met him. Jews are committed to creating a better world for all of humanity. I am proud to be part of this community. My soul has come home.

Meditation on Matthew 9:9–13

CHRISTIAN STAFFA

Introduction: Berlin, October 1994

It is very strange and at the same time challenging for me to write on issues of faith and belief after Auschwitz. Although I am increasingly distancing myself from some of the key points of Christian faith, nevertheless I still define myself as a Christian. When I started studying theology I soon became skeptical about the way Protestant theology is taught in Germany. With some exceptions, it is in the worst sense, academic. It seems to have nothing to do with the world; it remains untouched by politics and concrete injustice. I discovered a connection between this abstract theological teaching and the denial of biblical and modern Jewish thinking and belief. All that was left was the individual soul and ontology: "humans are sinners, how to escape from here." I then discovered, with the help of two professors (Peter von der Osten-Sacken and Friedrich Wilhelm Marquardt) and many fellow students, what I found most appalling: that after Auschwitz, Christian theology does not reflect on its participation in German anti-Semitism nor in Nazi ideology, which led to Auschwitz. Still today, I discover more and more of this guilt and I feel ashamed. I also feel challenged to uncover the key theological theories that are structurally anti-Semitic, or as Christians are tempted to say, anti-Judaistic.

This leads to a rather banal but important—and still unresolved—question. How was it possible that German Protestants and their institutions did not resist, and even worse, why did they support the oppression and the killing of European Jews? I know it is not a new question, but it is one that shakes every Christian belief or at least should shake it. Mine is shaken. How can a "religion" that is so focused on love terminology hate with such

310

ferocity? Did the Christian message not reach the people or was the message wrong?

When I started to reflect on these questions I thought that interpretation—the Hellenization and the Constantinism of the former Jewish-Christian tradition—underlay Christianity's power orientation and anti-Semitism. Although I still think this is partly right I also feel that it is an attempt to escape from the radical self-critical question whether something is wrong with the original teaching. I know that Paul did not think of a two thousand-year-long Christian institution. And I still think that it would help greatly if Christian theologians would take this into consideration—it is surprising that they do not—but despite this, isn't there a problem in thinking that someone died for our sins? Is this not so hard to believe that one has to conclude what Adorno did in his *Antisemitismus Thesen?* They repeat endlessly the sacrifice because they can't believe in its saving power. If you believe and at the same time do not really believe—which you cannot admit—then you have to find someone whom you can punish for "not believing"—the Jew. This is a simplification of a very complicated structure, but I want to make clear where my skepticism comes from.

If I now question the model of Jesus as the Christ and the Savior, two problems occur. First, Jesus is, to me, as a non-Jew, the historical and cultural access to the G'd of Israel and to "His" or "Her" history with His or Her people. He thereby introduced me to a way of dealing with secular power, which I call "transcendental anarchy"—meaning that by the acceptance of the rulership of G'd, all human beings have the same rights; no one has to obey another human being if or because they all obey G'd. We are in the best sense equal. What happens to this inspiring and, to me, fascinating way to think and organize a community and life in this world if I question the theological constructions around Jesus Christ?

Second, who am I? Am I still a Christian? Can I be a Christian after the history of Christian anti-Semitism, which culminated in Auschwitz? My answer for the moment is that there is no other way. There is no way to escape from this oppressing history. I still live in a Christian culture and I still gain from it, even if I don't like it. On the other hand, I still want to be heard among Christians as a member of the community. Even if I am on the edge of this community, I am still part of this tradition and I want to raise my critical voice.

Because I work on a biographical level with the descendants of the perpetrators and victims, I believe that part of my motivation to work on the Shoah is connected to my family history. In this I find an unresolved conflict between my Nazi grandfather and his wife, who comes from a Jewish background. I have not yet found out why I am so involved in Christian theology. I believe, though, that part of the answer is my family history. I might change my mind about identifying as a Christian if I discover what I am searching for.

The following article is a revised version of one I wrote for a book that was edited by Action Reconciliation Service for Peace. It was a reflection on the fiftieth anniversary of the liberation of Auschwitz. They asked me if I would be willing to write a meditation sermon to aid pastors and priests for their sermons on January 27, 1995.

I struggled with my task. As I said, I am someone who is increasingly distancing himself from Christianity. I asked myself, "How can I do this?" But even if I am no longer convinced of the messiahship of Jesus, I believe that only radical questioning of our Christian tradition can help the church confront the continuing issues raised by the Shoah, and to work for meaningful change.

Sermon Meditation

Living is
remembering my murdered relatives
The past
is eternity
their suffering—death
are the prism
through which I see and measure all things
all this is not only yesterday
it is tomorrow and today
pain, hatred of evil
and genuine love
—Halina Birenbaum[1]

Between Silence and Speech

A meditation on giving a sermon to commemorate the fiftieth anniversary of the liberation of Auschwitz is awkward and a sermon itself even more

---

1. "Geddenken," in *Der dumme Fuss will mich nach Deutschland tragen,* ed. Nea Weissberg-Bob (Berlin, 1992), 137, trans. Ellen Klein.

awkward. Silence would be another possibility. Silence, as is well known, was the only possibility that Helmut Gollwitzer saw for Christians, as he expressed in impressive language following the November pogrom of 1938.[2] The fact that sermons had failed for over nineteen hundred years hindered Gollwitzer from speaking at that time and this must also cause every contemporary attempt to speak to stick in our throats. Today, another motive for silence has appeared, besides the older one—the danger of the instrumentalization[3] of remembrance. It is still not unusual in Germany for the memory of the victims of the Shoah to be used for becoming free of the burden of history, especially after this had gained general social acceptance in the eighties. Yes, remembrance is certainly used frequently as a confirmation of one's own unchallenged Christian theology. For example, the listener hears this in a speech given by a high ranking member of the church council in Arnoldsheim reporting on a visit to Auschwitz. He saw a cross that had been carved into the wall in the death cell in Block 11 of the main camp. He understood this carved cross as symbolizing the presence of Jesus in Auschwitz and as a sign of hope. I call this blasphemy.

The failure of Christian theology and the church is also brought into play in remembering but without bearing consequences for its theological guilt. It is as if Christian theology could remain unchallenged after Auschwitz and the church's failure to act. This reminds me, in a state of helplessness, of the structure that also corrupts the theological notion of justification, where justification is used in a way that I feel myself justified without

2. "Who should give sermons today? . . . Are we not all hindered from speaking on this day? Can we do anything today other than be silent? How did all of the giving of and listening to sermons benefit us and our people and our church throughout the years and centuries? . . . What do we expect of God when we come to him now and sing and read the bible, pray, confess our sins, as if one could count on His still being there and not that only shallow religious activity is taking place? He must feel disgust at our audacity and presumptuousness. Why do we not at least remain silent?" (trans. by Ellen Klein). Sermon on Luke 3:3-14 delivered on 16 November 1938.

3. The word *instrumentalization* is, according to many of my American and English friends, not really understandable. In German it is used in a sense that someone uses someone to serve his or her purpose—to make him or her an instrument in one's own psycho or political system. This implies that you don't really listen, you don't take this "other" as a person. For example, politically the German government used the existence of Jewish communities in Germany since 1945 as an instrument to show the world "we are good again." They didn't really care how Jews felt in Germany after 1945, and I am afraid many people still do not. The "pride" to "host" Jewish communities in Germany did not relate to a way of communication with Jews in Germany.

knowing what my real transgressions are. Justification will stabilize my status quo, and not serve as a point of departure for change. But change, after all, is the object when justification and repentance interact. If one's own guilt—a guilt that, as it were, has been historically passed on—is covered up in remembering, the remembering becomes a cynical variant of the "liberation of Auschwitz." We dispose of the burden of history; we free ourselves of it without ever having really looked at it straight in the eye. This also means in many cases without ever having listened seriously to the victims of the Shoah and to their children and grandchildren talking about their past and present without having spoken to them. Thus, we see that this silence is a form of remaining untouched. Christianity in Germany today has, as a rule, proceeded in silence to the "normal agenda." It is difficult to deny that Christian faith and theology have not as yet allowed themselves to be stirred by Auschwitz. The churches, in any case, have not been dismayed by it, have not lost their form; they continue to be dominated by universal coldness and indifference. If, however, the voices of deeply moved individuals did speak out, they were not representative. For example, Bishop Dibelius dismissed the question whether it was still possible to pray after Auschwitz: "Nonsense. You just lost your nerves after Auschwitz."[4] This professing bishop, who in 1928 still referred to himself with solemn pride as an anti-Semite, is here warding off any kind of responsibility.

Defensive words such as these are followed by impassive silence. A perfect example of this for me is the much-used notion of responsibility, which is used without reflection in almost every memorial speech as a variable for the consequences to be drawn from the Shoah. Scarcely anyone knows what this means for each of the speakers and listeners. Sometimes it means that there will never be another Auschwitz; sometimes it means that Germany will never again, or better yet, will not continue, to be deluged by a flood of violence from the right; and sometimes it means that democracy will be strengthened. It is almost always the others who have to be opposed. But one's own answer as to what the situation with one's theology is, how much one knows of the mothers and fathers in the literal and proverbial senses, of their involvement with the Shoah, and the consequences of this for us today—this is almost never thought about nor expressed. And so the honorable concept of responsibility becomes a means of escape.

4. Friedrich-Wilhelm Marquardt, *Von Elend und Heimsuchung der Theologie* (On misery and affliction of theology): *Prolegommena zur Dogmatik* (Munich, 1988) 131.

Fritz Perls interpreted the word responsibility as 'response-ability,' as 'the ability to respond' or even better the ability to permit an inner resonance of an event."[5] In my view, after Auschwitz one should add the perception of the resonance of an event in others and the attempt to endure these resonances and to speak about them.

Therefore, the attempt to speak responsibly requires first that one is the opposite of impassive. It cannot be undertaken under the condition of feeling "unchallenged." The question that is addressed to us through Auschwitz is that of the truth of our faith and our theology. To make this attempt seems to me the duty of the church service, and not only on this day. Although we can only falter in such an attempt at speech, it brings us that much closer to the reality that has till now been obscured. I am increasingly convinced that the vapid nature of our theology and services is closely related to their being far removed from reality in relation to Auschwitz and its consequences. Facing the radical uncertainty of one's own theological traditions and family, and talking with Jewish survivors and their children and grandchildren, involves pain, but also may bring release and a new realism to theological concepts. I have never felt the true meaning of mercy more clearly than when in conversation with survivors. That they speak with me, take me seriously and even possibly like me illustrates the concept of mercy. The concept is, however, anything but simple. For me such an encounter is always accompanied by feelings of extreme guilt and requires effort. It is the same with most people I know. Here, it is not reconciliation like a shining light at the end of the path, but it is the path itself that becomes a perceptible experience of mercy and, as Paul would express it, the path becomes life.

Any serious attempt to face history in and around ourselves directly is therefore not—as often denounced—masochism, but a release from the set phrases and rigidity of our theology. Certainly, rigidities can also be observed in this process. They are connected with the temptation of "self-praise," which was resisted by Paul, or to express it in more modern terms, with instrumentalization.

For me, this means, in connection with church services, that I do not want to replace the formulas of "not perceiving" with formulas of

5. Richard Picker, "Psychotherapy and Nazi Past—An Attempt at Concrete Figures," p. 185, in Barbara Heimannsberg and Christoph Schmidt, *The Collective Silence* (Cologne, 1992), 175–93.

remembrance. Rather, I want to take as starting points my questions, doubts, and the areas where I feel challenged. This also prohibits a quick shift toward Bosnia or any other crisis area. With respect to Auschwitz, we ourselves, as Germans, Christians, and officials of this church, are the most immediate crisis area.

About the Text

The search for a suitable text for this Sunday seemed to me after a short while to be highly unsuitable. Which Bible passage really "suits" Auschwitz? The outrageousness of this question led me to "choose" the preassigned text, Matt. 9:9–13.[6]

> And as Jesus passed forth from thence, he saw a man, named Matthew, sitting at the receipt of custom: and he said unto him, Follow me. And he arose, and followed him.
>
> And it came to pass, as Jesus sat at meat in the house, behold many publicans and sinners came and sat down with him and his disciples.
>
> And when the Pharisees saw it, they said unto his disciples, Why eateth your Master with publicans and sinners?
>
> But when Jesus heard that, he said unto them, They that be whole need not a physician, but they that are sick.
>
> But go ye and learn what that meaneth, I will have mercy, and not sacrifice: for I'm not come to call the righteous, but sinners to repentance.

The Gospel According to St. Matthew is a testimony to the harsh conflict between his community and the Jews who lived next to them. This fact alone makes a passage from this gospel unwieldy for this Sunday sermon. In my opinion, there is much to support the interpretation of the Dutch theologian Ton Veerkamp that we are dealing here with a supercessionist theory.[7] Matthew does exactly what Paul is fighting against, namely, he forsakes Israel for the community of Jews and heathens. This is not with reference to the teaching "not a letter, nor a stroke, will disappear

---

6. In most of the Christian churches, there is an order of texts that is the basis of the sermon. It is not the whole Bible but only parts of it. Sometimes they are texts from the Hebrew Bible, sometimes from the so-called New Testament. Of course, in modern times the preacher is more or less free to choose other texts if he or she thinks that it fits better the occasion of the service.

7. *Texte & Kontexte* 3/93, 25–40.

from the law" (Matt. 5:18), but rather, with reference to the people. Whether you agree with this point of view, or whether you believe that there is a sharp inner-Jewish conflict about determining the path Israel is to follow: in either case, Matthew's polemics are contradicted by Paul, who stresses that Israel keeps its full heritage and all the promises (Rom. 9:1–5).[8] Relating to our passage, however, is a subtle tone, which—with the surely unjustified general criticism of the Pharisees at the back of my mind—must be noted and to which I will refer later. Now I would prefer to move around the passage with movements of association.

I cannot present the passage as a passage for a sermon without making clear its distance from Auschwitz and all of its consequences for the present day. Nevertheless, I can pose the question whether the passage speaks to our post-Shoah world. (In the following I use "we" as the subject most of the time, although I do not really care for this usage in an actual sermon. However, I do so consciously because I believe that we are dealing here with a collective connection; "we," meaning German Christians and members of the church—generation to generation.)

The Tax Collectors

The tax collector is a collaborator, a sympathizer. Someone who profits from unjustice. Therefore, he is not a poor man. But his profit has its price. For he is shunned by society. Are we collaborators of impassive silence? Of silence in our families, our congregations, and our society? When we ask these questions, do we really want to hear the answers? My accusations against the fathers and later also against the mothers—You did nothing against the Nazis, you were even bystanders, you still don't really think and feel that it was evil! I was fleeing from the question to what degree I, a member of the second generation, was involved. These accusations have their unconscious origin in the "grace of a late birth."[9] Generally, our material needs have been rather well satisfied. Is there a connection here also? A connection between repression, impassive silence and financial prosperity? Although I recognize a connection, it would be going too far to give

8. I quote verses 4 and 5: "Who are Israelites, whom belong the adoption, the presence of God, the covenants, and the giving of the Law and the service of God, and the promises. Whose are the fathers and of whom as concerning the flesh Christ came God who is over all, blessed forever."

9. This subsequently "famous" phrase was created by the chancellor of FRG at a visit in Israel to describe his (non) relationship to the Shoah and its consequences.

an exact description of it here. Yet, it would be worthwhile for our church to pursue this question in a sermon.

Do others keep their distance from us because of our history? Many Germans say that this is so. They tell of their "negative" experiences in foreign countries. This only shows that they were confronted there with their history, a confrontation that can be avoided when they are at home. It seems to me that this image of a suppressed German national conscious-ness is a reflex of an expected punishment that has not yet happened. People such as Oskar Schindler, who showed that the statement "We couldn't do anything" was and is a lie, were avoided in Germany. When called upon to follow, the tax collector rises and follows. Surprisingly, without any com-ment, without any profession of faith in Jesus Christ or confession of his past sins.

We remain seated. For a long time we have been called upon to change the way we have come to terms with our past, the way we profess our faith, but we look in a different direction. Or is something beginning to happen very slowly? Does the third generation have more freedom perhaps? We sit in church waiting for a promise that nothing will happen to us or to our basic structures. The tax collector did not know of any promises. Maybe there are some people in our congregations who will stand up. We should seek them.

Jesus

Jesus passes the tax collector's booth, sees Matthew, and asks him to accom-pany him on his way. Together, they go to eat with other tax collectors and sinners. Today, we encounter the Jew Jesus as a survivor of Auschwitz. Jews who were not in Europe between 1933 and 1945 are also survivors. The Nazis' plan was to exterminate all Jews. Today, for us Jesus is a survivor of the Shoah. Is he really still calling us or does he find us repugnant of God, as Gollwitzer in his 1938 sermon believes? I believe—still—that we of the second and third generations are being called. However, this is not anything to be taken for granted. And also that we eat with him, that life with him is still possible. Here we see a sign of hope, not of reconciliation, but of the possibility of communication.

The Pharisees appear during the meal. "Why," they ask, "is Jesus eating with those people there?" Jesus answers, "Not everyone needs me, but the ill and the sinners do." (If this were a sermon for another occasion, it would be worthwhile at this point to listen longer to that subtle tone mentioned above. Other than in the usual Christian reception, the Pharisees were really regarded here as healthy and righteous.)

Perhaps it is surprising for the tax gatherer to be suddenly declared ill. Did he already know this and was this the reason he was able to get up and follow him? If he didn't know beforehand what Jesus believes of him, he knows it at this point. And he remains. Are we aware of our illness? Here we are also confronted with the surprising discovery that the tax collector is able to learn about and experience himself without any comment on his previous history. But still it seems to me that by defining the tax collector as ill, Jesus confronts him with his history. As someone who is ill, he could only become healthy by looking at the reasons for his symptoms. The process of healing is a process of confronting the history of one's illness. At this point, it would be possible to reflect upon the double meaning of the two words "release from" in the sermon.

The Ill

We are the ill. What is our illness? Resistance, coldness, indifference toward Jews as partners in conversation and toward our own tradition. Politically obsessed with proving the guilt of Israel in its dealings with the Palestinians, reacting to stories of Jewish lives with stories of one's own suffering (and also with stories not experienced firsthand), needing clear black and white pictures to live. Jews are good, Jews are difficult to get along with, they are oversensitive, Jews are intelligent, they have enriched German culture— without Jews there is now something missing. And what of our memory gaps, too, in relation to our own family histories? All of these could be interpreted as symptoms of illness.

Compassion

"For I desire steadfast love and not sacrifice." This quotation from Hosea 6:6 is spoken by Jesus to the righteous ones, the Pharisees.[10] In recapitulation of what I have written so far, I want to ask what its message could be to those who are ill.

I find the opposition posed here difficult. It is usually the case when compassion and sacrifice are mentioned together that Christians quickly sort them into old anti-Judaistic stereotypes. The sacrifice is equated with the

10. In Hosea 6:6 it is written, "For love *(chesed)* is my desire, not sacrifice."

Torah, the Temple, the "old" covenant. Compassion is equated with mercy, the gospel, the "new" covenant. During two thousand years of Christian-Jewish relations, this opposition has been turned around by the Christian church; compassion has been forgotten. The desire of most Christian churches was sacrifice. The Jews were made victims of slaughter. Compassion is not at all an inherent quality of ours, but is something that must be relearned. In this respect, the prophet's words are really spoken to us, the ones who are ill.

But what form should compassion take today? What form should it have always had? Compassion is the ability to suffer with someone else; sympathy, participation. Seen against the background of the symptoms of illness already described, compassion would be a step toward acquiring the ability to act, toward recovery. Allowing history and stories to touch ourselves. Not as an onlooker, that is, not as someone being charitable in the negative sense, but as a participant, as someone participating. Compassion seeks encounter and for that reason has consequences for the way one deals with one's sense of normalcy. Thus, responding, response-ability, might be possible.

Working Through Doubtfulness

A Case Study of a Daughter of a Nazi

DAN BAR-ON AND ELKE ROTTGARDT

Through the analysis of the following case study we wish to show how "not knowing for sure" is extremely difficult to live with and work through. Whatever one assumes or reconstructs one's biography around ("he was a perpetrator," "he was not one") may not have simple consequences. Either it could mean trusting one's feelings, standing up against one's whole social web ("it can be, he may have done it"), or it could mean repressing them altogether ("it is all in my head"). The unresolved ambiguity, in turn, may easily be transmitted, unintentionally, into the following generations (Bar-On 1995).

Magne (pseudonym) contacted the first author after he finished conducting his interviews in Germany (Bar-On 1989). Here is the beginning of her self-presentation:

"I was born in a small town in northern Germany in 1950. My father, born in 1914, was a teacher and was well respected in town. My mother, born in 1925, is a housewife and brought two children into this world, my brother and me. The consequences of the war were still ever present in my hometown then; the grown-ups talked about this time a lot to each other. I thought I knew a lot about National Socialism. Nevertheless, I had the feeling that this was about a time in history that was long gone and didn't have anything to do with me."

Magne tells that she had a history teacher who was in the Wermacht during the war but he "strictly taught the text from the history book," and therefore she was not aware that he was talking about a time he had experienced himself. She had no need to ask questions as she knew a lot of that time from home and it was not relevant for her present life anyway.

"My psychoanalysis shook me awake from my sleeping beauty sleep." Magne was more than thirty at that time. When she remarked that her father behaved like a Nazi, her analyst responded: "Your father *was* a Nazi." This hit me like a bomb. But the first shock soon made way to a growing relief. In a diffused way I felt that she was right. Only then did Magne remember her father telling her, during her childhood, that he had given a "glowing speech in honor of the führer in front of his soldiers" as late as April 20, 1945. Though he tried to contextualize it as an example of how the Nazis took advantage of his young age and seduced him, she now reflected on "how happy and radiant he was each time he reported this. He pretended to complain about the Nazis when in fact he liked to remember his enthusiasm for them." Only then did Magne realize that in 1945 he was already thirty, long grown out of his adolescent innocent enthusiasm.

Now, other memories became meaningful. Her father used to emphasize how important for him was the fact that he married a woman with blonde hair and blue eyes (and so were his two children). "I don't think I am doing an injustice to my father when I assume he was a believer in the breeding philosophy of the Nazis as it was proclaimed by Lebensborn." He used to say: "The Nordic is still better." This feeling grew even stronger after talking with a friend. Magne reported how her father once told her and her brother "in an inhibited and trivial way" how he told the midwife who helped in the birth of her and her brother "about letting us die if we had been handicapped. The friend, a prosecutor, looked at me in total shock and said: 'That is murder!' Only through his response did I fully realize what had been discussed in my family as if it were normal."

Magne noticed that her parents made her, as a child, "an ally to their secret love of National Socialism." Father taught her the first (now forbidden) verse of the national anthem together with other Nazi songs, "not without emphasizing that you were not really allowed to sing these." Magne's favorite children's book was a National Socialist (NS) propaganda book with lots of photos: "I liked best the ones in which Hitler shows himself with children. I got the impression of a loving and lovable person. I know that Hitler was close and familiar to me and that I would have liked to belong to those children." Magne tried to draw the swastika, but it came out the wrong way. Her parents, amused, tried to correct her. "My mother even led my hand when I was drawing it. At the same time she winked at me that I was not really allowed to do that." Magne finally drew it on her school bench and "nobody ever reacted to that."

"I also developed a sensitivity regarding how easy it was for my father to speak about the death of a person." He would describe his job in the army during the war, being in the air force, watching bombers approaching Germany. "He did not seem to realize that people were killed in this." Magne started to question her mother about the wartime in Poland, where she had stayed with her father, who was a veterinarian of the Wermacht there. Magne asked about the persecution and extermination of the Jews, but her mother claimed she "had not noticed any of that." Who did the house they moved into in 1940 belong to? "Maybe it belonged to a Jew? My mother called this thought absurd." Magne did not pursue her questioning, "as I was afraid that the more critical I was in asking, the less I would find out." Anyway, she maintained the suspicion that her grandfather expropriated the house from Jews, because "how else could he have established a practice in such a short time that enabled him to feed a four-person family? There was no wealth in our family."

About five years after she confronted her parents' NS past for the first time, Magne decided to write a dissertation (Rottgardt 1993). "I was lying on the sofa, reading a book about the disappearing of childhood because of secrets being revealed in the media, and I suddenly realized what I was interested in. I wanted to know how other families dealt with the NS past, how other children had worked through their family's NS history. I took a piece of paper and wrote down the questions I had. I knew immediately what I wanted to know." When Magne studied the literature, she read again and again that there was silence in the families about this issue. "I had difficulties understanding that, because in my family a lot was said; I only had to learn to understand what was said." Magne remembered that during the fifties it was a frequent topic at her home and she believed she was relatively late (compared with other kids her age) in understanding the meaning of what she had heard. This is an example of the difference between knowing facts (to which she may have been exposed too early) and understanding their meaning (which, Magne felt, she grasped only many years later, through her dissertation). I describe elsewhere how these are two separate stages in the working-through process among descendants of Nazis (Bar-On 1989).

Magne started her study with the hypothesis that "taboo created distance":

"I reached this hypothesis through my own experience. I had the feeling that I was always kept at great emotional distance, especially by my father. I sensed his fear of closeness, because closeness could have implied the danger of me asking difficult questions. Nevertheless I knew—'something is there'—I had tremendous crying spells when I was confronted with NS crimes, which I could not keep under control. I only gave meaning to them when I started to confront my parents' NS past."

Magne searched for dialogue partners of her age and origin. "This choice seemed favorable because it helped me find out how much NS thinking was taken over by the children even after the end of the Third Reich." As Magne advanced with her study she found out "how many taboos surrounded this topic." She had no problems finding interview partners: She interviewed twenty-seven people altogether. "Many felt increasingly uneasy talking to me. Although I never exposed my view, they obviously sensed through my questions how little they had thought about their parents and how little they knew." The outcomes surprised Magne. Belonging to the critical student movement of the late sixties, "I had anticipated no dialogue between parents and their children concerning the personal NS past of the parents, but I still believed that the children had developed in the meantime their own thoughts about their parents. None of them formed a picture from their knowledge about their parents." This did not happen because the parents silenced that period. "In all families there was enough information for me to put together somewhat of a picture of the parents, showing a clear discrepancy between what they had done during the NS time and how they presented this afterward."

Despite her anticipation, Magne was surprised that there really was no dialogue between parents and children even in the four families in which the father had been in the Communist resistance during the NS time. "When the parents' actions were discussed it was always in an atmosphere of antagonism. Either the children used the NS topic to fight their parents or the parents mistook their children's questions for attacks." Only one(!) of the interviewees "took into consideration that the NS time could have an impact on him too, or that the attitudes that enabled these atrocities could have been passed on to him through his upbringing." Most interviewees were not interested in Magne's results. The one who asked for them "sent me an angry response, which was so chaotic that I did not quite understand it."

Magne encountered with her dissertation a much wider social defensiveness, "most of which took the form of silence." Her professor, who seemed to support her in her work, "avoided any discussion about the content of my dissertation. When it was finished it took him nearly a year to give me a date for the oral exam. His written evaluation showed me that he had not read my dissertation. Although the oral was a somewhat lively discussion, afterward there was an awkward atmosphere in the room . . . everybody, including my adviser, seemed to be relieved when they could say good-bye."

Magne had only two meetings with her adviser during the whole period of the dissertation, owing to his "scheduling problems." A similar pattern happened later with her colleagues. Magne asked for feedback but they never responded. One well-known psychoanalyst was very fond of her work and tried to have it published in a more popular version. He did not succeed having it published, but also could not answer Magne's question why he was so fond of it. Strangely enough, both Magne's parents responded with great interest, though she felt it was at first a "father-killer topic." Whenever they met, during the time of the dissertation, Magne's father was eager to hear of its progress, volunteering more information about his NS past. When Magne asked him about his experiences in Russia, she felt "the same kind of murderous rage that I was familiar with from other situations." He denounced the Russians for their brutal way of fighting, and talked "like an innocent victim who had to defend himself against his murderers." Later, he told Magne, a Jew who was a member of his denazification committee accused him of being a member of the SS. This caused a new spell of that rage in her father. Nobody, however, could prove this accusation and "my father was reestablished as a civil servant without any problems."

When Magne started her dissertation she could only sense that there was something concerning her parents NS time. She called her parents Nazis, independent of party membership. "I knew my father was in the party, but that was not my criterion. I called them Nazis because they clearly sympathized with National Socialism. This sympathy made it possible that the criminals among the Nazis could commit their atrocities without hindrance." Through her dissertation, Magne suddenly understood that "what had happened in my family was not 'normal.' I had not been aware so far that no other family glorified National Socialism as much as mine." She interviewed a son of a high-ranking Nazi, who made it clear that "the NS lived in his family without the slightest doubt. But even there it was not this goal-oriented, hidden praise of NS, with the cheerful tenor 'that it was still good' as it has been in my own family."

While conducting her dissertation, Magne also recognized that there was a growing discrepancy between what she has expected of her interviewees to know about their parents' NS past and what she herself has learned about her father's NS past. So she decided to find out if he was involved in NS crimes. She had obtained bits and pieces of his wartime experiences in Russia, but never got a clear picture of that time. Magne tried to approach her father, but he became very defensive as soon as he found out that this time she was asking in a more "critical and distant manner. He created now a picture of himself as a convinced anti-Nazi. When I realized that I would not find out more, I asked him the direct question—what he had known about NS crimes and if he had been involved in any of these situations." Magne had a vague assumption, "based on the contemptuous way my father had been talking about partisans and Russian warfare, that he probably did not have any problems with them being killed. I had read in a book that at the eastern front Russian civilians were sometimes randomly declared partisans and shot dead." In addition, Magne felt that her strong reactions whenever she heard about the extermination of the Jews had to do in some hidden way with her father. He responded to her direct question—what had he known about war crimes and NS crimes and had he been involved in these situations—that he did not kill partisans or Jews. He claimed never having killed anybody by declaring that he never shot anyone. He saw some Jews digging one time but he knew of nothing associated with their being killed or gassed.

"He said this with such indignation in his voice that for a moment I was wondering if I was doing him injustice in my thoughts." But then he added that "at the end of the war he returned his gun rusty because he did not shoot a single shot throughout the war." The reactions of Magne's father pointed in different directions, and Magne could not make up her mind. The indignation in his voice almost persuaded her to believe his words of honor, but then he said a cliché that suggested that he tried to deceive her once again. Magne's suspicion gained support from an unexpected side. Her mother did not take part in the conversation, "but from her body language, how she was suddenly distancing herself from my father, while he spoke of returning the rusty gun and never having shot with it, I knew again that I was not wrong but that he was lying. I said: 'I don't believe you.' He looked at me full of hatred and said: 'Are you saying I am a murderer?' Again he had a murderous rage in his face. How come he reacted with the term murderer instead of liar? It occurred to me that being a liar may be for him an accusation worse than being a murderer. This reminded me of Eichmann, who remained untouched during his trial as far as the crimes

he had organized were concerned, but became very upset when someone mentioned a wrong number of victims."

Magne's father cut off any relationships with her after that conversation.
"I was tormented by doubts whether I was right. Again and again I had to
struggle with the thoughts that I was crazy." Magne knew her father had spent
the last period of the war as a commandant of a Danish island. She deliberated
about going there and finding out what he had done, "but I realized I did
not have the strength to do that. I was torn between wanting to know what
it was that I sensed in him and feeling that it was too much for me."

Many years before Magne started to deal with the NS past of her father,
she had experienced once how he constructed absurd lie stories when he
felt he was being pushed into a corner. He had an illegitimate daughter
from the time before his marriage with Magne's mother. No one knew
anything about this child, as she lived with an adopting family. "At some
point the girl wanted to meet her biological father. The adopting mother
created the contact to him through her biological mother. So, one day this
daughter appeared when I was about eight. My father presented her as a
daughter of a dead war comrade, of whom he wanted now to take care."
For many years the girl was a frequent guest in Magne's family. When
Magne and her brother grew older, Magne was about sixteen, the father
told his son that the girl was purportedly his daughter, but he did not
believe it. Anyhow, it became evident that the girl could say to her father
"daddy," while they were all by themselves. When someone was present she
had to call him "uncle." This game went on for several years. To his family,
the father gave the feeling she was not his daughter, while to her his
message was "I am your father."

Magne was confused. "For many years I did not know who she really was.
Meanwhile, my half sister had stopped communicating with our family and
emigrated to the United States. After many years I found her and visited her.
By then she had a ten-year-old daughter. When I saw the daughter it became
clear to me that my father was the grandfather of this child. You could not
overlook the family resemblance. I realized my father was a terrible liar."

This earlier experience caused Magne to develop basic doubts concerning her father. It helped her create a critical distance from his self-presentation when she later started to work through his NS past. The question,
however—what did Magne sense in her father—was not yet resolved. The
answer came through a conversation she had with her half sister:

"She told me one day that my father had visited her several times when
she was an infant. He had introduced himself to the adopting family as a

war comrade. When I heard this the thought went through my head, The criminal comes back to the place of his crime. I was preoccupied with the fact that he had pretended to be someone else and a terrible connection dawned upon me. He told me two stories about other people's crimes when I was a child." When I was six my father thought he had to give me 'sexual education.' He told me in all detail about a man abusing a girl and then killing her. About two years later he told me also in detail how the Nazis gassed the Jews. Although I was still young then, I never forgot these stories and still remember them accurately today.

"Suddenly I felt as if a veil was lifted from my eyes. He had told me about his experiences. In the same way he could not keep his secret to have a daughter to himself, he could not keep his crimes to himself. I felt I could not endure this and again I had doubts if I was becoming crazy. After all, I did not have any proof. On the other hand I knew that I would not feel so terrible if this were only empty speculation. I went back to my psycho-analyst and she reinforced my suspicions about my father."

Magne contacted Simon Wiesenthal, but he could not help her find out any conclusive details concerning criminal activities of her father. Magne's final suspicions concentrated on a girl her father had probably abused and killed during the war. These are the last paragraphs of her paper:

"I try to take signals seriously and to put them into a picture. In doing so I also acknowledge those signals I find within myself. When I take care of a child the thought goes through my head how easy it would be to kill such a child. . . . My mother often mentioned that I had been very quiet as an infant. Nobody hardly ever heard me. Probably I had very good reasons to remain unnoticed. When my nephews were still young my father did not want them to visit without their parents. He felt the responsibility was too much. All this led me to assume that my father killed babies. The matter-of-fact attitude how he talked about not letting my brother and me live had we been handicapped fits into this picture.

"I am able to have these thoughts because I have no contacts with my parents. Only breaking the connections enabled me to give up my inhibitions to think. I assume this is true for many German families. . . . It took me ten years since my first realizing NS problems until what I know today.

"Probably I would not have taken this on if it had not been necessary for my psychological survival to realize this concrete burden of my father's stories and the necessity to rid myself of it. . . . My parents' denial certainly originated from their childhood history. In their personality development they both remained at the stage of children who put their hands in front of their eyes to hide and assume that if they cannot see, nobody else can see either.

"Their inability to control destructive personality traits that were reinforced during the NS time had probably reinforced their denial. When I was a child this denial often confused me. When I told my perception of something my parents did not like they told me with great conviction that I was wrong. I had to stop thinking and feeling and play my parents' game, although at the same time I perceived what was really happening. In a gigantic effort I suppressed my own perceptions and mechanically oriented myself to what I was told. In order not to become crazy in these two worlds I closed down to any information from the outside.

"I am sure my family history is not as unusual as it might appear here. I am sure there are many families with hidden secrets concerning the NS time. These could be brought to light because there are always signals which point to these secrets. On one hand I think it is important to deal with behavior that parents were accountable for, because the burden of the parents is the burden of the children especially if you don't know the burden. In addition, the destructive potential of the parents is the destructive potential of the children. In order to break the vicious cycle and to prevent anything like this happening in the future it would be desirable for us Germans to confront the denied sides of our family history. On the other hand this process of working through is tremendously difficult and painful. Who can give consolation to this process when we all need consolation, and who can give consolation to us in the face of the enormity of what had happened to the victims of Nazism?"

Magne tried for a while to keep contact with her mother, but her mother refused to accept Magne's position regarding her father. Finally, they broke off too. Magne felt that she could live now with the burden of being unaccepted and misled by her parents.

Epilogue

Dan Bar-On met Magne three times following the completion of her dissertation. He encouraged her to write down her story, and subsequently he would comment on it from his own perspective. Bar-On received a letter in which Magne felt totally misunderstood. Bar-On suggested to meet again, which they did in November 1995 in Cologne. Out of that meeting came a few additional corrections and clarifications but also her following text, which speaks for itself:

"In the meantime the developments, between me and my parents, moved forward. I felt I did not want to keep silent about what my father has entrusted me. Therefore I wrote my mother a letter telling her how my father told me a story, as a child, of a murder, and which lasting effects this story had on my life. She reacted, enraged, accusing me of inventing the whole thing. I learned from her reaction that with her I have neither a chance of being listened to nor of receiving any compassion.

"At that point our relationship broke up forever (that is what I thought then). But I felt this was tearing me up. Having no contact was for me more difficult than having the conflict with them. My bonds towards them were too strong, in spite of all the difficulties between us. As I thought then that I would never regain contact with my parents, I wanted to have at least some relations with other family members, with whom I lost contact since I moved to another city to study after finishing school. I called the siblings of my parents and was astonished how happy they were with my phone call. They partially did not know about the difficulties we had and the break of contact between me and my parents. The older brother of my father, who is very close to him, started right away to arrange a reconciliation between us. He was quite confused to find out that they absolutely refused his proposal to arrange a meeting between us. Only then did I inform him of the sexual murder which my father described to me [when I was] six."

"My uncle was first so shocked that he could not follow what I told him. Again and again he asked questions and said he could not believe it. But in his general approach he gave me the feeling that he did believe me. Till today he never, even indirectly, questioned the reliability of my story. It took a long time for him though, to overcome his initial shock. In their next encounter, my uncle told my father he knew now what the matter was. He did not mention the content—of what he knew now. My father became so furious about me that my uncle told me, fearfully: 'You cannot go there. Something terrible can happen.' My uncle also said that my father still felt unsuspecting. He asked my uncle, however, if I was angry that as a child I almost drowned in a lake.

"For me this was interesting information. There was a situation, in my childhood, in which my father observed how I almost drowned in a lake. This situation was created only owing to the fact that my parents severely ignored their responsibility of watching me in the water. Though he was a trained lifeguard, my father did not come to rescue me, but proposed my brother go and help me out. As I came out of the water my father approached me, laughing: 'So, sweety, did you want to drown?' Now, when my uncle mentioned my father's reaction, I was very astonished to learn that he remembered that incident, and that he obviously recognized what he had done.

"For me, a few other things were of importance:

—When I told the story of the murder to my uncle I felt I was completely sure of telling a true story. I knew for sure, that if I had made it up I would not be able to tell it to this uncle.

—I could feel how much more human the reaction of my uncle was, compared to that of my parents. I could experience how long it took him till he grasped that I was talking of a murder (my father spoke of murder before I could even conceive this word myself). I also liked the fact that my uncle did not speak badly of my father. Thereby, my uncle did not put himself above him.

—The most important fact was that my uncle believed me. I suddenly felt it became unimportant for me how my parents would react. It was enough for me that my uncle took me seriously.

"Slowly I developed an image how I could encounter my parents, without falling into the old dynamic of reciprocal complaints and hatred. What helped me here was the understanding that I can absolutely not expect any understanding for my situation from my mother's side, neither for any interest of hers—how I view these matters. Although I wished this to happen from my father's side, I did not really expect it. I knew I should not develop any hopes in this direction because this would create only frustration and complaints. I decided not to discuss this story any further with them.

"When I called my parents for the first time, my father responded. He reacted as if we spoke only recently (we did not talk for the last five years!). He spoke with me as if nothing has happened. However, towards the end of our conversation he wanted to know what I had in my mind against him "so I can justify myself." He did not let loose till I told him the story the way he had told it to me as a child. I could not sense clearly if he recalled his telling me this story. He, of course, refused to accept my version that it was his own experience, and gave all kinds of arguments why this could not be so (for example: if so, he would now be in prison). Then he asked me if I could believe he murdered someone. I said 'yes' and then he became angry and said I was not his daughter anymore. I was not very impressed by this reaction. I felt his reaction was one of not being seriously engaged. When he saw that he could not impress me with his anger he ended the conversation with the words 'so, yes, then I cannot do anything about it.'

"The next day I called my mother. She reacted similarly. She spoke with me as if nothing had happened. When I asked her if she knew what I told my father the day before, she said she knew everything of our conversation. She also tried to persuade me not to believe my version of the story. However, in our discussion she said one sentence which was important for me. It showed me that she believed my version of the story. She said: 'OK, so if this story did not kill you then we also have to live with it.' I believe she was not aware of what she just said. But I could feel she meant it seriously. She also gave me the feeling that she was not impressed by my story. She even used the occasion to remind me not to call while my father takes his nap.

"What really struck me was the fact that my mother would do anything for a little recognition. She said she was very happy that I called again though I just told her I believed her husband was a sexual murderer. I had the impression I could tell her the worst things and she would not reject it seriously. I could feel, after this conversation, how my mother was emotionally in deep hunger. She would do everything to receive some emotional attention.

"Since then we called each other several times. My father behaved first like a little insulted child, but when he saw that I did not react, he went back to his usual reactions. Both of my parents behave like in former times. My mother, however, is now more respectful with me. For my parents the story seems to have ended this way. I feel relieved and less tense, since I do not have to carry the NS past of my father alone anymore. Also my parents do not seem burdened, suggesting that I did not tell them anything new. It even seems as if they feel happy with the facts that the secret became disclosed, finally . Our relationships, in my view became better. We found now the distance we need to respect each other. I have not seen them yet. For this I need more time, and I guess, they need it as well."

References

Bar-On, Dan. *Legacy of Silence: Encounters with Children of the Third Reich*. Cambridge: Harvard Univ. Press. 1989. Also in German: *Die Last desSchweigens*. Frankfurt/Main: Campus Verlag, 1991.

———. *Fear and Hope: Three Generations and the Holocaust*. Cambridge, Mass.: Harvard Univ. Press, 1995.

Rottgardt, E. Elternhorigkeit. *Nationalsozialismus in der Generation Danach*. Hamburg: Verlag Dr. Kovac., 1993.

PART SEVEN

Is Dialogue Possible?

Introduction

Dialogue groups that are committed to authenticity and honesty form a crucial part of the attempt at working through their Shoah legacy by both second generations. Members of these generations recall being raised in silence about the Holocaust. Yet, as noted, the motivation for this silence is quite different. Moreover, there is a vast difference in how each generation views its parents. Survivors' children can admire and respect their parents. Children of perpetrators, however, must live with the fact that their forebears either committed or acquiesced in evil.

The struggle to reach the current state has not been easy. For example, while adult offspring of survivors are committed to bear witness to their parents' experience, offspring of perpetrators had, in the words of Gottfried Wagner, to be liberated from *not* speaking about the Holocaust. Consequently, second-generation dialogue groups are often tentative and fragile. Yet, they bear an important responsibility; by being willing to speak to each other, they help determine how future generations remember the Holocaust.

When Children of Holocaust Survivors Meet Children of Nazis

JULIE C. GOSCHALK

Picture this scene: I, a daughter of Jewish Holocaust survivors, sit in a room facing the descendants of the people who had murdered most of my family, my people. Why do such a thing? Who would even *want* to do such a thing? Well, *I* did—with a great deal of fear, apprehension, and rage.

Before World War II, there were more than 250 individuals in my father's huge extended family. When the dust settled over Europe, my father and ten members of his family were all that emerged from the rubble. And *he* was one of the few lucky ones, because, even though, at twenty, he was virtually a skeleton weighing just ninety pounds, he *did* survive. And so did two of his four siblings—truly a miracle!

My mother, too, came from a large extended family, although we are not sure exactly how many of them there were. None of the family historians survived and the surviving family members simply did not know everyone else. What I do know is that my mother's father was one of eight children and my mother's mother one of five or six, but most accurate information is lost for ever. The tiny remnant of her family consisted of herself and her only sister, and they are aware of only two other survivors in their family, a cousin and an uncle.

So much loss and so much grief that it is simply incomprehensible! Reason enough for several lifetimes worth of hatred, I think.

But that was not my parents' way of dealing with their grief. They did not teach me to hate Germans. In fact, the whole subject of their war experiences, their survival, and the role of Germany during the war was never discussed in my family. Instead, complete silence around this subject, a thick taboo, settled over my family, which was only rarely broken by tiny snippets of stories from their lives.

I understand now that this topic was simply too painful for them to talk about. So, to protect *themselves* from our questions and to protect *us* from their answers, the Holocaust became unmentionable in our home. Of course, just because a subject is taboo does not mean that children do not know about it! In fact, I cannot think of a time when I did *not* know that they had crossed an unnameable chasm, although I obviously could not understand, as a young child, what had happened to them. But because I could not ask questions, there was no way of clarifying matters, learning, or understanding.

So I remained as silent about these questions as my parents. Indeed, I did not have the courage to ask them about their lives until I was in my late twenties and already a mother myself.

It took me years to realize and fully acknowledge to myself how much seething, suspicious rage I bore toward Germans, because of what they had done to my family and to my people. I had a visceral response when I met Germans and even though I speak German, I would avoid contact with them, if possible.

But who was I hating? Most of them had been children during the war or had been born after it. Are they to blame for my family's pain and loss? Could I allow myself to see them as innocent, and not responsible for what their parents' generation had done?

I first had an opportunity to explore these questions when I became involved in a German-Jewish dialogue in Boston, in 1987. (This group is still meeting and I have been cofacilitating it for eight years). I had always wondered about how Germans cope with their past and I have learned a great deal during these ten years.

My questions about my feelings toward postwar Germans troubled me and they shook my entire belief system regarding Jews and Germans; who were the good guys and who were the bad guys? I learned that there are honest, decent Germans of all different backgrounds and all different ages, who feel intense shame and guilt for what their people perpetrated during World War II, as well as about the renewed neo-Nazi violence. Some of the younger ones are conscientious objectors who refuse to serve in the German army; many of them have chosen to go to Brandeis, a Jewish university, or they have become involved in Jewish projects, to learn about Jews and what the Nazis destroyed in Europe. Many of them have visited Israel to feel the presence of Jews, which is largely missing in Germany now. And all of them are painfully open about trying to learn about, understand, and work through the past of the country that they call home.

These meetings also made me confront my rage toward Germans, but that only surfaced bit by bit. None of the fifty or so Germans who have come and gone in this German-Jewish dialogue group have fathers who were in any way directly involved in the extermination process, although a substantial number of them had and have parents who are overtly or covertly anti-Semitic or try to minimize the actions of Hitler's regime. They describe their rage at their parents, the humiliation and sadness they feel at having parents who have such hateful beliefs, and the awful and fruitless fights and arguments they have had with their parents on this subject.

But because no truly outrageous stories were shared by these Germans, I did not feel too threatened and could keep my hatred, which was always bubbling just beneath the surface, at arm's length—at least most of the time.

The only times it became a real challenge for me was when one of the Germans in the group began to talk about their own family's suffering during the war. I would be beside myself. How *dare* they speak of German suffering when it was *their* country that had started it all and had caused so much devastation? And *who* had brought about the murder of millions of innocent men, women, and children, including most of my own people? I felt indignant and offended and thought they had no right to talk about their pain in the presence of sons and daughters of Holocaust survivors.

It took me years to be able to acknowledge that, indeed, Germans, too, had suffered during the war. And it took longer *still* to feel that not all of them had deserved it.

Then I met Prof. Dan Bar-On, an Israeli Holocaust scholar and psychologist, who had interviewed the children of many high-ranking Nazis. He invited me to attend a meeting of other children of Holocaust survivors, like myself, together with several of the descendants of perpetrators whom he had interviewed.

I was in a panic! I had always felt "marked" by the Holocaust, even though it had happened before I was born. But it had never occurred to me that the Holocaust might have impacted the lives of the descendants of the perpetrators. I was intrigued to see whether and how these children of my family's murderers carried Cain's mark, but I was also filled with all sorts of fears and doubts. I worried that these Germans would be loyal to their fathers and that they might find some way to minimize or justify their fathers' actions. I knew I would not be able to tolerate that under any circumstances. I also wondered how I would be able to sit in a room with people who had been touched by raw evil. And I feared the depth of my own rage toward them, given that their families had deprived me of grandparents, many aunts and uncles, and a huge extended family. I had nightmares and I worried that my parents might feel betrayed by my talking to these Germans.

Then I thought I might have done enough of my own work to be able to tolerate sitting in the same room with these sons and daughters of perpetrators, without having to pour all my disgust and endless fury onto them. But would we find enough common ground to talk to one another?

As it happened, I had nothing to worry about. During those four intense June days in 1992 in Germany, it took only a little while, after the initial awkward moments, for us to bond and to realize that we not only had a common language to think about the events of that horrible past that bound us together, but we also were firmly on the same side. That was what I needed, to be able to begin to let down my guard and start trusting them.

My first shock and surprise came when I noticed how deeply moved I was by their painful stories. I hate to admit this, but at first, when I had thought abut these Germans' shaken lives as a result of their fathers' actions, I heard this nasty little voice inside of me that said: "Good! They deserve it! That's just retribution!" But this little voice did not live long. It had been easy to feel vengeful toward an anonymous group of people, but it is quite a different matter when you sit face to face with individuals who are honest and filled with undeserved shame and guilt and who feel defiled as a result of being their parents' children. After all, they were totally innocent of their fathers' actions. So why be angry with them? Why blame them?

My next shock came when I realized that my pain and that of my family threw these Germans into the depth of despair, shame, and guilt, as though they personally had caused it. We learned together that this second generation, who are now in their forties, fifties, and sixties, bear the guilt and shame that their parents neither experienced nor acknowledged. And we learned that the deafening silence not only occurred in most of the survivor families, but also in the perpetrator families. Of course, the motivation for not speaking about the events of the war was quite different in the two sets of families, but the results were the same. It left a gaping hole of fear and confusion.

But here is the major difference between us, the children of the victims, and *them,* the children of the perpetrators. We are so very much connected by the legacy of the Shoah, yet the children of survivors, mostly, can look up to our parents with pride and admiration. The children of the perpetrators, however, see themselves reflected in the eyes of evil.

Again and again during those four days there were moments when none of the seventeen participants could hold back their tears, and crying together proved very healing.

One woman, who was born in 1941, was the illegitimate child of an SS general who was married and had several children. Her mother was a simple young German woman who had fallen in love with this officer. He was a very highly placed person in the Nazi regime, and was responsible for the murder of tens of thousands of Jews. After the war, this woman's mother told her that her father was missing in action, like so many other German soldiers, when in fact she knew very well that he had been executed in 1946 for crimes against humanity. As a child, my friend often dreamed of her father's return, at times leaving a piece of cake for him, just in case he might come back unexpectedly. As an adolescent, she suddenly stumbled across the fact that he had been dead for many years. This was a terrible blow to her, but what made it even more unbearable was the fact that she could not obtain any clear information about his death.

Not until she was in her thirties did she discover the first solid piece of evidence: she found his photograph in a book about the Nazi elite. This is when her systematic search for information about her father began, and the more she learned, the more distraught she became. She realized after about ten years of unearthing material about him that what she was really looking for was some information, even a tiny shred of evidence, that could explain why he had committed these terrible crimes, as well as some proof that maybe he had not been all bad. In the end, after having met survivors of one of the ghettos he had liquidated, as well as watching historical footage from his trial testimony, she had to come to the painful conclusion that her father, whom she had idolized most of her life, appeared to have had no redeeming virtues.

In some ways another woman's story is even more shocking, because, having been born in 1934, she knew her father while he was committing his crimes. She was five when the war broke out and eleven when it ended. Her father was a physician, in charge of the euthanasia operations in his district. He was a fierce, evil-tempered man, who would not allow his infant son to be treated when he developed pneumonia, because he had a club foot. The child died. My friend was a very nearsighted child, unable to see the blackboard at school, yet she was too frightened to tell her parents.

Another story concerns a nineteen-year-old girl coming home from the movies with her boyfriend to find a policeman waiting for her. The year is 1962 and the family is gathered in the living room to say good-bye to the father, who is being taken into custody. How devastated must she be to find out that her father was not just a simple policeman during the war, but the commander of an Einsatzgruppe, an elite killing unit. How does one live with the knowledge that one's father was a mass murderer and still love him? Is this possible? Of course, this woman has the additional burden of having had a loving relationship with her father before finding out the truth. To this day (she is now in her fifties), she finds it impossible to combine those two images in her mind: that of her daddy and that of the mass murderer.

To make matters worse, she has found additional information about him that has further increased her pain. She went to the document center in Germany and looked through the thick files of transcripts from her father's trial. She learned that her father *could* have chosen *not* to remain in his position as Einsatzgruppe commander. His predecessor had done so without any adverse consequences. Instead, her father had chosen to stay and continue his grizzly job.

I can well imagine how a person with such a father might find easy pride in becoming a neo-Nazi or simply hide away in a hole and never deal with the ugly truth—*anything* so as not to feel the shame, the guilt, the burden. But here are people who for years have struggled with how to come to terms with a father who in some cases was a good and loving parent, but whose hands, at the same time, were tainted with the blood of the innocent.

For this woman there is no solace, no explanation to help her understand her father. She is tormenting herself with the question, Why? Why did he do this? Why did he not request a transfer? And maybe he did not fully comprehend what it was that he was supposed to do—but surely, by the end of the first day, it was crystal clear. Then how did he go back the next day and issue those same horrendous orders again and again and again?

It is little wonder that these Germans feel marked by evil. I must admit, there were times during that first meeting when I would suddenly become aware of who was in this room with me, and I would shudder! Yet, we did lean on one another and were able to support and comfort one another. At one point, when we took one of the many needed breaks, a German woman came up to me and, putting her arm around my shoulder, she said ever so gently, "I am so glad that all my father's hatred could not prevent you from being born."

All of us in the group had experienced this first encounter as so healing that we decided to meet again. Indeed, we have had four more four-day encounters: two in Israel, one in Boston, and one in Berlin.

Each meeting has been stressful and challenging in a different way. For example, our first Israel encounter in 1993 proved to be very painful and scary for several of the Germans.

One woman described her sense of elation as she stepped off the airplane and saw "all these Jews." She felt it was a tremendous victory over Hitler. But her mood switched instantly when she realized that all the Jews in Israel were only half as many as were murdered by the Nazis.

Another woman spoke of her intense fear of being recognized as the daughter of her Nazi father. She described her anxiety when traveling through Israel in the days before our encounter, fearing that Israelis might identify her accent and become hostile. Again and again she encountered older German-speaking Israelis who, when noticing that she was German, would speak in German to her and were warm and friendly. This repeatedly reduced her to tears. She also described an unsettling incident where some young Israelis had been terribly rude to her and her husband. She was utterly unable to say anything to them, even though she was outraged at their behavior. She felt that as a German she had no right to be angry with a Jew, no matter what they had done.

Others in the group fantasized that they might be killed by terrorists in place of an Israeli, and they felt that this would be divine retribution, given what their fathers had done to the Jewish people. Of course, they realized that their death could not undo all the evil perpetrated by the Nazis against the Jewish people, and that they themselves were innocent of their fathers' crimes. Yet, they had the sense of it being "only fair" if they were to die on Israeli soil, possibly in place of a Jewish person.

It so happened that the last day of our meeting fell on Yom HaShoah, Holocaust Remembrance Day. We decided to spend our last few hours together as a group at Yad Vashem.

My feelings were in turmoil. The exhibits always touch me in the depth of my being. I experience wrenching sadness looking at the photographs. It feels almost beyond my strength to look at the devastating images of the children. That day at Yad Vashem, I kept being torn between wanting to be absorbed in my feelings, huddling with my kind, the other children of survivors for comfort, versus needing to reach out to the others who were crumbling in shame. I realized that I was receiving a tremendous amount of support in my sadness simply by being surrounded by hundreds of Jewish visitors to the museum. But how about the Germans? How lonely they felt in their grief, their despair over their nation's vicious destruction of a people. There were moments when I resented their presence, because I did not want to deal with their pain when I could barely handle mine. There were other moments when I looked up and saw one of them sobbing and it felt natural to put my arms around them and cry together. Then I was glad that they were there, because their courage to face their country's and their families' crimes gave me hope.

One of the most difficult moments for me occurred when I stood in front of the large wall of photographs showing the actions of the Einsatzgruppen. I was numb, reading the excerpts from a meticulously kept journal written by one of the murderers. I was trying to comprehend for the thousandth time what had taken place there—how they had been able to kill naked and innocent men, women, and children in such a heartless way. I averted my eyes for a moment and noticed one my German friends, the woman whose father had been the Einsatzgruppe commander, standing in a corner opposite the wall of photographs, sobbing. I was overwhelmed by my wrenching feelings, yet I felt terrible for this woman. When we held each other, crying together, I could feel her despair and her incredulous questions at how her father could have committed such crimes. At precisely these moments the two parts of our group touch, the German and the Jewish side. They need us and we need them to attempt to deal with our nations' legacies and to begin the long road toward healing the wounds, individual by individual.

Beyond working through one's history, I believe that dialogue, really listening to each others' stories, is the only way to bridge historical divides. It is a difficult way, demanding that both sides swallow their pride and come together with an open mind and heart, to share, listen, and learn. I have found this process to be tremendously enriching and deeply healing.

To Be German after the Holocaust

The Misused Concept of Identity

GOTTFRIED H. WAGNER

For children of German perpetrators and children of Jewish victims born after the Second World War, the starting point of a discussion about our identity is the Holocaust and its effect on our generation and those to come.[1] After the Holocaust the attempt to define our identity becomes an existential problem, because the very word *identity* pushes me toward the shadows of the past. After the Holocaust it is appropriate to doubt the conventional definition of the word *identity,* like the one in *Duden,* "a complete equality resp. agreement of two things or two persons,"[2] or in a psychological sense, "as the self-experienced inner unity of a person, as Self-Identity,[3] according to Meyer's *Grossem Taschenlexikon.* I consider attempts to define a new German identity after the Holocaust not only very problematical, but also dubious, because the shadow of the Holocaust overshadows our existence still too powerfully, and definitions of identity also contain the danger of limitations, conformity, and simplicity. The American publicist Leon Wieseltier argues rightfully for a multitude of identities and remarks that the truth lies in the plural. Therefore, I share Wieseltier's seemingly

1. This is a new version of a paper read at a conference in the evangelical Academy Arnoldsheim on the topic: "How Does a Nation Turn? 1994–1995: Half a Century after the End of the Second World War." Further development of my reflections on this topic can be found in my autobiography.

2. *Der Grosse Duden,* vol. 5: Fremdwörterbuch. (Mannheim: Bibliographisches Institut, 1966), 292.

3. *Meyers Grosses Taschenlexikon,* vol. 10 (Mannheim et.al: Bibliographisches Institut, 1987), 163.

polemic statement that "only someone . . . who possesses an identity . . . can understand why someone could have the desire to get rid of it."[4]

As an individual with a German past and passport who wants to define one's own identity anew, I am confronted with the following questions: Where do I find my identities? In my professional or private sphere, or in one in which profession or private life form a unity? In a national German character? In a German Europeanism? In cosmopolitanism? In Christianity? In which religion or ethics—or can one be only a humanistic atheist after the Holocaust? In which society, monocultural or multicultural? After the Holocaust I refuse to answer the question in which race I could find my identity, because in German history this question led to the Holocaust and is still part of an anachronistic discussion about a future mono- or multicultural society that has long become multicultural.

Because my identities have been codetermined or influenced by generations of parents and grandchildren, in my case by my parents, my family, and my son, I consider it proper to first use a historical psychological approach for the discussion about the generation of the National Socialist (NS) perpetrators.

A General German and Personal Family History

Before I address this topic, I would like to point out the connection of general German history and personal German family chronicle since 1945 that can neither be resolved nor concluded. I am alluding, among other things, to the *Historikerstreit* since 1980, provoked by Ernst Nolte and Andreas Hillgruber, and the so called Auschwitz lie in its infamous portrayal by Fred Leuchter, with the support of David Irving, in 1989. To avoid the danger of generalizing from my case as a descendant of an elitist NS family to all NS perpetrators, I consider it necessary to elucidate briefly the connection between general German history and my family chronicle in key events *before and after 1945* for the definition of my identity today and that of future German generations. The call for a differentiated perspective is not only generally valid for Germans, but also for German families that, in my case, did not consist only of NS opportunistic perpetrators but also of victims. The conflict within the family is a further reason I propose a multiplicity of identities; this conflict is shaped also by growing up in the West German miracle society.

4. Leon Wieseltier, essay in *Die Zeit* Feb. 17, 1995, p. 57.

False Identifications of the Germans Before and after 1945

Because the development of my postulate for multiple identities is closely intertwined with the aftermath of the Holocaust, I looked for intellectual influences that moved me toward a new ethics, one different from that of my parents or my grandmother, Winifried Wagner. One of the guiding figures during my student years was Bruno Bettelheim. In his book *The Informed Heart: Autonomy in a Mass Age* (1960), I found helpful guidance in a period when I completely lacked a sense of identity. As an eyewitness of the time and on the basis of his fate as a Jewish inmate in Buchenwald, Bettelheim gave me the first answers to my questions concerning the false identity of the German perpetrators' generation and to those troubling questions that my parents refused to answer or could not answer because they were not, or did not want to be, conscious of having lost their human orientation. In the chapter "Men are Not Ants," Bruno Bettelheim described the psychological-historical situation of the Germans in the Nazi period 1933–45 as follows:

> Thus most if not all Germans who were not convinced Nazis shrank severely in their own estimation for the following reasons: their denial of what they knew to be true; their living in constant fear; and their not fighting back where they felt it their duty to resist. These blows to their own image of themselves could be compensated in only one of two ways: through great satisfaction in their family lives, or through the rewards of achievement and recognition.
>
> Both sources were closed to most Germans who rejected National Socialism. Their family lives were seriously interfered with by the state. Their children were encouraged to spy on them and thus robbed the home of its intimacy. This wrecked even once stable and happy families. Status and social success were entirely dependent on party or state organizations. Even advancement in what many countries consider private enterprises or professions was subject to state control.
>
> There was still one easy way for these Germans to fortify their badly damaged pride and preserve even the semblance of an integrated personality. It was by just being a German, the citizen of a country that was day after day winning political and military successes. The fainter their sense of pride the more insistent the need for some other source of strength to lean on. The appealing solution . . . was to share power with the group one belonged to. And most Germans, both in and out of the concentration camps, availed themselves of this source of vicarious satisfaction and self-respect.

Only a few German citizens could withstand all the pressures of tyranny and survive in virtual isolation. To succeed, they had to have a particularly well integrated personality to begin with, and had to keep it intact through a satisfying family life or such achievements as gave them pride and satisfaction even when no one else knew about them.

In all other Germans who were not convinced Nazis, the concentration camp produced personality changes, however indirectly. They may not have been as radical as those produced in the camps, but were far reaching enough to fit the needs of the state. The new integration that came to characterize almost every German citizen was on a very low level of personal dignity. But as yet most people, when they must choose between integration on a low human level and intolerable inner strain, will probably take the first and forego the second to regain peace.[5]

Work of Recollection (Erinnerungsarbeit) (1987) by Margarete Mitscherlich reads like a continuation of Bettelheim's insight. Already in 1968 she had published, together with her husband, Alexander Mitscherlich, a social-critical stocktaking of the West German society entitled *The Inability to Mourn (Die Unfähigkeit zu trauern)*. This book was of great importance to me at the end of the 1960s; her publication *Work of Recollection* is based on it. In the chapter "In the Shadows of Repression" ("Im Schatten der Verdrängung") she arrived at the following judgment about West German society:

Instead of a thorough political and intellectual study of the past and the search for new ideas, ideals, concepts, there was an explosive development of the West German economy, as everybody knows. . . .[6] The psychic immobility which resulted from the inability to mourn is evident today above all in the fact that most Germans are not willing to even notice the discrepancy between ideal and reality in their own country. As a consequence, some view the person who points this out to them as an enemy, who should be ostracized from society. This inability to stand criticism is naturally closely interwoven with the Germans' precarious self-esteem. Only when Germans confront their past will it be possible to make a creative and

---

5. Bruno Bettelheim, *The Informed Heart: Autonomy in a Mass Age* (Glencoe, Ill.: The Free Press, 1960), 297–99. Bettelheim was arrested in 1938. Sent first to Dachau and then to Buchenwald, he was released and emigrated to the United States in 1939. [ALB]

6. Margarete Mitscherlich, *Erinnerungsarbeit. Zur Psychologie der Unfähigkeit zu trauern* (Frankfurt am Main: S. Fischer, 1987), 119. Subsequent page references to this text appear in parentheses after the quote. All quoted passages trans. G. K. S. and G. A. S.

intellectual new beginning, one that will enable them to connect to historical and cultural experience and traditions as well as deal with them critically. The present generation resists this confrontation with the past although
it did not participate in the events of the Third Reich. 124–25

The above extensive quotes by Bettelheim and Margarete Mitscherlich,
which could not yet consider the years since German reunification, make it
possible not only to understand and appreciate the behavior of the German
population during the Nazi period, but also to provide important insights
into the West German economic miracle from the 1960s to today. They
show me clearly how my family chronicle shares similarities and differences
with most Germans in the Nazi period and West German economic miracle
citizens.

My Parents' Lack of Identity

Contrary to Bettelheim's description of the Germans, my father—and also
my mother as an immature, dependent wife—was a Nazi as long as he
derived benefits from it. As a Wagner, Hitler protégé, and German elitist
member of the master race in Bayreuth's grail and Nazi shrine, he hardly
had anything to do with the Germans, only a little as a Wagner. After the
Third Reich, he found the most ample compensation for his damaged self-
confidence as a German and a Wagner by concentrating completely on the
social recognition of his achievements in the inherited family cultural enterprise from 1951 until today. My father's social degeneracy became more
evident to me through renewed reading of the studies by Alexander and
Magarete Mitscherlich at the end of the 1980s. With regard to Margarete
Mitscherlich, I must assert that my father—and with him, my mother—did
not (my father) or did not want to (my mother) perceive in their personal
and public sphere (father) "the discrepancy between ideal and reality in
their own country [owing to] the psychic immobility which resulted from
the inability to mourn" (143). Thus, I come to my father's refusal to
confront "critically and self-critically" his historical and cultural experiences
and traditions.

Richard Wagner's Ideological Bayreuthian Inheritance

My parents identified with Bayreuth's festivals and the poorly developed
worldview of Richard Wagner in Bayreuth, where the general German

repression mechanisms and perverted German idealism are closely linked to the family chronicle. I refer to Richard Wagner's anti-Semitism as the essence of his cultural-political concept for Bayreuth's festivals. It had its starting point, after years of latent anti-Semitism at the beginning of the 1840s, in the anti-Semitic inflammatory pamphlet *Judaism in Music,* of 1850 (*Das Judentum in der Musik*) and continued in his racist anti-Semitic writings until 1881. The culmination was reached with the "opera of salvation, *Parsifal*" as Wagner's gospel of his "new Christianity" for the world. In this he demanded compassion and salvation, but only in the sense of his own ideology. His Weltanschauung, as revealed in his *Know Thyself* (*Erkenne Dich selbst*), written under the influence of the racist French author Artur Compte de Gobineau, went from 1881 to the vision of a Germany free of Jews as the "great solution." On this poisoned soil, the "cultural tradition," in truth the Bayreuthian ideology for my ancestors' Germany, was built. It was founded by Richard Wagner, continued by Cosima Wagner (as the evidence of her diaries from 1869 to 1939 shows), then continued by his son-in-law Houston Stewart Chamberlain, who along with Wagner was one of the intellectual pioneers of Nazi-Germany, and finalized by his daughter-in-law Winifred Wagner, who was so close to Hitler that he wanted to marry her. The Bayreuthian ideology of Richard Wagner in his anti-Semitic inflammatory writings and operas *Ring of the Nibelungs* (*Der Ring des Nibelungen*), *Die Meistersinger von Nürnberg,* and *Parsifal* led to Chamberlain's *Foundations of the 19th Century* (*Grundlagen des 19. Jahrhunderts (1895)*, Hitler's *Mein Kampf* (1924), Rosenberg's *Myth of the 20th Century* (*mythos des 20. Jahrhunderts (1920)*, Goebbels's *Ten Principles of German Musical Compositions* (*10 Grundsätze deutschen Musikschaffens (1938)*, and the propagandistic essays for Hitler by Winifred Wagner since 1923. Thus, the way from Bayreuth led also to Auschwitz.

New Bayreuth's Pro-Semitic Anti-Semitism

Because an identification with the anti-Semitic legacy of Richard Wagner and his family in Bayreuth after 1945 was prohibited by the Allies and the new German Basic Law for the sake of the bankrupt family enterprise and West German industry, the Bayreuthian anti-Semitism changed to the more than questionable philo-Semitism of the compulsorily democratic New Bayreuth in the interest of preserving family power under the profitable motto "here prevails art." The former Aryan center of salvation from 1876 to 1945 was transformed overnight into the Bayreuthian Repression Company with limited liability as a moralistic-cultural purification factory for the West German society, in which, however, "old traditions" could be carried on. Whoever reads the Bayreuthian program notes, speeches for special occasions, and the exhibition catalogs in Bayreuth from 1951 until today will see confirmed the Bayreuthian repression:—A miracle with the respective portraits of an opportunistic ideological Wagner,—interpretations and phrases (from the psychoanalytic West German Wagner from 1951 to 1968, to the Wagner of all German leftists of 1968 to the end of the 1970s, to the utopian Wagner of the 1980s and the turncoat Wagner since 1989). This, however, also shows my parents' lack of identity as well as that of the Bayreuthian audience in the context of manipulated and changing content of the Wagnerian legacy in Bayreuth. Freud, Bloch, Adorno, and Hans Mayer are among those who have striven to repress the anti-Semitic Wagner cult and its effects on the intellectual German climate since 1951. They found themselves in the company of the old Wagnerians in the nonspirit *(Ungeist)* of *Judaism in Music* by Richard Wagner and that of the Third Reich. Winifred Wagner openly raved about her Wolf, to whom in 1923 she during his imprisonment in Landsberg had delivered the writing paper for *Mein Kampf.* She praised Hitler not only in Syberberg's movie of 1975 about USA = "our blessed Adolf," *(unser seliger Adolf)* but also during her "inner party rallies" since 1951, especially on the twentieth of April (Hitler's birthday). My father's production of *Parsifal* in 1994 constituted a high point of dubious repression and refusal to recognize the anti-Semitic family tradition; in this staging at the end of the opera he falsified Kundry, whom Richard Wagner, in conformity with his racist delusion, let die as a female Ahasverus and Jewess. He made her a living savior of the grail, a female messiah, evidently a "savior of the world," without protest from the Bayreuthian audience and the media. How could and can such "a creative, intellectual new beginning" in the sense of Margarete Mitscherlich occur for my father and his opportunistic circles? Also informative in this connection is my father's autobiography, *Life's Records (Lebensakte)*, of August 1994. If one reads critically the keywords "Wagner's anti-Semitism and the names of Wagner family" members who were opposed to the repression of anti-Semitic attitudes, one will see documented beyond any doubt the findings of Bettelheim and Mitscherlich about German behavior, and will also be reminded of passages contained in the book *In the Beginning Was Education (Am Anfang war die Erziehung)*, published by Alice Miller in 1980, and her discussion of "black pedagogy" *(schwarze Pädagogik)*. Alice Miller shows what still remains hidden behind the philo-Semitism à la Bayreuth from 1945 until today, which does not tolerate any contradiction. Of no help here are the false loyalties of Walter Jens, as for instance, in his speech on the eight hundredth anniversary of Bayreuth in January 1994, in which he painted the history of the festivals in Bayreuth and the people responsible for them in a manner that one has to call dishonest in Karl Popper's sense.

Ways Out of the Parents' Repression

Based on my experience, I have now arrived at a criterion for the behavior of the German majority, which I would like to characterize as a "disastrous separation of individual responsibility and private and public ethics after the Holocaust." It forms an insurmountable potential of conflict for the repression, denial, and falsification of one's past. This led children, who could no longer stand their parents' false identities, identifications, and ideals to hate their parents. As children of the Nazi perpetrators, we have, in my opinion, a single chance to show our hatred for our parents and their bitter legacy of making the Holocaust and the Second World War possible. Furthermore, we must oppose them openly with all means, even if this often leads to "unbearable inner stress" in Bettelheim's sense and to a periodic isolation and discrimination within existing society, even in my generation. I realize that the publication of my book *You Should Never Ask Me (Nie sollst du mich befragen)* in the spring of 1997 probably means the final break with Germany, because in this book I was no longer inclined to show false considerations for a family legacy that I find in its existing form not only anachronistic but also disastrous for German history and family chronology until today. I am not willing to feed my son (who has an Italian passport) and the coming generations with German background the lifelong lies of the typical German family Wagner and the falsified picture of history of some writers à la mode.

My Multiple Identities

The following perception of Margarete Mitscherlich surely has much to do with the Germans' search for their identity, Germans who were born after the Holocaust and who consider it the basis for the German-Jewish dialogue after the zero hour. Mitscherlich wrote in her Work of Recollection: "[T]he spiritual and intellectual liberation from false ideals and idealizations, from traditional prejudices is the precondition that an intellectual-spiritual development and new orientation can take place actually" (143).

My liberation and the development of my *Culture of Disobedience (Kultur des Ungehorsams)* only began with the hidden, then open rebellion against the totalitarian Bayreuthian idealism in the private and public spheres. This revolt had the following stages: the doctoral dissertation about Weill and Brecht, the time as director of the Weill Foundation in New York, the lecture tours about Wagner in Israel, the stays in Terezin and Auschwitz, and the founding of the Post-Holocaust Dialogue Group with Abraham Peck. All of these formed for me the irrevocable milestones of my multiple identities as a descendant of a prominent family of Nazi perpetrators. With these milestones I live in Italy—despite everything, still with a German passport—and that better than in the frosty turncoat country of Kohl and Jens. I experience my identities as a multicultural and social involvement for which I have to exert myself daily with the intensive consciousness of a German who was born after the Holocaust.

The Identity of My Son and My Values

Although the Germans' inability to mourn makes it impossible for me to identify with their values, still I attribute great significance to my son's search for identity with himself, with me, my wife, and with our Italian family. The facets of identity are complex for Eugenio, not only because my wife comes from an Italian Catholic family of craftsmen and I from a German atheistic bourgeois family. In addition, Eugenio has his life story as an adopted child from Rumania. Not until 1990, with the integration into our Italian family, could he begin slowly with his search for identity. Even in our otherwise children-friendly residence near Milano, we went through moments of discrimination with him that resulted from Eugenio's lack of family in his past. Eugenio was always conscious of being our adoptive child. Three years ago he asked me why Grandfather Wolfgang, that is, my father, never visited us. I avoided answering him because I did not yet want to darken his childhood with my own Bayreuthian history and said: "Grandfather sees many things in a different light from us. He has too many other things to do and therefore has no time for us." Eugenio guessed immediately that something was not in order and replied: "If he does not have time for us, then I have no desire to get to know him!" To soothe his pain, I nourished his hope for the moment that his grandfather would like to get to know him one day. Today, he no longer hopes to know his grandfather even though I have not spoken further about this. He has for some time accepted that I cannot be a self-denying career Wagner. I was almost the same age as Eugenio, ten, when I learned about the Holocaust without any preparation from my parents or teachers. At this age Eugenio had survived almost six years as an orphan under Ceaucescu. Despite his experiences, he is a sensitive, happy child commenting on the televised news from Bosnia or Rwanda in accordance with his life's experiences; this confirms for me that one can confront "the great fear with the great hope" in the sense of Ralph Giordano. As fifth generation, quite in the Jewish biblical sense, Eugenio has nothing whatever to do with the lack of identity of the super-man Wagner from Bayreuth. His search for identity is for the moment in our parental hands. He has understood: justice and compassion have much to do with the ethical values of his mother, individual moral courage with those of his father. Not long ago, he entered a dispute between a weak and a strong classmate; he sided with the weak one and came home from school with a bloody nose—quite in accordance with our educational values. To reward him for his supporting a just cause, I took him to an ice cream store. There I told him: "We both have to learn to box out of self-defense, because otherwise we will again get our noses bloodied." His laughing OK was a further confirmation that he has developed multiple identities: for him, for me, for us.

Gottfried H. Wagner
September 1996
To Teresina

This article was translated from the German into English by Gerd K. Schneider, professor of German at Syracuse University, and Georgia A. Schneider, professor of German and English as a Second Language (ESL) at Onondaga Community College.

Taking Leave of the Wrong Identities or An Inability to Mourn

Post-Holocaust Germans and Jews

ABRAHAM J. PECK

In their search for meaning, many of the children of Holocaust survivors, the second generation, have come to a dead end. Gone are the halcyon days of the late 1970s, when the children of the survivors took an oath in the shadows of Jerusalem's Temple Wall and declared "mir szeinen doh," we are here, mirroring their parents' affirmation of life in the weeks and months after the liberation.[1]

It was a heady slide into the abyss of inactivity, this decade-long pre-occupation with identity by a diverse group of young adults, long beyond their childhood years, who gratefully became children once again.

When they first started to come together, the children of survivors understood only that as different as they were from everyone else, among their own kind there was a sameness that gave them a warmth and under-standing that they had never before possessed.

And it was important that they reformulate their identities, because the same thing was happening to their parents.

Beginning in the early 1980s, survivors and their children began to occupy a unique role in the evolution of the Jewish presence in history. The Holocaust and its observance became in its rites and rituals an American concern. Indeed, the 1980s emerged as the "decade of the survivor," as

---

1. The author refers to the 1981 world gathering of Jewish Holocaust survivors held in Jerasulem [AB].

354

they were asked to speak in the classroom and in front of the video camera.

The 1980s was also the decade of the second generation. For the better part of that decade, the American children of survivors sought to implement a number of aims and ideas that connected them, perhaps without their knowing it, to the idealism of a group of Holocaust survivors, who immediately after the liberation had formulated a kind of neohumanistic response to the tragedy that had befallen European Jewry during the 1930s and 1940s.[2] They did so at individual levels, through their own involvement in the helping professions; they did so collectively, moving to a kind of political engagement that saw them demonstrate against unjust governments and ultimately take a "leap of faith" to conduct a dialogue with Yassir Arafat and the PLO in pursuit of peace in the Middle East.

But for the past several years, a kind of silence has characterized the activities of the children of survivors. The growing realization that many of us are nearing or have reached real middle age has made the "child of survivors" identity a difficult one to maintain.

Indeed, more than a half century after the beginning of the Second World War, the survivors, with few exceptions, have reached the end of their days. They face the prospect of death and of an old age separated from their children and grandchildren, and of all the traumas that come with being an aged member of society. As the psychologist Yael Danieli has pointed out, the aging survivor carries a double burden: not only is he or she preoccupied with the questions "who loves me?" or "who cares if I live?," the survivor must also ask, "Who will remember me? Will the memory of my people and of the Holocaust perish?"[3]

The burden of the aged survivor is no less easy to bear for the second generation. We are caught up not only in the dilemma of having to care for our parents, a burden of enormous consequences under normal, nonsurvivor conditions, but we must also face the situation of the survivors' efforts to confront their lives, to integrate their Holocaust experiences into the flow and memory of those lives, to try to come to grips with the fact that they have lost not only loved ones, but also an entire civilization and way of life.

2. I have written about this idealism in Abraham J. Peck, "She'erit Hapletah: The Purpose of the Legacy," in *Midstream* (Apr. 1991), 27–30.

3. Yael Danieli, "The Aging Survivor of the Holocaust. On the Achievement of Integration in Aging Survivors of the Nazi Holocaust," in *Journal of Geriatric Psychiatry*, vol. 14, no. 2, 1983:209.

2

Like many of my contemporaries, I became a child of Holocaust survivors long after I had grown into an adult. It was an overnight metamorphosis, almost as if that child in me had been waiting to emerge for a very long time. Helen Epstein has called it the opening of the "black box," the internal sense that children of survivors have of being different, of having grown up in a home with survivors, but without grandparents, uncles and aunts, or cousins.[4]

My uncles and aunts were shadow figures. There were thirteen of them, five on my father's side and eight on my mother's. They all bore traditional Jewish names: Abraham, Chaim, Rivka, Rachel, Pinchas, Yankel, Eli, Shmuel were just some of them. They all were murdered in the Holocaust.

For most of my life they have remained only names. I cannot identify them by facial features, idiosyncrasies, or any of the other lovable characteristics that make up the pleasure of the extended family. I never referred to them as Uncle "this" or Aunt "that." They were always "your brother" or "your sister."

In a strange, perhaps morbid, way, I was much more familiar with the tormentors of my parents, who had assumed the responsibility, no, the mission, of destroying them and the millions of other European Jews who were the targets of the Nazi "final solution" of the "Jewish problem" in Europe.

There was Paul Kuhnemann, a lame, dwarflike man who, as commandant of Skarzysko-Kamienna Factory Camp A, would shoot Jewish prisoners for amusement, or allow his German shepherd dog to tear a prisoner to bits.

There was also Hans Biebow, the Nazi administrator of the Lodz, Poland, ghetto, which the Nazis called Litzmannstadt. He was a rather handsome man, in a devious sort of way, who made tremendous amounts of money from the labor of the ghetto's Jewish inhabitants while at the same time helping deport them to the crematoria of the Chelmno death camp.

Then there was the "Monster." He was an SS doctor, a perverted member of the German medical community whose purpose was not to save life but to destroy it.

But he was rather decent to my father. When my father felt comfortable enough to ask him why the Germans were destroying the Jews, this SS

4. Helen Epstein, *Children of the Holocaust* (New York, 1979).

doctor shook from head to toe in an angry rage and replied, "Because the Jews are a superfluous race, forgotten by God!"

This assorted cast of killers and decent types took center stage when, on those rare instances, I would be allowed to have a friend visit my home. My father would "entertain" my friends of eleven and twelve years of age with full-fledged stories of the ghettos and the camps. My friends would sit in shock, perhaps in grief, looking first at my father, and then at me, with the question: "Why is he telling me this?" on their faces and in their eyes. They rarely returned to hear part two. I, too, questioned the purpose of my father's need to bear witness. I wanted desperately to hear about his child-hood days playing baseball or playing hooky from school. But deep down I knew that it was my duty to listen to the Holocaust stories, not only because it allowed my father to fulfill a desperate need to tell them, but also because they would one day become my stories to pass on to the next generation. They would become my legacy and my mission.

It was not an easy legacy. For years, I felt alone, believing that only I lived in the eye of a hurricane, surrounded by the shadows of death and destruction.

Now, many years later, I am convinced that there is an entire generation of children who shared my experience—those who belong to the families of the victims and those who belong to the families of their oppressors. Both of our groups have gone through confronting what we have become and we need to develop an understanding of who we are to be.

For me this realization came when I was in my early twenties and a university undergraduate. At the American University in Washington, D.C., I met Petra Kelly.

She was the first German with whom I was able to speak about the Holocaust. Even at that time, in the late 1960s, Petra Kelly was an idealist whose great skill was in turning this idealism into practical results. She would never accept a situation of social injustice and knew only a desire to overcome it.

Such an attitude was admirable, especially, I thought, for a German. And Petra was especially frank about the failures of her nation to confront the murder of European Jewry in the years after 1945. From Petra Kelly I first learned about a generation of German youth who would not accept their parents' crimes during the Holocaust nor their silence when their children confronted them with the facts.

I remember especially a conversation we once had where we discussed our legacies as children of survivors and of oppressors. Petra would not be satisfied with simply acknowledging our individual burdens. She wanted to know what we would do with them, how we would use them to make the world a better place.

Such questions, while intriguing, would have to wait. I needed to explore other areas of my identity. I needed to know more about the people who had condemned my people to a "superfluous" place in the family of nations.

But Petra Kelly could not wait. She went on to become one of the major forces in German and international society and politics. She co-founded a political party, the Greens, struggled on behalf of the oppressed of all nations, and sought to change the silence of her parents' generation after the Holocaust into a roar of protest against the increasing danger of nuclear annihilation. Her short life, ended in a murder-suicide, was an extraordinary one.

3

What made my relationship with Petra Kelly genuine was the mutual sharing of our family histories. Fifty years after Auschwitz, an entire generation of Germans and Jews continues to share a legacy and a burden that in the words of Sabine Reichel, born in 1946 in Hamburg, "is like [a] historical umbilical cord that can't be cut off and that pulls at the most unlikely moments."[5]

At the heart of this cord is family history. It is an obstacle to both Germans and Jews. For Germans it remains the great divide between silence and dialogue. It is a diseased branch on the pages of far too many family trees.

Every well-meaning German who wishes to engage in a frank discussion of German-Jewish relations is nearly always reduced to tears or to silence when the inevitable question is asked: "What did your father or grandfather do during the Second World War?" To argue that he was in the German Wehrmacht or armed forces is no longer much of a rejoinder: the collaboration of the frontline troops with the racial ideologues of the SS in the murder of Jews is by now a well-established fact.

Even more disarming is the question: "What did your parents or grandparents know about the Final Solution? the planned destruction of European Jewish life? Often the answer is one of genuine ignorance. German

5. Sabine Reichel, *What Did You Do in the War, Daddy?* (New York, 1989).

families in the main did not discuss this issue in the years after 1945. But we are beginning to learn that many more knew what was happening than have let on. Many more knew what was happening to the Jewish family that suddenly disappeared from their apartment building one fine day and never returned. Many more knew because their fathers, husbands, sons, and brothers could not keep a *Reichsgeheimsache,* a state secret, which the Final Solution was always intended to be. In letters from the front, from the concentration camp, or in drunken, sometimes terribly guilt-ridden confessions while on leave, these men told a great part of the home front just what was happening in the "east" to the Jews of Nazi-occupied Europe.

Family history is also a problem for the children of Holocaust survivors. We have grown up, many of us, in the eye of a hurricane, surrounded by shadows of the Holocaust. We have grown up knowing that the Holocaust is a part of our being, but often do not know why. Many have asked next to nothing about the suffering of their parents during the Holocaust years or the absence of grandparents, uncles, and aunts. These children of Holocaust survivors fear the trauma inherent in their parents' reply.

Family history was very much on the minds of those Jews living in Germany as they viewed the euphoria that swept across the city of Berlin and the Federal Republic on November 9, 1989, as the much-hated Berlin Wall was reduced to a collector's item. Amidst the calls that this day become a national holiday of German reunification between east and west, Germany's Jews could not join in the celebration. On November 9, these Jews were remembering the fifty-first anniversary of a national pogrom that marked the end of German-Jewish life and the beginning of the Holocaust.

How could an entire nation so easily forget one of the darkest chapters in its history? The answer lies somewhere between the oath of national silence that marked Germany's confrontation with its Nazi past and its willingness to pay billions of dollars in restitution to the survivors of the greatest tragedy in Jewish memory.

Only now have members of Germany's postwar generation spoken out about the silence that marked their early years. Sabine Reichel has described the "overdose of conscience killer" that was injected into German society in the immediate post-1945 period: "The demoralized Germans made a peace treaty with their souls for a new start: there would be no discussion of that shameful past, no analyzing, no reflecting, no mourning, and no regretting. There would be no need for answers because there would be no questions."

Further in her analysis of postwar German society, she writes that "it is no wonder that Germans have been incapable of mourning, since it requires sadness and a sense of loss. . . . But beyond the millions of people they killed, the Germans find any sort of mourning impossible."

Perhaps the most interesting of all is Reichel's contention that "I also began to discover some startling behavioral similarities between my generation and some of my Jewish peers. I learned that many children of Holocaust survivors grew up with a throttling silence and an inexplicable fear of a secret box that contained explosive materials and shouldn't be tampered with. These impressions, in turn, reminded me of my own upbringing. *The inability of both groups of parents, in my case an entire nation, to speak about the past—one because of pain, the other because of guilt—caused similar symptoms for their offspring."6*

For young Germans born after 1945, those symptoms included a wholesale rejection of the kind of Germany their parents had created for them, a Germany based on overnight change from criminal state to a nation credited with a *Wirtschaftswunder,* an economic miracle.

Two German psychotherapists, Alexander and Margarete Mitscherlich, have published a volume entitled *The Inability to Mourn.*7 In it they conclude that for most Germans there has been no real period of mourning, not for the crimes committed by the Hitler regime, not for the millions of Germans killed during the Second World War, not for the wholesale destruction of German cities and towns. And because their parents did not mourn, did not learn to overcome the loss of their loved ones, did not learn to accept responsibility for the crimes of the Nazi state, they handed their children a legacy that included denial, avoidance, and a feeling of nonguilt.

According to the Mitscherlichs, many of today's young Germans are "orphans with parents." A great spiritual vacuum separates mothers and fathers from their parents and from their children.

How interesting this notion of an inability to mourn by an entire generation of post-1945 Germans. And how interesting the statement by Helen Epstein that the sense of being different, of the greatest secret in the children of survivors' "iron box," was the knowledge that "our family tree had been burnt to a stump. Whole branches, great networks of leaves had disappeared into the sky and ground."

6. Ibid.

7. Alexander and Margarete Mitscherlich, *The Inability to Mourn* (New York, 1975).

Children of survivors as well as their parents have had a difficult time overcoming something by now very familiar, something the mental health professionals have described as a "genuine" impossibility of mourning for those lost branches on their family trees. This inability to mourn has impeded their ability to cope with and integrate the Holocaust into their lives. Survivors and their children have not yet discovered meaningful ways to mourn the loss of family and of their geographic and cultural roots. Hence, according to Epstein, "survivors' and their offsprings' pilgrimages to their [European] hometowns, to concentration camps, and to Holocaust monuments are informed by their search for roots and by their need to mourn."

Perhaps then Sabine Reichel's description of the legacy shared by Germans and Jews as a "historical umbilical cord that can't be cut off . . ." begins to become even more meaningful.

The thought that survivors and their children have anything in common with Germans, either the Nazi murderers or their children, is at first a repulsive thought. For the aged survivor generation, that question should not even be asked, an impossibility that should never be suggested.

But the post-1945 generation of Germans and Jews will face a kind of zero hour of new beginnings and new opportunities. New beginnings for what? New opportunities for whom?

4

No postwar German publication has aroused so much controversy as Ralph Giordano's *The Second Guilt or the Burden of Being German,* published in 1987.[8]

Indeed, the twelve hundred letters that Ralph Giordano received—most of them favorable—in the months after the book's publication probably make *The Second Guilt* the textual equivalent in public response to the late 1970s showing of the series "Holocaust" on German television.

The book is a clear, concise, and brilliant indictment of German history since 1871. Instead of simply detailing themes such as nationalism, the *völkisch* movement, Prussianism, the stab-in-the-back legend as the primary forces giving rise to the Nazi state, it focuses on a key issue that succinctly combines all of the above themes into one—the loss of a "humane orientation." This loss, which Giordano claims "comes from the depth of the

---

8. Ralph Giordano, *Die zweite Schuld oder Von der Last Deutscher zu sein* (Hamburg, 1987).

founding of the German nation-state in 1871," must be understood as the real indictment of the generation responsible for the creation of the Third Reich. The Nazi state must be seen as a continuation of the systematic dehumanization of the German nation and not as its beginning.

"How can this generation breathe?" asked a young veterinarian from Hamburg in a letter to Ralph Giordano. How can the generation of the first guilt, the murderers, continue to face each day? she wonders, but no less than the generation of the second guilt, the generation that suppressed and forgot the confrontation with the crimes of the first."[9]

Yet, I believe, the problem is not so much whether after 1945 the Nazi past was confronted or suppressed but what German society and its citizens have learned or wanted to learn from that history, whether the chance to develop an honest and wide-ranging dialogue between post-Holocaust Germans and Jews has a chance of ever becoming a real agenda item.

But family history, despite its ability to keep Germans and Jews from dialogue, has, at least in one case, brought them closer together.

In 1923, Adolf Hitler's attempt at a Nazi revolution in Bavaria failed. A few months after the abortive coup, Hitler appeared before a court on trial for treason. He recalled in his testimony that "when I stood for the first time before Richard Wagner's grave, my heart swelled with pride. He was one of the three greatest Germans nearest to the Volk." Hitler had become close to the Wagner family and visited them just a few months earlier at the Wagner family mansion, Villa Wahnfried, in the Bavarian town of Bayreuth. The town became for Hitler a kind of musical capital of the Nazi revolution. His showmanship, based on operatic devices from the Wagner Opera House in Bayreuth, used torchlight parades, mob choruses, ever-rising climaxes, and grand gestures of Nordic heroes to mesmerize his audiences.

Hitler was sentenced to five years in the Bavarian fortress prison at Landsberg am Lech. He spent only nine months there. Yet, he managed to complete the greater part of a manuscript, which he dictated to his faithful secretary, Rudolf Hess. The manuscript was an account of his past, present, and future plans for Germany and its great enemy, world Jewry. He entitled his work *Mein Kampf* (My struggle). Hitler received the paper upon which he dictated his manuscript from Winifred Wagner, the grandmother of Gottfried Wagner, my German dialogue partner, who traveled from Bayreuth to see him.

---

9. Ralph Giordano, ed., *"Wie kann these Generation eigentlich noch atmen?"*: *Briefe zu dem Buch: Die zweite Schuld oder Von der Last Deutscher zu sein* (Hamburg, 1990).

Is it coincidence that Gottfried Wagner was born in Bayreuth as the great-grandson of Richard Wagner and I was born in Landsberg am Lech as the son of Holocaust survivors?

Whatever the circumstances, we have been drawn together in dialogue for the past five years because I believe we share a common desire to understand each other's burden as a result of who we are and the consequences of our family histories.

But dialogue under any circumstances is a complicated matter. Dialogue between Germans and Jews is a minefield of missteps. We are both, I think, still uncertain what results we want to achieve as individuals and as Germans and Jews. Am I looking for a new kind of reparations, and is Gottfried's generation still responsible for confessional memories of guilt? Is Gottfried, even after I have told him it is not mine to give, secretly longing for the forgiveness of reconciliation with a hug and a tear?

Gottfried Wagner set out our guidelines at the very start of our dialogue. In June 1993, he wrote that "the spirit of all our future issues must be tolerant of the She'erith Hapletah," the name meaning "saving remnant" in Hebrew, which the survivors called themselves and their broadly-based plan to use their tragedy as the starting point for a moral revolution in Jewish and world history. "But," Gottfried continued, "we also have to base our dialogue and our group on a very concrete historical basis and clear, responsible programming for the future. It is not enough for me to say with pathos 'never again' but we should ask ourselves self-critically what could I, with good will, contribute to overcoming the 'negative symbiosis' between Germans and Jews. Our starting point," he concluded his letter, "is the common tragic memory of our past which will forever be part of our children's existence."

Is the possibility for dialogue worth the encounter? There are dialogue groups between post-Holocaust Germans and Jews in various places across the United States and to a smaller degree in Germany, Austria, England, and Israel. Their efforts are tentative, still open to widespread criticism from both Germans and Jews, especially within the survivor community.

Is the possibility worth the encounter? I was never certain of this until I met Gottfried. He represents for me the beginning of Germany's efforts to recapture its sense of a "humane orientation" as it is understood in the work of Ralph Giordano.

The beginning of Germany's misguided path into tyranny and inhumanity may be tied to the generation of Gottfried's great-grandfather, Richard, and to Richard Wagner himself. And what more appropriate representative of the need to reclaim for Germany its humane orientation than the great-grandson of the man who helped lose it?

I tremble as does Gottfried, and I suspect all those engaged in the German-Jewish dialogue, at the thought of the shadows that lurk over us. But we also know that our post-Holocaust world has not changed enough to allow us to withdraw from the challenge. We see the Holocaust all around us, in the brutalities that occur in national and international conflict, in the apathy with which we can view the victims of war, both young and old, and in our lack of trust in law, religion, medicine, and technology as important and immutable foundations of our civilization.

The Holocaust is a German and a Jewish nightmare that will not go away, because post-Holocaust Germans and Jews will not let it. It must be on the agenda of many groups but especially Germans and Jews with an intensity and ferocity of purpose that will keep it there for generations to come.

At the end of the twentieth century, I believe that the second generation can find a purpose that remains true to the oath we took to carry on for our parents and our murdered millions. We cannot let the absence of mourning, which defined the generation of Jews and Germans from the Holocaust, be a burden to us and to our children.

In ways that our parents can never understand, the Holocaust has shaped both Germans and Jews. It is responsible for who we are and what we have become. But we are in turn responsible for helping shape the way it is remembered by future generations. The fact that Germans and Jews are willing to talk to one another, to open the "iron boxes" of their souls, is as important as what they have to say.

The dialogue may never lead to reconciliation. But it will allow the second generation to renew its sense of purpose and in no way disturb the legacy handed to us by the survivor generation. Indeed, I believe in the notion of "never again." Both the second generation of Germans and Jews, their children and their children's children can and must vow to say "never again," and mean never again for all humanity.

A Concluding Meditation

At the millennium humanity has much to celebrate. Medical and techno-logical advances bring hope for both longevity and quality of life. Politically, the cold war has ended and many of the old political tensions and obstacles to peace have been removed. Nuclear arms are being dismantled. We may be near the time when swords will be beaten into plowshares. Tolerance and sensitivity to pluralism are the guidelines of official culture and discourse. Technologically, humanity is light-years ahead of where it began at the commencement of the twentieth century. Space stations, once only a dream, are now becoming a reality. At the beginning of the twenty-first century, the world appears to be a very different place than it was when Hitler and Nazism came to power. Viewed in one way, the planet seems poised on the brink of a new era in human relations.

Yet, as the contributors to this anthology attest, humanity is still chal-lenged by the need to learn tolerance and sensitivity to the *other*. The psychosocial and theological legacies of the Holocaust are palpable pres-ences in the lives of the second generation. Members of the Jewish and German second generation who have shared their reflections know what it means to walk through the biblical valley of the shadow of death. Like their counterparts of antiquity, they *fear* no evil. But they are immensely *conscious* of this evil, having been raised in its hovering presence. Moreover, this evil assumes many guises, both ancient and modern; anti-Semitism, homopho-bia, racism, prejudice, "ethnic cleansing," and other types of fanaticism are some of its names. The "rod and the staff" that this generation employ in seeking a way through the valley of evil include memory, compassion, empathy, a commitment to social justice, and the possibility of meaningful dialogue. They model a way of being that may encourage others in the eternal task of seeking to mend the world.

As the two second generations seek to confront and shape memory of the Holocaust, a pattern emerges in their efforts. Jewish adult offspring of survivors work through their legacy by visiting, or revisiting, countries of origin and by reconnecting with their parents and with Jewish history. Here the legacy of the Shoah is overt and unavoidable. The German second generation is different. Many identify with Jews, some convert to Judaism, and trust of parents is very fragile. The ramifications of the Holocaust on this generation tend to be more *covert;* one can choose, as it were, to deny its impact.

Authentic dialogue between the descendants of victims and offspring of perpetrators is crucial, although we have noted there is not unanimity on this position. Such dialogue tells the story of the Holocaust and its legacy, and encourages further discussion and reflection, thus helping shape how the Shoah is represented to future generations. Moreover, this dialogue may possibly motivate humanity to move away from genocidal modes of thinking and acting. We do not claim that the German second-generation contributors are representative. Indeed, the daughter of Heinrich Himmler is involved with neo-Nazis. Yet, the future of Holocaust memory will be shaped by those having the courage to honestly face the past. Elie Wiesel retells a hasidic tale in the prologue of *The Gates of the Forest* that illuminates the position of the second-generation and its possible salvific role in bearing witness.

When the great Rabbi Israel Baal Shem-Tov saw misfortune threatening the Jews it was his custom to go into a certain part of the forest to meditate. There he would light a fire, say a special prayer, and the miracle would be accomplished and the misfortune averted.

Later, when his disciple, the celebrated Magid of Mezritch, had occasion, for the same reason, to intercede with heaven, he would go to the same place in the forest and say: "Master of the Universe, listen! I do not know how to light the fire, but I am still able to say the prayer." And again the miracle would be accomplished.

Still later, Rabbi Moshe-Leib of Sasov, in order to save his people once more, would go into the forest and say: "I do not know how to light the fire, I do not know the prayer, but I know the place and this must be sufficient." It was sufficient and the miracle was accomplished.

Then it fell to Rabbi Israel of Rizhyn to overcome misfortune. Sitting in his armchair, his head in his hands, he spoke to God: "I am unable to light the fire and I do not know the prayer; I cannot even find the place in the forest. All I can do is to tell the story, and this must be sufficient." And it was sufficient.

Index